COMPLETE DELIVERANCE FROM WITCHCRAFT

THE GAME CHANGER

ALEXANDER ZABADINO

Copyright© 2024 Alexander Zabadino

All rights reserved. No part of this book may be reproduced or transmitted in any form or by any means, electronic or mechanical, including photocopying, recording or by any information storage and retrieval system without prior permission of the author.

This book is a work of non-fiction. The views expressed are solely those of the author and do not necessarily reflect the views of the publisher and thereby disclaims any responsibility for them.

Dedicated to God the father, God the Son, God the Holy Spirit.

Acknowledgement

This is acknowledgment to the immense assistance of Ms. Elaine Choi Fung Chan in the typesetting of this book "Complete Deliverance from Witchcraft" as it is in this present form.

Table of Contents

INTRODUCTION 7
CHAPTER ONE 9
    AN OVERVIEW TO WITCHCRAFT 9
CHAPTER TWO 13
    ORGANISATION OF WITCHCRAFT 13
CHAPTER THREE 15
    INITIATION INTO WITCHCRAFT. 15
CHAPTER FOUR 21
    WITCHCRAFT ATTACKS. 21
CHAPTER FIVE 25
    HOTSPOTS OF WITCHCRAFT INITIATION. 25
CHAPTER SIX 33
    FIFTY WITCHCRAFT DREAMS, CONNOTATIONS AND SOLUTIONS. 33
CHAPTER SEVEN 41
    EVIL WITCHCRAFT POWERS. 41
CHAPTER EIGHT 50
    FOUNDATIONAL WITCHCRAFT. 50
CHAPTER NINE 61
    MARINE WITCHCRAFT 61
CHAPTER TEN 70
    SPIRITUAL PURGING. 70
CHAPTER ELEVEN 72
    WITCHCRAFT IN CHILDREN 72
CHAPTER TWELVE 80
    TYPES OF WITCHCRAFT 80
CHAPTER THIRTEEN 99
    HOW DELIVERANCE WORKS 99

CHAPTER FOURTEEN	102
NOTES FOR DELIVERANCE MINISTERS	102
CHAPTER FIFTEEN	110
THE BASIC CONSIDERATIONS IN DELIVERANCE.	110
CHAPTER SIXTEEN	112
THE DELIVERANCE PROGRAM	112
CHAPTER SEVENTEEN	114
SALVATION	114
CHAPTER EIGHTEEN	117
THE WORD OF GOD	117
CHAPTER NINETEEN	119
COUNSELING	119
CHAPTER TWENTY	121
FAITH.	121
CHAPTER TWENTY-ONE	128
PRAISE AND WORSHIP	128
CHAPTER TWENTY-TWO	130
PRAYERS AND DELIVERANCE	130
CHAPTER TWENTY-THREE	155
COVENANTS	155
CHAPTER TWENTY-FOUR	162
HOUSEHELPS AND THIRD PARTIES	162
CURSES	170
CHAPTER TWENTY-SIX	179
PROSPERITY AND DELIVERANCE FROM THE SPIRIT OF POVERTY.	179
CHAPTER TWENTY-SEVEN	190
HEALING AND MIRACLES	190
CHAPTER TWENTY-EIGHT	198
THE SPIRIT OF DEATH AND HELL.	198

CHAPTER TWENTY-NINE	203
DELIVERANCE OF THE HEAD.	203
CHAPTER THIRTY	207
DELIVERANCE OF THE HANDS.	207
CHAPTER THIRTY-ONE	210
DELIVERANCE OF THE FEET.	210
CHAPTER THIRTY-TWO	212
THE HOLY GHOST BAPTISM.	212
CHAPTER THIRTY-THREE	217
HOW TO MAINTAIN YOUR DELIVERANCE.	217
CHAPTER THIRTY-FOUR	222
WHEN THE MARRIAGE VOW BACKFIRES.	222
CHAPTER THIRTY-FIVE	235
DELIVERANCE FOR ELIGIBLE SINGLES.	235
CHAPTER THIRTY-SIX	245
DELIVERANCE FROM THE SPIRIT OF INFIDELITY.	245
CHAPTER THIRTY-SEVEN	254
DELIVERANCE FROM WITCHCRAFT ATTACKS AGAINST YOUR CONCEPTION.	254
CHAPTER THIRTY-EIGHT	270
POWER OVER THE ENEMIES OF YOUR SAFE DELIVERY.	270

INTRODUCTION

Complete Deliverance from Witchcraft was written by the instruction of the Holy Ghost, and the spirit of the Lord came upon me severally to execute this assignment in a most phenomenal and unforgettable experience.

Many problems that affect mankind are rooted in witchcraft. This book unveils several obscure routes of witchcraft initiation observed in the deliverance ministry, and the "hotspots" of witchcraft initiation in the environment. There are hidden powers that witches go about with in their eyes, mouth, genitals and other parts. What are they and how can you fall victim?

An overview of witchcraft types and organisation is given, before exploring the details of each. Some old topics have been revisited by the inspiration of the Holy Ghost, and with an amazing practical insight. These include the topics like Foundational Witchcraft; Marine Witchcraft; Covenants; Curses; Salvation; Repentance and Deliverance; Praise worship; Counselling; Deliverance from the Spirit of Death and Hell; How to Maintain Your Deliverance; Deliverance of the Head, Feet, and Hands; and the Holy Ghost Baptism, to mention just a few discussed in the 38 chapters of this book. These write ups essentially discuss the causes of the problems, signs to look out for, and how to solve the problems.

New uncharted deliverance topics in high demand based on our experience are being discussed. These new chapters include a new chapter on "House Helps and Third Parties", helping many women who have been dealt with mercilessly by possessed third parties in their homes. The various steps that you need to take to know God's will have been adequately addressed in the chapter on "Deliverance for Eligible Singles". Many husbands and wives battling with infidelity in their marriages, can now heave a sigh of relief after reading the chapter on "Deliverance from the Spirit of Infidelity". Two insightful chapters have been included about how to receive deliverance from witchcraft to get pregnant seamlessly, and how to ensure safe labour and delivery. The issue of Assisted Reproductive Technology included.

Embattled couples can read the chapter "When the Marriage Vow Backfires" and even give the book as a gift to friends. They can discover why they are experiencing the present problems in their marriages, how to end the problems, and rekindle the fire of the agape love of God in their marriages. Furthermore, many couples are concerned about strange and unexplainable manifestations in the lives of their children, which can affect their destinies on long term. "Real" parents should strive to reverse this ugly trend. We are happy to present a chapter on "Children Deliverance", another uncharted and poorly documented topic.

The chapter on "Healing and Miracles" reviews my experience in the ministry of healing and miracles to churches and hospitals; and a review of the classics of great fathers in faith, that God used worldwide in great revivals and the working of miracles especially in the United States. Deliverance Ministers, can also benefit from the unravelling of great mysteries, revelations and practical experience that will step up your game in the deliverance ministry, and usher you into new consciousness, awakening and anointing.

Fifty common dreams added to help you to identify witchcraft attacks in your dreams, and close to 1,500 prayer points on the different topics, to help you to confidently, and victoriously wage war against the enemies of your purpose and destiny. This book is not just a read, but a "transformation", that it has been tagged "THE GAME CHANGER". It certainly promises to move you to a higher realm in redefining and revolutionising deliverance. My mission is to share my vast ministerial insights and experience with Christians worldwide, equipping champions.

The new deliverance topics that have been added are based on common and pressing problems that are encountered in the day-to-day practice in the deliverance ministry but to which little or no focus has been given. The youth do not know the steps to take to get delivered, identify their divine partners. Many couples are childless and are going about without a solution, when actually the answers are not farfetched. I have blended the benefits of the anointing and call of God upon my life with medical knowledge to provide some insight. As stated earlier, other virgin topics have been discussed.

There is no experience that matches being in a hall with a facilitator, sharing diverse practical insights that may not be found exhaustively in the book; the inspiration of the holy spirit to raise prayer points, word of knowledge, anointed worship, and most importantly, the privilege of asking directions from the source and satisfying curiosities. This is why we have given the opportunity for people from any part of the world to book public speaking appointments, enrol in our coaching or mentorship programs by sending emails to abayomi.olugbemiga@gmail.com. Savour the deliverance and enjoy the transformation. God bless you all in Jesus name.

CHAPTER ONE

AN OVERVIEW TO WITCHCRAFT

What is witchcraft?

Witchcraft is a wide and complex subject, but could simply be defined in these few ways:

1. It is an alliance of powers, principalities, rulers of the darkness of this world, and spiritual wickedness in high places, to steal, kill, and destroy the souls of men physically and spiritually (Ephesians 6:12).
2. The use of supernatural and diabolical means to rebel against God's plans for those who reject the word of God, through Christ our LORD.
3. The use of hypnotics, spells, deceptions, manipulations, and magical powers to destroy or arrest the destinies of men and women.
4. Obeisance and commitment to demonic spirits through the worship of idols, rivers, trees, animals, the earth, the sun, and other elements or figures, and clearly portraying themselves as enemies of God, demonstrating hatred to God. (Exodus 20:5).
5. Cruel operations and activities going on in the dark places of the world (Psalm 74:20).
6. Witchcraft is simply rebellion, and stubbornness against the will of God (1 Samuel 15:23).
7. The major agenda, being pursued by witchcraft is to steal, kill, and destroy:

    John 10:10

    The thief cometh not, but for to steal, and to kill, and to destroy I am come that they might have life, and that they might have it more abundantly.

A certain woman who renounced witchcraft, confessed that she was part of a group that would go to churches and teach women empowerment, but they subtly preach rebellion against their husbands. There are many programs in town that are misleading. The women folk have been misled by satanic agents to have a totally wrong perception about marriage.

Divisions of The Witchcraft Kingdom.

The witchcraft kingdom operates in the heavens, on earth, and under the earth, establishing their strongholds, and altars in these realms. The witches that operate in the heavenlies operate as birds of different types, including owls, vultures, the European black bird, and even as serpents which are usually "flying serpents". They make their abode on high trees and meet there. At night, humans transform into birds, and fly to these aerial destinations to meet. They conclude their meetings in the early hours of the morning and transform back from human beings to birds. The process of this dual transformation is known as "shapeshifting". Some witches go in human form on brooms, by astral projection, and attend these meetings. Astral projection, also known as the "out of body experience" is often used by witches and wizards to travel to carry out their activities.

When you are a prayer warrior, you tend to chain them down and deactivate their powers with your prayers. Many of them have confessed when a new neighbour packs into their neighbourhood, saying, since this couple came here, we have not been able to attend meetings regularly as we used to do. Some of them who are landlords simply refund your rent and beg you to find another accommodation. Witchcraft possessed persons can recognise God's presence and power upon the children of God, if you take your place through spiritual violence. They will respect you. Right from the days of John the Baptist until now, the kingdom of God suffereth violence and the violent take it by force (Matthew 11:12):

> *Matthew 13:25*
>
> *But while men slept, his enemy came and sowed tares among the wheat, and went his way.*

As children of God, the hours of the night are not hours to sleep all through the night. Anything from 12 midnight to around 3am should be used for prayer, praise and study of God's word. This makes you to charge your spiritual battery every night, and because you are on fire every night, they cannot attack you, if you live your life in righteousness. I take it upon myself to pray every night, continuously and this has continued for several months. An old witch that I knew very well has been trying to get at me. The daughter called me one day to my amazement as she asked, "so you have not been sleeping at night"? I wondered how someone in Africa could be aware of what I was doing in England. Contrary to what many do, trying to physically fight them is not scriptural and fruitless as the Bible does not encourage us to employ that approach:

> *2 Corinthians 10:4*
>
> *For the weapons of our warfare are not carnal, but mighty through God to the pulling down of strong holds;*

The night prayers you say is a coded message to tell them that they are not permitted to operate where you are in charge. We need the wisdom of God, as it is not by power or by might. It is left for you to draw the battle line. The Bible says it all:

> *Philippians 2:10*
>
> *That at the name of Jesus every knee should bow, of things in heaven, and things in earth, and things under the earth;*

Another realm of their operations is the earth! Many institutions in this world are dedicated to evil practices and cruel activities. There are societies termed as "secret societies" whose members can not reveal their identities openly, and they carry out their activities secretly, obviously because of their satanic activities. Many institutions that label themselves as institutions for economic and financial development, are actually the devil's workshop. Souls are initiated unconsciously, and by the time you get to discover, it is too late. Any invitation to go to secret places or carry out rituals especially in the night should be ignored.

There are cemeteries that if you go there at night, you will wonder what people are doing there at that odd hour. I met a woman who said she likes to meditate in the cemetery at night because of the silence. She told me that she is a Christian. There are also houses used as covens. People can only be seen there during the night-time. During the day, it is deserted and under lock and key. Be mindful of these satanic altars in the society, and the people that go in and out of such. The road junctions are places of serious demonic traffic, and that is where the witches and wizards meet, and wreak havoc on individual and group or business basis, most of the unprofitable enterprises are actually being attacked by witchcraft. I used to live on a street many years back, where a booming Cybercafe was situated. One night, I slept and saw that witchcraft powers came to raid that area, spiritually. In the dream, many shops were closed down, many things were vandalised in the spirit realm. The mast of this cybercafe standing distinctively in the skyline of that street was one of the structures that were vandalised. It didn't take more than a few days after that dream, that the Cybercafe started having technical problems, and was eventually closed down. The colossal investment went down the drain!

Many huge trees that you see around are altars of witchcraft. Evil powers meet inside them or around them and could be seen moving around. Someone noticed as some damsels moved out of a tree, and a tree was being cut in a town and people noticed that blood gushed out of the tree like a stream. They have been a shelter for the devil for many centuries. I relocated to a new area sometime in the year 2006. I started praying for God to destroy every evil influence in that area, I saw a tree in the spirit realm and in a trance, that a snail shell with a red cloth was hanging on it. I decided to burn it down with old tyres. I tried to cut it, and the machete bounced back severally. It was as if the tree was made of a special kind of plastic. That was why I decided to burn it. It took persistent burning for it to be eventually ignited and burnt down. What amazed me was that as I burnt it, a demon ran out of it, standing afar and looking at me as a homeless lad would. At that same period, the Lord told me to cut down three other very tall trees in my vicinity. These trees were about 20 metres tall. I decided to observe the trees more closely and discovered that three birds looking like vultures were living on the tree. I decided immediately to hire labourers who would cut down the trees.

There was a major river in Lagos, Nigeria, where I lived, that accidents were always happening at a particular spot close to the river, at the foot of the bridge. I was on a fast, and the Lord opened my eyes to see a blood sucking demon alighting from a vehicle, at that spot, where auto-accidents usually happen. All altars in a city where idols are worshipped are also "hotspots" of witchcraft activities, and places of great demonic traffic. In the next chapter, we shall examine in detail, "Witchcraft Organisation and Tactics" It is amazing to note that civilisation has given way to extensive witchcraft attacks against the souls of men in many nations of the world.

A lot of activities are happening even under the surface of the earth, beyond what we can see with our ordinary eyes. Under the earth, we have activities in the marine world. Particularly, the existence of mermaid spirits which we all know. The mysteries surrounding the disappearance of ships at the Bermuda Triangle is also well known and documented. The sea is associated traditionally with the belief that it is associated with wealth. This has drawn the interest and worship by many of the world's people. The splendour associated with the sea is another reason of attraction to water activities. Many of the slaves that migrated to South America during the Trans-Atlantic slave trade influenced many people in South America to embrace idolatry, and witchcraft practices associated with the worship of the river goddess, known as "Yemoja" in Africa, but which they know as "Yemaya".

In areas where the water goddesses are worshipped, there is immorality, promiscuity, violence, deceptions, sexual perversion, crime, and materialism. When you draw spiritual map of the world, you would discover that many coastal cities of the world are characterised by these afore-mentioned vices and other perversions. The Evangelists world-wide need to do a lot of work in order to be able to dismantle these strongholds. Even amongst the Pastors in these locations, spirituality is at its lowest ebb. These are the effects of massive witchcraft infiltration.

CHAPTER TWO

ORGANISATION OF WITCHCRAFT

The witchcraft kingdom is well organised, and they do not joke with their issues as many of us Christians do. Lateness to meetings, or compromise of any sort may attract serious penalties or consequences. Every member is dragged into an oath, usually a blood oath, which links all initiates that they can communicate at will. Breaking the oath could cost a member his or her life. They monitor world affairs and activities around them with so much commitment, and determination to execute their evil assignments. When it comes to wreaking havoc, a witch or wizard does not understand if you are a relative or not. For instance, your mother might be the one assigned to monitor you and bring you down. There are just like policemen and policewomen. Once your relative does something wrong, you must bring them to book and act according to what they have all agreed upon.

Close Marking.

There is "close marking" in the spiritual realm, and one of the signs that you have a glorious destiny is the attacks that you start receiving at a particular time. This should not intimidate you, but you should strive to fight and win. They can see you from their control room, the great things that are about to happen in your life. What is happening is that they are trying to stop you, and they are committed to doing just that. Many years before I travelled to England, someone very close that I knew very well, and would even sometimes stop to eat in their house was saying in a trance, "if we allow this one to get to the main road, he will be a problem". This normally happens in families too, as a member of the family, or in your neighbourhood is intimidated by your prospects, like Joseph and his brothers. It could be in your career, like Saul and David. The devil could use anyone, and that's why you need to be righteous in and out and try to always be at your best at all times. The attack against Joseph by his brothers is what is known as "household witchcraft" A man's foes shall be they of his own household (Matthew 10:36).

> *1 Corinthians 16:9*
>
> *For a great door and effectual is opened unto me, and there are many adversaries.*

If they can't get you down, they'll quickly look for someone that will do it. They try to accuse you before God, so that you can lose credibility, and your blessings, honour, and glory. If you are a man, they could inspire their daughter to offer you sex. If you are not dead to sin. It could be money. The devil who tried Jesus (Matthew 4:1-11). There is someone that the devil has assigned against you brighter future. Be careful, live righteous, holy and watch and pray. Do everything possible to flee from sin.

Groups.

Witches are usually grouped in odd numbers as a functional unit. They essentially have a Queen or Leader who is usually crowned and given immense powers. I had the privilege of delivering a marine queen many years ago. Groups of three, five, seven, nine and up to two hundred and one people are common. They normally have a leader, as well as duties assigned to individual members. As a sign of commitment to their groups, they are asked to donate the person that is dearest to them. Most times, a son, a daughter, a wife, a husband, a mother or father. The donated person may be killed for them to move up the ladder, or may simply take their place in the group, and spearhead their activities. It is not different in the occult, as the practice is same. The attire you always see in your dreams that they put on include white attire which commonly represents marine witchcraft. However, some marine witches are identified by red or black attire. Other types of witches are commonly identified by black and red attire.

Meetings.

Witches and wizards meet regularly at least once weekly on specific days which are significant to them. Mondays, Tuesdays are Thursdays are common days. Some combine membership in the occult with witchcraft society membership. The occult is more physical in its dispensations because they can be seen physically. I had a supposed member of our church who confessed to me that he had dual membership in the occult and marine witchcraft. He found himself in our church because he said he was in love with one of our members. Witchcraft meetings are held at road junctions, in the river, on trees, inside the rock, under the banana tree, and huge trees like the "Iroko", which is one of the mystical trees of the Yoruba tribe in Nigeria. Sometimes, they simply connect by "astral projection" and go on with their meeting. The meetings occur in their dreams, as they go online spiritually, so to speak. They may decide to be alone at that time and wouldn't feel like talking to anyone. Child witches usually do this. They go to a quiet place, usually at the back of the class, while they are in school, or alone in the room, if they are at home, even during the day, and they mutter inaudible words. If you can interrupt them, then you have successfully foiled the meeting, and they could curse you under their breath. This could be followed by a resistant or stubborn behaviour. We shall discuss witchcraft in children in a subsequent chapter. Prayers are very effective in stopping witchcraft meetings, even if they are not living in your house. If they live in your house, and you know the day of their meeting, try to involve them in the prayers. I had a house maid many years back who has witchcraft and possessed by different wild animal spirits. As I was praying deliverance prayers with her, her spiritual colleagues twisted her tongue and she couldn't speak clearly. They knew she would reveal vital information to me in the process. She was unable to speak clearly.

CHAPTER THREE

INITIATION INTO WITCHCRAFT.

Initiation into witchcraft could be involuntary or voluntary. In involuntary initiation, whether you like it or not, in as much as they have seen your star, and marked you for initiation or attack, they will try all possible means to ensure that you are initiated. Common means of initiation are through food and sex. Due to the innocence of children, many unfortunately are initiated unconsciously, without them knowing. I had a counselee and deliverance candidate that I prayed with. Suddenly, she fell to the ground under the anointing, and said mentioning the name of one of her childhood friends "the biscuit you gave me that day is what has put me in trouble now. She had been carrying that bondage since she was in the primary school, as she had a flashback of the experience, after recovering from the anointing that fell upon her. Initiation is the beginning or induction into witchcraft, but we still have oppression and obsession which shall be discussed in later chapters.

Who Could Possibly Initiate You?

Anybody can initiate you into witchcraft. It is not written on the forehead, but when the cv of some children, and their witchcraft achievements are read to your hearing, then you shrink into your seat. It is a common thing for mothers to initiate their children, and to kill them through witchcraft! Does that come to you as a surprise? It is common for people to be initiated cheaply in everyday life, including your favourite restaurant and your barber or hairdressers' shop. The new twist in the western world now is that they encourage you to join some groups that will make you rich. They drag you gradually into it, until you are sunken in it. It is like a frog placed in a cold beaker, and the fire is turned on. He enjoys it as the water gets warmer. It gets to a point where it becomes a little bit unbearable. He might say, let me endure, until eventually the water comes to the boil. He is destroyed. There is nothing as effective as exposing the devil as soon as you possibly can, even though the voice threatens to kill you.

Why Are People Initiated?

People are initiated into witchcraft, so that the plan of God for them, and their glorious destinies can be destinies can be destroyed. Once you are initiated, the powers that you have a covenant with, continues to be in total control of your life and can do anything. They also derive some form of promotion as their commission for initiating you, and at your expense. Some groups can initiate you and allow you to have everything, except one thing that you would feel the impact so much. A lady was initiated, and as we ran her through deliverance, the spirit spoke through her, "I will allow her to marry, but I will not allow her to have a child". The spirit was trying to negotiate with us. We rejected her proposal and told her it was unacceptable. We continued praying, casting out, binding, and loosing. Eventually the sister had a baby. An initiation could be for the purpose of initiating a child, making that child to be an agent to monitor the activities of the parents, and report to them, if the parents are actually the main target. They could also fly at night, and land into the life of the child, and from that child project into the body of the parents as they sleep together at night. I had a Deliverance candidate that was possessed, and as we continued, the demons in her spoke, and. I asked them, "what is your mission in her life?" They replied, her grandmother handed her over to us, so that she would never be settled in her life. The sister in question was always committing errors and receiving sack letters or leaving her employers under mysterious circumstances. They had fired the "arrow of error" and being vagabond into her life. She would always make mistakes, wherever she worked, and because she is in a blood covenant through her grandmother, they are always there to inspire her negatively to make mistakes, anyhow.

How Do People Get Initiated Unconsciously?

1. *Through what you eat, or drink*, you could get initiated. I mentioned the case of that sister who was initiated as a kid by her friend in school, who gave her biscuit. The problem remained with her till her early adulthood when she met Jesus and was ready to be delivered. Many are not ready to be delivered as they keep telling the Pastor that they are busy at work, and they squander their holidays in a useless manner. A child was given some sweets in school, which he decided to keep and show to his parents whenever they came back from work. He didn't remember to show it to them until the next morning. When he got to the shelf the next morning, the sweet had turned into a human thumb, and dripping fresh blood. If he took it immediately, he would have been initiated!

2. *Sex is another means of initiation*. A lady confessed some time ago, that they were out to offer "cheap sex" to men, in order to take control of their lives, introduce terrible spirits into their lives, and destroy their marriages or their careers. They could also introduce sickness into their system, through their body fluids. Once a lady has sex with you, you are connected directly to their kingdom. Many men are sick or jobless because of cheap sex. It could be in the office and not last more than 5 minutes, but it may give you a problem of a lifetime.

    1 Corinthians 6:16

    What? know ye not that he which is joined to a harlot is one body? for two, saith he, shall be one flesh.

    Nahum 3:4

    Because of the multitude of the whoredoms of the well-favoured harlot, the mistress of witchcrafts, that selleth nations through her whoredoms, and families through her witchcrafts.

3. *At birth*, many babies get initiated through direct contact with their blood. Many housewives in the hospitals have been commissioned by the devil, to initiate children. It will surprise you that even in state-of-the-art hospitals, you still find this happening. Recently in Europe, a Nurse developed a satanic means of killing babies for no reason, until she was discovered to be the serial killer! Babies were just dying mysteriously in her facility. She could have initiated them if that was the assignment given to her. At a time, I was involved in Hospital Chaplaincy in Africa, the Lord told me to always quickly dedicate newborn babies in the name of the Father, the Son, and the Holy Spirit, as soon as I could possibly do so.

4. *In a quest for power*, many are unconsciously initiated, because they are so desirous of political or organisational power that they do certain things, go to certain places, or do certain things which could transfer demons into their lives.

5. *Evil laying of hands* can also result to witchcraft initiation, just like laying of the hands of the presbytery could impact the anointing of the Holy Ghost. This is another method that is used to initiate babies in the hospitals, apart from the blood route. Witches who are into hairdressing too find it a good channel of initiation especially with repeated patronage. A woman that I knew many years back gave her hair to be attended to by another sister on the church. She started having nightmares right from that point onwards.

6. *Hospital procedure*, in the form of what you eat or drink, access to your blood, body fluid, and even your materials. It is not only the hospital staff, but also people that you meet and relate with in the hospital. The people you meet at the hospital came with the problem of infirmity, poverty, and possibly other problems. Most of these people's problems are sponsored by witchcraft too, and they too have monitoring spirits. In a place like the hospital, you have got to monitor whom you relate with, not just because of cross infection, but spiritual attacks.

7. *Star gazing and mediums*: those people that have interests in star gazing and horoscopes do not know that the ability to foretell comes from evil powers as well, and not just the holy spirit. Many people get initiated through these means.

8. *Mischief by unfriendly friends*. Many women are initiated through this means, either by the clothing they exchange with their friends or through food sharing at events and social gatherings. A handkerchief from a man of God can transfer spiritual power and so does a covenanted clothing from a stranger or unfriendly friend. A woman was lured into using a head cover given to her by a friend. She noticed that ever since then, things were never the same with her.

9. *Evil forests and forbidden places*. There are some places where you could go to and be possessed by evil spirits. Places like the Bennington Triangle in Vermont, USA, and Nahanni Valley in the Northwest Territories, Canada, are examples.

10. *Dream initiation*. This is another means employed by spiritually wicked forces. All they need do is to identify your weakness e.g. food or sex. They program night caterers or conduct and evil initiation whereby they make you to have sex with a demon. This will happen seamlessly, because you are prone to immorality.

> Proverbs 25:28
>
> He that hath no rule over his own spirit is like a city that is broken down, and without walls.

11. *Another type of unconscious initiation is initiation by heredity*. Some children are initiated whilst in the womb. This is because they inherited it, and at the time they were in the womb they were doing astral travel. The spirit was polluted from the womb.

Voluntary Initiation.

Voluntary initiation is knowingly and willingly agreeing to witchcraft initiation. This is usually because they desire wealth, materials, position, children and other things. One thing about these gifts is that sometime in your life, you would regret joining the cult, or witchcraft society. It is a way of putting your life on fast-forward or compressing your blessings. People who surrender to witchcraft initiation might shorten their lives. The devil has no free gift.

How does witchcraft initiation work?

Basically, the aim is to get the witchcraft spirit to enter into you and begin its work. Once it can enter into your spirit, you are now possessed, that you do not have control over your spirit of your volition. They have total control over you instead. Only Jesus can deliver you from them. Another thing is to establish a linkage and covenant to enable you to be one with them. Once the spirit can enter you, they can easily torment you to accept to "log in" at any time.

What do I mean by a "log in"? I mean you can join their meetings or gatherings using astral projection. Then also you can actively participate in their activities. When you are involuntarily initiated through sex, or blood, you are connected. When the voluntary initiates get initiated, usually by blood contact, each person that enters the group links the blood of all the others. This is a blood covenant, and linkage, and is very strong. They can all be in their different locations and do video conferencing. They can hold meetings spiritually and you cannot perceive with your bare senses, except you belong.

There is always a mechanism in place that is put in place to monitor their activities. Anything you say or do is known by all the others, because you are linked. Also, it may surprise you that all the thoughts of one are known by the rest. It is a serious type of bondage that gives you no freedom of your own, until you pray and fast to get delivered. If a lady belongs to a group consisting of seven initiates, and you have sex with her, you are having sex with seven people at the same time. How unlucky are you. If it is a large marine group consisting of up to two hundred and one people, then there you go! That is why marine witchcraft bondages are always very strong. It is not possible for a man that had sex with them to lie about his location at any time because the GPS is very strong monitoring you.

Signs of witchcraft initiation.

1. _Bad dreams_: witchcraft initiation will make you to have bad dreams like being pursued, and tormented. You may see dead people or other frightening figures.
2. _Terrifying visions:_ even when you are awake, you see terrifying images. A little boy of a few months old was initiated. The boy could not talk at that age, but the parents noticed that anytime he looked at a particular area in the room, he cried, and looked away. He was always not himself especially looking at that area. He had been initiated.
3. _Fear:_ an initiated person lives in constant fear, sometimes even of the unknown. They are used to a lifestyle of fear. The fear of death is common, because if they decline an evil assignment, they will be threatened that they would be killed, until they accept. However, it is a big lie! If they are determined and shun fear, all thigs are possible to them that believe. What you believe is what becomes of you. The best thing is to cry out and expose the rubbish!

4. _Hearing voices_: an initiate will hear all forms of voices threatening them. Even as an adult, they will threaten them. The funny thing is that even as a born-again Christian, and minister of God, they can attempt to initiate you, buy persistent attempts of intimidating you with death. If you fall for the nonsense, then they have you., if your faith is weak. They already got you probably through blood, or body fluids. Don't be surprised that if there is witchcraft in your husband or wife's root. They can still attempt to initiate you, in order to stop your ministry, as a child of God, through blood or food. However, if you are legally married, and you are not committing adultery, it would be a difficult task for them. Also, you need to remain on fire, prayer, and fasting.

5. _Strange behaviour:_ people who have been initiated exhibit strange behaviour like they are depressed and not always happy. They will always like to be alone. They may notice an increased libido or urge for sex. Some may have the urge to take alcohol or to even kill. You may feel like drinking blood. A woman came to me on a certain morning, and said "Pastor, I feel like killing someone". She was living in a stronghold and an area where witches were, and most probably by way of interaction, she was initiated. What is the strange behaviour that you are having, or that you occasionally have? This may be a sign, and an emergency.

6. _They mutter inaudible words_ and communicate with their sacred mates. An elderly man whom I met in England told me that it was a common thing in England, that people possessed usually have "sacred mates". These people they now begin to see and communicate with from time to time.

    Isaiah 8:19

    And when they shall say unto you, seek unto them that have familiar spirits, and unto wizards that peep, and that mutter: should not a people seek unto their God? for the living to the dead?

7. _They may fall sick constantly._ This is another thing that normally occurs with people who are initiated. When as a mother, you notice that your children who weren't falling sick regularly, suddenly begins to fall sick, then you need to review the situation. when you now see the doctors more frequently. Adults too fall sick after being initiated. In Africa, the parents add problem unto problem by taking them to traditional healers, who are predominantly witches and wizards themselves.

8. _Stubbornness and meanness_ are signs of an initiate. They have recently not received love and don't expect them to show love to anyone! They are mean and stubborn! However, some of them may look gentle on the face of it, not until you move to them more closely.

9. _They say words that convey despair, and frustration_. They tend to lose hope and give up easily. When others are trying to hold on, initiates give up. They may continue with that type of attitude for several years, and a husband or wife that has any of these attitudes needs help. If you are married to an initiate, they affect your shinning! There is the joy of salvation, which inspires inner strength and courage. They rob you of this.

All these signs do not need to be present before you can know that you are initiated. Only one or two are enough to confirm initiation into witchcraft or witchcraft oppression What do you do, when you notice witchcraft initiation?

Steps to Take to Cancel Witchcraft Initiation.

The rate at which the devil initiates children is alarming, through what they eat, or drink. Do you know that the same way that you respond to a "blue film" that you are sexually aroused, or the same way a little boy responds to a film of "Karate" by kicking and hitting his younger brother, or the same way you will react to horror films, or other obscene content, and you are frightened and dream about it? The devil just creeps into your dreams with the foundation of sin or unrighteous living you built in your mind, to activate your bondage.

Many initiates are unable to help themselves. They are drowning, and only someone who is not in the river, or knows how to swim, will be in the position to rescue them. As parents, husbands, wives, relatives, and significant others, we need to take the following steps:

1. *Discuss with a spiritual person*, because the problem cannot be solved physically. This might be discussed with a Deliverance Minister, Pastor, Evangelist, Christian Counsellor,
2. *Don't get irritable or condemn them*. Don't shout on them, but rather show love and understanding. Tackle with maturity. Many people possessed by witchcraft are people with glorious destinies that the devil is trying to stop them from manifesting gloriously. The battles of life, isn't it?
3. *Don't abandon them too.* I had the case of a husband, who suddenly discovered the wife was possessed, after many years of marriage, with 3 children, and abandoned her, not having sex with her. Try to give them all the necessary help and God will reward you. There is always a "spiritual reward" for every contribution to another person's deliverance. God himself rewards you. Don't abandon them, if they are your children. Try to help them as your hope for the future.
4. *Engage them in vigils*, otherwise known as "the night battle". Everyone in the family should agree on this. Let there be no dissentions with utterances like "they are going to school tomorrow, or I will get late to work. Husband and wife should plan their time. I have experienced it before. One or two hours at night daily is not too much. 12 midnight to 1am is perfect. All you need do is take dinner early, and go to bed a bit early, say 9pm. You would have had 3 hours to yourself before the alarm wakes you up by 12 midnight.
5. *During the day, engage them in Recreational activities.* An idle mind is the devil's workshop.
6. *Pray with them* and pray for them. Share the word of God with them. Show some love and kindness. It could be anyone! Anyone could be bewitched. Take it as a fall, help them to rise up (be delivered) and continue with life.
7. *Sacred Music is beneficial* because it has great potentials for deliverance from the spirit of heaviness.

    Isaiah 61:3 To appoint unto them that mourn in Zion, to give unto them beauty for ashes, the oil of joy for mourning, the garment of praise for the spirit of heaviness; that they might be called trees of righteousness, the planting of the LORD, that he might be glorified.

    Note the phrase "the garment of praise for the spirit of heaviness". When you put on the spirit of praise, it can lift away the spirit of heaviness.

8. *Confess the word.* When you are battling witchcraft, you need to study the word, meditate in the word and let it define your day-to-day activities.

9. *Aggressive fasting*: a person oppressed or possessed by witchcraft would always dare to fast. This makes the problem stronger. Except for health reasons, fasting need to be frequent and aggressive. Marathon fasts should be engaged in. Fasting weakens witchcraft spirits and forces them out of the body.
10. *Use your spiritual gifts.* Someone that needs their deliverance from witchcraft should use their spiritual gifts. This attracts the angels attached to the gifts and an advantage to the person that needs deliverance. Spiritual gifts edify, and do good works, and work against wicked witchcraft activities and goals.
11. *Dreams should be monitored and reported to the Deliverance Minister* periodically as an index of what is going on spiritually.
12. *Enrol in the Holy Ghost Baptismal Class.* Demonic spirits cannot cohabit with the fire of God. It is beneficial to enrol in the Holy Ghost Baptismal Class, and as soon as you receive the baptism, keep speaking with other tongues and watch out for any gifts that would follow.

CHAPTER FOUR

WITCHCRAFT ATTACKS.

It is possible for witchcraft spirits to oppress a person, without necessarily possessing that person. In oppression, witchcraft spirits attack you mainly in the dreams, by visions, and by "pressing" you down to your bed in the night, or other wicked acts. It means you are under the influence and control of demonic spirits. When they continue to oppress you, and you cannot do something to set yourself free, the memory lingers on, in your thoughts and emotions, and controls your life. This is known as obsession. When you have been oppressed and obsessed for too long, and you are not resisting all the attacks through prayer, fasting and the word of God, they move on to possess or initiate. When they attack you in the dream, and you do nothing about it, then the evil arrows they fired will prosper, and what they want can manifest. When they have confidently broken all your resistance, then they move in to possess, and live in you. This is demonic possession. At this stage, you have no say, they can do whatever they want with your life against your will.

Witchcraft attacks vary in manifestation and strength of manifestation, depending on where the arrows are coming from. Witchcraft attacks from people linked with you by blood are usually very strong, and vicious. However, if you are living a holy life, and are violent in prayer and fasting, it is difficult for them to attack you. Witchcraft attacks can only prosper, if there is sin, or iniquity, prayerlessness, or an open door. It ranges from waking life experiences, or experiences while men sleep.

Matthew 13:25

But while men slept, his enemy came and sowed tares among the wheat, and went his way.

Attacks in our everyday activities in the day light.

Real life arrows include bad experiences you have whilst you are awake. For example, you feel a gentle breeze right in front of you, as you were sitting around your house, and moments later, you have a weak leg as if something is moving around in your leg. You were having sex with your neighbour's daughter, and you noticed that your penis was paralysed, and couldn't function. Bringing in a prostitute to the house, and in the middle of the night, she turned into a coffin and disappeared into thin air, leaving no traces. A hairdresser made your hair, and you discovered that you got home, and you had a dream that the person came in your dream and made your hair, but this time around, in the dream, she was shaving your hair and not making it. Many years ago, I went to a local cafeteria to eat, and when I got home, I had a strange dream. In that dream, I was taken to the cafeteria once more in the dream, and instead of the delicious meal that I ate there in the afternoon, I discovered it was something different and dirty that I was served. I had been attacked in that cafeteria in the afternoon. There are sun and moon worshippers, and witchcraft agents that can attack. The Bible makes us to understand this in:

Psalm 121:6

The sun shall not smite thee by day, nor the moon by night.

Sometimes you might feel a peppery sensation in your hand or leg, and if you do not pray, it may grow worse. Consider a black bird that flew around your house with a very loud strange sound. Moments after, you started talking incoherently. A certain woman was walking past a T-junction in her neighbourhood, where a demonic ritual was placed. As she set her eyes on it, she felt as if her head was getting bigger. That was the beginning of her problems.

Mark 14:38

Watch ye and pray, lest ye enter into temptation. The spirit truly is ready, but the flesh is weak.

We need to keep watching and praying. Report every strange experience you have immediately to members of your family and giving details of what you think might be responsible. Also let your Pastor be aware. Invite the brethren to pray with you for up to a week. This could be organised at home or in the church. A stitch in time saves nine. Some of these signs could also be medical and help is urgently needed from a medical perspective. Leave no stone unturned. It is well known that some witchcraft activities might yield to medical care.

Attacks in the dream.

God in his infinite mercies has so designed dreams that he may reveal the activities of the wicked to us, so that we can make amends, repent, and avoid destruction. We do dream to receive god's instructions for our safety:

Job 33:15	*In a dream, in a vision of the night, when deep sleep falleth upon men, in slumberings upon the bed;*
Job 33:16	*Then he openeth the ears of men, and sealeth their instruction,*
Job 33:17	*That he may withdraw man from his purpose, and hide pride from man.*
Job 33:18	*He keepeth back his soul from the pit, and his life from perishing by the sword.*
Job 33:19	*He is chastened also with pain upon his bed, and the multitude of his bones with strong pain:*
Job 33:20	*So that his life abhorreth bread, and his soul dainty meat.*
Job 33:21	*His flesh is consumed away, that it cannot be seen; and his bones that were not seen stick out.*
Job 33:22	*Yea, his soul draweth near unto the grave, and his life to the destroyers.*
Job 33:23	*If there be a messenger with him, an interpreter, one among a thousand, to shew unto man his uprightness:*
Job 33:24	*Then he is gracious unto him, and saith, deliver him from going down to the pit: I have found a ransom.*

Studying verse 18 carefully, it shows that God always has us in mind, and wants to deliver us from going down into the pit or perishing by the sword. This is why he gives us information in our dreams (Job 33:16). Dreams are not to make you scared in any way but going by the scripture in Job 33 as you have now discovered, he wants you to strategize and get rescued. It is a message of mercy and kindness from God, no matter how scary it looks.

Whenever you have a witchcraft dream, there are a few things you need to do:

1. Surrender your life to Jesus by confessing him as your Lord and saviour
2. Decide to forsake every sin and unrighteousness.
3. Seek to know the meaning of your dreams that you have had, through your pastor or online resources. Sometimes the online resources are not reliable especially if they are not written by Christians.
4. When you know the meaning, then seek to know exactly what they are trying to do. A dream will always reveal how the enemy wants to attack you in real life e.g. maybe he wants to get you angry. I had a member who was not giving her tithe, but confidently came to a breakthrough service that I organised. As she prayed, she got home and discovered that in her dream, her shop was robbed. She came to report to me, and I asked her "madam, do you normally give your tithe"? Then she said was quiet for a while and said, "No Sir". I said, "there you go"! She was not giving tithe, and was robbing God, and was expecting blessings from God. Her prayers became sin as written in:

   Psalm 109:7
   When he shall be judged, let him be condemned and let his prayer become sin.

5. Try to judge all that you do with the word of God. If it is healing, then listen to messages on healing on YouTube. There are loads of resources on healing.
6. Look for corresponding actions and changes in your lifestyle, and sins you need to repent from. If you have disobeyed God in anyway, think about it. In the dream of Pharaoh, he acted by storing food. (Genesis 41:33-35)
7. It is also necessary to seek counsel from Counsellors and men of God, including your Pastor.
8. Meditate on the issue until you receive clarity as to what next steps you should take.

CHAPTER FIVE

HOTSPOTS OF WITCHCRAFT INITIATION.

There are particular areas and institutions in everyday life, where witchcraft activities thrive, and you may be a victim of witchcraft attacks, or completely initiated by witchcraft. This is to give you an idea of their activities and how to avoid their onslaughts.

Maternity Centres.

There are some people, immediately they arrive in this world, they are welcome by witches and wizards, and given a certificate of membership. In some maternity centres, owned by witches or members of the occult, they have covenants that initiate babies. God showed me many years back, a centre where the woman in charge made a covenant, that every baby born on her couch would be initiated. So, in as much as you deliver your baby on that couch, he or she is initiated. Another thing is the placenta. Immediately the placenta came out, what was done to it? Where did they take it? Don't allow anyone to take it away. Request for it, because it is very important. The placenta can be used diabolically to determine what happens to the child in his or her life.

Who has access to the blood? The linen and scrubs and all the other things containing blood, where would they go. Many of us do not know the power that blood has and what it can do. It might not be possible to collect all these things, but you pray for revelation and that every counsel of the wicked should be brought to nought. Who are the people that bathe the baby or combed the hair? The glory of most children are wiped off their head in the first few hours of life. These are the types of children that struggle endlessly in life, from cradle to grave, and never achieve anything. To make matters worse, they may always ignore the call to receive Christ, so that the possibility of their ever getting saved is rare or altogether impossible. What are the pronouncements that were made jokingly regarding the baby, as he or she was born? Pray at this juncture "I recover, every glory stolen from me in the first few days of life, in the name of Jesus." Finally, when the child was discharged from the hospital, and got home, who were the people that came to greet the baby. Which people were anxious to carry the baby? Why must you carry a baby as a visitor. All mothers should not only resist this but prevent it. In the light of recent knowledge and wisdom, it is no longer in fashion for people to visit a newborn baby and insist on carrying the baby before they leave.

Babysitters.

It is possible you may resume work as a mother, after six months, and the child is now left always with the babysitter! Choosing a babysitter requires prayers of inquiry for a few months before you finally decide on whom will baby sit. The choice of the babysitter could make or Mar a child's destiny, as many physical and spiritual tragedies could befall the baby, at the house of the babysitter. What is your baby eating? Who feeds him or her? What are their intentions. If you and your husband pray Until you receive an answer as to who would baby sit for you, it is worth it. You could always give instructions to the babysitter as to who carries the baby or feeds the baby. Regular crying, and sickness in a newborn baby, are signs that should not be overlooked. We shall go into details about this later.

Even mother in-laws have proved dangerous with past experiences. Some mother in-laws who are possessed will like to initiate a baby, so that in their group, she can put down someone who would continue after her. For some, it is out of sheer wickedness, because your demonic group needs a blood donation. What does that mean? They want you to donate a person. Some mother in-laws actually go ahead to do that, and the newborn baby is the target. House helps are not also left out of this. In fact, if the house help is possessed and the mother in-law is possessed, then, it takes tough spiritual warfare and determination to save the child. Couples need to pray and implement the instructions from the Holy Spirit with great caution. If you cannot pray alone to receive results, get other members in your church to pray with you or for you, with the aim of arriving at a Holy Ghost inspired decision as to who comes to take care of the baby.

Primary schools.

A lot of children that escaped initiation or witchcraft attacks in the first few days of life, and at the babysitter's place, may not be able to escape witchcraft attack or initiation in their 6 years of enrolment in the primary school. In an earlier example that I have given in this book, all it took to be initiated into witchcraft was for that child to eat biscuit from a possessed child. The witchcraft spirit was living in the girl and was not exposed until after almost 20 years later that the child, now an adult, went for a Deliverance program. The spirit manifested and revealed that the problem that the lady brought for deliverance was caused by the biscuit she took from her friend in the primary school, several years back. What if she never had the opportunity to go for deliverance? Would it be beneficial for us to allow our children to attend deliverance programs during the holidays? Certainly yes!

We should be interested in what these children do in school, and the kind of company they keep, whether as day students or boarders. As a student staying far away from home, you need to visit your ward occasionally and unannounced to them, so that you can track progress.

Secondary Schools.

In the secondary schools, teenagers tend to associate more closely with one another, and spiritual flows and transfers from one child to the other are easier. Starting from the food they share, the words they share, and many other ways. Based on experience over the years, there have been more cases of initiation reported in the secondary school stage than at any other stage in life. Food consumption is usually the pivot. It has been shown that single sex schools allow witchcraft tendencies more than mixed schools either all males or all females. That is where you have lesbianism and homosexuality, as well as cultism more predominantly. All sorts of deviant behaviour abound in single schools. Think about these things and more before you enrol your child in a school.

Higher Institutions

There is a lot of witchcraft activities going on in tertiary institutions. This includes initiation into various types of cults, with killing and maiming in between rival groups of cultists. Satanic empowerment by these cults, to be able to see visions, to be resistant to gun shots or machete cuts. Female students employ all forms of manipulation to seduce lecturers, so that they can earn cheap marks without reading.

Diverting the star of young men by the female students, as one of them openly confessed. She said that they were sent to the higher institutions to lure the students into having sex with them, so that their glory can be arrested. Young men like that may attain very good grades in the final exams, but wouldn't be able to find a job, or make headway in life. There is also all forms of spiritual manipulations and witchcraft activities amongst traders on the campuses, and against students.

Markets.

Markets are places of terrible demonic and witchcraft activities. Several seen and unseen altars, and demonic powers are seen in marketplaces. In some markets, human body parts are being sold, some traders are being lured into witchcraft deceiving them that they would be rich. Many of the wares are dedicated to demons. Some artificial hair and clothing are dedicated to demons. A closer look at the items on display for sale, will reveal demonic signs on them. There are objects with serpents drawn on them. Others have the picture of a skull, scorpion, coffin, mermaid, or other tiny pictures that have significant meanings. A man saw a woman who was standing upside down with her head down and her feet up. Yet another saw a woman, who was selling palm oil, but she was in the spirit realm washing her hair in the big container of palm oil she was selling. Strange demonic beings appear from the spirit world to transact business on market days. That is why you need to sanctify anything you buy from the market, especially in a place like England, when the market days are filled with people from several countries. I used to get baffled when I go to the market and see many food items too numerous to identify and describe. Some of these things are actually from the other side of the world. The same is the case with every market, big or small in America, especially the farmers markets, and crafts market, across the United States of America.

Pentecostal Witchcraft.

Witchcraft is well established in many churches, and is practised by Pastors, ministers and members alike. Many Senior Pastors try to suppress upcoming Pastors by posting them to areas where they would not be able to operate their gifts, or make sure they keep them in a place where they wouldn't be able to use their gifts. A Healing Minister who is highly anointed; his Senior Pastor has given the responsibility of ministering at burials, is a Witchcraft decision. Every time he is about to clinch a major achievement, you transfer him. He is indirectly destroying his star and preventing him for shining. He is trying to kill him whilst he is alive.

A minister who would always find fault, and not forgive is practicing witchcraft. If a Chorister in your choir comes late to church, you don't bother to ask why, you start complaining one you set your eyes on them. There are churches where members visit herbalists to get charms to harm other members. There are churches where powerful and promising ministers were poisoned.

Seduction in church, and cheap sex is another issue. They do this to quench the fire and reduce the power of God. Churches like that will never have good members. If they will ever have members, they will only be the unserious members. It is the agenda of witchcrafts.

Gossiping is another Witchcraft work of church member. Some church members peddle rumours about the Pastor, his family, ministers, and members, whether those statements are true or not. It is all in an extremely to cause prayerlessness, reduce the fire of God, and collapse the church. Be very careful about what you listen to, and what you say. All kinds of immoral tendencies and immorality should be condemned. Bible study should be taken seriously and the Pastor should guide against their words and actions. The Bible gives qualities of a good Pastor in (1 Timothy 3:1 – 7), and anything outside this this is not ideal.

Offices and Workplaces.

A lot of immoral activities go on in such a way as to manipulate leaders in the offices. Any leader who is so close to the opposite sex is trying to give way to witchcraft. The agenda of witchcraft is to sell nations and families to the devil.

> Nahum 3:4
>
> *Because of the multitude of the whoredoms of the well-favoured harlot, the mistress of witchcrafts, that selleth nations through her whoredoms, and families through her witchcrafts.*

An uneducated witch could use her witchcraft power to direct the affairs of an office, including elderly and well-educated people, if the leader can stoop low to have sex with her. They use the avenue to lobby for undeserved promotion.

Food is also a common weapon of witchcraft in the offices. Many celebrate the 40th Birthday, almost every year, using food to get at people. The rage of the devil in this regard is so much during the Christmas and New Year seasons where gifts are freely given. There was an attempt by witches to kill a man through poison during the Christmas time. The food he was given was used to feed his dog. Immediately, the dog ate it, it stretched on the floor and die. A Professor of Medicine was unfortunate as he ate the food he was given in his own case. He died before getting to the hospital.

Favouritism and tribalism are also ways of witchcraft practices in offices. It delays the promotion of other people and perpetually makes them frustrated.

Canteens.

Canteens are places where someone could be initiated into witchcraft, especially familiar spirit possession. Many staff who are working in a canteen are possessed by witchcraft. The fingers are snakes in the spirit realm. Their hairs are worm like if God opens your eyes spiritually to see them.

There was this case of a canteen owner, who would always put a basin for washing hands in the canteen. After food, she collects the spent water to take to the herbalist to convert their stars to herself. Meanwhile another woman, a canteen owner, would always wash her private part inside the big pot she has used to store food, in order to seduce men. She serves everyone from that pot as a form of ritual. It is always better to avoid eating outside, as a Christian, if you can.

Most of the food some of them sell have been dedicated to demons, and that is why you eat that type of food to discover that you may sleep and see yourself eating in that same canteen, but this time in the dream, you are eating pebbles! They do this to steal your glory.

Brothels and Pubs.

People in brothels and pubs are used to a rough life. Bewitched starts from the words they speak to one another, which could be untrue and misleading, yet has a great impact upon their lives. It manipulates them and shapes their character and destiny. In this way, your star could be stolen through misleading words and an inappropriate lifestyle.

For a lady to make up her mind to pursue a career as a prostitute, and go commercial, she most definitely has a sexual demon, that gives her the desire and energy. It is not normal. Normally, 90% of the girls you see in a place like that are heavily possessed by demons. If you join yourself to them, then you acquire their demons. Your life cannot be the same again. They sell the stars of these men or convert their progress in life. Such men may never get a job. When they now have a job, there is no saving. They depend on the wife and others. Whenever they save money, because they have been bought by prostitutes, they take the money back to prostitutes. When these witches catch you with the weapon of sex, it might take the help of your wife to release you from their grip. Most men that fall victim, beat and violate their lives and children, because nothing else matters in this world except sleeping with the whore! If you are a lady and find yourself in this situation, you have got to use every energy in you to wrestle in the place of prayer. A lot of prayer is needed for God to direct you as to what you need to do.

Hairdressers Place.

The hairdresser's place is another "hotspot" for witchcraft activities and operations, especially when the hairdresser himself or herself is possessed by evil powers. The approach is to barb your hair at home, as a man, if you don't mind. Some women cut their hair for this reason, and don't do anything flamboyant, and trust me, some of those shorn hair could be very beautiful on some women.

If a possessed person with a demonic hand and fingers makes your hair, their laying of hands impacts negative anointing of failure, reproach and death, physically and spiritually. One of the imminent signs after such an evil spiritual transaction is that you dream and see yourself repeating the hairdo in the dream, but this time around, the hair will be cut in a haphazard manner and very untidy. When you wake up, immediately you need to pray like a wounded lion, and recover your glory. There is no other language that these evil spirits understand, then a resilient spiritual attitude! Battle them until you get what you want.

The Marriage Institution.

This is another place where a person can be easily and cheaply attacked or initiated by witchcraft. It is not just about your wife or husband, but about other people significant to your husband or wife, that you would not like to step on their toes. Imagine your mother in-law is a witch and has been given an agenda to destroy you from the Kingdom of darkness. The Lord in his unsearchable mercy would reveal to you, every evil that is happening in your dream. However, it takes courage to say no, even when they are almost killing you. There is a need to pray for revelation, under the circumstances. Without the power of revelation in this world, witches would keep operating as they will.

If that kind of a woman gives you food, and you say you are not interested, the son or daughter may say, it is a culture in their town, if you are not from the same town. Brethren, if you want to be a Christian, be one, and never use culture to make the grace of God of no effect. Act according to your intuition. Many of us have played into the hands of witches, and wizards, when God actually wanted to deliver us, because we despised the word of God, owing to culture and tradition.

Matthew 15:3

But he answered and said unto them, why do ye also transgress the commandment of God by your tradition

If your father in-law or mother in-law "prays" for you, and lays hands on your head, and you are quite aware, would you tell him or her to stop it? These are things we should consider. Not every father or mother in-law is happy with your existence. For all they care, anything can happen to you. They are interested in only their child. That is why you need to prioritise your God and your welfare. Self-love is important.

I have heard a mother in-law, that was sent to destroy the son in-law, say she would be able to get at the son in-law, through her daughter. What was she depending on? The fact that she is connected to her daughter by blood, and the son in-law is connected to her daughter too through sexual intercourse and are one with her daughter. This same woman was heard by the mother in-law in a revelation say to some people that if we allow this boy to het to the main road, we are in trouble! The woman tried, but the son in-law is a covenant child. A mother in-law which could use their daughter to get at you. If you now see your wife in the dream saying "they sent me to destroy you" how would you feel? She was sent, but mind you, no one can stop God's agenda, because he is the Almighty, and the dreadful one! Some people call him "Erujeje" or "Onye na-atu egwu" meaning the dreadful one.

Depending on whether you know whom you know your wife is, you may be in the belly of the crocodile. When you marry a possessed lady, she will always control your life under different guises. If you resist the evil domination, you are in a bigger trouble. We always encourage in the Deliverance Ministry, that intending couples should court for about a year, before they endorse the relationship. It is not only because they have been able to pray and fast, but they have enjoined others to pray with them, and they have observed the character of the person in question, firsthand.

A poorly informed decision could frustrate you for the rest of your very life, and that is why you should be careful. Many people have the right partners, but the wrong in-laws. Witchcraft in your father or mother in-law will eventually manifest in your wife or husband.

A witch was confessing and has this to say. She said that the agenda of every witch is to run the husband down financially in every way possible, so that they can dominate and control the men. She went further to say that once he is down financially, that they abandon him and move on!

Cultural festivals.

It is possible to be attacked and oppressed after attending a festival dedicated to idols. The food that are eaten there are dedicated to idols. The people that cook the food are not clean either. Rituals done pertaining to the food might be unknown. In some parts of West Africa, things like kolanuts are used. Events in the Americas that make people dress in a sexually provocative manner are included in the festivals mentioned here. Negative sexual energy is developed, and such carnivals might make vulnerable men to play into the hands of the enemy.

If you contribute money to the cause of such festivals, you have I directly participated in the festival or served the deity with your money and are liable to be punished by God accordingly:

> *Exodus 20:5*
>
> *Thou shalt not bow down thyself to them, nor serve them: for I the LORD thy God am a jealous God, visiting the iniquity of the fathers upon the children unto the third and fourth generation of them that hate me;*

The act of worshipping idols is rebellious to God, and is seen as witchcraft:

> *1 Samuel 15:23*
>
> *For rebellion is as the sin of witchcraft, and stubbornness is as iniquity and idolatry. Because thou hast rejected the word of the LORD, he hath also rejected thee from being king.*

Some festivals are characterised by the use of bells, gongs, drums or other instruments that give characteristic sounds which could demonically inspire certain utterances or dance steps. The place where cultural festivals are being celebrated are loaded with demonic traffic, and you just need to abstain.

As a Christian, we are in the world buy not of the world, and should refrain from participating or showing any interests in traditional festivals.

Hospitals.

There is a noticeable demonic and witchcraft traffic in hospitals, if the Lord opens your spiritual eyes. Even after an accident, or the sickness, witchcraft spirits are not relenting as they continue the chase of their victims, right into the hospital. There they could cooperate with other witchcraft powers. This is called "demonic reinforcement". When God opens your eyes, you would see the demonic activities and movement of red witchcraft in an Orthopaedic Hospital, in particular, blood sucking spirits. I was administering therapy to a young man on a certain day, when he shouted on his bed. I asked him why he shouted. He said someone was using water sachet to collect his blood. Whenever I moved closer to him, he stopped shouting, as they would leave him alone.

The issue of using food, drinks and water by patients to initiate fellow patients and hospital staff alike is a common occurrence. When you are in the hospital, you try and share things less with people. Also study the word of God and pray for revelation.

Another open door to witchcraft attacks is that many people reveal their secrets to the enemy in the hospital by being too vocal about events in their life. Most times we give the enemy the key with which to enter our lives.

Government.

Ephesians 6:12

For we wrestle not against flesh and blood, but against principalities, against powers, against the rulers of the darkness of this world, against spiritual wickedness in high places.

The Bible makes mention of spiritual wickedness in high places, and this is not only true in the spiritual sense but also in the physical sense. The effect of this is what you see manifesting in the lives of the citizenry, all over the world. To say the least, there is great rancour and hatred between one politician and the other, with one party trying to pull down the other. Most governments do not have good plans for the masses, and the result is the poverty and unrest we see in the nations of the world. Chemical warfare and killings.

Many government leaders are into cultism whilst some are initiated into witchcraft, manifesting different kinds of destructive and deceptive tendencies because of money and power. Any Christian leader that joins then will soon be part of them. In many countries of the world, the citizens wouldn't have any problem, but their government is the cause of their problems. Any Saint that is involved in politics will not finish his tenure the same. He must have been bewitched and corrupted. This is not good enough.

The Internet.

The internet has played a terrible role in the oppression of individuals and initiation into witchcraft. To start with, you could gain knowledge on the Internet and familiarise yourself with witchcraft and destructive practices from all over the world.

Joining a witchcraft movement is just a click away for as long as you care. It is witchcraft for free! It is not for sale. The youth mainly are the victims and casualties of these. One great way of stopping this is to be cautious about how our youth use the Internet.

Social and cultural groups.

There are millions of social and cultural groups around the world, whose ideas are just to promote some ideas and make fun. Most cultures and traditions from different parts of the world are unchristian, and promote witchcraft activities. Some of this groups are outright satanic or occultic. We as Christians need to contest for leadership in these organisations so we can alter the existing paradigm. Unfortunately, some of them have grown to be very popular and influential. Evangelism provides an overall solution to problems like this, and still the most effective tool in the hands of Christians for social and cultural reformation.

CHAPTER SIX

FIFTY WITCHCRAFT DREAMS, CONNOTATIONS AND SOLUTIONS.

Here are fifty witchcraft dreams, connotations and solutions:

1. *Eating in the dream*: different kinds of food could be served in your dream. The mission is to pollute your spirit man, so that you would not be able to remember your dreams, so that you can have nightmares, or make you sick. The solution is to avoid eating late and control the portion of what you eat. Don't eat excessively. Pray against the source of the food e.g. O LORD, destroy the source of satanic food in my dream life, or O LORD, destroy every evil altar or power, feeding me with the bread of affliction.

2. *Sex in the dream*; this dream is to introduce a sexual demon into your life, and to cause sexual perversion, such that you wouldn't be satisfied sexually with only your wife or husband. Solution is to refrain from lust, and inordinate affection and play with the opposite sex. Pray to destroy evil soul tie and covenant with spirit wife.

3. *Seeing tomatoes, palm oil, or other red substances in your dreams* will make you to have irregular menstrual periods and difficulty in conception or safe delivery. Solution is to schedule a Deliverance program and visit a gynaecologist as further support.

4. *Red wine in dream.* When you dream that you are drinking red wine in the dream, they are actually feeding you with blood, and polluting your spirit man. People like that might not be able to pray or study the bible for more than 5 minutes at a go, before they fall asleep. Solution is to pray for one-week, breaking blood covenants that you have entered into unconsciously

5. *Wearing rags, and dirty clothing* is a dream of poverty. A good income is no guarantee. What have you achieved with the good income, is a question you should ask yourself. Solution is to see a Counsellor or contact our website. Make sure you work harder and be honest in your dealings at work. Pay your tithes and sow seeds (Isaiah 58).

6. *Nakedness in the dream* means that the enemy wants to expose you and disgrace you. Watch your actions and flee from any behaviour that will make you to come short of God's glory. Run from every sin. Break every curse and covenant of shame and reproach.

7. *Pregnancy in the dream:* the enemy is giving you spirit children so that you cannot have children. However, this condition yields to stubborn prayer if you can pray. Go to our website for further enquiries.

8. *Marriage in the dream:* this is also known as evil spiritual marriage. Once you are married in the spirit realm, it takes fasting and prayer repeatedly for several days to break the covenant. It is needful to break the covenant with spirit spouse, because in the realm of the spirit it would stand in between you and your husband, preventing you from enjoying your marriage.

9. *Injections in the dream*: witches and wizards are trying to inject spiritual toxins into your life. A pregnant woman thus injected could miscarry. A worker thus injected could commit errors. It could lead to strange behaviour. Solution in ALL these scenarios is to see a deliverance minister or contact our website to book a consultation.

10. *Bleeding in the dream* means you are losing virtues and life sustaining elements in your life. The Bible says that the life of the flesh is in the blood (Leviticus 17:11). This is a pointer that the enemy is stealing from you! It may be through sex, or even because of ignorance. If you feel sick, or are having other signs and symptoms, book a session on our website.

11. *Sickness in the dream* means that the arrow of infirmity has been fired into your life. Get our book entitled "Healing Miracles" on the Amazon website. The same advice is for all that are having one sickness or the other. If you have any queries after reading the book, then arrange an online consultation.

12. *Receiving coins in the dream, receiving torn notes, or losing money in the dream:* the enemy is targeting your finances. This is common if they can see that you have an impending financial breakthrough. If you have this type of dream and are expecting huge money, make sure you plan your finances very well, otherwise you won't achieve anything with the money. Also arrange a Deliverance session with a deliverance minister or visit our website.

13. *Seeing dead relatives in the dream* is an attack by ancestral witchcraft to disrupt the plan of God for your life. Familiar spirits (spirits in your lineage that know all your secrets), are behind this. They are very stubborn and frustrate their victims. Familiar spirit and foundational Deliverance is needed as urgent solutions to this problem. It might not mean death.

14. *When you dream about your former house, or former school*, it is a dream of backwardness. They want to return you back to the things you left behind. Pray against every spirit of backwardness and go for deliverance. Visit our website too to book a consultation.

15. *When you dream about your former place of work* especially in a negative way, it is an attack of backwardness in your career. Try to look at what you are doing wrong and needs to be changed. This applies to every witchcraft dream. This is all about the concept of repentance. God will give us grace to repent in Jesus' name. Also pray against backwardness and profiteers hardworking.

16. *Being pursued in the dream by human beings, or animals* like snakes, cows, lions or crocodiles, is a revelation that you have stubborn devouring enemies. But if you go for deliverance, all shall be well (Isaiah 49:24-26). Get our book on Healing Miracles on the Amazon Website and study Chapter 2. Schedule a deliverance session on our website.

17. *Destruction of your materials or belongings* means destruction of same in the waking life. If for example your smartphone is destroyed in the dream, then you need to be very careful with it. Pray against the spirit of the wasters too.

18. *Dreams of seeing yourself in the forest:* depicts a lonely and dejected state. It is similar to wearing rags, especially if there is no way out and you are lost. If there is a way out of the forest in that dream, it means there will be a solution to the problem. A deliverance session is needed.

19. *Dreams of a desert or lonely place* is similar to the dream of the forest. This means that a lonely era may be ushered in if you do not pray or act accordingly. These interpretations are given to you so that you can have an idea of the relevance if the dream to your situation when you consider it side by side.

20. *Dreaming of crossing a river or swimming* and can't cross is an attack by marine witchcraft. They use it to frustrate and make life to come to a standstill. The agenda of witches is to paralyse your finances so that other problems will emerge and frustrate you. People who are sexually loose or have fallen into the trap of marine strange women

will always experience things like this unless they arise with the spirit of enough is enough, then pray and reject it.

21. _Dreaming that you are paralysed in the dream_ means that the enemy will prevent you from achieving your desires if you do not pray. There's a need to exercise and build your muscles spiritually through prayer.

22. _When you dream that you are a child in the dream:_ witches are trying to retard your spiritual growth so that they can have you like chicken and chips! It is possible you may be making money, but they have cleverly diverted your interests from spiritual things and retarded your growth. This is just an example. How is your fasting life, study of the word of God, prayer, Evangelism? Watch it Sir/Ma.

23. _When you dream about idols_ and that you are wearing the paraphernalia of idol priests: this means you are connected to idols through covenant. It may be from your roots, your in-laws, or even your environment. Break idol covenants and set ablaze everything that pertain to idols in your house or environment as much as possible.

24. _Dreaming about the cemetery_ is telling you are in the shadow of death. Pray yourself out of it. Take care of your health and watch your habits. Watch driving habits, and others like smoking or drinking. Some of these dreams may take years to manifest, and that's why you should not lose track.

25. _Dream about mad people pursuing you_: this pertains to demonic spirits that have vowed not to give you rest. There's always a linkage or covenant, which you must break. Restitution is important if you have anything in your possession that is not yours.

26. _Eating meat in the dream_: when you eat meat in the dream, it is a sign that they are trying to initiate you by giving you meat. This meat usually is human flesh. It is to initiate. Pray to break the covenant of evil initiation and make sure you guide against all forms of initiation mentioned earlier on in this book.

27. _Swimming in the dream_ usually connotes involvement with marine powers and their covenants. It is possible for you to see a mermaid, or other marine animals like crabs, fishes, sea horses, oysters and the likes. If you do not have water worshippers in your root and you see it, then you and your spouse need to be checked. It is most likely to come from them. Both of you should go for deliverance and re-unite tightly. Dreams of the water can make a potentially glorious marriage look worthless from the surface.

28. *Seeing barriers in your dream* that you cannot cross means hindrance or fault that will not make you move forward. If you are going for a job interview and see a wall standing between you and a place you want to cross to, or a river, or masquerades preventing you, the dream has told you where the problem is coming from, that is water spirits or foundational masquerade. Pray to break curses and covenants and make sure you get ready made answers for any flaws in your certificates or work experience. If possible, go for deliverance.

29. *Carrying load and other forms of slavery in the dream* is the spirit of servitude. That type of dream will always position you where you would be enslaved in a ridiculous manner, no matter your certificate. It is deliverance and holiness (Obadiah verse 17) that you need, in order to possess your possessions.

30. *Dreaming about wild or terrible animals* are a similitude depicting stubborn witchcraft that are bent on carrying out evil agenda. They shall not prosper. Walk closely with God in the study of the word and prayer. Let God reveal secrets to you that will give you victory over every stubborn enemy.

31. *Dreams of seeing very close family members* like your wife, husband, mother, father or children attack you or do evil to you in the dream should just be prayed about normally and allow God to reveal to you. Many marriages have been scattered because of this evil people who will use your wife's image to attack you in the dream. Maybe they initiated her unconsciously as a blind with or have some form of access to her spirit. Her friend in the place of work, who is jealous about your accomplishments may use food. Be careful especially if it is a new trend, say after 3 years or more! If she is really evil, you would have been seeing traces since the beginning of your relationship. Even if true, love overcomes. What if she's your daughter? Don't scatter your future.

32. *Walking bare footed* is an attack against your marriage whereby the enemy wants to make you unmarried for a while, or for long or forever! Watch your attitude and character in the marriage carefully. Someone may not really know the value of what you have until you lose it. Small issues that you never imagined could scatter a marriage and turn their testimony to "had-I-known". That shall not be your portion in Jesus name. Amen.

33. *Seeing snakes in the dream* is a dream of a satanic and cunning evil person, just like a snake assigned to do evil to you. This is someone you might not even think could do such. Don't be surprised that a witch may not be an old woman, but that lady in your office who speaks English Language excellently and has chains of degrees locally and internationally. Watch and pray is the solution. In as much as you are careful about committing sin, then you are always protected.

34. *When your bag is stolen in the dream*, it is an attack against your finances. It is possible you may be duped or spend money on what you were not supposed to spend money on. Plan wisely and spend carefully.

35. *Dream about missing your way* means that you might take a wrong decision if you are not careful. When you are about to get married, get a new job, start a new business and you have a dream like this, pray very well, because witches want to mislead you. Seek counsel exhaustively and meditate carefully about anything that you may want to do.

36. *When you dream and see yourself in thick darkness or partial darkness in your place of work*, it means that there are certain things that are obscure to you that you need to know about your place of work. When you dream that there is darkness in your bedroom, it means there are certain things you need to know about your marriage. Don't conclude that your partner is into adultery, but pray, "O Lord, show me all that I need to know about my marriage". It might just be a stranger that is close to you wreaking havoc, or God wants to reveal to you "the treasures of darkness and hidden riches of secret places" (Isaiah 45:3).

37. *When you dream that people wearing red, off-white, or black garment are surrounding you in the dream* with you in the centre or in their midst, they might want to judge you, afflict you, or initiate you. Note whatever they do in that dream and pray accordingly. Visit our website and book a session or tell your Deliverance Minister.

38. *When you dream that your hair was shaved*, it means an attack on your glory. It is the same thing as wearing rags in the dream. Serious Deliverance prayers are needed under such circumstances. Also, be careful about illicit sex, or evil diversion. Receive clarity on your actions before you go ahead. There is a battle in Deliverance circles we refer to as the "battle of the wrong choice".

39. *Watching television in the dream* is pending shame and disgrace that will allow many people to ridicule you. Watch your conduct and control yourself. Anger making you to misbehave or commit sin is a No-No.

40. *When you see yourself in a toilet* that is very dirty, whether you are stained or not, then it is depicting rejection. No one wants to associate with faeces. Guide your actions and utterances as you pray against shame and disgrace.

41. <u>*Seeing a particular object or place in the dream*</u> always, means that you are in covenant with that person or place which is usually negative. The way it will appear in the dream will give you the impression that it is for evil. For example, before you got born again, you slept with a lady, who has been appearing to you in red, black, off-white, multi-coloured dress, then you have a witchcraft covenant with her. It will affect your progress and your marriage. In fact, that single dream can show you the reason why you have been having all other witchcraft dreams. It is very urgent for you to break the covenant, until you dream or see a sign that it is broken. Don't fight anyone for we wrestle not against flesh and blood (Ephesians 6:12). If you went for consultation with a medium or oracle, you may always see the Priest in your dream, or always see his room in your dream. This shows that something is fishing.

42. <u>*Any evil utterance against you in the dream*</u> in the course of your interaction should be taken seriously. Proceed on a prayer and fast to break demon inspired curses, decrees, or judgements. **Pray Until Something Happens.**

43. <u>*Dreaming that you saw yourself in a pit*</u> means destiny arrest, or a problem. It may mean impending death in some cases. The truth is that many are buried but are marking time. Only prayer can bring you out. A brother received the judgement of death and infirmity by witches, and he prayed for the resurrection power of God. He was sleeping on an afternoon, when suddenly, the power of God brought him out in a trance from the grave in which the dark powers had buried his spirit and waiting for him to die. There's nothing that the power of God can't do, if you believe.

44. <u>*Dreams about seeing yourself in the hospital*</u> means pending sickness and hospital admission. There's a need to watch your diets and habits as you pray deliverance prayers against the demons of infirmity and sickness.

45. <u>*Dreaming about padlocks and chains connote witchcraft bandage.*</u> Prayers to break every witchcraft chain and padlock are necessary, in military style, with warfare songs. It is so exciting praying this type of prayer if you know deliverance warfare songs that go with it. Put it into action prophetically as you shake your heads, hands and legs, setting yourself free. It works instant miracles when you seek God with all your heart.

46. <u>*Any dream that you have making an evil utterance against yourself*</u> should be taken seriously. Definitely, you cannot wish evil for yourself, but some evil spirits have entered and possessed your spirit, making you to curse yourself. Deliverance with many days of fasting and prayer is needed. It is a mark of witchcraft possession, which can ultimately be used to destroy you if you do not pray it out.

47. _Owls and vultures in the dream_ signify death. This type of dream could be had with dreams of skeletons, cemetery or grave. They all mean impending death which you must pray against.

48. _Breastfeeding and nursing children in the dream_ is a dream of barrenness. Pray against infertility and at the same time also register with a gynaecologist and follow all their directions and advise, except you have a contrary revelation.

49. _A collapsed building in your dream_ means an attack against your efforts. The enemy wants to return you to square one. Holiness and deliverance (Obadiah verse 17) is also relevant here.

50. _A blemish on your dress_ means an attack against your reputation and you must guard against soiling your reputation. This requires going for deliverance also as you shun every corrupt tendency.

CHAPTER SEVEN

EVIL WITCHCRAFT POWERS

Witches and wizards have been known for ages to operate using different types of evil powers and abilities. In many instances, they have exposed themselves, during services, after the Holy Ghost arrests them, either in an open service, or privately to Pastors. Some witches have even confessed to witchcraft, in public places like the marketplace. If you have someone who has been revealed to you as being a witch, or possessed by familiar spirits, or other similar possessions, these are the types of powers they usually have. It may not be all, but at least, some of the powers. These are evil anointing upon their lives with which they do evil.

These powers can only be destroyed or reversed by special prayers and ministrations, during deliverance. Also, a special act of God can cripple the power. When I say a reversal, some of them that were having evil visions and dreams will now start having good dreams and visions, when the demons giving evil visions have been cast out, and the Holy Ghost has taken over their temple. They wouldn't also be able to hear evil instructions, if the witchcraft covenant is broken. One of the things they guard jealously during deliverance is that covenant. That is why they cross their legs and refuse to let go. It is the covenant that is connecting them to the dark world and supplying the evil powers.

Another thing is to chase out the demon, supplying that power, and make sure the witchcraft spirit(s) are out. When they begin to shake their heads during Deliverance, then the spirit in them is telling you that it won't go. On a certain day, as I was ministering deliverance in church to a group of candidates, I caught a revelation about an evil spirit in a lady. I didn't want to address her in particular, so I raised a general prayer point for all of them to pray and gave them time for accumulation of holy fire. This spirit still did not go out. Then I knew she wouldn't let go easily except I helped her. They don't usually want to let go of the powers. I moved close to her, because I was convinced about what I had seen. I started commanding the fire to increase, and when I saw the fire was increased, I raised a dangerous prayer point that left the demon that was pretending crying and yelling, and eventually went out. Some of them keep the powers on nearby trees on inside a pot or in some other ways, before they enter the Deliverance ground. As you minister, don't just concentrate on the powers in the auditorium, but also address their powers wherever such powers are kept outside the auditorium. We shall see certain notes and precautions, that are useful to Deliverance ministers in a subsequent chapter in this book.

Power to know.

Witches have the powers to know what has happened, is happening or will happen in the future. They can plan evil, project or use some other powers to wreak havoc! They could manipulate you, if they see that you want to break through. If they cannot do it by deception, then they try food or sex in order to arrest and destroy. Many glorious destinies have been destroyed just by having sex, and under 5 minutes, the spiritual transaction is done. One power, they sometimes have is the eye on the forehead which they use to see into people's future.

Witchcraft Transportation Powers.

Witches and wizards employ diverse kinds of "transportation powers" depending on their geographical locations, assignment, tradition and culture. Witches and Wizards in African may adopt flying as birds, but European witches may prefer to fly on broomsticks. The idea is to be airborne and transport themselves seamlessly from place to place whilst carrying out their assignment.

A knowledge of their means of transportation and what to do, in order to stop them, from flying, is important. We are children of authority, and witches and wizards cannot be allowed to operate where true children of God are. It is a disregard for our authority as children of the King of Kings and Lord of Lords. The following are the methods of how witchcraft transportation is employed:

1. _The first method that they use is to send their power_ and the very basic is through news and threats. The first thing they want to do is to intimidate and scare you, even when they are grossly incapable of carrying out what they are bragging that they would do. By the time you grab their neck through prayer and violent faith, they suffocate completely. So, you learn to ignore and disregard their threats in words that you hear, your body feelings, imaginations, what you see, and dreams. When you have a dream, no matter how scary, God wants you to be sensitised to fight and win victoriously, (Job 33:15-18) as earlier on stated.

2. _The second form_ is through a disappear and appear method. This is used by occultists too. They virtually disappear from Lagos, Nigeria, to arrive in New York, USA, in record time. They sometimes get hanged on a tree, or crash land into a strange forest. Many of them die and not wake up. In the United States, in contemporary witchcraft academies, this method also known as apparition is taught to students. It involves concentration on where you want to be transported to so that if you are not concentrating fully, you could also get yourself trapped or leave behind part of your body. Prayer is a sure way of disallowing them to do this. Be suspicious of most people that leave instructions that you should not wake them up whatever the case may be. They hate been woken up, although it is medically not right to wake people who are sleeping up. Other signs like specific and strange positions of sleeping, muttering to themselves, accurate predilection of evil, and meanness are corroborating signs.

3. _Transportation through animals_ is another way. A witch may sleep, and project herself into a goat in the house. While she is asleep, the goat is propelled by a human spirit, and goes out to wherever they want them to go. When they get there, they can project into their target, especially if they gave you food or had sex with you before or both. When you meet some of them do not be mistaken that you are receiving care.
The precaution here is to watch your pets and animals around you for strange behaviour or misdemeanours. A goat that climbs a platform, opens a big iron pot, eats from the pot and covers it, again is not just an ordinary

goat. Sometimes they look scary, and you feel goose pimples all over your body is another confirmation that you are not seeing an ordinary animal. A bird that flies across with a strangely terrifying sound is not ordinary. A goat that can remove a padlock from the latches, as it was trained for months, is not ordinary.

4. *The use of Portkeys.* Portkeys are objects that could be used by witches and wizards to fly. They get attached to the objects and fly using those objects. They could get trapped as well. Regular prayers and fasting are effective in preventing them from flying.

5. *They could also use "the airport system".* In this system, they build "airports" in your body by giving you food, having sex with you, and turning you practically to an airport where they can land, because they make you compatible and compliant to their operations. Unfortunately, except you are spirit filled, and strong willed, how do you escape an attempt by your own mother, or your mother in-law, to strike you or initiate you. So, if they sense spiritually that you are somewhere, they could just project into you from wherever they are. It's as though you are micro-chipped. This allows them to transport themselves.

    When you live a prayer and fasted life, it would be impossible to use your life as a "Airport". Do not also allow then to know your whereabouts. If you tell them that you are attending a job interview at a particular time, they don't need to try to view your location in their demonic map. They already know you would be there and what you are up to. They just connect and for example make you to sleep off in such a way as to miss your interview. They could also make you to lose your memory so that you may momentarily forge your name, age or address.

6. *Never enter into a blood oath, have casual sex or eat casually anywhere, anytime.* You give them the chance to live inside you. It means you are possessed. So, they could easily start speaking to you without necessarily connecting. Because their spirit is in you, they can know your thoughts even if they are in San Francisco, and you are in New York. They can give you evil visions and dreams because they are living in you. It is like having a hyena in your bedroom! Any wild animal you dream that you see in your house depicts this situation.

7. *As birds.* One of the easiest ways to move from place to place is to "body shift" become a bird, and fly to wherever you want to be, using a witchcraft compass. They kind of bird is synonymous with your identity or assignment. A witch flying as an owl or vulture, or any other scavenging bird, is on assignment to kill. There are birds that eat flesh, that may cause infirmity. There are different kinds of birds that you may see in your vision, or in your dreams that interact with you, or try to peck you, pursue you or harm you.

Prayer and fasting is the key, and some prayer points to deal with witchcraft transportation are suggested in the chapter on prayer as we continue our journey in this book.

Powers of Communication.

Witches, wizards, members of the occult, and other dark agents communicate with one another and other people on the society in various ways. One of the basic ways of communication is through the print media. They do go to newspapers, tabloids, and bulletins to advertise their evil deeds. People who are interested can readily read these materials and if not careful, may be carried away by the contents and stumble.

The electronic media has been another means of communication in recent times. The radio, and television do announcements that promote witchcraft, and many people enter into their bondage. The worst in recent times is the Internet. Even if you were not intending to be initiated into witchcraft, an exploration of the Internet, and a few clicks could end you up in the bondage of occultism and witchcraft. The more you click, the deeper you sink into the abyss of witchcraft destruction.

Through blood oath, by Inheritance, by incision, the witchcraft seed is planted and flourishes. Through the blood connection, an initiate or a victim can receive messages and evil communication through dreams and visions.

Through sweat. A man took his sister to cohabit with him in his house. The man was a nominal Christian and was not so much spiritual. On a certain day he went to the mountain to have a prayer retreat. When he came back home, the sister sat him down and asked him, how was your journey to (mentioning the name of the town). He did not tell her anything but was surprised to discover that the lady knew where he went to. As if that was not enough, she went further to tell him everything he had prayed about on the mountain. The lady went further to confess that she had a mission and was sent to destroy the man. When asked how she got to know, she said that once she was able to lay her hands on the singlet or other clothing that the man's sweat was able to touch, she had access to whatever he did wherever he went.

Marks on different parts of the body: This could also be used to communicate amongst members of the same cult, or to send messages across to members of the society. A mark made with white paint or charcoal on the forehead, arms, legs, or red paint on the forehead is a sign of communication, that you belong to our sect. The people who do not belong and decide to be afraid ate hence intimidated, alienated or endangered themselves. All depends on your perception.

One of the victory ways is to disregard silly marks and stand up to your faith and your belief. When you really believe that they can't harm you, which they can't, then they wouldn't be able to. You become what you believe. Feel free to advance and talk to them normally. Bridge the gap physically but maintain a spiritual distance. Walk with faith and wisdom.

> Matthew 10:16
>
> Behold, I send you forth as sheep in the midst of wolves: be ye therefore wise as serpents, and harmless as doves.

The sexual route is another route. They have sex with you, deposit their seed in you, and manipulate your dream life showing you things that do not exist or that cannot happen at all. If you lose faith and confidence in yourself and believe those dreams, and you allow the dreams to hinder good things for your life and make them to pass negative information into your life, then you have fallen into their plans. You must ignore their visions and dreams (2 Corinthians 10:5).

There are certain signs too that are witchcraft signs sponsored by human beings. A man bought a piece of land, which some occultists wanted to take forcefully from him. What they did was to look for a red cloth, tied some cowrie shells, and snail shells with it, and together they hung it on a pole erected on the plot of land. When the man that bought the land came, he was totally confused and set in disarray. If you were the one, what would you have done?

One of the tricks of witchcraft is to intimidate. If you are afraid and intimidated, the battle is half lost. You should normally pray to God for leading. Then act accordingly. No Christian law neither does any law in the world allows the righteous to suffer. The law of Karma is well known all over the world, so also is the law of attraction. Do not fear when you are not doing evil, rather if you activate your faith the witches should fear you

Seductive powers.

Witches have seductive powers that could lure you into wanting to befriend them and surrender totally to whatever they tell you. There are ladies that would only wink at you, and from that moment, you are gone, because they have seductive powers in the eyes. In the scripture that follows, the bible makes us to know that it is possible for these whorish women to take people with their eyelids, and offers an advice, that you should never allow them to "take you" with their eyelids. How do you do that? They would always like to fix their gaze on you. The more you look, the more there is a connection, as they fire their arrows into your spirit through their eyelids. Then there is a fire of desire, that will burn in you. So simply look away, and don't connect!

Proverbs 6:25

Lust not after her beauty in thine heart; neither let her take thee with her eyelids.

It is well known that the eyes could carry seductive arrows, and many of these men and women are empowered in the eyes, in order to bewitch your career, business and marriage. They practically "take you" and control your life, no matter how hard you worked or suffered before you got to where you are. A gaze is enough to mess you up completely.

Nahum 3:4

Because of the multitude of the whoredoms of the well-favoured harlot, the mistress of witchcrafts, that selleth nations through her whoredoms, and families through her witchcrafts.

Proverbs 6:24-28

^{24}to keep thee from the evil woman, from the flattery of the tongue of a strange woman.

^{25}Lust not after her beauty in thine heart; neither let her take thee with her eyelids.

^{26}for by means of a whorish woman a man is brought to a piece of bread: and the adulteress will hunt for the precious life.

²⁷Can a man take fire in his bosom, and his clothes not be burned?

²⁸Can one go upon hot coals, and his feet not be burned?

Many businesses, parastatals, and countries sadly are being controlled by these ruthless satanic agents. They are in church, unfortunately to "pin down" those Pastors who cannot control themselves, and who get carried away by little things. They will shower you with gifts, bow and kneel for you, say seductive things, and invite you to their houses to pray for them. There are also Pastors wives too, who are agents, and offer cheap sex to members of the congregation where their husbands lead. The ministry will be greatly affected. Members lose confidence in you because of the conduct of your wife, irrespective of your innocence and there is powerlessness Agents like that would never allow Ministries to grow. A member in your church, either a man or woman who is empowered by the devil seductively, can wreak a lot of havoc. It is a dangerous power that we all need to be discerning and avoid seduction. They could use their looks to seduce, they could exhibit fake behaviour, too, so don't be carried away by first impressions. The men seduce with looks and money too. Some even speak very loud in public and tell lies about flamboyant experiences they never had, all in a bid to seduce.

Sexual powers.

Witches and wizards have sexual demons, that wouldn't let you go easily once you are trapped, irrespective of whatever they do to you. The devil knows the weakness of men for sex, so, many of these ladies offer free sex, and present themselves cheaply, to trap you down. By the time you know, it would be too late. Many marriages and businesses have been destroyed this way. I used to know a man, who had sex with an agent, and from that time, his Nursery School was deserted, as only about 4 students remained in a class. He sold all the trucks he used for haulage and he entered a huge debt.

Another man, a Director of International repute had sex with this agent, who pretended she was working on the laptop, but she put the camera on. She was able to prove that the man wanted to have sex with her and recorded other evidence against the man. The man lost all his local and international business connections because his naked picture was everywhere on the Internet. He was rubbished in social circles as well, and practically everywhere. As cheap as it may look sometimes, sex is the most expensive thing a man can pay for in life. Don't go near it.

Summoning powers.

Witchcraft powers are able to summon you if they have caged you through the food they gave you or if you had sex with one of their agents. With this, your spirit can appear in their meetings. They can ask you questions and if you are found wanting, be sure they will judge you as necessary. A rope has been created with they can pull you at will. When you see yourself in the midst of some people questioning you with regards to a sin that you committed, or judge you, that was a witchcraft summons. In as much as you avoid indiscriminate food and sex; and maintain a holy and fasted life.

Astral travel.

Witches and wizards can go outside their bodies at night to distant places, to attend meetings or carry out evil assignments. When this happens, the empty container they call their body is lying on the bed. Their soul is gone! No matter how you try to wake them, it will take time before they come around because they were not there in the first place. Even when you wake them, they are incoherent for up to 20 minutes or more sometimes, before they come around.

Physical and spiritual camouflage.

Some cultures have described witches as the creatures that tiptoe to enter the market, and the black cat on the roof top. All these point to the highly secretive nature and hidden lifestyle of witches. A stepmother who has had sex with your father, can put on the picture of your father, to fight you in the dream at night, if she has observed that your father loves you and the Intimacy is a threat to her.

A person can give your mother a bewitched food, so that she becomes one with your mother spiritually and will always use her picture to attack you at night, and even make her to turn to a snake and a lion. Justice has been miscarried severally in this manner. In cases like that, pray very well. Physically, a teacher who comes in to teach your children may be sent on assignment to scatter your marriage. If your husband normally comes in at 6pm, but she normally should close at 5pm, she will tell you she will offer free lessons for the good of your son, so that she can have access to your husband and seduce him. If she is a physician and a man has brought a sick person to the hospital, a witch on assignment will always follow patients to their cars and try to be intimate or look for a way of demonstrating that she is doing some special favours until you get attracted. We must be discerning to be able to unravel these camouflaging or masquerading tendencies.

Power of charms, amulets, and phylacteries.

These are magical objects worn on the neck, waist, wrist, ankles, or other parts of the body, or simply carried about by the agents of darkness to carry out their evil works. We should not be ignorant of the devices of the enemy.

There are beads worn around the wrist, or even rings worn on the finger, that when they shake you with it could make your male organ or breast to disappear immediately. There are charms worn around the waist, that could make a criminal to disappear and elude arrest. Police Officials watch it! There are rings you put in your mouth and when you use it to speak to someone, they do what you say and nothing else.

There are rings or sometimes eye pencils that if a man wants to sleep with you, he seduces you with the eye pencil and hits you with the ring, and he's got you. There are hats you could wear and you disappear into the hat. There are charms that could be worn by them that would make your money to disappear. So, Bank Officials should be careful. There are amulets that could be worn such that a machete cannot cut you nor a gun be able to kill you.

These materials sometimes are not only used to do evil works but as a means of communication or identification. There are certain sects that shake one another with their elbows or grab each other tongues during a handshake. Pray for God to reveal them and their plans to you, as well as being observant will reveal them to you and possibly frustrate their plans. Learn to speak in tongues as you pray and fast.

Shape shifting.

Most witches can change to an animal in your dreams and visions. They usually change to snakes, owls, vultures, cows, goats, cays, dogs, scorpions, sparrows, or other animals. They can also effectively change from an animal figure to humans in your dreams. They use the power also to attend meetings. It will amaze you that some animals behave as if they are humans, and this is because they have human spirits projected into them. Some do things that will make you to think twice if they really animals. A dog that ate up a baby, is not an ordinary dog. A goat I saw in Africa was opening the pot in the fireplace, or open doors to pantries in strange ways. One person that I know too was bitten by his monkey, and which led to the amputation of his leg. I heard one night shortly after midnight as a dog was speaking like a man. An elderly man said, "You people have entered into this dog tonight". What they do is to project a human soul into an animal body, thereby making such animals to behave like human beings.

Lying spirits.

Witches and familiar spirits do tell a lot of lies like their father, the devil. They do this in order to hide their atrocities. A man or a woman who is promiscuous will always tell lies to cover evil deeds. However, such powers destroy them at the end of the day of the day, because the truth sets you free and lies keep you in bondage.

Even when you have caught them through a CCTV Camera, they could still twist the story and the reason for doing what they did. As if this is not enough, they pretend to be angry, adding lies to lies.

Power to make evil decrees that come to pass.

Witchcraft possessed persons curse effectively. They have powers in their mouth that they can use to empower evil decrees, especially if they are linked with you through sex or blood (family member). Each time anyone says anything that is contrary, you reverse it immediately and if possible, in their presence, jokingly reverse it, but essentially you have said words that reverse it. When you get home, pray in your closet to reverse it too. This is why you need to avoid sin and anything that could provoke anger. Occultists also use this type of power in Africa, and in India, where it is known as a "do what I say charm". Anything you don't want to do that is coming like a command should be considered very well before doing it.

Power in their feet.

Anywhere they walk to, they use this power to cause evil. If they get married, the very day they pack into the house and walk in with the legs, trouble has started. The power in the legs is also used for seductive purposes. A lady confessed in church that her power was in her legs, and that if she stands by the roadside putting the leg forward, any man that sees her in that position must be charmed and lust after her!

Power in their hands.

The witches can touch anything, and rather than blessing, they curse. A lady who comes to stay in your house and has broken many plates, spoilt the door handle, damaged the refrigerator, and other things within the span of one day should be examines carefully. The hand instead of healing is used to transfer illness into people's lives. That is why it is not good to bring a newborn baby out, for everyone to touch. Allow your baby to rest in his or her bed. A baby was greeted like that on the day he was born. Unknown to the parents, all his stars were cleared away by a witch. Later in life, the witch confessed about what she did at the time the baby was born.

The hand is also used by some men and women to seduce. Once they touch you, you start feeling funny. Seductive powers reside in the hands.

Powers that make evil thoughts to come to pass.

A lady confessed to witchcraft that a couple was going for a wedding. The witch poured okra on the way spiritually and wished that the vehicle could be overturned. She had it and the way she was thinking and desiring in her mind. This is why you must be prayerful if you plan to do any good thing. Good things need prayers. Also, learn not to reveal all your plans to people, especially when it is not necessary.

False kindness.

I think I must mention this emphatically. Don't be carried away by false kindness, especially when it is not called for, and without any reasonable justification. These "kangaroo" acts of kindness are meant to mislead. Such acts of kindness are potential traps. Married men and women should be careful about these especially from the opposite sex, or people who stand to benefit from them, in which case it is known as a bribe.

CHAPTER EIGHT

FOUNDATIONAL WITCHCRAFT.

Every house that is built has a foundation that is first laid, and the blocks are arranged on that foundation to build the house. The size of the foundation determines the size of the house to be built, likewise, the strength of the foundation determines how far you may go, whether 2 storeys or 20 storeys. If the foundation is limited, the size of the house is limited. Many houses collapse because of a weak foundation and for some foundations you may not go more than 3 storeys, whilst for some you may go as far as 25 storeys, and a great spectacle is erected for all to see and admire. If you have a magnificent structure in mind, the best solution is for you to demolish an initial faulty foundation and erect a new one and build on it.

The bible makes us to know, and calls our attention to the fact, that the same principle of laying a good foundation in order to build a great structure applies to our lives.

> Psalms 11:3
>
> *If the foundations be destroyed, what can the righteous.*

Analysing the above scripture, we can arrive at the fact that human beings do have foundations, which could be faulty, or destroyed. One common thing presents in every family and affects outcomes is "FOUNDATIONAL WITCHCRAFT". Our foundations are consisting of the values, norms, sanctions, values, and activities of our forefathers. Many people are not able to enlarge their coasts in life, owing to a faulty foundation. A person who is supposed to build 10 houses may build only one or even die as a tenant because of certain things relating to how he was born and how he was brought up. Sometimes, the height that many are supposed to reach in life, they do not reach because of the witchcraft in their foundation. They may commit some shameful acts sponsored by foundational witchcraft and fall from grace to grass or their lives may be terminated by foundational witchcraft.

A person for these reasons needs to rebuild their foundation in life as quickly as possible. The word of God is the way and the truth to maximising our potentials. The only solid, sure and enduring foundation can only be built on Jesus Christ.

Matthew 7:24-25

²⁴Therefore whosoever heareth these sayings of mine, and doeth them, I will liken him unto a wise man, which built his house upon a rock:

²⁵and the rain descended, and the floods came, and the winds blew, and beat upon that house; and it fell not: for it was founded upon a rock.

When we accept Christ, believe in him, and live our lives strictly based on what the word of God says, then we have rebuilt our foundation on Christ and can be the best version of our lives that God has created us to be and wants us to be.

Witchcraft activities in our foundation.

When we talk about witchcraft in our foundation, we refer to wicked acts that our forefathers committed, and all evil practices, values or norms, that were against God's commandments and destructive or injurious to the destinies of others in the way they practiced it. What are these activities in our foundation that mean we have witchcraft in our foundation?

1. <u>Conscious initiation into occultic societies.</u> It is common for people in different parts of the world to voluntarily get initiated in dark societies. This results in being possessed by these spirits and using them to harm and manipulate individuals and groups of people transcending all ramifications and strata of the human society. Through the oaths they entered into, soul ties were formed and they were yoked to wicked powers.
2. <u>Marine Witchcraft.</u> Our forefathers engaged in a lot of practices because they wanted wealth and popularity. In other instances, they sought these powers to ask them for children or power. Marine witchcraft usually originates from the riverine and coastal areas of the world. These resulted into witchcraft covenants been transferred from generation to generation. People with this type of witchcraft in their foundations usually dream about rivers and seas as well as having spirit spouses sleep with them in their dreams.
3. <u>Black witchcraft.</u> These witchcraft powers were for vengeance, and wicked activities. They usually have birds, snakes and other animals that they operate with. They do in actual fact, fly in their dreams. They also turn to snakes and wear black apparels. They are vert wicked.
4. <u>Idolatry.</u> Idolatrous practices were common and are still common in several parts of the world, including the sacrifice of animals or human beings, and using their blood. Many of the descendants from these families have

names glorifying those idols. If you bear a name like that, it is wise to change it. The result is a foundational covenant against the descendants.

5. *Blood rituals.* At that time, whenever they kept people in a dungeon to be sacrificed, those men and women including pregnant women cried in agony and cursed. The blood of these people cry for vengeance (Genesis 4:10). This brings about foundational curses.

6. *Unlawful possession.* Many of our ancestors forcefully acquired what was not legally theirs including materials, farmlands, slaves and women. All these are rebellious against the commandments of God and are witchcraft practices.

7. *Necromancing* and relations with the dead. Some of our forefathers had profound relations with the dead and the graveyard. They drew a lot of power from the graveyards and the dead. They could either see visions, use it to improve palm produce, or gain popularity. When a person has an accord with the graveyard or the dead, they could have money, but they die before their time or fall sick for a greater part of their lives.

8. *Divination and Crystal balling.* These ones not only engage in trying to know the future for wicked reasons most times, but they join all types of cults, fraternities and dark societies, giving them direction and guidelines.

Foundational problem transfer.

How have these things been passed down to this generation?

1. *Curses.* When an atrocity is carried out and the victims curse the parents and their children for their grievous act of witchcraft and wickedness. The children are then by implication are "beneficiaries" of the problem. Many people are labouring under problems that they don't know how it started. In 2 Kings 5:27, Gehazi was not only cursed by Elisha, but his seed and descendants were cursed as well.

2. *Evil covenants.* God warned the Israelites in Exodus 20:5 not to bow themselves (worship) idols, because he is a jealous God visiting the iniquities of the fathers on the children up to the third and fourth generation of them that hate God (worship idols). The accord, covenant or contract that they have with idols, God says their sin shall be visited upon the children up to 90-120 years. A generation is 30 years.

3. *Soul ties.* As a result of evil covenants with people and idols, their souls are joined to those people and idols. In Hosea 4:16-19 the bible makes it clear that Ephraim is joined to idols. Where have you been joined to an idol too. In that scripture, the bible makes mention of drinks and sacrifices. Pray like this "I break every soul tie with foundational witchcraft in the name of Jesus Christ".

4. *Festivals.* Foundational battles can be transferred through festivals and indigenous practices that do not glorify God. When you participate and eat, demons are transferred. When you dance some dance, it transfers sexual demons. There are some kinds of dance in Africa and the Latino where the waists are twisted and moved rhythmically and seductively. If a person partakes in this type of dance with some people over a few days, demons

of seduction or lust can enter into their lives. These traditions and iniquities have moved from generation to generation through these festivals.

5. *History.* Negative faith comes with the continuous listening to evil words which inform strange practices. A lot of demonic activities of our parents are written in history books which are construed in seductive ways e.g. those history books narrate the fantasies of polygamy, and a male reader may find it interesting, not being ware however of the spiritual disasters that go with a practice like that.

6. *Culture.* Once a person reads such a history, then Culture is sustained, be it positive, or with negative repercussions. Some terrible cultures and traditions have kept many people in bondage for several hundreds of years.

7. *Marks and incisions.* A mark on a person is a form of identification physically and in the realm of the spirit. An incision even goes deeper to pollute the blood. This poison and evil ordination move along generations in a family line.

8. *Concoctions.* These are like incisions too, but for the fact that these are eaten or drank. They have an effect on the spiritual life of such people. I had a church member; whose husband was not alive to his responsibilities and was always misbehaving. Obviously, he was under witchcraft attack! When I took his history, he was from a family of diviners and from generation to generation they have used cola, and dry gin to appease the family oracle from time to time. Over the years, it became a family thing and it was difficult for him to quit. We conducted deliverance and the spirit departed. Alcoholism as medical science will call it was the problem, but a Pastor surely believes it is the spirit of non-achievement, and in this case, was rooted in the foundation of witchcraft.

9. *Marriage.* Marriage can take evil transfers to another level. It will not only transfer the bondage, but take it beyond the usual boundaries. God warned Solomon not to marry from other nations (1 Kings 11:1-3). God knew that the values, traditions and norms of the foreign women could be transferred into his life and cause problems. Solomon ignored the warning and these women turned his heart away from God and bewitched him. In what ways have you adopted lifestyles from your wife's/husband's hometown through food, drink, mannerisms, festivals, culture etc? This is why it is good for a born-again believer to marry a born-again believer, and in that case, there is no wall of partition. In Ephesians 2:14 the bible says "for his is our peace, who has made both one, and has broken down the middle wall of partition between us.

What are the signs of foundational witchcraft oppression and possession?

1. *Terrible nightmares and dreaming about strange objects and personalities that you never met in real life.* When you have regular sex in the dream, eating in the dream, being shot in the dream, missing the road in the dream, being chased in the dream, and others.

2. *Hearing strange voices when sleeping, or even when wide awake.* These voices threaten you, or command you to do things that are not right, though most times are alluring.
3. *Seeing terrifying visions.* One thing is for sure. The devil wants to intimidate you so that you can be afraid and submit to him. When you begin to see visions of dead relatives, coffins, cemeteries, dangerous animals, dream about scary festivals and the likes. Pray against these.
4. *Constant fear.* When things are not going fine with you and witchcraft powers are in, one sure sign is fear constantly. Fear devastates a person spiritually so that it can be difficult to stay focused on good things and achieve greatly.
5. *Depression.* When you are tired about everything and life seems not to have a meaning, then it is a sign of foundational witchcraft. When life is becoming meaningless because of your many experiences or for reasons you cannot explain.
6. *Evil patterns.* The same problem that you are having is happening in the lives of your siblings and your uncles and aunties. It may be a particular illness, habit or addiction. This is because you are all from the same foundation.
7. *Blood pollution.* There is pollution in your blood which may bring different kinds of manifestations.
8. *Strange behaviour.* Foundational witchcraft wants you to fail in life. One of the attacks is that of strange behaviour. For example, this strong unexplainable sexual desire that leads to polygamy in males or sexual waywardness and divorce in ladies. It could also come in the form of uncontrollable anger.
9. *Failure at the edge of breakthrough.* This makes people to fail when they are almost succeeding. For example, a man is about to be appointed as a Country Representative of a multinational concern. However, he is implicated in a fraud, or sexual scandal. He is then sacked from work.
10. *Business failure.* Wrong decisions in business, huge debts, low sales etc are all signs of business failure.
11. *Disfavour.* When people hate you everywhere you go, even as you try your best to behave normally. This could be due to an evil mark in your foundation, a specific strange behaviour, or evil monitoring by demonic spirits
12. *Difficulty to live a holy and righteous life.* When you are finding it difficult to be honest, to stay away from alcohol, finding it difficult to control your sexual desires, finding it difficult to remain at work or school, and many others, these are signs of foundational battles.
13. *Iron-like battles and problems.* When you keep praying about a particular problem, but it defies a quick solution, then you need to address foundational witchcraft curses, foundational witchcraft covenant, and evil dedication.
14. *Multiplication of bad luck.* When bad luck keeps multiplying, and especially when it affects members of your family, then you think about foundational witchcraft.
15. *When life is difficult and good doors and opportunities are closing, then it is foundational witchcraft.* When as a lady, your mother struggled to raise you, because your father was not a serious man, and now you and your sisters are struggling to raise your children too, it is a foundational witchcraft battle.

16. *When Christian living becomes a battle.* The foundational strongman is always giving you a reminder that you are in covenant with them, then you need to fight with aggression to fight the battle. They will never leave you to serve God if you don't act decisively.
17. *Stubborn embargoes.* When it is as if you have been barred from achieving something good, because you are always met with disappointment, then you have to pray against witchcraft in your foundation.
18. *Divorce repeatedly.* When you have had up to 3 marriages and you are now with the fourth husband, but you are already having issues with your present husband and seriously wish you could have another divorce. Also, you see a similar pattern in the family on your father's side or your mother's side.
19. *Chronic sickness.* When you are chronically ill and the disease defies healing, then you think about a foundational problem.
20. *Vagabond behaviour.* I had a house help many years back. We all decided to go for deliverance and she manifested. When we got home, she started praying as I helped her because she had difficulty praying in English. The demon in her spoke that the grandmother handed her over to her. When I asked, what is your assignment in this life, she said she was assigned to be pushing her from place to place.
21. *Delayed progress.* The things you are normally expected to achieve at the age of 30, when you have not achieved them even at 60, then there is a problem.
22. *Dry and deserted life.* Life is just dry and nothing seems to be happening really, though you may not be depressed.
23. *Falling from grace to grass.* When a person experiences demotion, then promotion then demotion and the cycle is repeated continuously. It is one of the signs of foundational battles.
24. *Soul-tie.* Always preoccupied with thoughts and imaginations of past occurrence, people in the past, remembering culture and tradition with nostalgia, this demonstrates a soul-tie. A mother possessed by witchcraft can always tie their soul to that of their children. The child is married but cannot stop thinking about her mother every minute, and vice-versa This can result to lack of commitment and failure in work and marriage if it becomes excessive.
25. *Spirit of rejection.* No matter their qualifications, nobody wants to employ them, and no matter how beautiful, no one wants to marry them. This occurs in other areas of their lives too.
26. *Repeated and frightening spiritual attacks.* A person possessed by spirit husband may be seeing this terrible witchcraft appear to them in a human form whilst wide awake. They may see demon idols too.
27. *Profitless hardworking.* People with foundational witchcraft battles have profitless hardworking. They will normally get jobs with very poor salaries, which might not be paid regularly. They fall into the hands of dubious employers.
28. *Regular backsliding.* With a foundational battle, you cannot be able to live a holy and righteous life. When there is powerlessness in the life of a Christian leader too, it may be due to foundational witchcraft.
29. *Anti-Success syndrome.* There is this battle working against their success that scatters whatever they gather. They make decisions that work contrary to achieving their success A person with foundational battles cannot save

money. They are the types of people that run into debts. As a Pastor, they may never be able to grow membership of a church more than 10 members, no matter how they try.

30. *Debts.* Since there is lack of performance, this impact results in what they do. They will invariably run unto debts.

How do we receive deliverance from foundational witchcraft?

1. *Surrender your life to Jesus.* Accept Jesus and believe. Jesus will show you the way, teach you the truth, and make you to live. God's own foundation for you is in his word.
2. *Repent from your sins and embrace righteous and holy living.* There are things that you are doing now, and you know some of them, that you need to forsake totally. This will weaken the power of foundational witchcraft.
3. *Ask for God's mercy and position yourself for God's mercy.* How do you position yourself for God's mercy? He who confesses his sins and forsake them will obtain mercy (Proverbs 28:13). Furthermore, you have to be merciful especially to the poor, needy, oppressed and despised, as it is written, blessed are the merciful, for they shall obtain mercy (Matthew 5:7). The mercy of God turns away judgement and the wrath of God.
4. *Study God's word and meditate, and act according to the word of God.* Even if you don't know the destination, trust the process.
5. *Be determined to do God's will,* whatever it will cost you – your friends, your time within good reason, your money, your comfort and all.
6. *Prayer and fasting.* Devote quality time for prayer and fasting. Pray the prayers of inquiry to know what your grandparents did. You will be surprised to see all the abominations your grandparents committed. As a student enrolled in the School of Deliverance, God showed me many things that transpired in my foundation. When you now know what transpired, then you pray for forgiveness on their behalf. Furthermore, you consider those things now happening in your life, then uproot where you need to uproot and plant where you need to plant. God told Jeremiah "See I have this day set thee over the nations, and over the kingdoms, to root out, and to pull down, and to destroy, and to throw down, to build and to plant (Jeremiah 1:10). For example, you could pray for God to uproot the spirit of poverty from your life, or the spirit of anger, or other spirits you do not like. Pray for example for God to plant helpers in your life. Pray to God to help you to build a 7- figure business for example or build a marriage that the storms of life cannot pull down. Pull down every investment of the enemy for your life.
7. *Ask questions from your parents.* Ask them the old family names that your ancestors bore. Ask them what types of idols that your forefathers worshipped. Ask them about the history of polygamy in your family. Ask them the name of your town and its meaning. Ask if there is any sickness in your family line. Ask them about the general beliefs and myths regarding your family line and hometown. Look at your life now. Ask them if things happening in your life right now happened to your grandparents and ancestors according to history. These are the battles you need to fight, determines what you need to resist e.g. polygamy, when you honestly discover you ate struggling

with the spirit of lust, just two years into your marriage. Then you can do further prayers and take humanly possible steps to stop it.

8. *Decide to resist the temptation* of following evil family patterns through words of advice, or discouragement, or evil precedents you are asked to follow by relatives. There are parents who advised their children to pack and leave their marriages when it wasn't right to do so. Relatives may tell you "Don't allow him/her to know your salary". How can you work together with your spouse in marriage if you continue to obey the wrong advice? Then they support it, by mentioning members of your family that got divorced, and that you should be like them. No, don't listen to what will not benefit your destiny.

9. *Have faith.* Do away with fear. Entertainment of evil thoughts open spiritual doors for those things to manifest in your life. Job said "the things which I greatly feared have come upon me, and that which I was afraid of is come upon me (Job 3:25). There may be storms in your business or marriage, but if you trust in God, study the scriptures, confess the scriptures and walk according to God's plans (word) for your life, he will strengthen you to fight and be victorious. However, ask yourself, am I in sin, what are my fears, why am I vulnerable?

10. *Evil inheritance.* Is there anything that I have inherited that may make foundational battles to prosper in your life. Have you inherited clothing, shoes, problematic piece of land, problematic piece of property, wall clock, or some other things you inherited from your parents that the spirit is leading you against and you are getting suspicious about them. Dash them out if they wouldn't be harmful to the beneficiaries. A piece of land or property could be given to a charity where people can benefit from it. You are trading your problems for greater blessings. Really you gave it away physically, but there is a spiritual principle that transfers blessings to you because of that which you give. At the right time, your life will be credited because you have simply done business with God and you cannot fail.

11. *Don't attend cultural festivals.* There are certain blessings that may not manifest if you do not come out of your kindred physically or spiritually. God told Abraham to get out of his kindred (Genesis 12:1-3), and in doing this you may relocate to another town, state or country.

12. *Don't make the word of God of no effect by your traditions (Mark 7:13)*, even when family pressure is much. Anyone desiring to be free from foundational witchcraft should desist from following culture and tradition, but instead focus on God's word.

Prayers that deliver from foundational witchcraft bondage:

1. Fire of the Holy Ghost, pass through my foundation and destroy every investment of the enemy in the name of Jesus Christ.
2. By the power in the blood of Jesus Christ, I arrest every evil arrester in my foundation in the name of Jesus Christ.
3. O Lord, arise in your mercy and repair my foundation.
4. Every voice of condemnation in my foundation, be silenced in the name of Jesus Christ.
5. Every power, sponsoring false visions in my foundation, be arrested in the name of Jesus Christ.
6. Spirit of error arising from my foundation be arrested and be bound in the name of Jesus Christ.

7. Foundation of marine witchcraft in my life, Scatter in the name of Jesus Christ.
8. Satanic priest from my mother's side, appearing in my dreams in order to trouble my destiny, lose your power over my life in the name of Jesus Christ.
9. Satanic Priest from my father's side, controlling my life through my dreams, receive confusion in the name of Jesus Christ.
10. Foundational battles fashioned against my marriage, collapse by fire in the name of Jesus Christ.
11. Every evil river from my hometown that has swallowed my virtues, vomit them now in the name of Jesus Christ.
12. Agenda of foundational witchcraft powers for my life, scatter by fire in the name of Jesus Christ.
13. I receive the grace to overcome foundational battles in the name of Jesus Christ.
14. Spirit husband/wife, troubling my life from my foundation, release me and my siblings in the name of Jesus Christ.
15. Evil mirror, satanic crystal ball in my foundation being used to monitor my life, shatter into pieces in the name of Jesus Christ.
16. Every mind-controlling spirit, attacking me from my foundation, lose your grip over my life in the name of Jesus Christ.
17. Evil veil of foundational powers, making me to lose my blessings, be destroyed by fire in the name of Jesus Christ.
18. Satanic python from my foundation, appearing in my dreams, be paralysed in the name of Jesus Christ.
19. According to the word of God which says in the name of Jesus Christ I shall cast out devils, I cast out every evil spirit on assignment to make my life miserable in the name of Jesus Christ.
20. Any power in my foundation to which I have been dedicated, release me by fire in the name of Jesus Christ.
21. Any power in my foundation using my face to attack my helpers, I strop you of your power in the name of Jesus Christ.
22. Evil foundational altars attacking my destiny, be destroyed by the fire and thunder of God in the name of Jesus Christ.
23. Evil foundational mark on my forehead, hands, chest, tummy, back, feet, chasing away my helpers, be wiped away by the power in the blood of Jesus Christ.
24. Blood bondage in my ancestral line, break in the name of Jesus Christ.
25. Evil foundational timer, set for my marriage, be destroyed in the name of Jesus Christ. I shall meet my divinely appointed partner, this year.
26. Evil foundational timer, monitoring my conception and safe delivery, be broken by the power in the blood of Jesus. I shall conceive this year in the name of Jesus Christ.
27. Evil foundational spirit wife, drinking my sperm, vomit my sperm and lose your power over my life in the name of Jesus Christ.
28. Any foundational power using my menstrual cycle to attack my destiny, I break your hold in the name of Jesus Christ.
29. Any of my body organs connected to any foundational altar and power, be set free and receive healing in the name of Jesus Christ.

30. Blood suckers and flesh eaters in my foundation, eat your flesh and drink your blood in the name of Jesus Christ.
31. Coffin from my foundation, fashioned against my life, appearing in my dreams and visions, I set you ablaze in the name of Jesus Christ.
32. Covenant of destruction in my foundation that wants to manifest in my life, break and release me now in the name of Jesus Christ.
33. Evil chain holding me down in my foundation, break and release me in the name of Jesus Christ.
34. Demonic serpent in my foundation, swallowing my money, vomit my money and lose your power in the name of Jesus Christ.
35. Evil monitoring power from my foundation monitoring my finances, receive the judgement of God in the name of Jesus Christ.
36. Satanic prisons in my foundation, release me now in the name of Jesus Christ.
37. Every satanic prison warden, fashioned against my life spiritually, I sack you by the power in the blood of Jesus Christ.
38. Any power in my foundation sitting upon my marriage certificate, be unseated now in the name of Jesus Christ.
39. Foundational embargo placed over my finances, be lifted forever in the name of Jesus Christ.
40. Any foundational evil pattern programmed into the cycle of the moon against my life and appearing with the new moon, break in the name of Jesus Christ.
41. I refuse to obey the instructions of wicked powers in my foundation in the name of Jesus Christ.
42. O Lord my father, give me the key to unlock every caged fortune in my foundation in the name of Jesus Christ.
43. Evil rag in my family line, I refuse to put you on in the name of Jesus Christ.
44. Any foundational power, that was the undoing of my ancestors, you shall not have your way in my life in the name of Jesus Christ.
45. All the accumulated and unspent blessing in my foundation, I gather you together and I begin to use you in the name of Jesus Christ. The height that my parents could not get to, I shall exceed it in the name of Jesus Christ.
46. Any power in my foundation that is using my glory to prosper, release my glory and be put to shame in the name of Jesus Christ.
47. I disappoint every evil foundational appointment in my foundation that wants to manifest against my marriage and finances in the name of Jesus Christ.
48. Curse of infirmity and untimely death from my foundation, break in the name of Jesus Christ.
49. Any power in my foundation, demanding my worship, be silenced forever in the name of Jesus Christ.
50. Every evil marital pattern in my foundation that wants to manifest in my life, be cancelled in the name of Jesus Christ.
51. My foundation, you shall not mock me at the time of my greatness in the name of Jesus Christ.
52. The arrow of error and mistake, sponsored by my foundation against my life, you shall not prosper in the name of Jesus Christ.
53. Curse of poverty in my foundation, break in the name of Jesus Christ.
54. Familiar spirit covenant of untimely death in my life, break in the name of Jesus Christ.

55. Any demon in my foundation, assigned to supervise affliction in my life, be arrested in the name of Jesus Christ.
56. Covenant of generational infirmity from my mother's side break and release me now in the name of Jesus Christ.
57. Evil dedication to mermaid and water spirits, break and release me in the name of Jesus Christ.
58. Curse of marital turbulence and divorce in my foundation, break in the name of Jesus Christ.
59. O Lord, show me that thing that I need to know in my foundation that will bring me total deliverance.
60. Evil dedication to the idols of my place of birth, break and release me in the name of Jesus.
61. Any demonic spirit of my in-law's house that is attacking the glory of my marriage, be disgraced in the name of Jesus.
62. Soul tie with familiar spirit in my foundation, break in the name of Jesus Christ.
63. Soul tie with water spirits in my foundation, break and release me in the name if Jesus Christ.
64. O Lord break me and remould my life on the name of Jesus Christ.
65. Fountain of sorrow in my foundation, be destroyed in the name of Jesus Christ.
66. Soul ties with any dead relative, break in the name of Jesus Christ.
67. I break the power of any unconscious witchcraft initiation in my foundation in the name of Jesus Christ.
68. Any power in my foundation, manipulating my dream life, break and release me in the name of Jesus Christ.
69. Genetic disorders in my family line, be reversed in the name of Jesus Christ.
70. Witchcraft animals in my foundation using my glory to prosper, release my glory in the name of Jesus Christ.
71. Witchcraft bird in my foundation on evil assignment against my life, catch fire, and be destroyed in the name of Jesus Christ.
72. I destroy every satanic linkage in my root in the name of Jesus Christ.
73. Every ritual by the graveside that has kept my family line in bondage, lose your power in the name of Jesus Christ.
74. Every human blood sacrifice in my foundation frustrating my destiny, be destroyed by the power in the blood of Jesus Christ.
75. Spirit of the necromancer in my foundation, break and release me by the power in the blood of Jesus Christ.
76. I withdraw the power and strength of foundational powers on assignment against my life in the name of Jesus Christ.
77. Ancient foundational trees harbouring witchcraft against my life be destroyed by the thunder fire of God in the name of Jesus Christ.
78. Any idol power in my foundation responsible for financial failure, be destroyed in the name of Jesus Christ.
79. Demon idol on assignment from my foundation on assignment to kill me, go back to your sender in the name of Jesus Christ.
80. Every voice of shame and disgrace speaking from my foundation, be silenced in the name of Jesus Christ.
81. Every evil inspiration from idolatrous family history that is keeping my life in bondage release me in the name of Jesus Christ.
82. I come out of every bondage in my imagination in the name of Jesus Christ.
83. Witchcraft network in my foundation, Scatter by fire in the name of Jesus Christ.

84. Foundational vampire, sponsoring infirmity in my life, be roasted by the fire of the Holy Ghost in the name of Jesus Christ.
85. Every name in my foundation that I am bearing now that is responsible for my problems, I break your power (change the name) in the name of Jesus Christ.
86. Every foundational power sucking the milk and honey of my life, I curse you in the name of Jesus Christ.
87. Any power in my foundation aborting God's glory in my life, be exposed and be disgraced in the name of Jesus Christ.
88. Foundational Goliath, your time is up in my life, lose your power in the name of Jesus Christ.
89. Every mask of darkness in my foundation covering up my face, that is making me to lose my glory, I pull you off in the name of Jesus Christ.
90. I bind the strongman in my foundation and possess all my possession in the name of Jesus Christ.
91. Garment of non-achievement in my life, be roasted in the name of Jesus Christ.
92. I break the power of strange behaviour over my life in the name of Jesus Christ.
93. Every intimidating power assigned to create fear and deflate my faith, fall down and be arrested in the name of Jesus Christ.
94. Every evil river from my foundation, flowing into my life, dry up from your source in the name of Jesus Christ.
95. By the mercy of God, I cancel every judgement of foundational witchcraft upon my life in the name of Jesus Christ.
96. Every door opened to foundational witchcraft in my life, be exposed and be closed for ever in the name of Jesus Christ.
97. Every unconscious evil paradigm in my root, be exposed and be broken in the name of Jesus Christ.
98. By the power of the Holy Ghost, I break every evil limitation created for me by my foundation in the name of Jesus Christ.
99. Powers assigned against the glorious children of my father's house and my mother's house lose your power in the name of Jesus Christ.
100. Any foundational power saying no to my international breakthrough lose your power in the name of Jesus Christ.
101. Familiar spirit foundation, break and release me in the name of Jesus Christ.

CHAPTER NINE

MARINE WITCHCRAFT

Marine witchcraft refers to wickedness and rebellion to God that is characteristic of riverine and coastal dwellers, and the spirits and other personalities in their domain. Marine spirits are one of the most devastating demonic spirits that exist. Every riverine city in every part of the world has their presence, and every coastal city has their presence as well. Riverine cities have rivers passing through them, and coastal cities are those that are close by the sea or ocean. When you think about relaxing and chilling, you think about the beach. At the beach, people wear different sorts of bikini, and may even lose themselves in some form of ecstasy and it is not uncommon for people to loosely have sex by the beach. This sort of behaviour has come to stay with people that live in coastal and riverine areas. One major characteristic of marine witchcraft is that of sexual perversion. Let's see what the features are for people who are from riverine and coastal areas.

Features of people who are from marine environments or are possessed by marine spirits:

1. *Sexual perversion.* The sea and riverine areas as explained above are vulnerable when it comes to sexual perversion, sexual crimes and the consequences of sexual perverseness.
2. *Seductive tendencies.* These too are common in people from marine backgrounds.
3. *Divorce.* Due to sexual perversion and various types of inordinate affection, marriages don't last in these regions and people from these areas. This is why it is good to carry out intensive deliverance before you marry.
4. *Alcoholism.* Many people from riverine areas believe that the areas are breezy and cold. The only way that majority of the people fight this is to take alcohol and smoke. These are prevalent and this brings about violence and certain health conditions.
5. *Violence.* There is a lot of violence in riverine and coastal areas due to alcoholism and other substance abuse. Cannabis, marijuana, cocaine and others are common within the youth.
6. *Medical problems.* These substances cause cardiovascular and breathing problems. High blood pressure and stroke are common. As a result of sexual perverseness, sexually transferred infections are also common.
7. *Materialism.* There is a lot of wealth in these areas as the bible talks about the abundance of the sea (Isaiah 60:5). This wealth attracts different kinds of people, and there is bound to be crime in these areas. In women, this worsens the sexual perverseness.
8. *Marital turbulence.* There are problems in marriages as adultery is prevalent.
9. *Marine worship.* There are cities in Africa where you get to and what you see almost in every house is a white pot, with cowrie shells turned upside down on a mound. Many of the rich men there put on white apparel, as they believe the colour of the goddess is white.
10. *Prevalence of lying spirits and fake lives.* People possessed by marine spirits are mostly liars and live a fake life. In order to boost their ego, they tell lies. They also cover their sexual escapades by telling lies.

When you notice that you are from a riverine or coastal area, and these traits are common in your area, you have parents that exhibit same, and can see that you already manifesting same, then you need to go for deliverance.

How can someone acquire marine spirits?

1. *By inheritance.* A person can inherit marine spirits from one or both parents.
2. *Through sex.* One of the most terrible and easy means of transferring marine spirits is sex, within and outside marriage. However, it is easy to overcome with prayers if you are legally married. When you are not married, marine agents usually render their victims to be poor or kill them.
3. *Through food.* When you eat from the devil by accepting food anytime, anywhere, anyhow, you are likely to enter into trouble. These spirits will enter easily. I know a girl who took food from a friend when she was in the primary school. She was possessed by marine spirits, living a poor-quality life, without a husband. The husband issue was the main thing that brought her for deliverance. The spirit inside her cried out during deliverance as she mentioned the name of her friend "Abike", the biscuit you gave me when we were in the primary school has put me into all this trouble. I pray for you that every food the enemy fed you with and are troubling your life shall lose their power over your life in Jesus Name.
4. *Festivals.* When you celebrate marine idol festivals, then you are bound to be possessed by marine spirits. This is because there is great demonic density and traffic. You perform rights and are possessed unconsciously by marine spirits.
5. *Incisions.* Any strange material you allow into your blood can drag you into the bondage of the enemy, and evil spirits can possess you or oppress you.
6. *Consultations.* If you have problems and go to them for solution. They normally require you to carry out certain acts. In your deprivation and desperation, you are ready to do anything they tell you to do, even when they are pushing you into bondage.
7. *Concoctions.* One of the things is to give you concoctions to drink and rub your body with. It can make you to be possessed. Do you know what is used to prepare these concoctions?
8. *Clothing and textiles.* Just like a garment from a Pastor is anointed and can transfer the power of God, the same thing can happen from the Kingdom of darkness. Clothing is imported from different countries. In most cases, these clothing are dedicated to marine deities. Then do you notice the style and design? Are they short and above the knees, do they reveal your cleavage and your breaststroke, are they tight and seductive? Are they unnecessarily flashy? Now what are the signs and symbols on these dresses? Can you see a fish there, can you see a sea horse, mermaids, lobster shells, prawns and other aquatic signs? These are all strategies of the devil in addition to dedication of the clothing and evil laying of hands to transfer demons into the clothing.

How do you know that you as a person may be harbouring marine spirits?

1. When you *dream about rivers and seas* a lot. In that dream, what they normally see is impossibility and torment e.g. swimming in dirty water, trying to cross a river without success, or picking snails by the riverbank. It is also common to see people putting on white to come and torment you in the dream

2. *Spirit husband and wife*. One of the first things when you are initiated is to have a spirit husband assigned to you. Sexual lust and inordinate affection will give more power to the spirit. What do they cause?
3. *Excessive sexual craving*. People possessed by spirit spouses have excessive sexual appetite even when they are in a marriage.
4. *Hatred for your physical wife or husband* when they are trying all possible bests to please them.
5. *Strife and quarrels in marriage.* As a result of the poison of the serpentine spirit.
6. *Attraction instead to other people's husbands.* All your desires when directed to other people's husbands and wives even when you are in marriage.
7. *Struggling to live a holy life.* Marine spirits don't let go easily because they have a strong grip on their victims. Persistent fasting and prayer is an effective way out. A person possessed by marine spirits could commit adultery in marriage, and encourage their married daughters to do the same, all in a quest for more money. When they discover that the husband of that child is not happy about it, they know different kinds of tricks to make the truth hidden. A person possessed with marine spirits will give you a thousand and one reasons not to fast. They are always weak when it comes to fasting.
8. *Stubbornness.* People who are possessed by marine spirits tend to be very stubborn. They are stubborn in the sense that they disobey the commandments of God.
9. *False visions.* When you begin to see frightening visions, bad visions, or even make evil decrees that come to pass. Then watch it.
10. *Dominating spirit.* When people tell you a lot that you have a domineering spirit, then this is a mark of witchcraft, most especially marine witchcraft.
11. *Superstitious.* Deception is the main ingredient in their superstitions. A woman may tell you that she is missing you and feels like rubbing hearts with you, and that it is not right for a child to stay far from the mother. But in fact, she's trying to strengthen the soul tie with the daughter. It is even worse when that child wants to travel abroad for any reason, they will mobilise every resource to stop it. They have dedicated that child in the coven even the child may not know. Watch every of these tendencies. If you are a child, this will be useful.
12. *Afraid of true men of God, especially Prophets.* When you discover that you are just afraid of being in the presence of highly anointed men of God, but instead like going to churches where there is not much of spiritual activities, then you need to watch it. A person possessed by marine witchcraft is only interested in churches where they can seduce people, even the Pastor himself.
13. When you are afraid when you see a river or at the beach, or you see a large mass of water.
14. When you dream about seeing mermaids in your dreams.

Mermaid Spirits.

Mermaid spirits are often encountered and cast out from many deliverance candidates who are possessed by marine spirits. The mermaid spirit is one of the major actors in the marine world. According to a revelation that I was given, she marries off the victims to spirit husbands and wives; and supervises that union. Mermaids have been seen by sailors in many parts of the world, and the belief about mermaids is global extending to Japan, North and South Korea, Florid USA, Alberta, Brazil, Cuba, Uruguay, Denmark, Spain, etc.

People were originally drawn to these half humans, half fish creatures because of the magical powers they are believed to possess. They are believed to Prophesy, to kiss people and heal them to the extent that these people in turn, heal other people or raise people who are almost dying. However, after this encounter, what happens to the people? The devil has no free gift. This is why you should be careful about prophecy, signs and wonders. Many churches are being controlled by marine spirits. They are also believed to have the ability to control the sea, influence weather, and enchant with their voices. They are believed to be very good singers and that they seduce sailors with their voices, eventually captivating them and killing them, or luring them to the bottom of the sea to dwell there with them. One may wonder why floods carry many people at the same time, why boats capsize or why so much of gory tales has been heard about the Bermuda Triangle. Marine spirits are terrible and wicked. Sometimes a person could just wake up from his sleep and go straight to the river to drown. All the gifts are to arrest souls to steal, to kill and to destroy.

As a result of the powers, many people from many parts of the world have come to believe so much in the mermaids and that is the foundation and reason for the worship of the water goddess all over the world. Unfortunately, many have wealth and benefit from these false wonders, but their lives are polluted. I was conducting deliverance for a sister, and the spirit inside her was trying to negotiate. She said we should tell her that she will give her money but no children. They we told her that the deal is not sealed and is totally unacceptable to is the deliverance ministers. We quoted many scriptures, for example Lamentations 3:37 which says: "Who is he that saith and it cometh to pass, when the Lord commanded it not". He has also given us power to trample upon serpents and scorpions and upon every power of the enemy (Luke 10:19). Christ hath redeemed us from the curse of the law, being made a curse for us, for it is written that cursed is every man that hangeth on the tree, that the blessings of Abraham shall come upon the Gentiles through Jesus Christ and that we may receive the promise of the spirit through faith (Galatians 3:13-14). We were on deliverance ground a few months later and we saw the lady passing by and carrying a baby on her back, as it is the culture in Africa where I was then.

How to receive deliverance from marine witchcraft:

1. Surrender your life to Jesus.
2. Repent from every known sin.
3. Make the word of God your friend. Study to show yourself approved.
4. Take time to meditate on God's word
5. Pray and fast to break marine Covenants, break curses, break every evil dedication, ask for forgiveness of every sin, ask for God's fire afresh, and ask for God's favour and mercy. Deal decisively by breaking every covenant with spirit husband or wife.

6. Resist every tendency to commit any sexual immorality. The devil makes it enticing for you to commit sexual immorality so that you will not be free.
7. Learn to confess God's word.
8. Have faith. Back up faith with works.
9. Seek every knowledge that will move your life forward.
10. Identify God's gift for your life and use it. It attracts more angels to you and opens the door of God's favour and mercy.
11. Be a cheerful giver.
12. Evangelise regularly.

Prayers to deliver from marine witchcraft:

1. I break every covenant with the waters in the name of Jesus Christ.
2. Every water spirit, supervising affliction in my life, be arrested and be bound in the name of Jesus Christ.
3. Evil dedication to water idols, break and release me in the name of Jesus Christ.
4. Marine serpent in my body, be roasted by fire in the name of Jesus Christ.
5. Thou spirit of sexual perversion, lose me and let me go in the name of Jesus Christ.
6. Evil summons from the waters against my life, backfire in the name of Jesus Christ.
7. Let the yoke of spirit husband/wife in my life be broken in the name of Jesus Christ.
8. I withdraw my marriage certificate from every evil altar in the name of Jesus Christ.
9. I withdraw my wedding gown from every marine witchcraft in the name of Jesus Christ.
10. I recover every virtue stolen from my life by marine witchcraft in the name of Jesus Christ.
11. Anything representing me on any marine witchcraft altar, be destroyed by fire in the name of Jesus Christ.
12. Blood covenant linking me with marine spirits, break in the name of Jesus Christ.
13. Spiritual robbers from the marine world on assignment against my life, be arrested in the name of Jesus Christ.
14. Arrows of infirmity, fired into my life by marine witchcraft, I shake you off by fire in the name of Jesus Christ.
15. Covenant of untimely death, fashioned against my life by marine witchcraft, break by the power in the blood of Jesus Christ.
16. Covenant of shame and disgrace fashioned against my life by marine witchcraft, break in the name of Jesus Christ.
17. Covenant of marital misfortune and failure, fashioned against my life from the waters, break in the name of Jesus Christ.

18. Covenant of marine witchcraft initiation, break and release me in the name of Jesus Christ.
19. Marine witchcraft serpent monitoring my life, be roasted by fire in the name of Jesus Christ.
20. Evil mirror and calabash, monitoring my life from the waters, break into irredeemable pieces in the name of Jesus Christ.
21. Every marine witchcraft pot caging my money, break and scatter in the name of Jesus Christ.
22. Marine witchcraft bird flying for my sake, crash-land and die in the name of Jesus Christ.
23. Every blood sucker and flesh eaters raging against my life from the waters, eat your own flesh and drink your own blood in the name of Jesus Christ.
24. Any marine power, sponsoring fake vision in my life, lose your power in the name of Jesus Christ.
25. Every attack against my conception, be disgraced on the name of Jesus Christ.
26. I break every linkage with water spirits in the name of Jesus Christ.
27. Every poison of spirit husband/wife in my life, be purged by the power in the blood of Jesus Christ.
28. Marine witchcraft agent, drinking the milk and honey of my life, vomit them and lose your power over my life in the name of Jesus Christ.
29. Every curse of marine witchcraft against my business, break in the name of Jesus Christ.
30. Marine witchcraft covenant saying no to my conception and safe delivery, break in the name of Jesus Christ.
31. Marine witchcraft curse against my marriage, break in the name of Jesus Christ.
32. Serpent from the waters, stimulating me sexually, I announce your obituary in the name of Jesus Christ.
33. Ring of spirit husband on my finger, I remove you in the name of Jesus Christ.
34. Every mark of spirit husband/spirit wife on my forehead or any part of my body chasing away my marriage suitors, clear away by the power in the blood of Jesus Christ.
35. I withdraw my marriage certificate from the waters on the name of Jesus Christ.
36. Spirit children appearing to me in the dream, receive the judgement of God in the name of Jesus Christ.
37. Soul tie with the mermaid, break and release me in the name of Jesus Christ.
38. Covenant with the mermaid in my life, break and release me in the name of Jesus Christ.
39. Marine witchcraft altar, fashioned against me in the waters, horrible tempest of the Almighty, pull them down in the name of Jesus Christ.
40. Any water of sprinkling, ever sprinkled on my property, on my life, on my children, lose your power in the name of Jesus Christ.
41. I render null and void every spiritual attack against my head in the name of Jesus Christ.
42. Every marine witchcraft decree against my life, be reversed in the name of Jesus Christ.
43. Marine witchcraft supervisor, supervising my affliction, be put to shame in the name of Jesus Christ.
44. Angels of the living God, locate and recover for me, every lost benefit in the marine kingdom in the name of Jesus Christ.
45. The key of my prosperity on marine witchcraft altar, I recover you in the name of Jesus Christ.
46. Marine witchcraft embargo upon my business and marriage be lifted by fire in the name of Jesus Christ.
47. I break and release myself from every marine witchcraft bondage in the name of Jesus Christ.

48. I break every marine witchcraft limitation in the name of Jesus Christ.
49. Marine witchcraft strategy against my life, fail woefully in the name of Jesus Christ.
50. O Lord increase my speed against every witchcraft pursuer in the name of Jesus Christ.
51. Every power of the dog, sponsored against my life from the waters, expire in the name of Jesus Christ.
52. Expectations of marine enemies against my life be disappointed in the name of Jesus Christ.
53. Enchantment from the waters against my life, be reversed in the name of Jesus Christ.
54. Every marine witchcraft strongman boasting against my life, be arrested and be disgraced in the name of Jesus Christ.
55. Soul tie with marine witchcraft agent of destruction.
56. Fire of God, destroy every marine witchcraft foundation in my life in the name of Jesus Christ.
57. Spirit of poverty sponsored by marine witchcraft loose me and let me go in the name of Jesus Christ.
58. I shut every door open to marine witchcraft attack in my life in the name of Jesus Christ.
59. By the mercy of God, I cancel every marine witchcraft judgment over my life in the name of Jesus Christ.
60. Bulldozer of God's deliverance run through my foundation in the name of Jesus Christ.
61. I blot out every handwriting of marine witchcraft against my life in the name of Jesus Christ.
62. Arrow of death and hell sponsored by marine witchcraft against my life backfire in the name of Jesus Christ.
63. Food covenant strengthening marine witchcraft in my life, break in the name of Jesus Christ.
64. I break every curse of limitation and backwardness in the name of Jesus Christ.
65. Power of wrong choices sponsored against my life from the waters break in the name of Jesus Christ.
66. Fountain of affliction, constructed against my life, dry up in the name of Jesus Christ.
67. Every ritual done at the riverbank against my life, I break your power I the name of Jesus Christ.
68. Marine witchcraft gathering and conspiracy against my life scatter by fire in the name of Jesus Christ.
69. I break every environmental marine witchcraft law in the name of Jesus Christ.
70. Marine witchcraft altar of my in-law's house caging my glory, I pull you down in the name if Jesus Christ.
71. Marine witchcraft weapon fashioned against my life receive destruction by fire in the name of Jesus Christ.
72. Every evil connection between me and marine altars, break and release me in the name of Jesus Christ.
73. Marine priest or priestess sitting upon an evil throne to judge my life, receive the judgement of God in the name of Jesus Christ.
74. Any hidden marine witchcraft agent assigned to destroy my destiny, be disgraced in the name of Jesus Christ.
75. Evil arrow fired against me in the dream, I shake you off by fire in the name of Jesus Christ.
76. I refuse to enter into any sexual trap created for my life by marine witchcraft in the name of Jesus Christ.
77. Wisdom of marine witches against my life, be turned to foolishness in the name of Jesus Christ.
78. Agenda of the mermaid against my life, be scattered in the name of Jesus Christ.
79. Hook of fire from God, arrest every mermaid swimming in the ocean in order to destroy my destiny in the name of Jesus Christ.
80. Evil installation and power in the Atlantic Ocean against my life scatter by fire in the name of Jesus Christ.

81. Evil altar in the Indian Ocean erected against my success, be destroyed by the thunder fire of God in the name of Jesus Christ.
82. Every evil plan by marine witchcraft in the Pacific Ocean against my life, scatter by fire in the name of Jesus Christ.
83. I break into evert marine witchcraft warehouse and plunder my goods in the name of Jesus Christ.
84. Arrows of insanity fired against my life from the waters backfire in the name of Jesus Christ.
85. Marine witchcraft serpents assigned to trouble my life, come out with all your root in the name of Jesus Christ.
86. Chains and shackles of witchcraft tying me down to one spot, break and release me in the name if Jesus Christ.
87. I silence every roaring of lions from the Kingdom of darkness against my life in the name of Jesus Christ.
88. Arrow of insanity fired into my life from the waters backfire in the name of Jesus Christ.
89. Marine witchcraft timetable fashioned against my life be destroyed in the name of Jesus Christ.
90. Marine witchcraft clock fashioned against my life, in the name of Jesus Christ.
91. Every evil decree from the waters against my children, I cancel you by fire in the name of Jesus Christ.
92. Fire of the Holy Ghost, destroy every marine witchcraft plantation against my life in the name of Jesus Christ.
93. Marine witchcraft crown on my head, be shaken off by fire in the name of Jesus Christ.
94. Every marine witchcraft pot cooking my destiny, break and scatter by fire in the name of Jesus Christ.
95. Every marine witchcraft dog fashioned against my life, receive destruction by the sword of fire of the Holy Ghost in the name of Jesus Christ.
96. Marine witchcraft python suffocating me and making my life uncomfortable, be destroyed by the fire of the Holy Ghost, in the name of Jesus Christ.
97. Any power from the waters, claiming ownership over my life, I break your power in the name of Jesus Christ.
98. Evil cooperation between marine witchcraft, celestial witchcraft, and terrestrial witchcraft against my life, scatter in the name of Jesus Christ.
99. Marine witchcraft coffin, fashioned against my life, break and burn to ashes in the name of Jesus Christ.
100. I reverse every marine witchcraft burial fashioned against my life in the name of Jesus Christ.

CHAPTER TEN

SPIRITUAL PURGING.

The enemy can plant or program materials, arrows, spirits, and sometimes physical objects like needles, combs, cowrie shells. These materials could be programmed there to trouble your life, or to serve as a point of contact or ladder for them to climb into your life. They may cause pain, sickness, make you to have nightmares or hear strange voices. It could also lead to strange behaviour, and cause you to commit errors, and the list is endless. In deliverance, we sometimes need to come with the mindset that I want to purge a vessel and make it clean and useful to God, the candidate and the world at large. Any human being can be polluted, and strange materials programmed. The enemy can also program things in animals so that they can come in through your pets in your house to reach you. They use them like "helipads" so to say.

> *Matthew 13:25*
>
> *But while men slept, his enemy came and sowed tares among the wheat, and went his way.*

Furthermore,

> *Matthew 15:13*
>
> *But he answered and said, every plant, which my heavenly Father hath not planted, shall be rooted up.*
>
> *Matthew 3:10*
>
> *And now also the axe is laid unto the root of the trees: therefore, every tree which bringeth not forth good fruit is hewn down, and cast into the fire.*

The bible shows that the enemy is responsible for planting trees and the gimmick of the enemy is to do it secretly. He comes when you are asleep in a spiritual sense and cannot prevent him. When you are most vulnerable. Spiritual sleep could be when you are not studying your Bible, at a time you are not praying, you don't speak in tongues, you are supposed to use your gift and are not, no Evangelism, etc. It could also be physical sleep, when you sleep too much and there are no spiritual activities. If you must get rid of the trees, it must be through uprooting. This means you investigate, dig deep, and uproot.

10 ways that the enemy sows' tares:

1. *During dreams.* As been pointed above, during dreams. People dream that they eat in the dream, have sex in the dream, are being injected in the dream, spit upon in the dream, etc. Some of this manifest in real life.
2. *Through food in parties.* As a matter of fact, there are people that the wicked ones wait for to come to a party and strike them. That is why you must pray for divine approval if you want to attend a party. Pray for days ahead before attending. When you attend too, it is not compulsory for you to eat if you are not led to.
3. *Sex outside marriage.* Marriage is the only premise for sex. If you are having sex with anyone that you are not married to, your life is a fertile ground for affliction. The way of the transgressors is hard (Proverbs 13:15).
4. *The air.* The Bible makes us to know that there is a power of the air (Ephesians 2:2). The enemy can manipulate the air to afflict a person.
5. *The water.* The enemy can manipulate the water to programme evil into a person's life. The whole of the river in a town can be polluted to afflict people in the town. Some also manipulate Wells and bore holes in order to plant things. Witches have confessed that they made accord with the river in a town to program sickness in the lives of the people.
6. *The wind.* When air moves with a force, it becomes a wind. Demonic spirits have been demonstrated to move in the wind, some of which could be very strong. Someone may just feel a cool breeze blow on them and they fall to the ground and have a stroke.
7. *Enchantment.* An evil Priest may say some evil words and incantations right in his room, mentioning a person's name, and he could be afflicting someone many kilometres away.
8. *Evil plantations* can be inherited.
9. *Concoction.* Concoctions are magical preparations, purported to be medicinal, but prepared with different types of fetish materials that could be bewitching.
10. *Incisions.* These are prepared using different kinds of herbs and roots, with different animal organs from reptiles, amphibians etc but are rubbed into razor cuts made on the body. They can bewitching too.

What are the signs of evil plantation?

1. *Sickness.* Immediately the arrow enters, you feel some sickness and may feel nauseated and dizzy. It then progresses to other signs.
2. *Bad dreams.* Once the evil programme success, you will have a confirmation in your dream life. The pollution of the spirit will not go unconfirmed. Once you confirm it, then you need to pray and fast.
3. *Discomfort in the affected area.* If the arrow is fired into an organ in your body, you will feel pains there. It's a terrible headache if it is fired into the head, and this is very common.
4. *Strange behaviour.* Strange arrows will pollute your spirit and provoke strange behaviour.
5. *Strange voices.* A woman said she collected an accursed money with which the evil ones planted a spirit in her life. The spirit continued following her about and commanding her. She started hearing strange voices from inside her intimidating her.

6. *Seeing frightening visions.* When you see frightening and intimidating visions it is a sign of spiritual pollution.
7. *Constant dizziness.* The presence of strange materials will give you arrange feelings like dizziness.
8. *Limitation.* When you are being troubled by an evil arrow or spiritual stranger, you cannot be at your best. There is a slowing down of destiny.
9. *Poverty* is the result of a compromised destiny in many cases.
10. *Isolation.* People will keep a distance when you have a problem. That's why it is good to resist evil plantations.
11. *Depression.* Evil plantations can cause depression, anxiety and other psychological problems.
12. *Prayer life.* There is frustration, discouragement, fear, and the prayer life and desire for God's word may decline.

How then do we deal with spiritual pollution or evil plantations?

1. Accept Jesus as your Lord and saviour say.
2. Repent from every sin. If you don't live a holy life, the enemy will make your life a fertile land for planting affliction. If you are used to committing adultery, the devil will always make you to have sex in the dream, so that evil seed will be planted in your life. When you are covetous and greedy about food, the enemy will rely on that.
3. Forgive those that have sinned against you.
4. Watch what you eat and drink.
5. Be careful about what you look at. Looking at half naked ladies on the streets can cultivate a plantation of lust in your life, or spirit of covetousness. Everything should be looked at in moderation. Over-look is a sin.
6. Be watchful about what you listen to e.g. immoral music can pollute you with idol spirits, sexual demons. Or even the plantation of the spirit of anger.
7. Beware of visits to herbalist's houses or cultural festivals.
8. Ceaseless prayers bring ceaseless revelation and ceaseless protection and deliverance.
9. Do not allow the opposite sex to touch you carelessly. We all know what it is when the opposite sex touches you especially those that touch intentionally to seduce.
10. Study the word with deep understanding.

CHAPTER ELEVEN

WITCHCRAFT IN CHILDREN

Children are highly vulnerable to witchcraft attacks, and one of the major strategies of the witchcraft kingdom to expand its frontiers is to massively initiate children. The initiation of children starts from the womb, when the enemy may target the mother, through food and concoctions during pregnancy. The mother would immediately sense this, as she may dream that a strange animal entered her tummy, mysteriously, or that someone brought out the baby, and manipulated the baby.

A mother in-law, or a friend may have seen the star of the foetus, and they are interested in initiating the baby in order to attack and steal, kill or destroy the star. If this fails, owing to the fact that the mother does not eat from strangers anyhow, or wouldn't even eat in restaurants, then they device other means.

One of those other means is to launch the attempt at initiating the baby at birth. Many midwives are already demonic, and many of their staff, equipment and facilities are initiation friendly. There are some staff that the enemy have planted in the Labour Room, to monitor the stars of these babies and initiate them as soon as possible. The Lord told me a secret in a program, Balm of Gilead, that I was part of, in the year 2007. Balm of Gilead was a program, whereby we served as Healthcare Chaplains, visiting hospitals in the regions to pray with the sick, support them with gifts, and minister healing. The LORD told me that as soon as a child is born and I arrive there, that I should dedicate the child to God the Father, the Son, and the Holy Spirit.

This is very simple to do and does not require any thing ceremonial. All you need to do is to explain your mission to the parents as ethics demand. Ask them for their oil or water if they have. If they don't have, then take permission to use your personal oil, then they could easily get water around. Then you pray with the child pouring some water and oil on his or her head, and declaring the baby dedicated in the name of God the Father, the Son, and the Holy Spirit.

The house of the babysitter is another place where a child may be initiated, after which the next place is the primary school, and the community at large, as they grow up. A research carried out in Europe shows that a large number of children actually confessed to attending the "Witches Sabbath", including male and female children. A "Witch Sabbath" is a night meeting of witches. In Africa, many of these children confess to witchcraft and say many strange things. One of them once confessed that she did not want to have a competitor, and that was why she blocked her mother's womb, and prevented her from having a baby.

I had a first-hand experience with one of the children. The father suspected her and brought her for deliverance, together with the other children. At the peak of the Deliverance service, when she was overwhelmed by God's awesome power, then she confessed. She said she connived with her auntie who lived about 500 kilometres away, to make the father poor and wretched. She confessed they had removed the father's fortunes and hung it on a tree in their hometown. The auntie had visited them and stayed for a while. She also confessed that they used to have meetings in the uncompleted sitting room of her dad. Her dad couldn't continue the building project.

Her dad was a hardworking man and was trying to cater for his family. He had a car and business of his own, until the daughter struck. Even though she was out of school as the father could no longer sponsor her education, she was not bothered. The father suspected her and brought her for prayers, and that was it.

Witchcraft is a widespread phenomenon, all over the world, but it should be addressed in the proper context. Many children are not possessed but have fallen victims of child abuse. Culture and faith have been contributing factors to defining who a witch child is. The Bible says stubbornness is as iniquity as witchcraft, but a mere act of disobedience does not qualify a child as a witch. Disability, academic performance, bedwetting, and other unfounded reasons do not qualify a child as a witch. Different cultures and different faith have different perceptions and approaches regarding witchcraft generally, and specifically in children.

What are the signs that likely indicate witchcraft possession in children?

1. <u>Fear constantly.</u> When a child is always afraid, and cannot go into the room alone, without the mother following her. Or like the case of the baby, that I earlier on mentioned on this book, who was always afraid to look at a particular direction. The parents were discerning and were able to address the problem appropriately.

    2 Timothy 1:7
    For God hath not given us the spirit of fear; but of power, and of love, and of a sound mind.

    When a child is always afraid, then it is a bad sign, and is reflecting some conscious or subconscious bad phenomenon.

2. <u>Refusal to suck.</u> When a baby refuses to suck and is always crying. When little babies are being tormented by witchcraft spirits, they are not emotionally stable and can manifest a variety of symptoms in the demonstration of this. A refusal or inability of a baby to suck the mother's breast is a problem that shouldn't be lightly addressed.

3. <u>Seeing things, you cannot see.</u> When a child sees what you cannot see, and tells you, or you can see that the child is reacting to something unpleasant, then you must address it. The child might say something like "see them wearing white" and he or she cries and attempts to run. He could also just focus on a particular spot and gradually he cries out. The reaction sometimes is for the spirit to retreat and the baby stops crying. A child may suddenly give a loud cry, for example after seeing a large python, which you cannot see.

4. <u>Hearing things you cannot hear.</u> A possessed child may hear what you do not hear, and he or she may be trying to respond, or you see that he or she is bewildered. Visual impressions instil more fear in a child than auditory inputs.

5. <u>Disoriented, confused or withdrawn.</u> A child who is possesses or oppressed will normally be disoriented, confused, and sometimes withdrawn. That is their own way of expressing their frustration. The next thing you should do is to call them and ask why they are withdrawn. He or she might not say anything, then you continue by saying something you know the child will be interested in. You can change the channel to a station that they like. The key to the prompt deliverance is however discussing with the Pastor as soon as possible to organise a deliverance session.

6. <u>Strange behaviour</u> is common in children who are possessed, as majority of them are incessantly stubborn and daring occasionally. They receive all kinds of demonic inspiration and prompting to misbehave. These children tend to hear a voice that tells them to do what they do. There was a case of a child who was born to well-to-do

parents. She was always going around to steal panties spread on the line to dry outside. It may be that they do not like to stay in class. Some of them even as kids are possessed by sexual demons, and you see it in their behaviour.

7. *Crying from the sleep.* A possessed child will always be tormented in the dream, seeing all sorts of images and being prompted in the spirit to find himself or herself in strange places. When this happens and they are overwhelmed, they cry out from the sleep.

8. *Wicked utterances* concerning their situations, people around them, animals, or things. A possessed child may just look at the direction of a dog, and say "how I wish I can blow off the head of this dog" or look at a beautiful car, and ask you that "Daddy, if this car summersaults, what would happen"?

9. *Alone muttering inaudible words.* Like to be alone somewhere, muttering inaudible words. Some of them meet in broad daylight, and you may not know. At this stage, they have adapted to the witchcraft possession, and wouldn't resist it any longer by crying. Time of adaptation varies depending on the kinds of things they see or how frequently they attack.

10. *Frequent sickness, loss of appetite, and loss of weight.* A child oppressed or possessed by witchcraft spirits will usually encounter health problems, on and off. The mystery of it all is that it is usually difficult to diagnose or treat such diseases in the hospital through conventional means. All the laboratory tests would prove negative whilst there is an illness. The drugs will not bring relief.

11. *Nightmares* are also common. This may make the child not to sleep at night, and the child will feel embittered and not like to listen to anyone.

12. *Poor academic performance* is another reason to suspect demonic possession. The parents should try to uncover the reason why the child is not performing well in school. Try to discuss with the teacher in school on the one side, and your Pastor in church on the other side. As a parent you should pray enough and fast to solve the problem, together with the child making them happy and reassuring them.

Tips on effective deliverance strategies in children:

1. A person that wants to deliver a child possessed by witchcraft spirits must be observant. Children are undiscerning and even when they can discern, cannot communicate. It is important to monitor then at night and during the day. A further step is to be able to ask them questions to elicit responses.

2. As soon as you have been able to elicit concrete evidence or two, you've got to discuss your observations and fears with a Deliverance Pastor.

3. Have a small notepad, to jot the instructions of the Deliverance Minister and document your daily experience with the child, and everything they do.

4. Share stories about the miracles in the Old Testament, Miracles of Jesus, and teach on how the power of God can lead to victory.

5. Enrol them in a children's class to listen to the word of God. Engage them with the study of God's word.

6. Enrol him or her in a Music Class, so that they can learn how to play an instrument of Music. One of the most profitable ways of engaging and delivering a child is by singing and playing an instrument of music. The role of music in the Deliverance Ministry cannot be over-emphasised.
7. Always "pray with" the child and teach him or her the various types of prayers that are available. Point out to them the great things your prayers have done. Make them to appreciate the power of God, build their faith and share testimonies.
8. Both parents should "pray for" the children. The effectual fervent prayer of a righteous man availeth much.
9. Make sure you always show love and encouragement. The Bible says a merry heart doeth good like medicine and a broken spirit drieth the bones.
10. Don't ever treat them harshly but try to bring out the best in them. This problem is not their wish, but unfortunately it has happened, and it need to be addressed faithfully. Most cultures have very weird beliefs about witchcraft. Of a fact, many children are really possessed that a parent who is not in the faith could be terrified. Don't, take them to places where they will be cut, burnt, beaten, or things like that. The living word of God does not prescribe any of such. We walk by faith in God's word, and

Isaiah 8:20

To the law and to the testimony: if they speak not according to this word, it is because there is no light in them.

Since witchcraft is inherited sometimes, and could be transferred by initiation, if one person has it, then they all the family may need to go for a deliverance session.

Build up the child's faith and let them know after the Deliverance that the battle is over.

11. Before you could do a very good work, you need to lead the child to Christ for him or her to be saved. I am putting this at the end of this discussion because not all children are able to understand salvation and give their lives to Christ.
12. The devil finds it easy to operate where parents are not united and quarrel all the time. Parents should always show good examples to their kids.

Prayers to Deliver Your Children from Witchcraft:

1. I remove the name of my Children from every witchcraft register in the name of Jesus Christ.
2. I remove the name of my children from every list of the mortuary and graveyard in the name of Jesus Christ.
3. You my children, you shall not enter Witchcraft vehicle of sudden or untimely death in the name of Jesus Christ.
4. Witchcraft covenant of untimely death over the life of my children, be broken in the name of Jesus Christ.

5. Witchcraft plantation of untimely death in the life of my children, be uprooted completely in the name of Jesus Christ.
6. Plantation of infirmity in the life of my children, be uprooted completely in the name of Jesus Christ.
7. Evil blood connection fashioned against the blood of my children, be broken in the name of Jesus Christ.
8. Agenda of blood suckers and flesh eaters for the life of my children, fail woefully in the name of Jesus Christ.
9. You the brain of my children, receive deliverance in the name of Jesus Christ.
10. Every stolen virtue, from the life of my children, be restored in the name of Jesus Christ.
11. Every tongue, cursing the destiny of my children, wither by fire in the name of Jesus Christ.
12. Call the names of your children and command them to come out of witchcraft graveyard in the name of Jesus Christ.
13. You my children, become the head and not the tail in the name of Jesus Christ.
14. Satanic drum sounding for my children to dance, be busted in the name of Jesus Christ.
15. Blood bondage tying down my children to one spot, break and release then in the name of Jesus Christ.
16. Witchcraft network fashioned against the life of my children, crumble by fire in the name of Jesus Christ.
17. No matter how long that I live on earth, I shall not Bury any of my children in the name of Jesus Christ.
18. Witchcraft powers using the glory of my children to prosper, lose your authority and power in the name of Jesus Christ.
19. Sacred mates appearing to my children in the dream, I shut the door against you in the name of Jesus Christ.
20. Weapons of marine witchcraft fashioned against my children, you shall not prosper in the name of Jesus Christ.
21. Anointing that breaks the yoke, fall upon the life of my children in the name of Jesus Christ.
22. Power of unconscious evil dedication through food, or drink, break and release my children in the name of Jesus Christ.
23. Automatic failure mechanism programmed into the life of my children, be broken in the name of Jesus Christ.
24. Inherited witchcraft, lose your grip over my children in the name of Jesus Christ.
25. Evil anointing over the life of my children, dry up now in the name of Jesus Christ.
26. Witchcraft food strengthening the activities of witchcraft in the life of my children be melted in the name of Jesus Christ.
27. Monitoring spirits on assignment against the life of my children, be blinded in the name of Jesus Christ.
28. Thunder fire of God, locate and render impotent any witchcraft agent assigned to torment my children in the name of Jesus Christ.
29. Yoke of evil dedication by satanic midwives over the life of my children, be broken in the name of Jesus Christ.

30. Evil visitation at night or during the day against the life of my children, be aborted in the name of Jesus Christ.
31. Evil arrow that entered my child in the house of the babysitter, your time is up, come out by fire in the name of Jesus Christ.
32. Evil concoctions of witchcraft eaten by my children, be purged by fire in the name of Jesus Christ.
33. Witchcraft attack against the placenta of my children at the time of birth, be nullified in the name of Jesus Christ.
34. Every witchcraft attack against the life of my children, using their hair, be nullified in the name of Jesus Christ.
35. Every bewitched breastmilk that my children took in the house of the babysitter, lose your power in the name of Jesus Christ.
36. Sexual manipulation against the life of my child, I break your power in the name of Jesus Christ.
37. Satanic glory exchange in the life of my child, be reversed in the name of Jesus Christ.
38. Wicked spirit programmed into my child secretly in order to torment my destiny, be exposed and be disgraced in the name of Jesus Christ.
39. Any witchcraft power multiplying inside my children, your end has come, be arrested by fire in the name of Jesus Christ.
40. Any witchcraft power manipulating my children against me, I break your power in the name of Jesus Christ.
41. O Lord, separate my children from agents that want to influence them negatively.
42. Cultural loopholes waiting to bewitch my children, be covered in the name of Jesus Christ.
43. Spirit of disobedience, lose your power in the life of my children in the name of Jesus Christ.
44. Thou prince of the power of the air, lose your hold over the life of …………(mention the names of your children) in the name of Jesus Christ.
45. Satanic visions tormenting the life of my children, clear away by fire in the name of Jesus Christ.
46. Every spirit uttering strange voice into the ears of my children, be silenced in the name of Jesus Christ.
47. Angels of the living God, fight the enemies of my children unto surrender in the name of Jesus Christ.
48. Every power, sponsoring academic failure in the life of my children, lose your power in the name of Jesus Christ.
49. Witchcraft garment of reproach over my children, be roasted by fire in the name of Jesus Christ.
50. You my children, be released from the captivity of the spirit of depression in the name of Jesus Christ.
51. Evil spiritual nanny, assigned to my children be frustrated by fire in the name of Jesus Christ.
52. Evil spirit transporting my children spiritually by Witchcraft means, lose your power in the name of Jesus Christ.
53. Witchcraft animal on assignment against the life of my children, be roasted by fire in the name of Jesus Christ.
54. Rock of Ages, hide my children in you in the name of Jesus Christ.
55. O Lord, send your word and deliver my children from every destruction in the name of Jesus Christ.

56. Coven judgement over the life of my children, be cancelled by the power in the blood of Jesus Christ.
57. Every witchcraft power commanding my children to do evil, I break your power in the name of Jesus Christ.
58. Witchcraft chain tying my children to one spot be broken in the name of Jesus Christ.
59. Witchcraft garment designed for my children catch fire and burn to ashes in the name of Jesus Christ.
60. Ring and bangle of spirit husband/wife on my children, be destroyed by fire in the name of Jesus Christ.
61. You my children, come out of the waters in the name of Jesus Christ.
62. Familiar spirit covenant over my children, break in the name of Jesus Christ.
63. Every owl and vulture on assignment against my children, be destroyed in the name of Jesus Christ.
64. Witchcraft serpent programmed into the life of my children be roasted by fire in the name of Jesus Christ.
65. Blood sucking demon living inside my son/daughter, that is assigned to attack me, be roasted by fire in the in the name of Jesus Christ.

CHAPTER TWELVE

TYPES OF WITCHCRAFT

There are different classes of witchcraft with regards to their characteristics. In the foregoing, we are going to look at the different types and their descriptions, and what to do to be victorious over then. They are interwoven though, and the activities of one can be similar to the other, sometimes.

Environmental Witchcraft.

This has to do with witches and wizards that operate in your geographical location, and environment. Several years back, we were trying to plant a church, an carried out a survey in the environment. Suddenly, a crocodile appeared to one of us in the dream and was telling him that he was a landlord over the area, and that we were not allowed to plant a church in his territory. We went ahead, and that place has become a Regional Headquarters with several branches in the location. Their work is to deceive and manipulate, in order to steal, kill and destroy. In that same area, we had a river that was overflowing its banks. The worshippers believed that the goddess was angry, and that was why she was overflowing the banks. A mighty bridge was constructed over the place, and the river goddess kept quiet. All the altars and shrines, and evil powers that demand worship and blood, and the adherents attribute tragedies and calamities to their works in order to intimidate people and restrict their movements and activities are all environmental witchcraft.

What do we have in the scriptures:

> *Psalms 24:1-2*
>
> *The earth is the LORD'S, and the fulness thereof; the world, and they that dwell therein.*

For he hath founded it upon the seas, and established it upon the floods

It is very clear from the above scriptures that everything and every person in the world are under the authority of the living God. He reigns supreme in the affairs of men. These powers even when they appear in the dream are liars. The scripture can readily be used to check and stall their activities like in the scriptures above. Jesus Christ also applied the scriptures in a similar way when he was tempted by the devil in Matthew 4:1-11.

In that scripture the devil was acting as the "Prince of this world". Another thing after following the scriptures is to be holy and walk righteously.

> *John 14:30*
>
> *Hereafter I will not talk much with you: for the prince of this world cometh, and hath nothing in me.*

Another relevant scripture pertaining to environmental powers is:

> *Matthew 10:16*
>
> *Behold, I send you forth as sheep in the midst of wolves: be ye therefore wise as serpents, and harmless as doves.*

In the midst of all the battles with the World, Jesus encourages us to be as wise as serpents and gentle as doves. We need to study God's word and apply it. The fear of the Lord is the beginning of wisdom. Wisdom of Law and Medicine and other fields are important. The serpent is an animal that is unpredictable and full of strategy. Someone can't predict when a serpent will strike, or where or how. They should not know where we are coming from or where we are going to, like the wind (John 3:8) and so is everyone that is born of the spirit. This is the type of wisdom that the serpent has, and Jesus wants us to apply in our activities and dealing with the World. However, we should be harmless. The scriptures encourage us to be not overcome by evil but overcome evil with good (Romans 12:21).

Furthermore:

> *Romans 12:20-21*
>
> *[20]Therefore if thine enemy hunger, feed him; if he thirsts, give him drink: for in so doing thou shalt heap coals of fire on his head.*
>
> *[21]Be not overcome of evil, but overcome evil with good.*

We are the light of the world. Men should always see our good deeds and praise our Father in heaven.

Marine Witchcraft

These are witchcraft powers that reside in the waters and control every riverine area. These are found in riverine and coastal regions of the world. This type of witchcraft has been associated with various cultures in the countries of the Scandinavia. During the Transatlantic Slave Trade between the 16th century and the 19th century, marine witchcraft was massively transferred from Africa to the countries of South America. There is a water deity called "Yemoja" which literally translates to "mother of the children of fishes" which was later known as "Yemaya" in South Americas and the Caribbean. Olokun was another deity which was worshipped by the Yoruba and the culture was exported to the South Americas and exist up till today.

Marine witchcraft is common in coastal cities of the world, and many riverine areas. In Hinduism, the River Ganges is considered sacred and of spiritual significance. The Japanese Shintoism also is a religion that believes in the worship of waters. All over the world and in many nations, the seas are considered a religious symbol, contrary to the scriptures and the word of God. Even in areas that not very much of marine worship was observed historically, migrant populations have exported the culture.

There are certain evil trends associated with marine areas. These include:

- Prostitution
- Divorce
- Unstable marriages
- Violence
- Materialism
- Sexual perversion
- Alcoholism and drug abuse
- Difficulty in some cases to have children.

Many of the ladies from riverine areas have spirit husbands. A woman is said to have a spirit husband, when you dream of having sex in the dream, or you are always feeling wet or sexually excited. A man is said to have a spirit wife, if he normally has sex in the dream, or experiences things like premature ejaculation. When any man or woman experiences this, the marriage is not stable. It causes promiscuity. The result is divorce at the end of the day. Marriages in riverine areas all over the world are unstable. The presence of the mermaid is common in all these areas and it is worshipped. People from riverine areas need to go through deliverance sessions, severally before they can have a good marriage.

I used to have a counselee in Africa, who had the worship of Olokun, a water deity of African origin, in her ancestral line. She had three beautiful ladies who had good jobs, and eligible, buy could not get suitors. They couldn't have men who propose to them propose marriage. Something will surely happen and the relationship will break. Some of the ladies are highly materialistic too, because those marine regions of the world have a buoyant economy due to wealth from crude oil. Their ladies are materialistic and sometimes wayward, and promiscuous, adding to their problems.

I had another counselee who was at the time I knew her over 50 years old, but without a suitor for many years. When I prayed, I kept seeing a pot on the high seas, laden with cowrie shells. It marvels me, that at that time, a singles program was organised for only singles over 50 years old. The majority of the attendees mostly came from a particular region known for marine worship. Q.E.D. As from that time, I had reasonable evidence that would help me deal better with mu candidates. I handled their cases with extra ruggedness. These types of cases need relentless deliverance, and that's it.

The same trend is obtainable in the Scandinavia. There were countries that doubled their divorce rates in the year 2020. These are countries with good economies and peaceful countries too. Why the increasing divorce rates? It is beyond logic. It is spiritual. Unfortunately, many of these countries are ignorant about the activities of the devil in the marine world. The Bible has concluded it all in Hosea 4:6:

Hosea 4:6

> *My people are destroyed for lack of knowledge: because thou hast rejected knowledge, I will also reject thee, that thou shalt be no priest to me: seeing thou hast forgotten the law of thy God, I will also forget thy children.*

The solution to this is for anyone from these regions to surrender to Jesus. Jesus is always ready to give rest to the weary.

> *Matthew 11:28*
>
> *Come unto me, all ye that labour and are heavy laden, and I will give you rest.*

It is worthy to note that you will fundamentally need to resist every immoral sexual tendency which are the real cause of the problem. If you can fast and pray, fasting on a daily basis will make you dead gradually to immorality. A dead man (hungry during fasting) cannot have erection or have libido. It will be brought low! There is no sin that targeted fasting cannot conquer if that is your desire. I wanted to conquer anger sometime in 2005. I started fasting to go to work. I discovered I could not really reply to all provocations at work. I became very gentle and now had the very nature of God in me. One day as I came back from work, ate my supper and was relaxing, then I heard a voice in the spirit that roared "so you want to chase me out of your life"? From that moment, not only was I able to conquer anger, but I had peace and was able to focus, think and decide constructively, thereby making progress. So, the spirit of anger was stealing from me.

Covenants with the marine spirits also need to be broken. Most times, when you dream about seeing the waters, having sex in the dream, eating in the dream, seeing mad people in your dream, and dreams like that, it is an indication that marine witchcraft powers are at work. Some other signs are when you are afraid of seeing a large body of water, or river, and when you just hate the idea of marriage. Sometimes you feel like being a single parent, even if honestly there's no case for it because your husband or wife is trying his or her best. Marine spirits manifest through your parents and family members because they will always act on the inspiration of the marine spirits inside them. When you mention an issue, you are not happy with in your marriage, they advise you to institute a divorce. They are not interested in solving the matter.

Polygamous Witchcraft.

Polygamy is the practice of a man marrying more than one wife. This is common in Africa, the Middle East and Asia. It is difficult to treat all women equally with precision. If you cannot then achieve that, foreseeably because of their background and mindset, then there will be problems. There tends to be envy, and where envy is, there will be resentment, hatred and all evil works. This culture is gradually giving way to monogamy, that is one husband, and one wife. That is perfect and that is what the Bible recommends. It is practically workable.

In a polygamous setting, if a wife is displeased, and not happy, she forms a faction with her kids. The other wife too forms another faction. The husband is in between them as a Lone ranger and umpire. There is competition, rivalry and antagonism between the factions. Most times there is a problem of who sleeps with the husband or who doesn't. The loser then feels bad and may be revengeful. There have been cases of wives who have completely eliminated one another or their children through diabolic means. At other times, a wife may acquire witchcraft powers from various witchcraft groups in order to enforce justice. A wife whose children are not prospering sees the other as a threat and enemy. The rancour and hostilities continue. At other times, the wife who feels cheated may poison the husband, so that the one-sided game stops and they go their ways. All these are the works of polygamous witchcraft.

There are yet some others that wouldn't say a thing openly, but are utilising dark powers underground or in the background. One of the wives may even wreak havoc and still be the first person to come out to sympathise. When the wives are up to three or four, it is now a complex battle! Two wives may now conspire against the third wife, who is the apple of the husband's eye, usually the last wife. There are times that the fictionalised extends beyond the four walls of their home. The different wives have favourites outside the house, who may demonstrate enmity against the other women in the environment. In this case, it transforms from polygamous witchcraft to a combination of polygamous and environmental witchcraft.

It is usually not a healthy practice and, in some cases, especially if the couples are stricken in age, some may decide to live separately, whilst some may remain. Sometimes there is "restitution", whereby the last wife has to leave. The first wife now has the husband to herself, if she was legally wedded, whilst the second wife leaves and remarries. This way everyone can break the cycle of unending hostilities. It is not a good experience, but in each case, the Holy Spirit will lead, once they are now Christians.

Pentecostal Witchcraft.

A lot of witchcraft activities go on in some churches to varying extents. In Galatians 3: 1, Paul the apostle told the Galatians, O foolish Galatians, who hath bewitched you? He was referring to preachers (Galatians 3:5). When there is Pentecostal witchcraft practiced in a church, it wouldn't be different from a club downtown, or most times, such churches bring hardship in the lives of the people that are purportedly worshipping there.

What are the things that happen under Pentecostal Witchcraft?

The so-called Pastors do not have enough training in Theology, and neither do they have a knowledge or understanding of the scriptures. Some of them are members of cults who have access to money to establish a church for commercial reasons and not because of a passion for souls.

These Pastors and their ministers make use diabolical means and have procedures not in tandem with the scriptures. They could use slangs on the altar and put on crazy haircuts. Their wives and children abuse church ethics with impunity.

The love of money is not hidden, but clearly demonstrated. Materialism is the order of the day. The leadership rewards Pastors that bring more money or erect gigantic structures, even if they do not have a passion for souls. The rich members occupy exalted positions in the church, even though they don't understand scriptures and don't have spiritual qualifications. They can teach nothing because you cannot pour from an empty cup! The trend is annoyance and not the anointing.

The truth is hidden to give way to fleshly lusts. Events like the Valentine's Day are celebrated, spending huge sums of money. Many years back, I was in a vehicle in the midst of some church members, on St. Valentine's Day, and a man of about 35 years old was excitedly carrying a girl of about 21 years old on his laps, as the others were carrying out various obscene activities. Bad doctrines or poorly implemented doctrines give way to the operations of the antichrist which is witchcraft proper.

The Prophecies are manipulated, and the Prophets are saying what God has not said. The messages from the pulpit do not reproof. Instead, it teaches what the people want to hear. Charms and magic are freely used. Sometimes they poison one another in the quest for positions. The Senior Pastor plays the good man and looks the other way.

In churches like that, the Senior Pastor does not confirm anything he has heard from the people who are involved. He is always happy to receive false information and act upon them. The Ministries of many promising ministers are murdered, and ministers whose "fruits" are questionable continue to administer the loyal and committed ministers.

Sexual scandals flourish and are not punished as standards decay. All these are just a few of the things that happen in Witchcraft Pentecostalism.

1 Corinthians 5:1-2

¹It is reported commonly that there is fornication among you, and such fornication as is not so much as named among the Gentiles, that one should have his father's wife.

²and ye are puffed up, and have not rather mourned, that he that hath done this deed might be taken away from among you.

Such a church destroys faith and encourages spiritual lukewarmness and wickedness. The solution to Pentecostal Witchcraft is that you try as much as possible to contribute your own quota with all your heart. Be bold and courageous to say the truth. The world is waiting for you to speak the truth, so that the situation will be corrected. God will take the glory. The "hero worship" in church these days, is so much that many church leaders violate the rights of the members and the leaders in church support such actions. This is the height of witchcraft, and witches and wizards couldn't do worse. In many times, the leaders are men pleasers and not lovers of God. The best thing to do when the witchcraft is so much, is to quit the church. If your church cannot change you, then change your church.

Ancestral Witchcraft.

There is something known as "ancestral witchcraft", also known as "foundational witchcraft" or "inherited witchcraft". Witchcraft seed like a genetic disease is in the blood, and manifests at birth. This explains why a child who was born and bred in the United States, would sleep, and dream about witches and wizards, or dream about masquerades pursuing him in the dream. If they belonged to a marine witchcraft setting, the child would always dream about people adorned in white, putting on their wrists and ankles, cowrie shells. If there is a family spirit husband for example, they would see themselves having sex in the dream. However, remember that they never travelled to their country.

A little boy was angry on a certain day, and he was hitting his head against the wall. The grandmother demanded that they should bring palm oil to be used as a ritual to pour on his head and for him to drink some. She went further to say it was a common thing in the father's lineage, and started to chant some panegyrics, and trying to pacify the child. The mother from the Eastern part of the country gave him some serious spanking and he came to himself immediately. The grandmother was simply promoting a foundational misnomer, acting as a witchcraft agent. Spare the rod and spoil the child.

Proverbs 13:24

He that spareth his rod hateth his son: but he that loveth him chasteneth him betimes.

I think Christian parents should nip these foundational tendencies with the word and with the rod at an early stage.

Proverbs 22:6

Train up a child in the way he should go: and when he is old, he will not depart from it.

Some government policies are not helping the situation. I have a fourteen-year-old boy who was taken into custody and taken care of, because the mother spanked him, and the teacher got to know. The teacher informed Social Care. The child spent some months there, and on coming out, he grew worse academically and behaviourally. There is nothing that can be compared to parental care. In actual terms the mother is afraid that this child may not catch up with the normal behaviour expected of him. He will soon turn 18 and an adult. Social care should weigh the pros and cons carefully before taking a child into custody. Many Government policies in different parts of the world violate the faith and norms of the people. I feel these should be respected.

When there is foundational witchcraft manifesting in a child, which is ready made and very common, there are several possibilities until the person in question is delivered. How do you know if there is foundational witchcraft?

The dream life is important, and we need to encourage the children in Christian families to take their dreams seriously. The child may dream of seeing people wearing white. The other one may share the same experience. This is confirmed that it is in the root as they share the same experience. Another experience is being pressed in the sleep. In this type of experience, the child cannot move, and some of these experiences come with an image in your visual field spiritually.

As you are being pressed, you may see a dog. This is a sign of ancestral witchcraft. Children do experience sex in the dream, but they might not be able to explain clearly until when they are in the primary school. Some of them even in the primary school fees guilty discussing about sex. Try and assure them that it would help them to reveal the truth.

As they begin to grow, these will not only manifest in their dream life, but also begin to manifest as patterns in their destiny. A parent should watch out for these as the children grow up. It will manifest in their academics. All of them may have academic problems. When you look back, you may discover that you or the father had the same issue as youth and students. The issue of the sex in the dream may now become more pronounced in all your children. When you reflect once more, you discover that you or the mother had the same issue as young people. Foundational witchcraft will always reveal itself by way of an evil pattern which you have noticed in the life of your parents as a child and is now manifesting in your own life. It is amazing when a candidate comes to you for Counselling and needs deliverance for imminent divorce, and you ask them about their parents, and they say that they are divorced. When someone comes to you for deliverance from the spirit of poverty, and you ask them to tell you more about their parents. It might amaze you to observe that even the parents were poor! They may go further to tell you that there is asthma in the family, and that people usually die at 50 years old. It means you need to break this evil pattern. There is a saying that says: "the death that killed your parents might be a parable pointing to the type of death you are likely to die".

A sister had that experience that witches in their family line were killing the members of the family between ages 49-53 years. She tapped into her knowledge of deliverance from witchcraft and purposed in her life not to die early. She went for repeated deliverance until she had spiritual knowledge that the problem was solved. As at the time she gave this testimony, she was over 60 years of age and still counting. Jesus can "undo" every work of darkness if you surrender to him and walk with him, trusting and obeying him.

Foundational problems are long standing and requires great spirituality and revelation wisdom. A particular sister was pregnant and was afraid of the pattern in their family. What was the pattern? It was discovered that after about 2 kids, the female members of the family would always die during labour. She was already having dreams and voices in her dream. That was the pattern. It is common with many people with familiar spirits which we shall discuss soon. The sister discussed with her doctor, if it was possible under her own circumstances to do elective Caesarean Section. She was also praying fervently at this time for God's perfect wish to be done in her life. The doctor said yes. The witches were expecting to wreak havoc on the day of her delivery. A month preceding that time, she sent news to them that she had her baby last night, and that they should rejoice with her.

Some families that are tired of being tired would normally discuss this with their Pastor who would organise deliverance force few days counselling them and leveraging on the peculiarities of their circumstances to prayerfully beseech the Holy Spirit for what to do.

Familiar Spirits.

Deuteronomy 18:10-11

¹⁰There shall not be found among you any one that maketh his son or his daughter to pass through the fire, or that useth divination, or an observer of times, or an enchanter, or a witch,

¹¹or a charmer, or a consulter with familiar spirits, or a wizard, or a necromancer.

A stubborn, callous and very wicked group of witchcraft agents that we need to mention here are the "familiar spirits". All these groups mentioned together above belong to the witchcraft category because of their evil works, and destruction to human life. As the name suggests, they are familiar with their victims. What they depend on is blood or body fluid relationships as in through birth and sex in marriage. They are usually patient. It can only get stronger the more the know you and relate with you. They monitor your mistakes and your actions. They can always predict your actions accurately. They are very precise seers who can see only evil. Familiar Spirits are behind the most wicked witchcraft activities know to humans. In some areas, they are known as the husband to witches.

Familiar spirit possessed children keep dying and coming back to the family where they belong. Some of them are given marks on their heads, lips, ears or other parts of their bodies. They then die. When the mother is pregnant and gives birth again, the same mark given to them appears on the lips, ears, head or other parts of the body. Exactly the same way it was given to the child born before them.

Familiar spirits have strong ties with the spirits of the dead in the family where they are born, or in their environments. It is common place for them to faint from time to time if they are really deep into it. They vary in the magnitude of the power they have and demonstrate. They inflict so much sorrow on their parents and would usually fall sick continuously and die before they attain an age of 5, by means of an evil covenant. They reincarnate and are born again. Some of them have been in the family for up to 300 - 400 years. They have a file and maintain evil records about everything that has happened in the lineage. They are very ruthless and merciless. They are very wise, deceptive, liars and very rugged. In Nigeria, they are given names like "Onwubiko" as a plea meaning "death, please" or Ropo (a replacement), or "Remilekun" meaning "wipe my tears away". They have strong ties with the spirit of the necromancers, because death and reincarnation are a regular event in their lives.

Based on their confessions, before they come to the world, they make covenants that they would die on the day of their graduation from the university, the day they will give birth, the day of their marriage or other happy days or a particular time. There was one of them who told the husband in parables that she was going to die. She died during childbirth. She loved her husband. Another one was having a baby, and at a few minutes to 1 am, she was feeling uncomfortable and crying. When it was exactly 1 am, she clapped 3 times, and died. There have been cases that I was there when they were mentioned as a word of knowledge. The man of God said, "if you know you have a covenant with death, come out". People kept rushing out and at the end of it, the count was about a hundred women! All those people had various covenants with death.

A lady possessed by familiar spirit who wants to track you and harm you, would pretend they love you so much. The Lying spirit is one major attribute of familiar spirit possessed persons, which makes them skilful deceivers. They capitalise on food and sex to weaken you spiritually, and that is why you shouldn't have either in excess. Unfortunately, the bible talks about the wine of fornication.

Revelation 17:1 *And there came one of the seven angels which had the seven vials, and talked with me, saying unto me, come hither; I will shew unto thee the judgment of the great whore that sitteth upon many waters:*

17:2 *With whom the kings of the earth have committed fornication, and the inhabitants of the earth have been made drunk with the wine of her fornication.*

You could discover that you have so much of soft spot that the things they do is without disdain to you or impunity. They now begin their assignment. The first thing you might see is that they are sexually promiscuous. That will be your first shock! The next thing is that their behaviour towards you would change completely that you keep asking yourself if this is the same woman. Many of them already entered an evil covenant before they marry you. They were definitely given an assignment before they married you. One of the things they do is to cause poverty, bad luck, difficulties, and very terrible problems in your life to frustrate you or make you to tend to commit suicide. They provoke you to misbehave and sin against your God. This is why in the midst of your affliction, you must be temperate and learn how to control your temper and your instincts. After all these, because they programmed their software (evil spirit) inside you, they may make you sick of a very terrible sickness which lingers for a long time. You may die mysteriously afterwards if you do not have Christ and the Holy Ghost Fire in you.

In England an elderly man says it is a common phenomenon. He told me that in the English culture that they call them sacred groups. It will surprise you that many English ladies have familiar spirits, but nothing scriptural has been done to deliver them. The situation becomes worse daily. I have seen some of them spiritually in my spiritual exploration in Britain who are Brits. People from other nationalities also have this spirit. It is called "Emere" or "Ogbanje" in Nigeria.

As from the age of about 1 - 2 years old, they start manifesting their spiritual characteristics by falling sick frequently, getting lean and emaciated, always vomiting, running a high temperature, having a stunted growth, having marks all over their body, frightening looks, and sometimes tend to separate themselves and mutter inaudible words behind the walls.

At the time they are born, they see visions for their parents and siblings. When they go to school, they make these predictions very accurately too. Their teachers may fear them and reverence them greatly. Whatsoever things they say may come to pass. They are a famous breed. They talk like adults. However, if they have troublesome adults around, who know so much about familiar spirits, those ones indirectly intimidate them and makes them quiet.

In their adult life, they are endowed with seductive powers that make them look attractive to men, because of their evil assignment in life, and in some cases, very beautiful. The more beautiful they are, the more problems they give you. They may just faint or die completely in your hands in the hotel, if you are a sex freak. As from that day, your life wouldn't remain the same again. People possessed by familiar spirits have no control over themselves because they meet the wrong people, choose the wrong jobs and go to the wrong places. They also suffer sickness and infirmity from time to time. They see strange visions and hear strange voices. The spirit also attracts bad luck to them that people tend to resent them. They may subtly threaten you by saying certain things. If you are not a Christian, you become afraid, submissive, and begin to dance to their tune. That means you have been swallowed. However, if you know how to quote the bible, good for you. They may drag you into a covenant subtly and they ask you to promise them that you will never do this, or that you will always do this. For example, they may tell you to promise that you would never offend them. If you make the mistake of saying you promise, then you have sunken yourself. How is it possible not to offend someone you sleep and wake up with? Many unserious young men who are carnal and love drunk would have said yes before they realise. It will now require a serious battle before that single covenant can be broken. Once you say it, you are bound by it. Watch everything you say, in case you suspect a wife or a lady you want to marry. If you are really on fire, they are no issue for you. Make sure you are married properly. Unfortunately, unknown to many men, they are married to some persons with familiar spirit. A good percentage of people up to 50% or even more in riverine areas are married to people possessed by familiar spirits.

Many of them have their roots in the waters and are marine. If you have ever been taken to the river force ritual, you may be one of them. They are usually attached to people who have great destinies, in order to mark them down. They always have a cross to carry in form of a problem or disease that wouldn't be healed easily.

One major problem about their life is that they transfer their problems very easily. Anyone that is in any relationship with them must have a share of the covenant of sorrow that they have entered into, except God is really behind him to help him. If you like free sex, as a man, you may start seeing coffins. Just know that your time has come to go to the great beyond. Some of them get delivered and make very good wives living successfully with their husband or wife.

Diviners.

Another group under the witchcraft category are the people possessed by the spirit of divination. This happened in the Bible in the scriptural account that we have below. A person with the spirit of divination is able to say what happened to you in the past, and what is happening to you at the moment as well as predict what would happen in the future. It is not everybody that calls himself a Prophet or Prophetess is one. Many of them have the spirit of divination, usually working in conjunction with familiar spirits.

> Acts 16:16-18
>
> ¹⁶*and it came to pass, as we went to prayer, a certain damsel possessed with a spirit of divination met us, which brought her masters much gain by soothsaying:*
>
> ¹⁷*the same followed Paul and us, and cried, saying, these men are the servants of the most high God, which shew unto us the way of salvation.*
>
> ¹⁸*and this did she many days. But Paul, being grieved, turned and said to the spirit, I command thee in the name of Jesus Christ to come out of her. And he came out the same hour.*

We can see in the scripture above that Peter cast out the spirit of divination. Why did he do that? That spirit is of the devil, because the person using it is not a believer and Christ is not the source. The scriptures say she brought her masters so much gain by soothsaying, meaning it the spirit was for a commercial purpose. The spirit was definitely not of God.

We have to know that it is not everyone that can give you predictions that is doing that using the spirit of God. That is the pitfall of many people today and they have been initiated through evil manipulation premises on satanically inspired revelations. Anyone that sees a thing about you can easily manipulate you to do anything. They can even sleep with you or tell you to swallow concoctions. Anything they tell you about your marriage or husband, whether true or false, because he is trying to have an affair with you, you wouldn't know. With the diabolical powers he could foresee financial breakthrough and manipulate you into bringing same for his benefits.

So, we need to be careful about revelations, and the things we are told to do by these fake seers and witches. Unfortunately, many have established a church and using evil powers. Like in the example above, anyone that is commercialising the gifts of God is a witch, because they would always manipulate you to get more money. Sometimes they project evil spirits into you. You may need to go for deliverance to cast such spirits out.

Occupational Witchcraft.

These are people who come together to form a witchcraft group for the evil enhancement of their occupations. There are societies in many markets in the world, that you need to join, for you to be able to do business with the larger group. They have a process of initiation for you to become a member. They may need to enter into different types of covenants.

There are also secret societies in Europe and the United States which people join for the alleged purpose of moving their business forward. However, there are wicked practices, taking concoctions, swearing oaths and other strange things. They try to control government policies and suppress religion. One of the strategies of Satan, which was used in Matthew 4:1 is that of money and power. Unfortunately, many bow to Satan technically.

> *Matthew 4:8-10*
>
> *Again, the devil taketh him up into an exceeding high mountain, and sheweth him all the kingdoms of the world, and the glory of them;*
>
> *And saith unto him, all these things will I give thee, if thou wilt fall down and worship me.*
>
> *Then saith Jesus unto him, get thee hence, Satan: for it is written, thou shalt worship the Lord thy God, and him only shalt thou serve.*

In the Far East of the world, there is a company that manufactures cars, and the manufacturers are alleged to be dedicating the cars manufactured to some idols or gods. The effect is that if the vehicle users are not connected to a higher power, which obviously is the power of Jehovah, then definitely they would have spiritual deficits or experiences things like nightmares or fall sick regularly when using the vehicle.

Most occupational groups and associations that come together to implement policies that are contrary to the wellbeing of fellow human beings, that steal from or destroy their fellow human beings belong to the group of occupational witches and wizards.

All the manufacturers that use substances that are harmful for human consumption are practicing occupational witchcraft. Furthermore, exorbitant prices fixed on items because there are no alternatives, amounts to oppression and witchcraft.

Another great mystery about occupational witchcraft practices is the issue of jealousy and envy, leading to the spiritual destruction or elimination of glorious, hardworking, intelligent and promising workers. A Professor sometime many years back was invited to a party, only to poison him at the end of the day, because of his envious position. Many workers are into the occult because of their quest for high positions in their places of work. Unfortunately, many of them end their lives in shambles because there is no free gift from the devil.

The way out is to be careful about which associations you join. Check their laws very well, to be sure that they are not satanic or are contrary to the Christian Faith. The laws also should not be compulsory at least to a reasonable extent. Also, in the place of work, especially in government when the positions there are contestable and not permanent, when you occupy a position always have in mind that somebody is not happy seeing you there. Anything contrary to this is dangerous. Watch it. Even Judas betrayed Jesus. To every shining star in any place of work, there is a Judas.

Check yourself always, pertaining to how you operate your business. Do your operations in any way operate against your conscience? Is it fair to your customers, if you are to put them in your shoes?

Household Witchcraft.

A household consists of people linked by blood, by birth or by marriage. Sometimes, an employee is closely linked to you could be said to be a member of the household. All these people described above have access to things that outsiders would not normally have access to. For example, they have access to all the rooms in your house, they have access to what you eat or drink, they have access to your clothing, and have access even to the keys of your house. Most importantly, they have access to most of your vital information, or secrets.

Bob Marley of blessed memory sang in one of his songs, that only your friend knows your secrets, so only he could reveal it. There have been cases in the past where a member of the household, or an employee, leveraged on information or access to the space, property or keys to conspire with outsiders. There is an African proverb that says, "if your death does not originate from inside your house, then outsiders cannot kill you". The Bible also rightly and accurately observes:

> Matthew 10:36
>
> *And a man's foes shall be they of his own household.*

A typical example we can extract from the bible is that of Joseph and his brothers. They had information about his dreams and the knowledge of what he can become. They saw him as a threat. There are people in your household, who are in your household, or close to you, that are envious and uncomfortable about your present achievements, or even your potentials. Each time it crosses their minds, they feel like harming you or like you should be taken far away. They might think that something evil should happen to you. Some of them will even show it openly!

What then is the way out? There is a wise saying that says, "if God shows one his enemies, then the problem is over". I tend to agree with that saying. The best thing you can do is to pray for revelation, so that God will show you your enemies. Once you know your enemies, and the power they are using, or the potential harm they could do, then you can overcome easily. These are close people you possibly could not avoid. Don't be surprised it may be your wife, husband or even son. We are quite familiar with the story of David and Absalom (2 Samuel 13-18).

One thing about household witchcraft is that the enemy may operate for years, and you would never know. I earlier on mentioned the case of a daughter who hanged her father's fortunes on a tree in their hometown. How would you possibly suspect that the child that you are responsible for paying his school fees is the one making you to be poor, through witchcraft.

There have been husbands who used the menstrual pad of the wife for money rituals. The woman will fall sick, but he would be the one to take her to the hospital and spend money on drugs and other procedures.

There was a counselee of mine that was sent to bring the husband's sperm to do evil things to him. I was treating a certain couple's son in year 2005. The house help was the culprit. She confessed to witchcraft that she was the one that was always aborting the pregnancy of the woman anytime she was pregnant. She had aborted series of pregnancies because she was close to them and with her witchcraft eyes, she knew anytime the woman was pregnant. This couple were attending a holiness church that did not really believe in many revelations. The straw that broke the camel's back was when the man of the house lost his job, and the wife's mother, a Pentecostal started praying. The girl was able to confess that she was responsible for the sack letter that the husband received, and that she was sent from the kingdom of darkness to destroy the family.

There was also a Pastor's wife, that was in my deliverance ministration. She would always accompany the husband for deliverance ministration. The husband was doing well, until the time that he lost all both of his vehicles. He was also victimised in the church where he was a Pastor. He was posted to a jungle. Things were very rough for him.

One day, they came for deliverance, and we prayed for them. When I got home, the Lord showed me in a vision that she was responsible, and the modality she was using to attack the husband. I didn't ask her anything as I greeted them normally the next morning of their 5-day deliverance. As deliverance started, I raised a prayer point based on the vision that I saw, well harmed with revelation knowledge.

The first time I called the prayer point, she was feeling drowsy and was about manifesting under the anointing. It wouldn't be good for me to leave her to go home with the spirit. I raised the prayer point one more time for everyone to pray, because it was a group deliverance. The Pastor's wife began to scatter the whole church as the demon in her manifested. I increased the fire. I decreed and ejected the demon in Jesus name. The next day, she couldn't look at me straight into my eyes, but she knew, and I knew. Both of us knew what was going on, though I did not reveal it to the husband, but I was satisfied that I did the needful.

Occultism.

What is occultism? Occultism is a type of witchcraft. It is knowledge, conviction, and activities that do not fall within the purview of known scientific or religious assertions. This branch of witchcraft embraces necromancy, astrology, rituals, soul travel, magic, charming and other dark practices. Armed with these, they intimidate sometimes innocent people and miscarry justice, opening up opportunities for their initiates.

Occultism is an old trend in the witchcraft space getting increasingly relevant by the day. Social Scientists in the United Kingdom believe there is a revival of the Occult in the United States of America. Invariably, in many other parts of the world that many Christians hold dual memberships of their faith groups and occultist groups. Some churches in the United States only carry the name "Church", but in reality, they are occult societies. Outside these churches, you still have Pastors who work all kinds of signs and wonders, using dark powers. Pastors like these "commercialise" their signs and wonders and preach strange doctrines. They may tell you for instance to come naked to church, or do not talk to anyone. They use sign language. These societies are increasing in number in an unprecedented manner in recent times. It is shocking to note that key players in politics, entertainment, sports, medicine, law and most disappointingly people in government, all belong to one occultist group or the other.

Why are these societies then on the increase? Many people are facing the consequences of sin in a sinful world, but they do not want to follow the due process of salvation through Jesus Christ, repentance from sins, prayer, faith and practice of the word. They believe they should be able to commit atrocities and get away with them. They unite to as a group to commit illegalities. Those of them in the legal system miscarry justice, and those in government demonstrate favouritism, tribalism and nepotism, instead of justice and fair play. The churches that are occultic tend to modernise the Christian faith, so that their activities can be attractive to people who commit one sin or the other. They want to continue in their sins whilst still identifying themselves with the description of "Church".

In these occultist groups, necromancy is highly promoted and practiced with the use of humans and human flesh and blood for rituals. The Bible has a word for them:

> *Isaiah 49:24-26*
>
> *²⁴Shall the prey be taken from the mighty, or the lawful captive delivered?*
>
> *²⁵but thus saith the LORD, Even the captives of the mighty shall be taken away, and the prey of the terrible shall be delivered: for I will contend with him that contended with thee, and I will save thy children.*
>
> *²⁶And I will feed them that oppress thee with their own flesh; and they shall be drunken with their own blood, as with sweet wine: and all flesh shall know that I the LORD am thy Saviour and thy Redeemer, the mighty One of Jacob.*

They go to the graveyard for rituals and eat all forms of rotten animals in their rituals. Majority of the people that get enlisted regret it somewhere along the line. But thank God for sending Jesus Christ to save the world. In all these things, the earlier you seek attention the better. Some of them dabble into various cults with devastating spiritual and physical consequences. Demons are cast out of them, if they surrender themselves for deliverance.

At the point of initiation, many of these cults require that you bring your wife or first son for initiation so that they can succeed you. If they fail to surrender themselves for initiation, they will be killed! So, you are exposing your family to danger by being initiated in these groups.

The Bible records:

> *2 Timothy 3:13*
>
> *But evil men and seducers shall wax worse and worse, deceiving, and being deceived.*

One of the greatest deceptions and manipulations of all times by the devil of men and women, is the occult. Many have dabbled into it before realising their follies. We however thank God for his deliverance power, even in spite of their oaths. It takes a higher authority to silence a lower one. It takes the power of the most high God to silence the power of the devil., no matter the dispensation from which they are operating, whether from the heavenlies, or earth or under the earth:

Philippians 2:10-11

¹⁰That at the name of Jesus every knee should bow, of things in heaven, and things in earth, and things under the earth;

¹¹and that every tongue should confess that Jesus Christ is Lord, to the glory of God the Father.

What then can you do if you are contemplating to enrol in an occultic or secret society? Stop. Don't go ahead! Pray to God to release the secret of your prosperity to you. All you need afterwards is to follow what God's word says.

If you are already enrolled in one and want to revoke the covenant, then see a Pastor indeed for Counselling and deliverance. Pastor indeed in the sense that some Pastors are in the occult, but by their fruits you shall know them. Be careful in choosing a church to attend or go for deliverance.

If you are the child or spouse of an initiate, don't hide it and don't keep quiet. Go to your Pastors and tell them. If you are there and are not planning to come out. It is deception, and you need to come out before it is too late.

The Multitude of the Slain.

Nahum 3:1-4

¹Woe to the bloody city! it is all full of lies and robbery; the prey departeth not;

²the noise of a whip, and the noise of the rattling of the wheels, and of the prancing horses, and of the jumping chariots.

³the horseman lifteth up both the bright sword and the glittering spear: and there is a multitude of slain, and a great number of carcases; and there is none end of their corpses; they stumble upon their corpses:

⁴Because of the multitude of the whoredoms of the well-favoured harlot, the mistress of witchcrafts, that selleth nations through her whoredoms, and families through her witchcrafts.

In this discussion, we want to assess the extent of damage that witches and wizards have done to people's lives and property through personal experience in the ministry, and from confessions of witches and wizards. The scripture above refers to the mistress of witchcrafts, that selleth nations and families. It also refers to slaying and corpses with reference to a bloody city. All these are more characterise witchcraft.

The works of witchcraft include blood sucking and flesh eating. Most diseases involving the loss of blood, are sponsored by blood suckers. Some suck blood to make you lean and sick. They are known as vampire spirits. The flesh eaters take it upon them to eat human organs spiritually. Any human organ that is diseased or is malfunctioning has been eaten by witchcraft powers. Witches confess openly to eating human organs like the heart, the brain and kidneys.

A lot of barren women are like that because their wombs were eaten up in the witchcraft coven, sometimes by their own fellow witches, or by witches from other extractions

Witches are responsible for making people blind or mad, if they want to waste the destiny of that person. They know that without seeing or a good mind you cannot function properly, and to your best. A lot of people who are mentally ill were afflicted by witches and wizards. What a tyrannical group. I pray we shall not be trapped and afflicted by the enemy in the mighty name of Jesus.

Witches and wizards are sometimes responsible for epidemics. A group of witches confessed many years ago that they were responsible for the Cholera epidemic in the hospitals. The hospitals were filled with people who were sick with cholera, vomiting and stooling, until the witches confessed that they were the people who harboured an evil power on an evil tree, and which was responsible for the epidemic.

Witches and wizards possess trees and use those trees as a base to do evil. A particular palm tree very close to my house, sometime in 1978, caught fire all of a sudden in the middle of a heavy rain. The palm tree was burnt completely as it rained with large hot coals left after the inferno. Witchcraft spirits had possessed the tree, but the fire of God located it for destruction. The thunder fire of God shall locate and destroy all your problems in Jesus name.

Another group of witches confessed that they poured okra on the road in order to make a truck to have an accident, in which the truck was overturned. Other vehicles had accidents in that single witchcraft attack. They have altars on the major roads where blood sucking demons operate. Such altars continue to drink the blood of commuters.

Failure in business is one of the major assignments of witches and wizards. They fire the arrow of error to cause major losses in business. They could close a shop spiritually, and the owner wouldn't know that they are selling wares in a closed shop. They could place an evil mark on your shop or salesperson, so that people wouldn't buy from them.

I conducted deliverance for a Pastor's wife in 2008. She was being attacked by foundational witchcraft, to the extent that no one was coming to buy from her shop, despite all the investments of her husband on the business. She told me and as the Deliverance prayers progressed, she fell into a deep sleep under the influence of the anointing. She entered a trance where a mask was pulled off from her face.

A lot of students who are stuck in a particular class have had their brains eaten by witchcraft. Majority of these cases are polygamous witchcraft in which case, of many wives of the same man is responsible for afflicting the children of the other, so that their own children can outshine the others. It could also be as a result of occupational witchcraft in which a particular worker in a place of work has vowed to grind the destinies of others to a halt, so that they may outshine the rest. All the episodes of very bright and promising workers or students, who suddenly crash mysteriously are due to the activities of witchcraft, if investigated thoroughly. Other undergraduates through cheap sex have had their progress arrested or stopped forever by witchcraft powers.

Many uncompleted buildings are the product of witchcraft powers, like in the earlier example of the child that connived with the Auntie in the spirit to suspend the father's fortunes. They hanged his fortunes on a tree in Benin

City, a city in Nigeria. The same thing is prevalent in Portugal as a co-worker with me on the field of Evangelism recounts. She told me about how they even tried to initiate her, but she did not cooperate with their mission. The tragedy about witchcraft in Europe is that there are many witches and wizards who are winning and dining on the souls of men, because of spiritual Luke warmness.

Many great companies, including a Steel Company and blue-elephant project in Nigeria were sunken by witches and wizards. Can you imagine the number of people that were rendered jobless, and many people that stopped their education due indirectly to the work of witchcraft in that company?

In the above scripture, we can see it talks about selling nations and families. When the enemy sees that the future of a husband and wife is bright, then they may arrange a secondary school girl, who would seduce the husband and scatter the glorious destiny. If they can't forgive one another and move on, then the witches have won. In marriage, not everything should lead to divorce. An ability to be able to forgive after the most terrible offence by your partner, is the most terrible blow you could give the devil.

Forgiveness is for the strong and special people. Don't get tired of forgiving him or her. We shall not labour in vain in Jesus name. The devil can rubbish your gains in marriage of up to 20 years if you are unforgiving. Witchcraft is the brain behind every failing economy. Due to their selfishness, manipulative tendencies, lies, sexual manipulations by members of the opposite sex and the likes. This has untold effects on the progress of a nation.

One thing that the devil uses most easily is the weapon of poverty. Once familiar spirits can get to sleep with a breadwinner, that is the end of the story. A witch confessed that once they can have access to a man's semen, they can control virtually everything about his life. The same thing is through about the having access to a person's blood. They could also use an employee as a ladder to get into the business using co-workers or business associates against that person to bring poverty. They could stand on the fact that they are linked by blood and manipulate him or her to make the wrong choices through "soul ties". A soul tie is a spiritual connection that makes you to resonate with another person's thoughts, feel like being with them, think about them, or see them in your dreams always.

Through dream attacks, they capitalise on your weaknesses and sins. If you are greedy, they'll keep feeding you in the dream. If you are sexually loose, they keep sending spirit husband or wife to sleep with you. Some are not able to marry because they have a soul tie with sexual demons that makes them to always have sex indiscriminately. I have had a number of cases where the spirit husband will come and have sex with a woman at the time she's pregnant. Guess what? She would see blood the next morning, and the baby will be miscarried. That is how many women keep having miscarriages and remain barren for many years. For most women having miscarriages, there's always a code or pattern that the enemy uses. Some will not have sex in the dream, but will dream and see tomatoes, red chilli or palm oil and immediately they bleed and miscarry.

CHAPTER THIRTEEN

HOW DELIVERANCE WORKS

I would like to acknowledge that all power belongs to the almighty God, and the "Spirit of God" is the sole worker of the deliverance, lest any man should take the glory. However, there are certain things a deliverance minister must note well, in order to be able to conduct deliverance ethically, scripturally and effectively.

A deliverance program could run for a day, two days or any number of days, in as much as you give yourself to be led by the Holy Spirit. I have seen people who prepared for a five-day deliverance, but received deliverance in the second day of their deliverance, in as much as they come with righteousness and high expectation.

A certain man I met in the year 2003 came for deliverance from household witchcraft. He had an issue with his sister, over the sharing of their late father's property. The sister was using witchcraft to torment him. He was not really a committed Christian though, but he came to the deliverance program with the spirit of enough is enough and very high expectations. He had so much faith in what God's power could do and was ready to give it anything it demanded. He prayed like someone who would never have another opportunity to pray. He had focus. He had roamed about for months without a job and life was losing value. He decided to come for deliverance. Behold, the next morning after the first day of his planned 5-day deliverance he got a letter, which offered him a job with a Telecommunications Giant and multinational company. His testimony stopped the continuation of his deliverance, for heaven answered him. He was to start with the necessary health checks, pre-employment protocol, and start immediately.

Another lady was also believing God for career breakthrough and peace in her marriage. She was a graduate and had not worked with her certificates for upwards of five years that she graduated. The financial situation was now having a toll on her marriage, as the financial burden was now on the husband alone. I want you to note that in majority of the cases, if your finances can be improved, your marriage would be delivered considerably. Financial problems can strengthen demons in marriage.

She attended a deliverance program and got chatting with a particular lady she didn't know from anywhere, but they met on the deliverance ground, and they were friendly and got talking. When you come for deliverance, many people dress casually and you never could know who would be that God ordained angel with the passcode to unlock your fortunes. That is why it is good to have clean hands and a pure heart. Think before you say things, because it is not everything you have to say. Whatever you say, you must have a good reason for saying it, and it must bring an answer to your "needs". The Holy spirit used her good disposition and friendly nature to ignite compassion in the other lady. She was a "top notcher" in the multinational company where she worked, unknown to the other lady. There was a vacancy in that company. A good heart fetched her deliverance and not her prayers. Be good and be ready to seek help. One secret of deliverance that many people don't know is that with God and with man, the "ASK" principle works! What is the principle all about? "A" for ask, "S" for seek, and "K" for knock. God could use anybody or anything to answer your prayers in the week of your deliverance. So be open and be very inquisitive. Many of those people you meet on deliverance ground had firsthand experience of your predicament, many years back. They don't need to crack their brain or see any vision, but make sure that the information is valid by verifying from your Pastor or Deliverance Minister. Ask in this way: Pastor, is it right if I ... (mention what you plan to do). Depending on how you see it, the Deliverance Ground is a "Commonwealth" if you go there in love, optimism, and an open mind.

Matthew 7:7

Ask, and it shall be given you; seek, and ye shall find; knock, and it shall be opened unto you:

A closed mouth is a closed destiny. There is no crime in asking, and no punishment for wanting to know what would promote your destiny. It could only make you better. Be bold and courageous. The worst that could happen is that your request may be declined, but you have tried. Many people are willing to help you, but help wouldn't come until you ask, seek, or knock.

In our dealings with God, many will not knock but will expect a door to open! When you pray, you are knocking on heaven's gate, and the compassionate father who is loving and caring will always answer (Jeremiah 33:3). Jesus himself has promised rest to all who come to him (Matthew 11:28).

Jeremiah 33:3

Call unto me, and I will answer thee, and shew thee great and mighty things, which thou knowest not.

Matthew 11:28

Come unto me, all ye that labour and are heavy laden, and I will give you rest.

When you have knocked, another principle you need to apply is the "PUSH" principle. When you knock a door in everyday life, you wait for a reply. When you ask someone for something, courtesy demands that you wait for the next instructions. He wants to help you, so allow him to figure it out. It means simply that you keep Praying (and believing), Until Something happens. It pays to tarry until you achieve your desires. In 1 Kings 18:41-45, Elijah was believing God for rain. He never stopped believing until he saw the manifestation of what he was asking for. Rain! Jacob has an encounter with an angel and needed blessings. He made a resolve that he would never allow the angel to go until he was blessed.

Genesis 32:26-28

^{26}and he said, let me go, for the day breaketh. And he said, I will not let thee go, except thou bless me.

^{27}and he said unto him, what is thy name? And he said, Jacob.

^{28}and he said, thy name shall be called no more Jacob, but Israel: for as a prince hast thou power with God and with men, and hast prevailed.

Jacob did not allow the angel to go. He wrestled with the angel until he was blessed. God expects you to stay on the queue and he will answer at the right time. It amazes me the kind of impatience that I see in many people. When people are praying for healing, they expect it to happen immediately, without waiting. They get discouraged and lose their miracles. They walk out on God rudely because of their unbelief and impatience. A similar scenario occurred as the Israelites were going to the promised land. Even if your deliverance did not happen on the Deliverance ground, you can be sure that God has got your back.

Elisha prayed for the Shunamite woman, but she wouldn't get pregnant right there and then. It has to be at a season according to the time of life.

> *2 Kings 4:16*
>
> *And he said, about this season, according to the time of life, thou shalt embrace a son. And she said, Nay, my lord, thou man of God, do not lie unto thine handmaid.*

If God has a reason to open a way for you in "Chevron" he knows the best time to do it. For example, you would need to wait for the next recruitment season. If you failed an exam and you prayed to God, and God promises that you would pass the exam, you still need to fill the registration forms and wait for the next examination period. However, you can be sure he would do it. God does have his timing that he will make it happen. If you want the best results, wait for God's time. Sometimes, he may block some ways, because he does not want you to go through that way. At a time, God wanted me to settle down as an entrepreneur, but I was bent on pursuing a career with the NHS. I never knew he had better plans. There's a need to be patient when some things don't work, believing in God that he will give you the best possible. He works with an appointed time.

> *Habakkuk 2:3*
>
> *For the vision is yet for an appointed time, but at the end it shall speak, and not lie though it tarries, wait for it; because it will surely come, it will not tarry.*

In your quest for deliverance, you need to know that you have a predestination (Romans 8:30), and that God has plans for you, and one of the reasons that you have come for deliverance is to discover his plans and work towards the actualisation of those plans. The belief in the plans, and determination to make the plans and promises to come to pass in your life is what we call FAITH.

> *Jeremiah 29:11*
>
> *For I know the plans I have for you," declares the LORD, "plans to prosper you and not to harm you, plans to give you hope and a future. (NIV)*

CHAPTER FOURTEEN

NOTES FOR DELIVERANCE MINISTERS

The deliverance ministry is a sensitive one, and you need to work intimately with the Holy Spirit. Prayer and fasting daily for a deliverance minister are ideal and are desirable. A deliverance minister should be able to fast daily for the period he would be busy ministering. This deals with the flesh, helps your perceptibility of the Holy Spirit and gives you a good intuition and leading to do your work. As you minister, there's a need to pause occasionally and close your eyes to receive guidance from him. Then obey the leading he gives to you. It also keeps you safe and prevents you from receiving arrows. For example, candidates possessed by marine spirits are dangerous and do fire the arrow of seduction very well. If you are fasting, you can never be a casualty.

The Study of God's word.

Another thing is that you need to work with a knowledge of the written word and revealed word. Take your deliverance scriptures and meditate upon them as you teach. Try to improve your messages as you counsel on a weekly basis. It might become very boring to you and your candidates if you already have a typed message that you preach all the time, word-for-word. Variety is needed. Learn how to weigh individual issues side by side with the word of God.

Casting out devils.

Observation is key in the deliverance ministry. As you observe and explore, the Lord will give you more insight. That is why the bible admonishes us to "watch and pray". There is a part that prayer will play in the deliverance ministry, and there is a role that your observation will play. The two roles are not interchangeable. If you are not observant on the deliverance ground, you wouldn't know when a demon is about jumping out of a candidate. It would just start with for example, yawning, seeming weakness, or "swaying" body movements which initially may come very slightly. As you move closer to the candidate, the demon can feel you, and the manifestation is becoming more, as the body "swaying" increases, and the manifestation is now full-fledged. Some stubborn demons might just remain static and may wait for you to challenge it. Then you move closer to challenge it, head on. When you get closer, you begin to say blood of Jesus, Blood of Jesus repeatedly, or Holy Ghost Fire, Holy Ghost Fire repeatedly, then when you are satisfied that the Holy Spirit has overwhelmed that candidate, then you command the demon simply to leave. At this point, your faith is what finally sends the demon packing. Do not doubt but believe that the demon has left according to your word.

Mark 11:23

For verily I say unto you, that whosoever shall say unto this mountain, be thou removed, and be thou cast into the sea; and shall not doubt in his heart but shall believe that those things which he saith shall come to pass; he shall have whatsoever he saith.

The word of God has established it, that as soon as they hear of you, they shall obey you and submit themselves to you.

Psalms 18:44-45

⁴⁴as soon as they hear of me, they shall obey me: the strangers shall submit themselves unto me.

⁴⁵the strangers shall fade away and be afraid out of their close places.

Just continue to say into the ear of that person, as you address the demon, "come out in the name of Jesus Christ of Nazareth". The name of Jesus frightens them so much, that if they want to prove stubborn still, just continue to say "Jesus Christ", "Jesus Christ" or "Blood of Jesus", "Blood of Jesus". If you doubt or are naive as you issue your decrees or commands, they can feel it in your voice. However, they respect you if you speak with authority, quoting a few scriptures, they can also feel it. A highly legalistic demon may refuse to leave if you say in the name of Jesus, and you do not add the post-fix. That is why you need to address it clearly "In the name of Jesus Christ. By the time you quote a few scriptures, the demon is already out, pushing the candidate on the floor! If you are still not satisfied, because some demons are stubborn, then you may go ahead and release a few drops of anointing oil on the head or other parts of the body as led by the Holy Spirit. Anointing oil should be applied with a witness because of legal reasons. Some candidates might say what you don't mean or mean what you didn't say.

A mistake that many deliverance ministers and deliverance candidates make is that they believe that until somebody manifests and rolls on the ground, that the power of God has not moved. This makes deliverance ministers to shout and yell repeatedly in annoyance. Ministry without anointing will only bring annoyance. Many deliverance candidates too feel dissatisfied if they don't roll on the floor. It is not always necessary for you to manifest and roll on the floor. It is your faith in God that works the miracles. If you fall to the ground, at that moment, but do not have faith to maintain the deliverance, it means nothing. Also, if you continue in sin, your rolling on the ground at that time means nothing. What is important is your faith. Furthermore, yawning only might be a manifestation. When the blind see, and the lame walk, they don't necessarily fall to the ground, but function is restored quietly, and that's it.

Manifestations During Deliverance.

There are different forms of manifestations during Deliverance. It starts from yawning, coughing, swaying, shouting, jumping, violent running around usually by marine spirits. A patient may fall to the ground, and pass out for a while. This is quite normal. Don't panic but leave the candidate alone. When he or she comes around, the first question should be what did you see. Many of them go into a spiritual journey of deep revelations, and many of which leads to deliverance. I went to conduct deliverance for a Pastors family. The woman wasn't doing well in her business, because people wouldn't buy from her. On that day she fell down and slept off during Deliverance. I left her to sleep. When she woke up, I asked her, what happened. She said that a mask was being pulled off from her face. That was the mask that the enemy was using to scare away potential buyers spiritually. Does your boss in your place of work tend to repel you, or just like this woman, your clients or customers? Deliverance is needed urgently.

One thing you should note is that you need to guard against falls and injuries. Demons are very wicked sometimes. A demon may carry a deliverance candidate and make her to forcefully sit on a nail. Some may make a candidate delirious, that they may run out of the auditorium into the main road, mimicking a temporary insanity. Also, be careful not to allow then to injure other people going about their business or their deliverance. Legally speaking, you are responsible for any injuries sustained by any candidate, and it counts against your ministry. Make sure that there is enough space in between the seats if you are conducting a group deliverance, and also that you keep watch over the doors of the auditorium, or lock them. It is easier to control if you are conducting deliverance for an individual.

Demons Speaking.

Some demons are conversational, and may not want to obey you, and will like to engage you in a conversation. Be not ignorant of their lies and gimmicks as they speak. They could really confuse you if you are not careful. A demon may tell you, "I will deal with you". It would like to know if you are confident. Otherwise you may think about a sin that you committed recently, and feel guilty. He may even mention it because they can see. If you now start shivering, and stammering, then he has got you. It is a bad thing for a Deliverance Minister to live in sin. In the worst situations, let the demon know that Christ has redeemed you from the curse of the law, and that he hath borne your griefs and carried your sorrows. Let the demon know we are justified of faith and not of works:

Galatians 3:13-14

¹³Christ hath redeemed us from the curse of the law, being made a curse for us: for it is written, cursed is every one that hangeth on a tree:

¹⁴That the blessing of Abraham might come on the Gentiles through Jesus Christ; that we might receive the promise of the Spirit through faith.

There is a need for you to let them know that justification is by faith in Jesus Christ. If you say it but you do not believe the scripture or have faith, then he has got you. They could attack you if your faith is not strong in Christ.

Galatians 2:16

¹⁶Knowing that a man is not justified by the works of the law, but by the faith of Jesus Christ, even we have believed in Jesus Christ, that we might be justified by the faith of Christ, and not by the works of the law: for by the works of the law shall no flesh be justified.

Be sensitive to the Holy Spirit.

Another reason why observation is important for a deliverance minister is not just because of the candidate, but for yourself as a deliverance minister. There is a spirit that abides in you that is stirred in you, and there is a spirit upon that stirs you.

Luke 4:18

¹⁸The Spirit of the Lord is upon me, because he hath anointed me to preach the gospel to the poor; he hath sent me to heal the broken-hearted, to preach deliverance to the captives, and recovering of sight to the blind, to set at liberty them that are bruised,

The above scripture describes the spirit upon, and it comes for the purpose of. initiation as described above. When you study the scriptures at home, or you are convicted of evil in your spirit due to sin, the spirit of God within does thus. There is however a relationship between both the spirit that abideth in you and the spirit that comes upon you. They seek to perform the same function.

1 John 2:27

But the anointing which ye have received of him abideth in you, and ye need not that any man teach you: but as the same anointing teacheth you of all things, and is truth, and is no lie, and even as it hath taught you, ye shall abide in him.

It is important for you to note when the spirit upon is released from above. This is when you feel goose pimples all over you, or you just start shedding tears, or your countenance changes. Then you need to close your eyes because he wants to do something and is giving you a nudge. Close your eyes for a while and listen to the next instruction. Any action you take at that point matters.

When I am going out to minister and feel that goose pimples on the way, I know he is going to work mightily. When I am saying something, and I feel the goose pimples, I know he is confirming what I am saying. When someone is telling me something and the goose pimples come, I know it is a confirmation that what that person is saying is the truth and he probably wants me to act on that piece of information. Sometimes I feel the goose pimples and burst into tongues and begin to Prophesy uncontrollably.

When I minister healing, and I begin to cry, it is a sign that the healing power of God is upon me. Many ministers called into the office of Miracles follow this same shedding of tears of joy. It takes you to another world and gives you sharp unction. At that time the connection with the throne of grace is very strong. Thank you holy spirit. Any song that comes into your spirit at that stage, just continue to sing it freely. You don't need any external effort, just listen and follow his promptings as he does the work for you to the Glory of God.

Another thing is that you may be feeling weak and sleepy after a ministration. Look for somewhere to lie down comfortably. On a certain day, a woman brought a gift for me, to give to my children. I took it and prayed with her. Not quite long, I was feeling drowsy. I went into the Mission House close to the Deliverance Ground to take a nap. As I lay down, the Lord opened my eyes to see that these items were bewitched.

That takes me to another point, which is the receiving of gifts from counselees. Many of them are agents sent to the Deliverance Ground to strike powerless and unsuspecting ministers. Many of them will present battle to you in form of gifts. A woman brought a bag of rice to me, and as I got home, I discovered that the whole bag was filled with ants. They will test you with things like that sometimes. The Holy spirit can show you after you may have collected it, or he would have told you that morning that you should not collect any gift from anyone. I was going to minister in a church under my supervision as a Zonal Pastor. The gift was so massive and prepared to honour me. The Holy Spirit had told me earlier not to collect a gift. I didn't. There may be a temptation from a spouse that it does not mean, or the person, or members may impress you to take it. Please don't entertain sentiments. Obey the last order! The safety you and your family will enjoy is to the extent that you obey him. The people that you least think about may be your undoing one way or the other.

A Provincial Pastor's wife from another denomination blessed me with some items, including some drinks. I kept it on the fridge in my room, but my spirit was against the packs of juice. I still maintained keeping it there because I trusted her in my mind. I didn't listen to my heart. I should have thrown it away. That day, that thing pushed me, and I "accidentally" (laughs) opened and accidentally drank juice from one of the packs. That night, to my utter surprise, I was pressed down in my sleep. Something that never happened to me for several years. Many of us allow battles in our lives. What I think is that she must have been given by someone, not trustworthy, but instead of her to throw it away, she thought she could give it out. That is why the bible says we should love our neighbours as ourselves. What you cannot eat, you should not present to others.

Lying is another pitfall that a deliverance minister should be aware of. Many of the candidates are liars in many ways. They tell lies for many reasons. Some tell lies because they want to give you the impression that they are well to do. Some tell lies to hide the negative spiritual side of them. For example, if you ask some candidates, that, do you fly in your dream, they hesitate for a while and say hmmm, no. This might not be because of you only but they perceive that someone may overhear. This is why privacy is important when you are Counselling. It is best to counsel where people would see you from afar but are not able to hear what you are saying. Some tell lies to outshine their spouses or paint him or her badly. There is one golden rule that I use in Counselling couples. If possible, I like to invite the husband or wife of the person that I am Counselling, to cross examine them, so to say. Then you can get the issue in proper perspective. However, sometimes you can ask leading questions to ascertain the truth or try to make them to corroborate what they have said. Sometimes you may treat a counselee as a hostile witness in court, because some of them can be truly hostile.

Seduction by marine spirits and other demons.

Majority of your deliverance candidates are marine spirits. One major characteristic is their seductive nature. They are also stubborn. Mostly you see people possessed by dress strangely and seductively. They are mainly the category of these candidates may not close their eyes during prayers, they may never do assignments, or participate in anything meaningfully.

Try and establish the possession of witchcraft spirits by asking them questions, because this will help your deliverance as well as help you to play safe. They could discuss about sex with you between them and their husband or in past relationships. They invade your "ear gate" because they are aware that what you ear can be an evil arrow in your spirit. They could always wear short dresses to the deliverance ground, exploiting your eye gate. Listening to them mainly and not to look is the way out here. Tell them not to wear skimpy dresses to the deliverance ground. Some of them may be talking and touching you too, as they explain themselves to you. The way you react will save you from this. If you continue to laugh at it, they will say in their mind, this one is easy to catch. However, if you maintain a stern look, they will perceive you are not cut for that. The attitude you display will speak volumes about how they relate with you.

Beware also of seductive gestures. Kneeling all the time for you, smiling at you all the time, and trying to catch your attention to spend time with you unnecessarily are all things you should beware of. When you have answered all the answers of a candidate, and you ask them anything else, and they say no. That's it. If they now come again, and you say anything else in a calm manner, and they still say no, but pause to continue to talk about the rain that fell 3 days back, then you begin to suspect if they are satanic agents.

Specific patterns of manifestation and their meanings.

There are certain known patterns of manifestations by demonic spirits. For example, a spirit that keeps spinning and falling is a marine spirit. Any spirit that falls on the ground and wriggles like a snake is a marine spirit. Then you say, "you serpentine spirit, I break your power in the name of Jesus". Or you say, you serpent of darkness, come out of him or her in the name of Jesus Christ. If it is the symptom of breathlessness or weakness, then you will say serpent of infirmity, loose your captive in the name of Jesus Christ. It is also possible to command the poison of the serpent to be neutralised by the blood of Jesus. Then close your eyes for a few minutes to connect.

A spirit that is facing the wall or any other object and moving the hips as if they are having sex is a spirit husband or spirit wife, depending on if the candidate is a woman or a man. Then you pray prayers relevant to spirit husband or wife. For example, as they manifest, you say that you spirit wife, I break your covenant in this life. If the person is yet to have a baby, you command them to release the baby of that person.

A spirit that falls to the ground and starts flipping the wings is a proper witchcraft spirit. Mind you there is a difference between a snake and a bird and address them accordingly. When you see a flipping action of the shoulders (wings) then you break the covenant of witchcraft. Then you destroy the powers of astral projection, then arrest every witchcraft bird by fire, as you know it is only birds that fly. In all these cases you need to dwell on your knowledge of each manifesting spirit to raise the appropriate prayer points.

Strong faith.

Strong faith is one of the requirements for the working of miracles under which exorcism is. Healing Miracles require a lot of word of God and violent faith. For example, stopping a rain requires unwavering faith. If your faith shakes for more than 5 minutes, even though you did not say it out, you will see the rain fall as soon as possible. It will drench you before you get to where you are going. However, if you maintain a steady faith, it will never fall until you get to where you are going.

Once you have addressed a demon on the first day, of the Deliverance, there's no need to address it in subsequent days if you are really exercising faith. The worst part of it is when you casted out spirit husband on Tuesday, and the candidate comes to you on Thursday and says Pastor, hope you are praying for me, and you tell her, "Come, let me pray about it with you one more time". What you just did is that you just succeeded portraying yourself as a faithless

Pastor, because that is not the prescription of the bible. Mark 11:23 quoted above is the real prescription. It says when you say it, and do not doubt, but believe, that you already have them, it says you have what you say. The word of God says on Jeremiah 33:3 that when you call, he has answered you, then why are you asking again the third day if he has given it to you. It simply means you do not believe that you have it. Once you have asked and you believe, all you need do is to substantiate your faith according to what you have asked for and hoping for, and add works, for faith without works is dead.

Hebrews 11:1

Now faith is the substance of things hoped for, the evidence of things not seen.

The subject of faith needs to be taught and thoroughly supervised for the students and trainee Pastors in Deliverance to be able to increase their faith considerably to minister to deliverance candidates, and to teach Deliverance candidates.

Follow-ups.

After the deliverance program, candidates should be able to follow up, and ask any further questions regarding things they are not clear about. Sometimes depending on the country, you should note that it is unethical to have the phone numbers of your candidates. Healthcare Chaplains in the NHS and Care Homes, as well as immigrant workers should note this. Also feel free to give them addresses of places where they could seek help where necessary. Many Catholic churches in Europe have the Legio Mariae (Legion of Mary) where people could seek further help.

CHAPTER FIFTEEN

THE BASIC CONSIDERATIONS IN DELIVERANCE.

This would have been a very long chapter, as the topic is versatile, but let us break it down into different chapters. There can be no single deliverance procedure, because God is awesome and infinite. Generally speaking, God has called every minister into deliverance one way or the other, though the way and manner in which deliverance occurs are diversified. God can call 10 people into the same ministry, for example, healing, but the way he uses them differs greatly. We cannot give specific guidelines, but general. We shall try to exhaustively describe what we have seen happening in a period of 25 years in one of the greatest deliverance ministries in the world. They key, or the covenant he has given to the ten ministers may vary. Some are given the key of praise. Some are given prayers. Some are given anointing with oil and water like a man in Africa known as Apostle Ayo Babalola. Some beating people to raise the dead, like Smith Wigglesworth. Different covenants, methods and approaches. A deliverance minister must discover the covenant of God for his calling.

Where deliverance begins.

Where does deliverance start? God can move in the life of an unbeliever, and give him words of wisdom that will deliver a believer. For example, that is why the Bible says, that children should honour their parents. The Bible does not say categorically, if the parents should be Christians, before you can honour them. Furthermore, the Bible does not give a prescribed age that a child should be for them to consider honouring the parents. A child may be 50 years old, and the father is 75 years old, but if he says something in as much as God gives him grace to be in the right frame of mind, he should be respected and listened to by that son. Parents are always years ahead, at any point in time, and there is certain wisdom that you do not have that they can afford. They are authorities ordained of God. A parent, a leader, an employer a teacher, a religious leader, a husband, are all authorities ordained by God. Why? The bible may use words like we should honour them, submit unto them, obey them, or some other similar connotations. No matter the civilisation in the world today, when you carefully look at it with humility and honesty, these things are true. In as much as what they say or advise agrees with the word of God, they have said the mind of God. God has also given them immense powers to influence your life, during that relationship, and the influence may have an impact upon your life forever. I wouldn't like to dwell too long on this, but let's see what Romans 13:2 has to say:

Romans 13:1-2

¹Let every soul be subject unto the higher powers. For there is no power but of God: the powers that be are ordained of God.

²Whosoever therefore resisteth the power, resisteth the ordinance of God: and they that resist shall receive to themselves damnation.

The Bible foresees a tendency to resist these ordained personalities and forewarns in verse 2, that they that resist that ordinance shall receive to themselves damnation! For example, women are so favoured and loved by their husbands and children. They have the ability to determine their welfare. I must be very factual here to say that the extent to which you enjoy your old age depends on the cooperation between you and your wife. However, for both of you to enjoy your old age to the fullest, a woman still has to see her husband as the head of the family and respect him. That is when he will love you the more, and this is the mistake that many make to not to submit to their husbands. Many unbelieving women are not ready to accept it, but it is the truth. A child who does not honour the parent's words has received damnation to himself. An employee who does not obey the master, or employer has received damnation to himself.

I listen to divorced men and women or single parents, when they narrate their ordeals and lament bitterly. Maybe you are a divorced or single parent now, God can still show you mercy if you can swallow your ego and retrace your steps. James 5:14 says we should confess our faults one to the other, that we may be healed. They would only realise the mistake by experience. Unfortunately, women bear it more. We admit that some men could be terrible, likewise some women, but we need to pray for wisdom and be patient. If most men and women who are divorced are able to enter a quiet room in a neighbouring town, shut the doors and windows, and left alone with God, and ask themselves "was it a mistake that I divorced my husband or my wife"? They will hear a recurring yes.

There are responsibilities that we owe ourselves, our family, in our career as an employer or employee, as a church member, or as a member of the community. If we are unable to meet up with this, then we cannot be truly delivered. As I drove to work one day, the Lord told me, the greatest deliverance a man could enjoy in life is deliverance from sin. What is sin?

James 4:17

Therefore, to him that knoweth to do good, and doeth it not, to him it is sin.

We would have seen that basically, our deliverance lies in the word of God, and an understanding of God's covenant for his servant, and our obedience.

CHAPTER SIXTEEN

THE DELIVERANCE PROGRAM

The deliverance program should be a fasting program, and the candidate should be prepared to pray and fast round the clock. The week of your deliverance should always be seen as a special week, and a retreat. All phones are better switched off to avoid distractions, and diversions. If you can have the privilege of staying away from home and observe it as a residential program, it is worth the efforts. I am going to base my deliverance plan on a 5-day program which has brought wonderful results across the world, that I have used for many years and familiar with.

The first 3 days are for a dry fast, making sure you do not eat, drink or have sex round the clock. This is also referred to as a "marathon fast". The marathon fast should be stopped by around 12 noon or 2pm on Wednesday of the same week. For example, if you are to start the program on a Monday morning, then you would have stopped eating, drinking, or having any conjugal union by 10pm on Sunday night. It is advisable to arrange to get yourself to the venue by about 8pm on Sunday evening, for security reasons and to be well rested physically, and mentally before your program starts early the next morning. The fasting and the program generally may be hectic, but it will definitely change your game, if you are consecrated and give your best to it. Keep Praying to God "O Lord, give me the grace to do beyond what I think I can. Affirm to yourself, "I shall get there". I can do all things through Christ which strengthens me (Philippians 4:13) When you focus on prayers continuously during the program, you won't feel hungry. Draw a voluminous prayer program that will keep you busy, and make every moment of it a blessing indeed. Study and meditate in the bible too. However, when you are idle, the temptation to be hungry will come.

Marathon fasting is usually safer for three days, and many people do it for 3 days, after which they take water, fruit or food, at a specific time of the day at least. If you decide to break by 2pm, then you break at that time daily. My very first attempt at 7 days without food, water or sex was a bit hectic. However, since that time, 3 days dry fast has been like a child's play. When you begin to have good dreams and revelations from heaven, that will reposition life for great blessings, you will thank God that you were able to fast. Many problems will automatically be destroyed. You will practically see your problems crumbling before your very eyes.

A sister had a spirit husband that was preventing her from getting married. She was believing God for a partner and went for deliverance. After a 3-day dry fast, she saw the spirit husband, dressed in a track suit, and was waving at her as he went out of her body. A spirit spouse will always bring the face of someone you are in relationship with or you lust after. Another man who was battling with poverty went for deliverance, and after the second night, he saw a stunted, crippled man go out of his body. That was the power that was retarding his progress.

Another man was lacking and went for deliverance, and fasted and prayed. A dirty man and very sluggish appeared to him. That was the spirit of poverty, programmed into his life by witches and wizards. He clicked a very profitable contract afterwards. God is always ready to answer if we care to call upon him

Jeremiah 33:3

Call unto me, and I will answer thee, and shew thee great and mighty things, which thou knowest not.

Based on the covenant that I personally received for my ministry, use of ear rings, bangles, rings, hair attachments, lipsticks and make up generally are not acceptable not only for deliverance, but in church services. The use of oil and water was emphasised in that covenant as ways through which God wants to deliver his children.

The schedule of the deliverance program should always be for at least 3-5 days. One of the very important aspects that need to be emphasised is that of faith. There is a lot that the deliverance candidates need to know, that will make their program effective. The bible talks about the effective fervent prayer of the righteous man availeth much. This means that some prayers are effective by design, whilst others aren't.

Candidates need to know how to maintain their deliverance, because sin, prayerlessness, lack of study and meditation of God's word, insensitivity to revelation, all could make deliverance to be ineffective. The baptism of the Holy Ghost is also a necessity for every Christian. When a person receives the baptism of the Holy Ghost, the more they speak with other tongues, the stronger they become spiritually.

Let's see how a weekly deliverance program should be scheduled.

DAYS	8.00am-9am	9am- 10.30am	10.30am-12pm	12pm-1.30pm	1.30pm +
Mondays	Opening prayers and	What is deliverance?	Sin and Salvation through our	Faith. Announcements	Counselling

	praise worship		Lord Jesus Christ.		
Tuesdays	Opening prayers and praise worship	Foundation	Covenants	Curses. Announcements	Counselling
Wednesdays	Opening prayers and praise worship	Healing	Holy Ghost Baptism	Deliverance of the Head, Hands and Feet	Break the fast gently. Counselling
Thursdays	Opening prayers and praise worship	Prosperity	Marriage and Infidelity	Spiritual purging. Announcements	Counselling.
Fridays	Opening prayers and praise worship	Deliverance from Witchcraft	How to maintain your deliverance.	Testimonies. Announcements.	Closing.

CHAPTER SEVENTEEN

SALVATION

The first thing that should happen to a person in life before you can receive any blessing from God is to get saved. Jesus is the way that leads to God. After the fall of Adam and Eve in the garden of Eden, he came to reconcile:

Colossians 1:21

And you, that were sometime alienated and enemies in your mind by wicked works, yet now hath he reconciled.

This process involves believing that Jesus is the Son of God and confessing him as your Lord and saviour.

Romans 10:10

CHAPTER EIGHTEEN

THE WORD OF GOD

An important tool during Deliverance is the word of God. The fervour and passion with which the word of God is preached is important. The preaching of the word impacts the spirit and completely transforms the candidate's mindset and drives his faith. The word of God is the foundation on which our convictions and actions stand.

Romans 10:17

So, then faith cometh by hearing, and hearing by the word of God.

The word of God should be heard, spoken, meditated upon, put into action and taught. The written word of God is sourced from the Bible. The Rhema is the revealed word of God which we receive through revelations. The former is derived from the later and both of them are applicable in deliverance.

Whatever we desire on earth is premised on God's word if we believe in it. Every day on the Deliverance Ground, the word of God is taught give knowledge to the people. As the word of God is being taught, the Rhema is revealed, as words of knowledge, words of wisdom and prophecy, depending on how gifted the officiating minister is. The minister should therefore be at alert during the teaching to receive from God.

The Holy Spirit might reveal the word as a song or as prayer point, or a specific instruction. If the Holy Spirit gives you a song, then as you sing it, be observant and trust that something is about to happen. If he drops a prayer point in your spirit, all of a sudden in the middle of a teaching, raise the prayer point and give it time for the power of God to manifest. Get your anointing oil in your pocket always in a small ampoule and be ready to lay hands as led. Deliverance is a seamless experience if you listen and allow the Holy Spirit to lead you as you do the work. This is why deliverance candidates should not joke with any Prophetic actions as well. For example, the minister tells you to form a circle round the deliverance ground 7 times. There's definitely a reason.

Another channel of the word of God is through Praise and Worship. Apart from the lyrics of the song (words of the song), the Holy Spirit leads you into the realm of the Prophetic. Praise and worship inspire revelations and the Pastors should allow the singers to release words of knowledge or words of wisdom to edify the congregation. This is not the Old Testament time as everyone has access to revelation. In some cases, a deliverance candidate may Prophesy, for example during the session for Holy Ghost baptism, though it is not allowed in some congregations.

During Counselling, every advice you give to the candidates must be backed up with scriptures and examples given. This is what we call Biblical Counselling.

Assignments should be given to the candidates to be able to meditate in the word and learn by heart the word of God. Give up to 5 scriptural references per day, for them to study and learn by heart. The next morning, you could call them to recite the words they have learnt.

Candidates should be encouraged to teach the word of God. This is very beneficial and a win-win situation for the teacher and the church. It gives you an opportunity to study the word deeper. I got more familiarised with the word as a "Search the Scriptures" teacher. As a Pastor, then, I always took delight in teaching God's word by myself most times. I discovered that people from other branches came to our "word study". It is a very good time to make the word practical, as you address real life issues in the light of the word. It was always a good experience. I had to close the service because many people were not ready to go home.

The teaching of the word of God is one vital area where deliverance occurs passively and actively. If you are working as a team, the strengths of each minister should be identified and they should be allowed to demonstrate the grace upon their lives. Let the glory be to God and not man.

CHAPTER NINETEEN

COUNSELING

This is a part of the deliverance procedure that is very important and brings much benefit. Counsellors should be versatile in acquisition of knowledge and should try to read extensively. My background in Medicine gives me a world of understanding about the sick. It has helped me seamlessly in providing accurate Counselling to the sick. A candidate was about travelling out to another country and was confused about the procedure. I was able to help through my knowledge of Aviation. Likewise, it is important to know about government policies as it relates to the citizenry. Many times, I could tell people about Education and the best choices for their children, because my late mother was in the Educational Sector.

Every deliverance candidate should go through counselling, so that the root of their problems could be identified and solutions preferred based on the scriptures. The big question is that, is Counselling scriptural?

Proverbs 11:14

Where no counsel is, the people fall: but in the multitude of counsellors there is safety.

Counselling is to guide candidates based on what the scriptures say so that they do not make mistake. According to the scripture below, even in spiritual warfare, you need guidance of the counsellors to win. In the war against the devil, and for you to win in life, guidance is essential.

Proverbs 20:18

Every purpose is established by counsel: and with good advice make war.

Proverbs 24:6

For by wise counsel thou shalt make thy war: and in multitude of counsellors there is safety.

Ministers should be careful not to spend too much time than necessarily. Some candidates can ask the same question up to 3 or 4 times and talk about irrelevant things. For example, you may ask if they ever had a difficult delivery. They might go on telling you the history of how the hospital was founded, and a description of every staff. Remember you may have up to 20-30 candidates to be attended to in just 2 hours. Time is essential.

Do not get too familiar with candidates, and do not seek favours from them. This is unethical, as there should be boundaries in every relationship. When you get over-familiar, your role as a Counsellor could be abused. Do not ask for financial favours. It is scriptural, and not out of place for your candidates to bless you, but you should be led in your receiving of it. There are organisations where it is frowned at, and you should obey the laws in that case. Gifts could be used to attack you spiritually, likewise something like even snacks and drinks or other items of food. It is unethical to try to force your candidate to divulge secrets they may not be willing to share with you. Be careful!

The privacy of the counselees should be respected. The best approach is to attend to counselees in a far corner, but where everybody can see you. It may amaze you to note that there is sensitive information that a husband or wife may cherish privacy regarding certain issues. For example, a husband may be seeking advice regarding a potentially dangerous relationship in the office with the opposite sex and vice versa. The wife may also be experiencing the same thing and would like to ask questions. However, the bible says two have become one. Wisdom is important in cases like that. Try as much as possible to encourage husband and wife to be open to one another in order not to allow the devil into their marriage.

In your role as Counsellor, you should take notes on each candidate. Ask them how the problem started, frequency of the problem, their perception of the cause of the problem, the help sought in the past.

Try as much as possible to provide scriptural backing for all advice that you have given. A minister should ponder prayerfully on the notes they have taken concerning each candidate, when they get home. This could be done at midnight when there is absolute silence. Candidates should also be able to share information with their Counsellors freely.

CHAPTER TWENTY

FAITH.

Faith is the absolute confidence in God's word, in spite of whatever you are experiencing, or that you think may happen in the near or distant future.

There are certain traits that are demonstrated by people that have faith, and which were demonstrated in the scriptures. If a man can have this mindset, then the devil cannot overcome the person. Faith is necessary for us to receive Jesus as our Lord Jesus, and to walk with God fully. In the discussions following, we shall look at notable attributes in the bible and how the people that demonstrated these attributes were victorious through faith.

Word of God.

Faith involves receiving the word of God, and Faith will not be set in motion, except you hear God's word, or you have received God's word. God's word may come in written form, that is the word of God you read in the bible. Then you meditate in it and turn it over in your spirit. At some point, it aligns with your expectations. It gives you confidence.

> *Romans 10:17*
>
> *So, then faith cometh by hearing, and hearing by the word of God.*

Other ways of hearing from God are through visions, dreams, intuition, verbal instructions from the Holy spirit, revelations from the church of God, and others. God may just give you a word of knowledge, that he will heal, you. God told me twice, concerning a certain woman, that he will make a way where there was no way. In the case of another person, he told me to give the person some oil on the head, and some to drink. That is a word of wisdom, because it tells you exactly what to do. Really, according to Hebrews 1:1, God can talk to people in various ways, and at various times, but it is left to you to discover how and when he speaks to you. Then you act according to the word.

For God to give you an assurance concerning a particular issue, it means he has perfected it and made it fool-proof. So, you need not doubt or fear at all regarding the word. Meditate on it, together with other scriptures, but not logic, and at a time it will click in your heart, as settled. At this type you know peace. Logic tells you to consider and try to justify God's word by medical, or scientific knowledge. The more you do that, the more unrealistic and vulnerable you are.

> *Romans 4:17-21*

17 (As it is written, I have made thee a father of many nations,) before him whom he believed, even God, who quickened the dead, and calleth those things which be not as though they were.

18Who against hope believed in hope, that he might become the father of many nations; according to that which was spoken, so shall thy seed be.

19and being not weak in faith, he considered not his own body now dead, when he was about a hundred years old, neither yet the deadness of Sarah's womb:

20He staggered not at the promise of God through unbelief; but was strong in faith, giving glory to God;

21and being fully persuaded that, what he had promised, he was able also to perform.

Abraham had sexual relations with his wife and kept believing, even at the age of about 100, because God has said. He did not consider his old age or deadness of Sarah's womb. He did not consider that obstetric or gynaecological complications could arise.

Faith does not fear.

When you have read and received the promise of God in his word, you don't have to entertain any fear, because he has authority over evert thing and can do all things. Fear is an emotional, biological, behavioural, or physical response to a perceived danger. Whereby, faith is the substance of good things hoped for and evidence of God's awesome miracles yet to manifest (Hebrews 11:1), in the contrary, fear is the substance for negative occurrence imagined against God's promises and evidence of what God has not said concerning you, making you to agree and align absolutely with the devil's plan for your life. When you entertain fear, you lose spiritual stamina to confront the devil and walk through your signs and wonders. It is good to learn to trust God, and let our minds be stayed on God as a little child would to the mother.

Isaiah 26:3

Thou wilt keep him in perfect peace, whose mind is stayed on thee: because he trusteth in thee.

Once the Lord sees that you trust in him, he himself as a responsibility will keep you in perfect peace. However, if your mind is strayed away from the confidence and trust in God, then that is when you don't have peace and he can't reward you with a miracle. All good things come with absolute trust in God.

Faith does not doubt.

When there is a swing in your faith or belief that makes your conviction unstable, then doubt is said to have set in. When you are filled with faith on a moment, and the other moment, you experience fear, that is doubt.

James 1:6-8

⁶but let him ask in faith, nothing wavering. For he that wavereth is like a wave of the sea driven with the wind and tossed.

⁷for let not that man think that he shall receive any thing of the Lord.

⁸A double minded man is unstable in all his ways.

The bible describes doubt as double mindedness and an unstable attitude. It's like building a house and demolishing it then rebuilding and demolishing it.

Peter was in a boat and saw Jesus walking on the sea. He told Jesus if he could come with him. Jesus gave him word that he should come. He was walking on the sea, until the wind became boisterous. He was afraid, and doubted, and made the words of Jesus of no effect. Each time you doubt God's word, you make it of no effect. A doubting individual is like a wave of the sea, and because of that he cannot retain anything or have any miracle.

Faith is about taking risks, ignoring what you see believing God's word.

In 2 Kings 7:1-20, three types of faith were demonstrated.

1. Complete Faith
2. Partial Faith
3. Zero Faith

The lepers believed the words of Elisha and were ready to take the risk. They fell into the host of the Syrians though they were not sure if they were going to live or if they were going to die (1 Kings 7:4). Theirs was complete faith. When they entered into the uttermost part of the camp of the Syrians, behold there was no man there! For God to send you a word, he will go before you and perfect everything.

They went to tell the Porters, and the Porters told it to the Kings House (1 Kings 7:11). The King demonstrated negative faith, by his imagination. He and his servants doubted and limited their blessings. This is partial faith.

The man that said how could it be? was trodden upon and he died (1 Kings 7:19-20). He had Zero Faith.

Looking at the two accounts above, they recklessly believed the word of God, and did not care what could happen.

The widow of Zarephath (1 Kings 17:11-15) gave all that she and her child had left at home to Elijah, acting strictly on God's word (1 Kings 17:14 – For thus saith the LORD GOD of Israel of Israel, The barrel of meal shall not waste, neither shall the cruse of oil fail, until the day that the LORD senders rain upon the earth". Verse 15 says she went and did accordingly.

Add works to your faith.

Another thing to note about faith is that we need to add works to faith.

> James 2:17-18
>
> ¹⁷Even so faith, if it hath not works, is dead, being alone.
>
> ¹⁸Yea, a man may say, thou hast faith, and I have works: shew me thy faith without thy works, and I will shew thee my faith by my works.

In Acts 3:1-10, Peter healed the man at the Beautiful Gate. Peter commanded him to arise and walk in the name of Jesus Christ (verse 6). Even though power was released into his life, through the word in the name of Jesus Christ, he couldn't walk until Peter held him by the hand (verse 7). The Bible says that his ankle bones received strength immediately, and from that time he leaped, walking and praising God.

Peter helped him to add substance to his faith, by holding his hand and raising him up to walk. He needed to show the evidence that he is already living in the promise he was anticipating.

> Hebrews 11:1
>
> Now faith is the substance of things hoped for, the evidence of things not seen.

When God tells you that you will get a job in a company, you need to apply, and study hard for your job interview. If God promises but you fail to act, your testimony will not materialise. There is a part you need to play as a human being to make your faith work.

When we are ministering healing, I am led to tell people to pray and shake their bodies, or their heads, saying "I break every chain of infirmity". Most of the patients look at you as some of them are thinking about how long on earth they have been on a wheelchair. They probably think it cannot happen. Each time there is a miracle service, there is a force in the direction of your expected miracle. If your desire is walking again, there is a force that tends to push you up from the wheelchair during prayer which you need to follow. Sometimes you might just need to lay your hand on the affected part and say "I receive my healing in the name of Jesus Christ". In the past there are people who wanted to be pregnant and the Minister of God will tell them, even without getting pregnant yet, go and buy baby things. When they buy baby things, then they need to wake up every morning and decree upon the baby things, "I shall conceive and deliver safely".

Speak to your mountain.

> Mark 11:23
>
> For verily I say unto you, that whosoever shall say unto this mountain, be thou removed, and be thou cast into the sea; and shall not doubt in his heart, but shall believe that those things which he saith shall come to pass; he shall have whatsoever he saith.

When you speak to a problem repeatedly, and do not doubt but believe that the things you have said will be manifested, then you will see them manifesting. It could be healing of diseases, may be to your marriage, could be to your business or anything at all. When you wake up in the morning and you go to your wedding picture laying your hands on it, and saying "your marriage, you shall not fail in the name of Jesus".

The bible also tells us that we shall decree a thing and it shall be established.

Job 22:28

Thou shalt also decree a thing, and it shall be established unto thee: and the light shall shine upon thy ways.

So, you decree upon your business, every morning, that it shall go around the world. "I decree that I shall have branches in many countries of the world",

Don't walk by sight.

When you are walking with God, you don't walk by what you see, but by what the word of God says.

2 Corinthians 5:7

For we walk by faith, not by sight.

A certain woman was given a revelation by God about where to site her business. The place at that time was underdeveloped and there were other many houses around there. The woman thought, "after all, business will not flourish here". She went to rent a shop in another place. About a year later, a very big Secondary School was sited in that place, with hundreds of students and dozens of teachers. We cannot walk by what we see, but we need to seek God's counsel and walk by it.

A lady came to me for counsel as to who to marry in life. She had a young man in mind, who was working in a blue-chip company, but meanwhile, where she was working, the driver of that school was proposing to her. Judging by her dreams and revelations, the driver was the choice of God for her, but she was so much in love with the white-collar young man. She continued to ignore the driver. The driver unknown to her already had a big house of his own, had vehicles he was operating as commercial vehicles, and was a successful man. He was just planning to work in that organisation where he was working for a short time. All these came to limelight at the time he was preparing for his wedding to another lady. Then the lady came to me to tell me that he would be taking another lady to the altar very soon. It was too late! I told her, I can't stop the marriage.

This is a mistake that many ladies that come for deliverance from foundational witchcraft make who are believing God for a husband. Most times, ladies are more concerned about financial security in marriage, but then think about the present, and not the future or potentials. Many ladies who are ripe to marry make mistakes because they walk by what they see.

Many miraculous workings of the Holy Ghost have defied medical diagnosis, that for a child of God; both the diagnosis, and the signs and symptoms of disease are irrelevant. There have been cases of tumour that disappeared completely. People with HIV or other diagnosis going back to the doctor, to bring a negative result, terrible body mutilation receiving healing, previously shortened limbs increasing in length, and other medical prophecies contrary to health and wellbeing have been nullified but the power of the most high God. Many people that were given reports that they should go home and die, lived for many years after. Kenneth Hagin of blessed memory had a heart condition which made him bedridden was told by the doctors to go home and die. He received his healing at the age of 17 and died about 70 years later at the age of 86.

Faith doesn't give up.

I prayed for a number of people in England and observed that many people lack the patience to receive, and this is a great disaster and very tragic for people who are believing God for miracles! After praying for a few minutes, and nothing has happened, you see disgust in their faces. Real faith doesn't get tired and neither does it surrender.

I was to relocate to a new property in year 2006. However, I gathered intelligence that there was a vampire serpent, living in a gigantic "termite mound". It would be dangerous to move there with my family. I decided to wait upon God in a 70 day fast. The 70 days fasting ended in November, but yet I couldn't see any result. My faith could not wane, as I continued fasting and praying. All of a sudden, one morning in January, the LORD opened my eyes, and I saw the mighty serpent's head was roasted and was red hot in that revelation. "Mission accomplished", I said happily. The devil respects holy stubbornness, on the altar of prayer.

> 1 Kings 18:41-45
>
> ⁴¹And Elijah said unto Ahab, get thee up, eat and drink; for there is a sound of abundance of rain.
>
> ⁴²So Ahab went up to eat and to drink. And Elijah went up to the top of Carmel; and he cast himself down upon the earth, and put his face between his knees,
>
> ⁴³and said to his servant, go up now, look toward the sea. And he went up, and looked, and said, there is nothing. And he said, Go again seven times.
>
> ⁴⁴and it came to pass at the seventh time, that he said, Behold, there ariseth a little cloud out of the sea, like a man's hand. And he said, go up, say unto Ahab, prepare thy chariot, and get thee down, that the rain stop thee not.
>
> ⁴⁵and it came to pass in the meanwhile, that the heaven was black with clouds and wind, and there was a great rain. And Ahab rode, and went to Jezreel.

In this account, Elijah continued praying and wouldn't have stopped until he saw that there was a cloud which eventually brought about a great rain.

Faith is unstoppable.

It's one thing for you to want to stop believing something, willingly. It is a different story when people stop you. Many people will try to stop you on your faith mission through their advice, attitudes, actions and in many other ways, especially those who are close to you, who don't understand you.

When the Lord called me to leave my secular job for full time ministry, I was faced with a lot of comments, advice and actions from people who were members of my family, and other people in the household of God who did not have spiritual eyes. Mind you, your Pastor may not know everything that God wants you to do, no matter how highly ranked they may be. What matters is for you to be convinced about what God is leading you to do, and what you want to do. Don't allow anyone to stop you. Remember the story of the old prophet who convinced the young prophet to the extent that the young prophet died for lack of conviction (1 Kings 13:11-25). I thank God that I did not allow them to stop my calling and my ministry. I can remember I was called to a meeting of Overseers who tried to advise me to go back and resume my secular job. I did it secretly like a suicide bombing mission because I knew someone might try to stop me. I did it just like Abraham who did not tell his wife before going to offer Isaac. As a man of faith, you don't discuss everything with people. My late mother and my General Overseer were the only two people that supported my vision, prayed for me, and encouraged me to carry on.

In the story of blind Bartimaeus in Mark 10:46-52, he was begging by the roadside, until Jesus came passing by. Immediately he heard it was Jesus Christ of Nazareth, he started crying, "Jesus, thou son of David, have mercy on me". The bible records that the people tried to stop him, but he cried the more, until Jesus gave him attention and healed him. In the process, he cast away his garment as he ran to Jesus for healing. What is the voice that is trying to stop you, which garment may delay you? Cast then away.

In the story of David too, as he warmed up to fight Goliath, his brothers and King Saul tried to stop him, but he refused to be stopped. He eventually killed Goliath. Real faith is unstoppable.

Real faith doesn't get tired but endures.

When you are faced with a child who is not doing well at school, keep on believing for God answers prayers. When you believe God and keep trusting him, somewhere along the line, you will receive enlightenment from the word as to what to do. Stay on the lane!

Proverbs 24:10

If thou faint in the day of adversity, thy strength is small.

Isaiah 40:31

But they that wait upon the LORD shall renew their strength; they shall mount up with wings as eagles; they shall run, and not be weary; and they shall walk, and not faint.

The same thing is with your marriage. Don't entertain disgust, or despair, but keep renewing your strength. When you prayerfully "stay on the lane", you receive ideas and Illumination giving g you a solution out of the problem.

CHAPTER TWENTY-ONE

PRAISE AND WORSHIP

Praise is thanking God for what he has done, and worship is thanking him for who he is. In the ministry of deliverance, there are other spiritual songs as well, depending on the spirits leading that could be employed during deliverance ministrations. These include hymns mainly, native or traditional songs, and contemporary genres like rap, reggae gospel, calypso gospel, hip-hop, southern music and the likes. Most relevant however is praise and worship with a hymn or two at the beginning of the deliverance service.

Particular emphasis should be given to warfare songs, which are sort of Militant in nature and very important when you are breaking curses, covenants, evil dedication, or simply praying against witchcraft powers. These are songs like:

1. *Holy Ghost send down fire (x2), Respond: send down fire*
2. *Deliver me, deliver me, deliver me O Lord, by your power, by your fire, deliver me O Lord*
3. *Holy Ghost descend your fire (x2), respond; descend your fire........*
4. *Strongman submit your power; respond: submit your power; Strongman submit your power; respond: submit your power*
5. *I need fire, I need fire; Holy Ghost fire fall upon me (x2); fall upon me, fall upon me..........*

The praise and worship session should take about 45 minutes to one hour. Be mindful that your voice, the tempo of your song, the rhythm of your songs, and emphasis in your voice will determine how effective you would be as a minister. The countenance on your face is another factor that will affect the response and flow of the Holy spirit. If you are tired and weak, it will reflect in your ministration. Likewise, if you have domestic or personal problems that overwhelm you, it will affect your ministration.

A bit of moral adjuration is needed in form of words, as you start to minister worship, or at the end of the session. This goes on with prophecy, if you have any. A lot of deliverance occurs during this session and you would only get the best from it if you focus and consecrate during the session as a deliverance candidate. Meditate on the songs as the session goes on, and commune with your heart (Psalm 4:4). There should be no worries or distractions. Praise and worship God with great expectations. Worship should be solemn.

When I minister Praise and worship, candidates manifest in various ways, and demons leave. Sometimes, the word of prophecy is released. As a Praise and worship leader, you have to be observant during your ministrations, and watch out for candidates that may manifest. Manifestation shows that the Holy Spirit is at work in the life of an individual. Try to possibly influence them to experience deeper his presence and power. During the session, you could continue singing, the song that is bringing that manifestation. At the peak of the manifestation, you pause for a few seconds like 30 seconds, then you see the Holy Spirit really swing into action as different things begin to happen. The Holy Spirit does not like to struggle, and that is why you should always give him chance by pausing. Many don't understand that a pause is necessary during ministrations.

Psalms 4:4

Stand in awe, and sin not: commune with your own heart upon your bed, and be still. Selah.

Every deliverance minister should meditate on the above scripture and use it for their advantage. Deliverance Ministers should teach their candidates. When you stand in awe in the presence of the Lord, you don't discuss with friends, look outside the auditorium, go out to make calls, check your phones and the likes. All you do is concentrate and be in holiness. When you commune with your hearts, you are asking a question like how to handle a difficult work colleague, how to improve your finances and overcome poverty etc.

The Bible recommends that as you ask these questions, pause and be still. Listen to your heart, and what the Holy Spirit will drop there. That is why you need to be still. In the scripture below, you might wonder what was the significance of silence in heaven.

Revelation 8:1

And when he had opened the seventh seal, there was silence in heaven about the space of half an hour.

CHAPTER TWENTY-TWO

PRAYERS AND DELIVERANCE

What is prayer?

Prayer is communication with God. When you commune with someone, you speak with that person, and you wait for a response. The word of God says we should ask that we may receive (Matthew 7:7). God also says when we call unto him, he shall answer and do great and mighty things that we have not known (Jeremiah 33:3).

Even though prayer is a channel of communication with God, most people just talk to God and walk away, not expecting a response. That is why they do not get a response and prayer may be unfruitful. It is an abuse of your sonship. As many as are led by the spirit of God are the sons of God.

Romans 8:14

For as many as are led by the Spirit of God, they are the sons of God.

As you pray to God, you are expected to have a leading by the spirit of God which abides in you, and that's why you have to be still to hear from him after prayer. The Bible says he will teach us everything.

1 John 2:27

But the anointing which ye have received of him abideth in you, and ye need not that any man teach you: but as the same anointing teacheth you of all things, and is truth, and is no lie, and even as it hath taught you, ye shall abide in him.

Another pitfall in the place of prayer is that people pray for the wrong things or do not follow the right procedure as taught by Jesus with reference to the LORD'S prayer. That is another reason why many people's prayers are unfruitful.

James 4:3

Ye ask, and receive not, because ye ask amiss, that ye may consume it upon your lusts.

Jesus has already given us a pattern to follow when we pray, which is very complete:

Matthew 6:9-13

⁹After this manner therefore pray ye: Our Father which art in heaven, hallowed be thy name.

¹⁰Thy kingdom come. Thy will be done in earth, as it is in heaven.

¹¹Give us this day our daily bread.

¹²and forgive us our debts, as we forgive our debtors.

¹³and lead us not into temptation, but deliver us from evil: For thine is the kingdom, and the power, and the glory, for ever. Amen.

Prayers for Forgiveness.

One important aspect that many deliverance candidates overlook is that which talks about forgiveness of sins in verse 12. Sin can be a hindrance to our deliverance, and the prayers for forgiveness is important. As we go for deliverance, we must ask ourselves, who and who have we not forgiven? Who am I having grudges with. This excess burden on your spiritual life will hinder your deliverance. According to the LORD'S prayer, I'd you have not forgiven someone, it will be hard for your prayers to be forgiven. If you are not forgiven, it difficult for you to receive from God. However, God wants us to confess our faults. He said in 1 John 1:9, starting with "IF".

1 John 1:9

If we confess our sins, he is faithful and just to forgive us our sins, and to cleanse us from all unrighteousness.

The condition is stated and so simple; "if we confess our sins". That is the first prayer we need to pray. I know a man many years back who offended his brother's wife. He did not know that she was a witch, but that one used household witchcraft against him and sentenced him to poverty, backwardness and non-achievement until God knows when. He started roaming the streets, and when he was tired of being tired in their town, he came to the town where we met. He came for deliverance. I listened to his account carefully and the spirit of God led me to tell him to ask for forgiveness from God. That very night, the brother's wife came through the wall, to confront him, that "so you want to be free?" She tried to resist his deliverance but it was too late. The promise of God and mercy to a lawful captive forbids it. The word says that if we confess our sins, that we are forgiven. That's it! Who is the person that you have offended? Are you sure that the person is a witch or wizard or not? Would you pray forgiveness prayers tonight?

It is profitable to pray in the hours of the night, when the witches are having their meetings. They would see you are not available for attack. The spirit of God can use you effectively to scatter their apparatuses that they have set.

Prayers against witchcraft should be accompanied with fasting and should be done vigorously, loudly, freely and with great expectations. The Bible says, right from the time of John the Baptist, the Kingdom of God suffered violence and the violence taketh it by force.

Matthew 11:12

¹²and from the days of John the Baptist until now the kingdom of heaven suffered violence, and the violent take it by force.

If there is anything that witchcraft powers respect, it is spiritual violence, especially the familiar spirits and marine witchcraft. Regular fasting and prayer, daily vigils, in-depth study of God's word, confession of dangerous scriptures, and your uncompromising attitude in the place of prayer.

Covenant Breaking Prayers.

The second type of prayer on deliverance is covenant breaking prayers. This you have to pray violently and aggressively. Since covenants are like the contract papers for a type of business, cancelling the contract is breaking the covenant. Pray aggressively to break the covenant. Once you demonstrate that you detest their covenant and put all your energy into it, success follows. They withdraw all the wicked powers they have given to you, and if they have a covenant of death against you, it is immediately cancelled. If you have been sick for a while, you receive healing immediately the covenant is broken. If they have assigned a spirit husband to you, immediately the covenant is broken, he bids you goodbye with impunity. They cannot punish you because Christ paid for your sins. One important covenant to break is the sexual covenant. When you sleep with a witch, you tend to have more sex in the dream. The food covenant is another covenant to break, if you have been attacked or possessed through food. It will be seen that you will be eating more in the dream.

Prayers to Break Curses.

Witches can effectively make pronouncements and curse people with their mouth, because they have the power that they can use to do this. One of the ways they trouble people's lives is to place their hands on one another or join hands in their coven and curse. They seal it and it comes into operation. If they are also with you physically, they do curse. There is a need to tell them immediately that you reverse the curse by the power in the blood of Jesus.

Destroy their Transportation System.

Witches and wizards transport themselves in various ways. One notable form is by astral projection. Then you pray "I destroy every evil transportation system that the enemies are using against me in the name of Jesus.

Destroy their communication systems.

Witchcraft communication systems exist that allows them to communicate one with another or to conference with many participants. One of the prayers to destroy this communication system is to pray to break the powers of communication. Render them spiritually blind, deaf and dumb. Always anoint the house too with oil and water. Always release the blood of Jesus inside the food that the family will eat.

Break Soul-Tie and Covenant.

There is always a soul tie that makes the covenant even stronger. The main difference between a person possessed by witchcraft and a blind witch, lies in the strength of the soul tie. A soul tie will make you to see the other members of the sacred group more readily, easily and frequently. It creates a soul attachment. I know a witch who will always tell the daughter, I want my body to always touch yours, and will like to see you more frequently. She will also tell the husband of the daughter, to call her frequently. To the unlearned, you might think she's showing love, but in actual terms she's trying to strengthen a soul-tie, so that she can wreak her havoc more easily.

Pray frequently to destroy the soul ties depending on what you see in your dreams and the physical desires that you experience that are strange. These are indicative of witchcraft soul-ties.

Destroy their altars.

There are witchcraft altars where transactions are carried out. An altar is a place of worship and evil exchange. Some of these altars are on the top of huge and sacred trees, some of them are at the road junctions, some at the graveyard, some at the public cemetery, some may even be inside your house. A girl confessed that they were meeting inside the father's refrigerator.

Some altars may be the reproductive organ of the initiate serving as the place of exchange. The power in their sexual organ is usually a serpent! As they give you pleasure, the serpent steals your virtues, progress, promotions, your joy, your health or whatsoever that they have decided to strip you off. What an unprofitable exchange!

Release the fire of God, blood of Jesus, brimstone of fire, hails stones of fire, sword of God, anger of God, against the altars. Then don't forget to destroy the principality on the throne. I moved into a newly acquired property several years back. There was a serpent on an environmental witchcraft altar that I got to discover, which made it unsafe for me and my family to live there. I sought the face of God for the destruction of the serpentine altar, in a 70 day fast.

When it wasn't getting destroyed, I continued praying and fasting. A month into the new year 2007, I was lying on my bed and the Lord showed me the vision of the massive serpent, which had caught fire and was destroyed.

Destroy every animal that they are using.

Witchcraft powers do body shifting spiritually, whereby they change their shape into that of an animal in a dream or vision. They can also astral-project into an animal physically, such that their spirit control's the activities of the animal. Such an animal that they project into will behave like a human being and could talk like a human being. On a certain night, I heard dogs speak like human beings, and an elderly man in the neighbourhood exclaimed, you people have entered into these dogs tonight.

Animals that they commonly use include goats, dogs, chicken, birds like the owl and vulture, cats, mice, rats, snakes, or monkeys. A monkey was controlled by the powers of witchcraft, and it bit the owner in the leg. That leg was amputated eventually when the wound couldn't heal and the leg was getting gangrenous or rotten. A dog was possessed and pounced on the toddler child of its owner, and removed the scalp, and tore the child to pieces.

Cockroaches and insects generally are not left out. A swarm of insects could be possessed to destroy a farm, a poultry, or other economic ventures. The wall gecko is another animal that they use for evil purposes. The wall gecko harbours monitoring demons and does monitor effectively. They can also stay in the corner in the room up the wall to strike. For example, a visitor or house help who wants to attack people could just project into the wall gecko, move inside your room and operate. She can monitor you, read your stars, and strike if need be.

Pray to render them paralysed, and their powers demobilised. Command the fire of God to consume them. Scatter every plan that they have with the fire of God. Pray that the animals should receive confusion or send them back to their senders.

Destroy their powers.

When two nations are fighting, they try to bomb each other's power bases. The same way, you should try to destroy their power and what is important to them. A lady confessed to me that she had a third eye in the front of her head. She cried as I positioned hands on either sides of her cheeks, and positioned my two thumbs on the third eye on her forehead, and commanded it to go blind in the name of Jesus. That was what she was using to monitor people for destruction. When you break witchcraft covenants, you automatically destroy any power they were given. However, you need to back-up and uproot the powers completely by addressing the individual powers. Then you do a perfect and excellent job. The power in the eyes should be destroyed. Serpent in the private parts should be commanded to catch fire. Power in their hand sponsoring poverty in your life should receive destruction. Command them to lose any power they are using to curse you. Command them to get trapped inside the body of any animal that they are using to attack you.

Use the weapons of spiritual warfare against them.

There are very potent weapons in the bible that can be used against witchcraft to destroy, their altars, destroy their transportation and communication systems, uproot their trees, spell collective disaster in their camps and many more. These include brimstones of fire (Genesis 19:24), sulphur (Revelation 9:17), hailstones of fire (Ezekiel 38:22), horrible tempest of God (Ezekiel 13:11), horrible tempest of God (Ezekiel 13:11), earthquake of God (Revelation 6:12), anger of God (Romans 1:18), flaming fire (2 Thessalonians 1:8), arrows of lightening (Zechariah 9:14), thunder and hail (Exodus 9:23), whirlwind (Nahum 1:3), fiery serpents (Numbers 21:6), Consuming fire (Hebrews 12:29).

Recover your lost possessions.

Don't forget that the bible says that the devil has come to steal, to kill and to destroy. The Bible also gives illumination about recovering our possessions from dark powers. One of the scriptures is in

> *Mark 3:27*
>
> *No man can enter into a strong man's house, and spoil his goods, except he will first bind the strong man; and then he will spoil his house.*

It is the will of God to call forth your hidden riches, wherever they have hidden it. That girl told me that they hidden the father's fortunes on a tree in their hometown. Effective prayers and revelation will be a flashlight to lead you to what prayers you need to pray to recover. God in his infinite mercies will also show you the things you need to pray about or act upon. That is why he gives us dreams, so that he can guide and direct us.

> *Isaiah 45:3*
>
> *And I will give thee the treasures of darkness, and hidden riches of secret places, that thou mayest know that I, the LORD, which call thee by thy name, am the God of Israel.*

They could also bury you spiritually. Some years ago, some very close enemies tried to attack me using an evil decree. They passed a Kangaroo judgement and told me that I was guilty of death and sickness. I knew that contradicted the promises of God for my life. The word of God says mercy rejoiceth against judgement and that he will bring me out of any grave. I remembered what the resurrection power of Jesus did. I prayed and fasted aggressively for a few months. My main prayer point was that the power of resurrection should possess my life. That faithful afternoon, I was having a nap when all of a sudden, I was lifted and brought out of the grave, in the spirit. That was the victory. At a time 25 years ago, my finances were arrested, and I got it back. I pray that the Lord shall bring you out of your grave in the mighty name of Jesus.

Ezekiel 37:12

Therefore, prophesy and say unto them, thus saith the Lord GOD; Behold, O my people, I will open your graves, and cause you to come up out of your graves, and bring you into the land of Israel.

Any man or woman that has swallowed any organ of your body and attacking your health shall vomit it by fire in the name of Jesus. Many folks believing God for a child had their reproductive organ swallowed or kept on an evil altar. If you sleep with their daughter, they could seize your manhood forever if you don't pray. It earns the witch you slept with some promotion in their kingdom, or they give her another power to add to what she already has. You paid for it.

Pray to recover your letter of promotion, as well as other letters that they have kept. Many people have the paper copy of their certificates in their files, but the real copy which is the spiritual copy is on witchcraft altars, probably because of your sin. A woman built a house and couldn't have people to rent the house. I was led to give her a prayer point to recover the Certificate of Occupancy from the evil altar. A few days after that prayer point, people started coming to ask her to let the apartments to them.

There are landlord spirits that lay claim over property. If you are dealing with landlord spirits, you cannot have your desires on the property unless you deal with them spiritually. The massive serpent I mentioned earlier was a landlord spirit. The crocodile I mentioned in the first few chapters of this book that wanted to prevent us from planting a church was another landlord spirit. If you don't have the Certificate of Occupancy, you cannot admit tenants into "another man's house" spiritually speaking.

Purge evil seeds.

The enemies delight in planting the seed of problems in someone's life that will grow and bring problems.

Matthew 13:25

But while men slept, his enemy came and sowed tares among the wheat, and went his way.

One of the things that witchcraft power does is to plant evil seed into your life when you go asleep. The hours of the night are dangerous powers and Christians should use vital parts of these hours between 12 midnight and 3am for spiritual warfare. When you eat all sorts of food on the dream, it is a means of planting evil seeds and they do it for various reasons. For example, it may make you sick, or tired or confused. It may also affect your virility. They could always use it to give you nightmares because your spirit is now polluted. When you drink all sorts of drink in the dream, they plant evil in your life. It is not good to eat and drink in the dream.

When you are having sex in the dream, it is an evil seed that the enemy uses to pollute your spirit. It might increase your appetite for sex irrationally that you feel like having sex with everyone you come across. It could be used to make you sad or exhibit anger. It could be used to disrupt your hormonal levels, thereby preventing you from conceiving.

Furthermore, injections in the dream, wet kissing in the dream, and laying of hands, in the dream are all methods of planting evil seeds. You need to uproot every evil seed planted into your life through food to affect your marriage. Every evil plantation planted sexually into your life to prevent you from conceiving, or evil plantation bearing the fruit of sorrow in your life should be uprooted.

Scatter their network.

> *Proverbs 11:21*
>
> *Though hand join in hand, the wicked shall not be unpunished: but the seed of the righteous shall be delivered.*

The witchcraft powers work hand in hand and have a network. They usually have marks placed upon people, that even when you travel out of your country, there's someone to monitor and tackle you, because you carry their mark. This is why some people experience the same problem, everywhere they go.

If they are after you in Africa, if you do not pray well, there's nowhere you travel to in Europe that you would be free from their network. There's every need to break their network with prayers. For example, you pray that every witchcraft network that is against me in the waters, receive the judgement of God in the name of Jesus. Evil conspiracy against my progress, Scatter by fire in the name of Jesus Christ.

Prayers Against Marine Witchcraft.

Marine witchcraft is one of the most terrible departments of witches and wizards. People possessed by marine witchcraft are usually lured into it by friends, through food as children, or inherit it from their parents. They have held many men captive through sex and ripped them of their virtues. People possessed by marine witchcraft are usually very crafty, deceptive, slippery and stubborn.

One very common feature is that they have spirit spouses which makes then to be sexually reckless. All kinds of sexual perversion are seen in this group, and divorce and alcoholism are the order of the day. All the coastal cities and riverine cities around the world have the same characteristics. Evangelism is a tug of war in places like this. There are some places too that are not coastal cities, but historically the ancestors were devotees of the marine idols and deities. I once had a counselee whose two daughters had good jobs, of marriageable age and wiling to marry, but their relationships always got broken as they prepared for marriage, and for several years were unmarried. The spirit husband and wife problem always frustrates their lives. A lady may get pregnant, but spirit husband will come and sleep with then in the dream, with spontaneous abortion.

I had a man who was from a marine witchcraft foundation. Anytime he applied for a job and was given an interview letter, spirit wife will come and have sex with him. The next day, he must commit an error that will make him to be rejected at the interview. He attended several interviews with the same result. Sometimes, spirit husband will practically appear to a suitor and warn them, and the groom reverses his decision and will not continue with the marriage. The spirit spouses are usually the ones commonly bringing problems to the victims, followed by the mermaid spirits. The mermaids are the mothers in the marine world and have strong control over the affairs in the marine world. They marry the victims off and supervise the marriage to demonic spirits. Many people from marine backgrounds marry and remain childless for up to 18 years or more. The secret is love between couples, regardless of family pressure in some traditions. The testimony is usually a huge one after the wait. Many have twins or triplets after the long wait. Hallelujah!

Prayer and fasting, with intentional attention to breaking of covenants with the spirit spouse and mermaid is key. They will always manifest, shaking their heads in disagreement each time you address their covenants. They make their victims to go through a lot of problems during deliverance as they violently throw them around the deliverance hall. Don't give then a hearing during deliverance, else all they will tell you are lies. However, as a deliverance minister, and as a deliverance candidate, pray for revelation, and use the key of revelation. I have seen a lady that they harassed that she will never have a baby, carrying a baby about a year after her deliverance. I was so over joyed. I have seen people that they caged their jobs having a fantastic job.

Destroy witchcraft in your foundation.

Many people have witchcraft in their foundation due to occultic practices, or simply inherited witchcraft in the blood. Our parents may have entered into witchcraft covenants unconsciously too, and these witchcraft seeds have existed for centuries. Idolatry is another way through which our parents acquired witchcraft and it has come to stay with us.

Lamentations 5:7

Our fathers have sinned, and are not; and we have borne their iniquities.

Praying against foundational witchcraft covenant, and foundational curses, foundational evil dedication, foundational witchcraft serpents, foundational witchcraft birds, foundational evil seed, and foundational evil patterns are all ways of praying against foundational witchcraft.

Destroy poverty.

Poverty is one of the most terrible weapons that witchcraft powers use against their victims, once you can play into their hands. They kill you before you are dead. Once you begin to dream about wearing rags, seeing snails in your dreams, going back to your old house you lived as a Bachelor or Spinster, seeing yourself in your Secondary School you attended 20 years ago, receiving coins or torn notes, all these are a few examples of the dreams indicating the spirit of poverty is inside you already and that you have a battle to fight with witchcraft.

In cases like this, one of the most effective prayers is to ask for the mercy of God, break the curse and covenant of poverty. Arrest every spirit of poverty and recover your lost possessions. Promise God never to go back to sin. Then ask God for new revelation to take your career to higher levels. Though you may not believe this, but God can take you higher than what you were before, if you are now more committed, even though it was sin that made you to fall into the hands of witchcraft. God is awesome and most merciful.

Pray against untimely and sudden death.

When you begin to see dead relatives frequently in your dreams, you see coffins in the dream, cemetery in the dream, graveyard in the dream, you have a feeling that you are going to die, you are afraid when you see white cloth, or you are strangely and unusually disturbed when someone dies, or you can perceive odours that smell rotten. They so present these images to you in a disturbing manner. At this stage, the flesh eaters and blood suckers may have set in and eaten an organ of the body.

At this stage, pray against coffin spirits, break the covenant of death, break the curse of untimely and sudden death, command the power of resurrection to fall upon you, or break the yoke of untimely death, as well as setting spiritual vultures and owls assigned against you on fire.

Pray for your healing.

When witchcraft attacks a person with sickness through food, sex, or by the activities of blood suckers and flesh eaters, you tend to fall sick frequently, even though the doctors cannot arrive at a definitive diagnosis. Then you pray against the personality of flesh eaters and blood suckers, and their covenants. Pray to destroy every seed of infirmity in your life.

Prayers of healing requires audacity and faith. To be able to exercise faith, you need to ignore every symptom of infirmity as if they are not there, even when you can feel them. Every thought and imagination of infirmity has to leave.

> *2 Corinthians 10:5*
>
> *Casting down imaginations, and every high thing that exalteth itself against the knowledge of God, and bringing into captivity every thought to the obedience of Christ;*

Rather you adopt Philippians 4:8:

> *Philippians 4:8*

Finally, brethren, whatsoever things are true, whatsoever things are honest, whatsoever things are just, whatsoever things are pure, whatsoever things are lovely, whatsoever things are of good report; if there be any virtue, and if there be any praise, think on these things.

The only thing that can be true, honest, just, pure, lovely and of good report is the word of God. Then you think on these, confess the word, and put them into action. Holiness and righteousness will give you an incorruptible body. The next thing is to add works to faith. When you attend a healing service or go for deliverance and the Pastor says arise and walk, and you are in a wheelchair, then you arise and walk. The power of God is always available to do the unthinkable. Once you have knocked the door with your prayer, have faith that him who has promised is able to perform. Just keep believing because he answers prayers.

During Deliverance when the Holy Ghost baptism is going on, the Holy Spirit dies many miraculous works. I will not forget to mention the importance of faith objects. The anointing with oil, and use of holy water in the Pentecostal and Catholic beliefs. As a Catholic, the Miraculous medal and other faith items do work a lot of miracles if you put them on in faith. The same thing is true when you use a mantle.

Prayers of forgiveness and power over sin:

1. Father, forgive me for everything I ought to have done but did not do in the name of Jesus
2. O Lord, forgive me for every bad thing that I ought not to have done, but that I did in the name of Jesus Christ.
3. Every evil thought and imagination against my brethren, O Lord forgive me in the name of Jesus.
4. Every evil word that came out of my mouth, Father forgive me in the name of Jesus Christ.
5. O Lord, forgive every sin of my parents and grandparents that are working against my life in the name of Jesus.
6. O Lord, forgive everything that I ever did that caused harm to my fellow human being in the name of Jesus Christ.
7. Power to sin no more, fall upon me in the name of Jesus Christ.
8. Father, forgive every sexual sin that allowed the enemy in my life in the name of Jesus Christ.
9. O Lord my father, deliver me from the bandage of sin in the name of Jesus Christ.
10. O Lord, forgive every sin of my husband/wife that is affecting me negatively in the name of Jesus Christ.
11. Blood of Jesus that speaketh better things than the blood of Abel, wipe away all my sins in the name of Jesus Christ.
12. I confess all my sins (list them one-by-one) and ask for forgiveness in the name of Jesus Christ.
13. Every accusation hanging upon my life in the spirit realm, I deposit such at the foot of the cross in the name of Jesus.
14. Every sin in my life that caused me witchcraft judgement of infirmity, be forgiven in the name of Jesus Crust.
15. By the power in the blood of Jesus, I wash off evert spotted linen in my life in the name of Jesus Christ.
16. O Lord, by your power, separate me from every close associate luring me into sin in the name of Jesus.
17. Mercy of God, rejoice against every judgement of the enemy upon my life as a result of my sins.
18. O Lord, wake me up from every spiritual slumber in the name of Jesus Christ.
19. Every presumptuous sin in my life, be exposed and lose your power in the name of Jesus Christ.

20. Begin to think about anything that is in your possession that is not yours now, and say, Father, as I return this thing, forgive me.
21. Any person you are having grudges against, begin to ask them for forgiveness now.
22. O Lord, let your grace abound much more than any sin in my life in the name of Jesus Christ.
23. I recover now, every good thing in my life that I have lost to witches and wizard through sin.
24. Every financial sin like not paying my tithes and giving to the poor, father forgive me in the name of Jesus Christ.
25. Power not to go back to sin, fall upon me now in the name of Jesus Christ.
26. In any way that I have opened my eyes to evil sight, opened my ears to evil words, or participated in evil, O Lord forgive me in Jesus mighty name.
27. I break loose from the power of sin in the ne of Jesus Christ.
28. Any mind controlling demon, invading my thoughts and making me to commit sin, be arrested and be cast out in the name of Jesus Christ.
29. Father Lord, break me, melt me, and remould me for your use in the name of Jesus Christ.
30. I purge my life of every sin making me unworthy of God's love and kindness in the name of Jesus Christ.
31. Holy Spirit, make me dead to sin in the name of Jesus Christ
32. I refuse to be a slave to sin, I claim dominion over every stubborn sin in the name of Jesus Christ.
33. O Lord, give me the strength, determination, and will power to say no to sin and accept to follow you all the days of my life in the name of Jesus Christ.
34. Every man or woman that I have offended, that has vowed not to show me mercy and forgiveness, the mercy of God shall be far from them in the name of Jesus Christ.
35. Mercy of the most high God, vindicate me from every terrible accusation in the name of Jesus Christ.
36. Witchcraft finger of accusation pointed against my life, wuthering by the power in the blood of Jesus Christ.
37. Blood of Jesus Christ, redeem me from every self-acquired curse as a result of my sins in the name of Jesus Christ.
38. O Lord my father, forgive me, and make a way for me where there seems to be no way in the name of Jesus Christ.
39. Father, forgive my sins and restore all that I have lost to witchcraft in the name of Jesus Christ.
40. O Lord, forgive me every sin and release me from the bondage of every witchcraft sponsored sin in my life in the name of Jesus Christ.

Prayers on covenant breaking:

1. I break every sexual covenant with any witchcraft agent in the name of Jesus Christ.
2. Every sexual covenant with any witchcraft agent that has caged my life, break and release me now in the name of Jesus Christ.
3. Evil blood covenant with witchcraft powers caging my destiny, break and release me in the name of Jesus Christ.
4. Witchcraft covenant manifesting on my marriage, break in the name of Jesus Christ.
5. Every foundational witchcraft blood crying against my life, be silenced by the power in the blood of Jesus Christ
6. Covenant with foundational idol, break and release me in the name of Jesus Christ.

7. I remove my name from the list of evil witchcraft covenant in the name of Jesus Christ.
8. Any certificate of linking me with evil covenant, break and release me in the name of Jesus Christ.
9. Covenant with spirit husband/wife break and release me in the name of Jesus Christ.
10. Covenant with spirit children, preventing my conception and assigned against my safe delivery, break by the power in the blood of Jesus Christ.
11. Every evil agreement with the water idol of my father's town, break and release me in the name of Jesus Christ.
12. Every evil agreement with any idol of my mother's town, break and release me in the name of Jesus Christ.
13. Every witchcraft covenant in my blood, break and release me now in the name of Jesus Christ.
14. Every unconscious evil covenant that I entered into through food, break and release me now in the name of Jesus Christ.
15. Forest covenant that I entered into by virtue of Visitation in ignorance, break and release me now on the name of Jesus Christ.
16. Covenant with motor accident, assigned to claim my life, I break you by the power in the blood of Jesus Christ.
17. I receive deliverance from the covenant with blood suckers and flesh eaters and I claim my healing in the name of Jesus Christ.
18. Evil covenant with the graveyard, break and release me in the name of Jesus Christ.
19. Evil covenant with Iroko, Mahogany, Obeche trees, break and release me now in the name of Jesus Christ.
20. Untimely death, I break every evil covenant with you in the name of Jesus Christ.
21. Covenant of marital failure and divorce, working g against my marriage, break in the name of Jesus Christ.
22. Evil covenant that I entered into through satanic mantle, clothing or garment, break in the name of Jesus Christ.
23. I reverse every evil covenant of the wicked transferring my riches to an evil location in the name of Jesus Christ.
24. Covenant with destiny swallowers, my life is not your candidate, break and release me now in the name of Jesus Christ.
25. Covenant with the Queen of the Coast, break and release me in the name of Jesus Christ.
26. Evil agreement with night caterers, break and release my destiny in the name of Jesus Christ.
27. Familiar spirit agreement in the lives of my children, I break you by the power in the blood of Jesus Christ.
28. Covenant sponsoring the spirit of almost there and failure at the edge of breakthrough in my life, break and release me in the name of Jesus Christ.
29. Covenant of destruction with any witchcraft spirit, break and release me now in the name of Jesus Christ.
30. Covenant with the spirit of divination giving the enemies access to my secrets, break and release me in the name of Jesus Christ.
31. Evil covenant that I entered into unconsciously immediately I landed in the hands of satanic Midwife, break and release me in the name of Jesus Christ.
32. Evil covenant that I entered into through the water that I drank and concoctions I was fed with from evil nannies, break and release me in the name of Jesus Christ.
33. Evil gifts that I was given at birth that has followed me with evil covenant till today, I break that covenant in the blood of Jesus Christ.

34. Evil unconscious agreement that I entered into on the day of my wedding consciously and unconsciously, I break your covenant and power in the name of Jesus Christ.
35. Every inherited evil covenant that entered my life through any inherited gift item, or property, I break your power in the name of Jesus Christ.
36. Satanic covenant sponsoring evil pattern in my father's house or mother's house, break in the name of Jesus Christ.
37. Covenant with the spirit of the snail through any snail concoctions I ate as a child, break in the name of Jesus Christ.
38. Witchcraft covenant that I entered into through evil laying of hands, break by the power in the blood of Jesus Christ.
39. Evil sexual covenant that I entered into through sexual perversion e.g. oral sex, two-some, vibrators etc., break and release me in the ne of Jesus Christ.
40. Covenant with the mediums e.g. star gazers, palmists, crystal ball, etc. Break in the name of Jesus Christ.
41. Covenant with witchcraft bird in my chest or in my tummy, break and release me by fire in the name of Jesus Christ.
42. Covenant with any satanic barber or hairdresser, break and release me in the name of Jesus.
43. Evil covenant that I entered into through ear piercing or tattoo making, break in the name of Jesus Christ.
44. Every evil covenant that I entered into through borrowed clothing or shoes, break in the name of Jesus Christ.
45. Evil covenant with my former school, break and release me in the name of Jesus Christ.
46. Evil covenant with my former house, break and release me in the name of Jesus Christ.
47. Covenant with shame and reproach (if you always see yourself naked in the dream), break and release me in the name of Jesus Christ.
48. Covenant with the burial ground, break and release me in the name of Jesus Christ.
49. Every evil power that wants to manifest evil covenant in my life through the wind, I break your covenant in the name of Jesus Christ.
50. Evil covenant with the cycle of the moon, manifesting consciously or unconsciously against my life, break in the name of Jesus Christ.
51. Demonic covenant waiting to manifest at childbirth in my life, break in the name of Jesus Christ.
52. Evil covenant that wants me to work and not eat the fruit of my labour, break in the name of Jesus Christ.
53. Covenant of bad luck that has vowed to follow me from cradle to grave, break by the power in the blood of Jesus Christ.
54. I cancel every inherited evil covenant of sickness in my family line in the name of Jesus Christ.
55. I destroy every evil inherited covenant of marital failure of my father's house and mothers house in the name of Jesus Christ.
56. Yoke of hardship in my life, break and scatter by the power on the blood of Jesus Christ.
57. Every evil covenant with landlord spirits that says I will never achieve any good thing in my present location, break in the name of Jesus.

58. Any evil covenant that I am labouring under by virtue of the name my city or my street is known and called by, break and release me in the name of Jesus Christ.
59. Covenant with any witchcraft statue or image in my environment, break and release me in the name of Jesus Christ.
60. O Lord my father, if I have been sold unconsciously to witchcraft by virtue of any covenant festival or ritual in my environment, blood of Jesus Christ, redeem me.
61. I single myself out by the power in the blood of Jesus Christ from any collective environmental evil covenant that I have entered into through the purchase of textiles, shoes, jewels etc in the name of Jesus.
62. Any evil word spoken into the materials that have indirectly dragged me into evil covenant, I break your power in the name of Jesus Christ.
63. Evil marriage covenant in my dream (see yourself wedding in the dream), break by the power in the blood of Jesus Christ.
64. Covenanted materials in my place of work that I do use at work, I break that covenant in the name of Jesus.
65. Occupational covenant of my employers, demanding my blood and my life, break and be disgraced by the power in the blood of Jesus Christ.
66. Covent with the spirit of disability or the lame spirit, break and release me in the name of Jesus Christ.
67. Conscious and unconscious witchcraft covenant with satanic in-laws, break by the power in the blood of Jesus Christ.
68. Covenant with destiny diverting witchcraft, break and release me in the name of Jesus Christ
69. Evil polygamous covenant with my step-mother, your time is up, break in the name of Jesus Christ.
70. Covenant with barrenness, break and release me in the name of Jesus Christ.
71. Familiar spirit agreement assigned to take my life at the time of my joy, break by the power in the blood of Jesus Christ.
72. Any evil spirit, monitoring, enforcing and supervising any evil covenant in my life, go blind and be paralysed by the power of the Holy Ghost in the name of Jesus Christ.
73. Evil witchcraft covenant made with my semen/vaginal fluid, be broken by the power in the blood of Jesus Christ.
74. Every problem transferred into my life through saliva covenant, and kissing of witchcraft agent, I break your covenant today by the power in the blood of Jesus Christ.
75. Covenant of error and mistake assigned to bury my star and put me to shame, break in the name of Jesus Christ.
76. Every evil object that has been covenanted against my life appearing in my dreams, catch fire and burn to ashes in Jesus name.
77. Conscious and unconscious familiar spirit in my life, I break your covenant in Jesus Christ.
78. Every evil covenant speaking against my health be broken in the name of Jesus Christ.
79. Covenant of initiation into witchcraft in my life, break in the name of Jesus Christ.
80. Evil covenant assigned to take back to square one, break and release me in the name of Jesus Christ.
81. Covenant of death and hell, inherited from my family line, waiting to manifest in my life, break in the name of Jesus Christ.

82. Covenant of sorrow, in my home town, shall not swallow me or any member of my family.
83. Every evil covenant that I entered as a result of evil utterances, on my part, break and release me in the name of Jesus Christ.
84. Collective evil food covenant, assigned to transfer my fortunes, break by the power in the blood of Jesus Christ.
85. Covenant of environmental vampires assigned against my blood and that of my family members, break in the name of Jesus Christ.
86. Every evil covenant that I have entered in any restaurant, break and release me by the power in the blood of Jesus Christ.
87. Any evil covenant that my children and husband were dragged into, that witches and wizards are using as a ladder to steal from my life, be broken in the name of Jesus
88. Occultic covenant, entered into on my behalf by anybody in my blood line, Scatter like a pack of cards in Jesus name.
89. Any man or woman that has covenanted any vital organ in their body in order to trouble my life, I break your covenant in the name of Jesus Christ.
90. Covenant of slavery, fashioned against my life by any occultist employer in order to be sucking the milk and honey of my life, break in the name of Jesus Christ.
91. Unconscious covenant that I entered into in error and is secretly tormenting my destiny, be exposed and be disgraced in the name of Jesus Christ.
92. Covenant of poverty, and backwardness, sponsored by marine spirits in my life, break asunder in the name of Jesus Christ.
93. Any unconscious evil covenant with the sun, moon and stars, that says I will not have rest in my life, break in the name of Jesus Christ.
94. Any evil name glorifying idols, that is strengthening idol covenants in my life, I break your power in the name of Jesus Christ (change the name)
95. Familiar spirit covenant making me to see any dead relative, in my dreams, break and release me in the name of Jesus.
96. Evil covenants empowering monitoring demons in my life, break by the power in the blood of Jesus Christ.
97. Witchcraft covenant of manipulations fashioned against my dreams and visions and making me to see what is non-existent, break in the name of Jesus Christ.
98. I reverse every covenant of sickness and untimely death fashioned against me or any member of my family in the name of Jesus Christ.
99. Covenant traps in my environment (those things that you use, sit upon, restaurants that could make you to enter a covenant unknowingly), be exposed and be disgraced in the name of Jesus.
100. I shall share testimony and glorify God as a result of these prayers in the mighty name of Jesus Christ.
101. Covenant of destruction fashioned against my marriage, break in the name of Jesus Christ.

Prayers to shatter iron-like witchcraft curses:

1. Curse of poverty issued against my life by familiar spirits, break in the name of Jesus Christ.
2. Every curse issued against my destiny by envious witchcraft, break by the power in the blood of Jesus Christ.
3. Curse of you shall not get there fashioned against me by envious witchcraft, break in the name of Jesus Christ.
4. Negative decree from the waters, against my peace, joy and comfort, be broken in the name of Jesus Christ.
5. Father Lord, forgive me every sin strengthening curses in my life in the name of Jesus Christ.
6. Foundational witchcraft Curse over my life, break in the name of Jesus Christ.
7. Curse of collective death fashioned against my life and family, break in the name of Jesus Christ.
8. Curse of insanity issued against my life, break and release me in the name of Jesus Christ.
9. I break and release myself from the yoke of every self-imposed Curse in the name of Jesus Christ.
10. Every curse fashioned against my helpers, break and release my helpers in the name of Jesus Christ.
11. Familiar spirit curse of untimely death, fashioned against my life, break in the name of Jesus Christ.
12. Iron-like curses in the foundation of my house where I live now, be broken in the mighty name of Jesus Christ.
13. By the power in the blood of Jesus Christ, I redeem myself from every parental curse.
14. Every curse issued against my life by any witchcraft in-law, backfire in the name of Jesus Christ.
15. Witchcraft curses in the foundation of my place of work, break by the power in the blood of Jesus Christ.
16. Curse of "you shall not find helpers" targeted against my destiny, break in the name of Jesus Christ.
17. O Lord, deliver me from any curse attacking my life as a result of blood guiltiness (e.g. abortion, drinking blood, oath with blood etc.) in the name of Jesus Christ.
18. Curse of foundational idols against my life, break in the name of Jesus Christ.
19. Every curse issued against my life at the burial ground in the day or in the night, backfire in the name of Jesus Christ.
20. Every acidic curse issued against my life by the Riverside, break by the power in the blood of Jesus Christ.
21. Every curse in my imagination and thinking that wants to manifest in my life, break in the name of Jesus Christ.
22. Every cursed food that I ate from the enemy that is affecting my life, break in the name of Jesus Christ.
23. Every cursed money that I received from the hands of the enemy, I break the power of that curse in the name of Jesus Christ.
24. Any curse working against my life as a result of a broken agreement, Lord, redeem me from such a curse.
25. I walk out of every environmental curse by the power in the blood of Jesus.
26. Curse of error and mistake fashioned against my marriage, break in the name of Jesus Christ.
27. Curse of error and mistake, fashioned against my career, break in the name of Jesus Christ.
28. Evil altars, cursing my destiny, receive destruction by fire in the name of Jesus Christ.
29. Any witchcraft anointed mouth cursing my destiny, wither in the name of Jesus Christ.
30. With the shield of faith, I arrest and send back the curse of untimely death to their senders in the mighty name of Jesus Christ.
31. Every curse attached to my name, lose your power in the mighty name of Jesus Christ (Change idol glorifying names).
32. I break the powers of any cursed item in my life in the name of Jesus Christ.

33. Every Jonah, in the boat of my destiny, bringing misfortune upon my life, be thrown into the sea, and let my problems seize in the name of Jesus Christ.
34. Every Achan in my family, be exposed and be disgraced in the name of Jesus Christ.
35. Every power supervising the curse of poverty on my life, I bind you in the mighty name of Jesus Christ.
36. Any possessed pet animal in my life assigned to cause destruction to my destiny, receive deliverance in the name of Jesus Christ.
37. Cursed mantle, Cursed garment (for many reasons) in my wardrobe, I break your power over my life in the name of Jesus Christ.
38. Anything, any power, any man, bringing curses upon my life, blood of Jesus, fire of the Holy Ghost, separate us in the name of Jesus Christ.
39. O Lord, eject me from every cursed career that is against your will for my life in the name of Jesus Christ.
40. Curse of environmental disaster and tragedy, fashioned against my location, break in the name of Jesus Christ.
41. Every flying curse at the road junction, you shall not locate me in the name of Jesus Christ.
42. Any witchcraft curse programmed into any material that I bought from the market, be de-programmed in the name of Jesus Christ.
43. Any Cursed gift given to me in my first 8 days in life, break in the name of Jesus Christ.
44. Every blood ritual done by my parents at the time I was born that has brought a curse upon my life, I break your power in the name of Jesus Christ.
45. Every curse programmed into the first soap I used to bath after I was born, break in the name of Jesus Christ.
46. Every curse that entered my life as I was born into the hands of evil Midwife, break in the name of Jesus Christ.
47. Wicked elders of my father's house, cursing my destiny, carry your evil load in the name of Jesus Christ.
48. Any occultist cursing my life naked, run mad in the name of Jesus Christ.
49. Every Haman, assigned against my Mordecai, carry you evil load in the name of Jesus Christ.
50. Any Prince of Persia, withstanding my prayers, receive disgrace in the name of Jesus Christ.
51. Inherited curse of poverty, break and release me in the name of Jesus Christ.
52. Inherited curse of infirmity, high blood pressure and diabetes, break and release me in the name of Jesus Christ.
53. Inherited curse of Cancer and genetic anomaly, break and release me in the name of Jesus Christ.
54. Every internal voice within me cursing my destiny, lose your hold in the name of Jesus Christ.
55. Curses in my life manifesting periodically, break in the name of Jesus Christ.
56. Every cursed tree, animal or person harbouring bewitchment for my life, I break your power in the name of Jesus Christ.
57. Cursed feet in my life, walk out by fire in the name of Jesus Christ.
58. Every curse fashioned against my growth and expansion in life, break and release me in the name of Jesus Christ.
59. Every curse of disobedience to God's word, wherever I have cheated the poor and the weak, Lord have mercy and forgive me in the name of Jesus Christ.
60. Every embargo-like curse placed upon my destiny, break in the name of Jesus Christ.
61. Generational curse of slavery in my family line, break by the power in the blood of Jesus Christ.

62. Curse of suicide, suicidal thoughts and self-harm, fashioned against my life, you shall not prosper in the mighty name of Jesus Christ.
63. Every curse that has released devourer into my finances, be broken by the power on the blood of Jesus Christ.
64. O Lord, wherever I have robbed you, (Haggai 1&2; Malachi 3:8-9) which made demons of poverty to enter into my life, father forgive me and have mercy in the name of Jesus Christ.
65. Mercy of God, begin to rejoice against every witchcraft judgemental curse in my life on the name of Jesus Christ.
66. Satanic curses of familiar spirits assigned to grind my career to a halt, be broken in the name of Jesus Christ.
67. Curse of confusion, and instability issued by marine spirits against my life, backfire in the name of Jesus.
68. Curse of everyday strange illnesses without a diagnosis affecting my life, break by the power in the blood of Jesus.
69. O Lord, you bore my griefs and carried my sorrows, I refuse to suffer the consequences of sin. Power of any curse attacking my destiny, break, break, break in the name of Jesus Christ.
70. In any way that I have broken my marital vow secretly with the strange man or woman, father forgive me and have mercy in the name of Jesus Christ.
71. Every curse, issued against me in any witchcraft cauldron as a result of my sexual recklessness, be broken by the power in the blood of Jesus Christ.
72. Every curse issued against life by an anointed man of God, singly or collectively, blood of Jesus, wash it away now.
73. All terrible and iron-like curses operating against my success on life, break by the power in the blood of Jesus Christ.
74. Curses working against my life as a result of rebellion and evil deeds against a servant of God, O God forgive me and have mercy in the name of Jesus Christ.
75. Every curse working against me as a result of my sin of abortion, murder, and shedding of innocent blood, be broken by the power in the blood of Jesus Christ.
76. Every curse of infirmity working against my life as a result of unforgiveness to my neighbour, be broken by the power in the blood of Jesus Christ.
77. Curse of family disaster and tragedy, break and release my family in the mighty ne of Jesus Christ.
78. Every curse of poor harvest working against my efforts, break by the power in the blood of Jesus Christ.
79. Every curse of desolation (you are alone, no helper, no friend) issued against my life by witches and wizards, break in the name of Jesus Christ. (desolation and loneliness can lead to sickness, insanity, poor quality of life and sudden death).
80. Every cursed object allowing failure to prosper in my life, catch the fire of the Holy Ghost and be destroyed in the name of Jesus Christ.
81. Every curse of except, issued by witches (if they helped you before, they could go naked and issue the curse of except) against my prosperity, backfire in the name of Jesus Christ.
82. Any curse of except, issued against my life by any woman, living or dead, holding her private part break by the power in the blood of Jesus Christ.
83. Any curse working against my life as a result of my participation in any fetish festival or ritual, break by the power in the blood of Jesus Christ.

84. In any ways that I have made the word of God of no effect through my culture and tradition, O God, forgive me in the name of Jesus Christ.
85. Evil pictures and images of serpents and other satanic animals bringing curses upon my life lose you power in the name of Jesus Christ (pull them down and destroy them).
86. Every curse upon my life as a result of any material dedicated to idols, that I bought and used (e.g. hair attachment), break by the power in the blood of Jesus Christ.
87. Every curse against my life as a result of any statue or shrine in my locality, break by the power in the blood of Jesus Christ.
88. Every curse working against my life as a result of my use of any second-hand material (do you know if it was stolen?), break by the power in the blood of Jesus Christ.
89. Every curse that entered my life through evil laying of hands, break by fire in the name of Jesus Christ.
90. Every curse that entered into my life through any witchcraft incision on my body, break by the power in the blood of Jesus Christ.
91. Curses issued against me by any witch in the dream, be broken by the power in the blood of Jesus Christ.
92. I shall not beg before I eat in the name of Jesus Christ.
93. I refuse to cooperate with the curse of shame and reproach in my life in the mighty name of Jesus Christ.
94. Occupational curses e.g. (divorce, untimely death) disaster and tragedy, my life is not your candidate, break and release me in the name of Jesus Christ.
95. Unspoken and imagined curses, telepathic curses issued against me by witchcraft, break by the power in the blood of Jesus Christ.
96. I refuse to click on the abominable, and reject to be caged by online courses in the name of Jesus Christ.
97. I refuse to be caged by the spirit of the end times in the name of Jesus Christ.
98. Curses assigned to make me a vagabond, break in the name of Jesus Christ.
99. Curses of non-achievement, break and release me in the name of Jesus Christ.
100. Every cursed organ in my body by witchcraft powers, receive deliverance in the name of Jesus Christ.

Prayers for destruction of Witchcraft Altars:

1. I destroy evert marine witchcraft altar, raised against my life in the name of Jesus Christ.
2. Every strongman, upon any evil altar sitting on my blessings, thunder fire of God, unsit them in the name of Jesus Christ.
3. Occultic altars, fashioned against my wellbeing, be destroyed by fire in the name of Jesus Christ.
4. My blessings, my virtues caged upon any evil altar, receive deliverance in the name of Jesus Christ.
5. Evil altar demanding for my blood or that of my children, be destroyed by fire in the name of Jesus Christ.
6. Any material or photograph belonging to me or any member of my family, be withdrawn by fire in the name of Jesus Christ.
7. Evil decision upon any evil covenant against my life, be utterly cancelled in the name of Jesus Christ.

8. Altars of darkness, in my place of birth, release my blessings in the mighty name of Jesus Christ.
9. Any evil bird, drawing power from any evil altar against my destiny, receive disgrace in the name of Jesus Christ.
10. Environmental evil altar, swallowing my virtues, vomit then by fire in the name of Jesus Christ.
11. Foundational witchcraft altar, holding my life captive, release me now in the name of Jesus Christ.
12. Any graven image that is representing me on any evil altar, be destroyed by the power of the Holy Ghost in the name of Jesus Christ.
13. Altars of the devourer in my environment, swallowing my finances, vomit if by fire in the name of Jesus Christ.
14. Holy Ghost, deliver me from every altar of sickness that I have been tied in the name of Jesus Christ.
15. Every evil vampire altar sucking my blood, I cut you off in the name of Jesus Christ.
16. Altars located in the moon or stars that are being consulted against my life, I pull you down in the name of Jesus Christ.
17. Altars of witchcraft birds, raised to destroy my portion, receive destruction in the name of Jesus Christ.
18. Every satanic altar, swallowing my money, be destroyed in the name of Jesus Christ.
19. Evil altars interacting on my case, receive the judgement of God by fire in the name of Jesus Christ.
20. Witchcraft altar of death and hell assigned to judge my life for destruction, be heavily destroyed in the name of Jesus Christ.
21. Every evil human altar assigned against me to run me dry, catch fire and be destroyed in the name of Jesus Christ.
22. Every evil personality on an evil altar, saying no to my greatness in life, be arrested and be bound for ever in the name of Jesus Christ.
23. My money on an evil altar, receive deliverance in the name of Jesus Christ.
24. My glory, buried on an evil altar, resurrect by fire in the name of Jesus Christ.
25. Evil altar, asking for my blood or the blood of my spouse and children, be dismantled by fire in the mighty name of Jesus Christ.
26. Every evil tree in my environment harbouring evil altar against my peace and progress, be destroyed by the thunder and fire of God.
27. Evil altar, speaking impossibility into my life, lose your power, by the power in the blood of Jesus Christ.
28. Serpentine altar in my locality, swallowing good things in my life, be destroyed in the name of Jesus Christ.
29. Every evil pot, on any evil altar, cooking my destiny, break and scatter in the name of Jesus Christ.
30. Any key to my breakthrough, captured by any evil altar, be released by fire in the name of Jesus Christ.
31. Marine altars, caging my blessings, release them by fire in the name of Jesus Christ.
32. Evil altars in my home town, demanding my worship, be destroyed by fire in the name of Jesus Christ.
33. Evil powers, summoning me for judgement upon any evil altar, Scatter unto desolation in the mighty name of Jesus Christ.
34. Every evil dream attack, sponsored by any witchcraft altar against my life and my family, backfire in the mighty name of Jesus Christ.
35. Any witchcraft image on any witchcraft altar, representing me, be destroyed by fire in the name of Jesus Christ.
36. I break and release myself from the bondage of evil altars in the mighty name of Jesus Christ.

37. Unconscious covenant tying me down to an evil altar, break and release me in the mighty name of Jesus Christ.
38. My marriage certificate, receive deliverance from every evil altar in the name of Jesus Christ.
39. My testimony, that is caged upon any evil altar, receive deliverance and locate me now in the name of Jesus Christ.
40. Any foundational witchcraft personality on an evil altar, using my glory to prosper, release me and be put to shame bin the mighty name of Jesus Christ.
41. Every evil altar, sponsoring affliction and poverty in my life, be destroyed by fire in the mighty name of Jesus Christ.
42. Weapons of satanic warfare, on any evil altar, fashioned against me and my family shall not prosper in the name of Jesus Christ.
43. Satanic remote control of marine witchcraft, controlling my life from any evil altar, be destroyed by fire in the mighty name of Jesus Christ.
44. Evil mirror on any evil altar assigned to monitor my life, break and shatter to pieces in the mighty name of Jesus Christ.
45. Evil altar, holding my life captive, demanding sacrifice from me, Scatter unto desolation by fire in the name of Jesus Christ.
46. Altars of satanic caterers, in my environment, I dismantle you on the mighty name of Jesus Christ.
47. Evil altars, stealing from my children at school, be exposed and be disgraced in the name of Jesus Christ.
48. Every evil Priest, ministering on an evil altar, in order to make my life miserable, be paralysed in the name of Jesus Christ.
49. By the power of resurrection of our Lord and saviour Jesus Christ, I withdraw my organ from the altar of witches and wizards in the name of Jesus Christ.
50. Every occultist altar in any burial ground, attacking my destiny or the destiny of any member of my family, be destroyed by fire in the name of Jesus Christ.

Prayers Against Witchcraft Transportation Systems:

1. Every appear and disappear power of witchcraft that is targeted against my life, fail woefully in the name of Jesus Christ.
2. Every Transportation strategy of the enemies of my life, be turned to foolishness in the mighty name of Jesus Christ.
3. Every power engaging in incantations in order to move and harm me, I suspend your memory in the mighty name of Jesus Christ.
4. Let the sun, moon, and stars refuse to cooperate with every transportation strategy of witchcraft against me in the name of Jesus Christ.
5. Every power appearing and disappearing to harm me or any member of my family, be hanged on a tree in the name of Jesus Christ.

6. Any man or woman, projecting into an animal, in order to harm me, hang forever in that animal and be destroyed in the name of Jesus Christ.
7. Any man or woman, embarking upon witchcraft sleep in order to destroy me or any member of my family, you shall not wake up in the name of Jesus Christ.
8. Every evil bird that witchcraft powers are hiding inside spiritually in order to attack my soul, receive the fire of the Holy Ghost in the name of Jesus Christ.
9. Every threat and dreadful communication by witchcraft transported into my life to intimidate me, be frustrated in the name of Jesus Christ.
10. Every spirit of fear in me, cooperating with the threats of witchcraft, be arrested in the name of Jesus Christ.
11. Any evil object, anytime, anywhere that witches and wizards are using to transport themselves in order to harm me, refuse to cooperate with witches and wizards in the name of Jesus Christ.
12. Every blood oath and covenant, empowering witches and wizard to transport themselves into my life, fail woefully in the mighty name of Jesus Christ.
13. Arrow of error, locate overwhelm any witchcraft power on assignment against my destiny in the name of Jesus Christ.
14. Let the air water and elements, work against every animal agent, transporting witches and wizards against my life in the name of Jesus Christ.
15. Let the wind refuse to cooperate with every witchcraft transportation system fashioned against my life in the name of Jesus Christ.
16. Holy Ghost, mount a wall of fire, around me, and let every witchcraft power on assignment against me meet their Waterloo in Jesus Christ mighty name.
17. Witchcraft powers transporting themselves against my life, tender fire of God, locate them for destruction in the name of Jesus Christ.
18. Evil airport of witchcraft powers against my life, catch fire and be rendered desolate in the name of Jesus Christ.
19. I withdraw the power and strength of marine witchcraft powers targeting my destiny in the name of Jesus Christ.
20. Every power, turning into a fish, in order to attack me in my dreams, be microwaved by the power of the Holy Ghost, in the name of Jesus Christ.
21. Transportation power of mermaid spirits, attacking my life, fail woefully in the name of Jesus Christ.
22. I block the route of every witchcraft power flying against me by the power in the blood of Jesus Christ.
23. Every witchcraft landing facility, witchcraft altars in my house, be destroyed by fire in the name of Jesus Christ.
24. Every man or woman, flying in space in order to harm me, be located by the fire of God, crash-land and be disgraced in the name of Jesus Christ.
25. Witchcraft owl with the message of sudden death against my life, go back to your sender in the name of Jesus Christ.
26. I pull down every signpost useful to the enemy in my life in the name of Jesus Christ.
27. Any evil witchcraft driver, on assignment against my life, collide with the rock of ages in the name of Jesus Christ.

28. O Lord my father, disappoint every transportation device of witchcraft fashioned against my life in the name of Jesus Christ.
29. Every evil boat in the dream, targeted against my life, to convey me to the coast of destruction, be destroyed in the mighty name of Jesus Christ.
30. Power of satanic summons, assigned to carry me to coven meeting, break by fire in the name of Jesus Christ.
31. Every evil done to me through witchcraft transportation in the womb of my mother, be undone in the name of Jesus Christ.
32. Witchcraft transportation agreement against my life that I entered into unconsciously, be cancelled by the power in the blood of Jesus Christ.
33. Anything in my tummy, that I ate on witchcraft dining table, that is giving witches right of passage in my life, catch fire and lose your power in the name of Jesus Christ.
34. By the power in the blood of Jesus, I change every genetic password, allowing witchcraft powers into my life in the name of Jesus Christ.
35. Transportation system of spiritual robbers on assignment against my life, fail woefully in the name of Jesus Christ.
36. Every witchcraft vehicle, assigned to convey satanic cargo into my dream life, receive destruction in the mighty name of Jesus Christ.
37. Transportation system of night caterers assigned against my life, catch fire in the name of Jesus Christ.
38. Heavenly traffic angels, arrest every witch or wizard on assignment against my life from the Kingdom of darkness.

Communication.

1. Every blood covenant that the enemy is using as a Communication Facility against my life, be broken by the power in the blood of Jesus Christ.
2. Every published or electronic communication empowering my enemies, be destroyed by the fire of the Holy Ghost in the name of Jesus Christ.
3. Witchcraft animal, monitoring and reporting me to the Kingdom of darkness, die suddenly in the name of Jesus Christ.
4. Any sign on my face, lines on my palm, giving the enemy valuable clue with regards to my life, be rendered inaccessible in the name of Jesus Christ.
5. Witchcraft Communication hub in my house, be destroyed by the thunder fire of God in the name of Jesus Christ.
6. Strangers of darkness programmed into my family, reporting me to witchcraft coven, receive blindness in the name of Jesus Christ.
7. Anything in my life, acting as a microchip for the enemy to access my location and destiny, be deprogrammed in the name of Jesus Christ.

8. Agents of darkness, monitoring the progress of my work and reporting me to the kingdom of darkness, be blind and be paralysed in the name of Jesus Christ.
9. Communication network of darkness over my life, scatter by fire in the name of Jesus Christ.
10. Every power of the diviner, established against my life, crumble in the name of Jesus Christ.
11. Every spirit of the loose tongue in my life, making me to expose myself to the enemy, I bind you in the name of Jesus Christ.
12. O Lord my father, confuse every evil observer, monitoring my life for evil in the name of Jesus Christ.
13. Communication technology of witchcraft against my life, be frustrated in the name of Jesus Christ.
14. I block every Communication Channel open to the enemy in my life in the name of Jesus Christ.
15. Witchcraft Communication signal against my life, be cut off in the name of Jesus Christ.
16. Every animal, acting as witchcraft satellite against my life, be roasted by fire in the name of Jesus Christ.
17. I erase every written witchcraft Communication against my destiny in the name of Jesus Christ.
18. Witchcraft radar in my birthplace, be destroyed by fire in the name of Jesus Christ.
19. You my life, reject every evil Communication, command, and summons in the dream in the name of Jesus Christ.
20. Messenger of death assigned against my life, go back to your sender in the name of Jesus Christ.
21. Every witchcraft sound and audio engineer, monitoring the affairs and signals of my life, die in the name of Jesus Christ.
22. O Lord send terrifying noise to the camp of my stubborn enemies in the name of Jesus Christ.

CHAPTER TWENTY-THREE

COVENANTS

What is a covenant?

A covenant is an agreement between two or more people defining the terms and conditions of their relationship.

A covenant could be good, in the sense that it is from God and blesses the lives of men and women. There could also be an "evil covenant" in the sense that it is from the devil, and it is usually unto death, destruction, shame and poverty.

Witchcraft covenants address a lot of issues about the activities of witchcraft and what each witch can do. Witches so much have regards for their covenants that they punish errant members for breaches by making them to fall sick, experience poverty or kill them. Evil covenants are regarded by dark powers to be permanent, but we thank God for sending Jesus Christ through which we can cancel evil covenants through the power in the blood of Jesus Christ.

What are the types of witchcraft covenant we have?

1. <u>Covenant of satanic initiation.</u> This admits you to be a member of the group. With the covenant of satanic initiation, you have some powers and can link up through this covenant with then and have meetings wherever you are, on the surface of the earth. This covenant is usually a blood covenant whereby every member is linked up with the blood of the new member. Other methods could be employed for example, food, drink or sex. Biscuits and sweets are the most common for children, and they are being recruited massively on daily basis. Other types of covenants follow to complement this covenant.

2. <u>Covenant with the spirit of infirmity.</u> Witches receive spiritual power or other things that they need by paying dearly for it. One of those ways is by paying with their health. Some may receive power to be more vile and wicked, but they may need to donate an organ in their body in order to achieve this. If they donate their kidney, they have kidney disease going forward. If they donate their womb, then they become barren going forwards. Most times they confess that they have donated an organ to acquire wealth. This is the process in some confraternities. The devil has no free gift!

3. <u>Another one is the covenant with death and hell.</u> There are many witches and wizards that make covenant with death, and hell in exchange for wicked spiritual powers. They covenant themselves to die on the day they are going to have their first baby, or perhaps their fourth baby. All these happens in dreams, and they know it and must not disclose it to anyone. On a certain morning, I went for a program after I just gave my life to Christ. The man of God announced from the pulpit that some of you here are pregnant, and you have made a covenant to die on

the day of your delivery, and that if you are here, come out for prayers, so that you wouldn't die. It would amaze you that scores of women came out for prayers. The same thing occurred also in yet another church. The church was so large, and sat on a space of land of 1 Km by 1 km. The man of God said that people who made any form of covenant with death should come out. They massively came out too. We used to have a neighbour, who died during child birth many years back. She made a covenant with death and hell. She had revealed to her husband in parables, but he didn't understand until this woman died, and it dawned on him that she was telling him about his impending death. Many people you see moving about have already made a covenant with death and they cannot say it to anybody, else they will kill them. I want you to know that, if you are like that, if you reveal it, you would struggle and fight, but live at the end, and if you don't reveal it, you die witchcraft death. So why don't you reveal it and damn the consequences. Familiar spirit possessed people do this often making a covenant with death.

4. *Evil marriage covenant.* When a person has a spirit spouse, naturally they won't be able to have an earthly marriage in order not to offend the spiritual husband. What will now happen is that they allow them to get married physically, but would have to demonstrate their loyalty to the spirit husband by making evil marriage covenants, like she would be barren and not have a child for the earthly husband, or that they will make him poor all his life, that they will make him blind, have stroke or suffer one misfortune or the other. She might pretend as if she loves the earthly husband, but a lot is going on in the spirit world that she dares not tell anyone. She may simply make the covenant that she wouldn't know happiness in the marriage. Any couple who has a problem of spirit spouse should deal with it decisively if you want to enjoy your marriage. It is worth praying and fasting for several days about.

5. *Ancestral witchcraft covenant.* This is to perpetuate the witchcraft covenant in the family line from generation to generation and often comes with a package of "evil pattern". If the covenant is not broken, all the children in that family will have witchcraft and manifest the evil pattern. The evil pattern may be untimely death in the family, or an evil marriage pattern, or an inherited disease. The doctors would say it is a genetic or hereditary disease, but the partial pact believes it is a demon that goes from generation to generation backing up an evil covenant of infirmity. Any evil pattern in a family line that is happening in the lives of many people related by blood is usually indicative of an ancestral witchcraft covenant. This requires urgent prayers by the family members, although it might be possible for just one person in the family to pray and make a petition to God. Thorough repentance and belief in the redemptive power of our Lord Jesus Christ is also important.

6. *Environmental witchcraft covenant.* This is covenant binding witches and wizards in an area. They come together, as a united body in that area, for example to trouble businesses and health of the people, or trouble marriages. They have a common altar and a common voice. So, when you observe an evil trend in an area, say people are dying and you see graveyards in front of almost every house as you go there to buy a piece of land. If the Holy Spirit

opens your understanding, you will know that there is an environmental witchcraft altar, and you need to think twice before buying land there if you don't want to fight battles. Anyways if the Holy Spirit is leading you to go ahead, he's got your back. I lived in an environment like that, but Christ protected me and my family and I had his assurance because he told me.

7. *Idol Covenants.* The witches and occultists do form alignment with idols and various shrines. Within a group of people or in an environment, they may form a covenant to worship an idol for certain demonic favours. They go there to bow to the idols and offer sacrifices. They do this to protect themselves or ask for certain evils to be done to a person or group of persons. In many religious cultures in the world, Satan himself is deified and worshipped, and you can imagine if he will ever give peace. No. They consult him to do evil. So many of these idol Priests do not only bow to one idol, but many idols including satanic. In order to be able to get things from these idols, the Priests drag you into a covenant. This covenant can be easily broken by praying and withdrawing from the worship of the idols. It may also be necessary to change any name that glorifies an idol.

8. *Blood Covenant.* This is the most common and most potent covenant in the kingdom of darkness. It connects man to a deity and connects man to man. Blood is usually offered to idols and deities in exchange for some favours. In the olden days, they used the blood of human beings which they believed carried a higher premium relative to the blood of animals. They would kidnap people at night and lock them up to be sacrificed. The practice is changing gradually now as animals are being uses more commonly, especially cows. The blood is sacrificed to the deity. In the covenant between man and man, only a contact with the blood, and backed up with an agreement is necessary. This is the type uses by many witchcraft societies. It applies to environmental witchcraft as blood can be sacrificed at the market square for satanic rituals. In marriage and business, people enter an oath. In ancestral covenants, the tragedy lies in the blood and goes from generation to generation. When you are praying against witchcraft and you sit down or stand and break blood covenants for two hours or more in a day until something happens, you are striking a good bargain. Some landlords drag tenants into a blood covenant through killing a goat, ram, pig or some other animals at specific periods of the year. It may allegedly be for protection, according to them, but the truth is that the devil has no free gift. If ever there is any protection, be sure you'll pay for it and run at a loss. It might be possible that no robberies take place, but occupants of the house are losing their jobs and falling sick frequently! When you break blood covenants decisively there's a lot of progress that comes with it.

9. *Graveyard Covenants.* There are people that draw power from the grave, and apart from blood covenants, graveyard covenants are high ranking and common.

Hosea 13:14

I will ransom them from the power of the grave; I will redeem them from death: O death, I will be thy plagues; O grave, I will be thy destruction: repentance shall be hid from mine eyes.

God himself makes us to know that the grave has power which can be used against man. There are witchcraft and occultism societies that draw their power from the grave to do different things. There is a celebrated case many years back of a man, who hypnotised a lady and took her to a graveyard to commit immorality with her. After that time, he started getting richer and richer, but the lady started getting lean and emaciated. This is a case of a blood covenant again, working in conjunction with a graveyard covenant. Many celebrities draw their power for fame from the graveyard through the many occultic societies that they belong to. Eventually at the end of their lives, they die shamefully and mysteriously. Necromancers and people possessed by familiar spirits also draw power from the grave and cemeteries.

10. <u>Marine Covenants.</u> These are evil agreements with the waters, which may be inherited or acquired, but most times inherited. It is inherited when you have a parent or ancestors that worshipped the river goddess, mainly in riverine areas of the world. It is acquired by unconscious initiation, when a person is initiated through food, drink, or sex. Some people go to the priestess to get initiated voluntarily. Once you get initiated, you have entered into a marine initiation covenant. Other marine Covenants follow which may be to empower you with seductive and sexual demons. This is an area where marine agents are very active. They also have spirit husbands attached to them that have sex with them in the night. If you dream a lot about the river, and do have sex in your dreams, then you are being oppressed or possessed by marine witchcraft. Many marine agents are in the "sex industry" and are mean and wicked standing by the roadside, smoking, drinking, chewing gum, and soliciting for customers. They approach you for sex and entice you with very dirty inducements shamelessly. They could stab or kill their customers. If you see yourself actually having meetings in your dreams, doing wicked things like killing people, ability to be able to transform to different animals, especially animals in the waters, seeing mermaids etc, then you are likely to be possessed by marine spirits. People who are possessed by marine spirits may have or may not have money, but they do not usually enjoy their marriages, or have wayward children, as well as making wrong choices in life. A marine initiate cannot be the wife of one man, or husband of one woman. They flirt around and they are ready to remarry once the slightest mistake arises in marriage. They have zero tolerance and do not wait patiently to solve marital problems. They are sorrowful and easily frustrated, and that is another thing that the devil does to them. Many of them dodge the truth during Counselling in deliverance. Like if you ask, "do you see yourself swimming in your dream"? They hesitate for a long time, stare at you, to see your reaction, then they say no. But if you say what about 5 years ago, then they say yes, and quickly add, but it is not very serious. However, the experience they are having in marriage confirms it is an urgent situation. Thorough deliverance with fasting and prayer is needed. Marine spirits are stubborn, so you may need to put them through an intensive fast. Even at that they may keep troubling them in the spirit to go and eat.

11. <u>Familiar spirits.</u> These are by far the most wicked spirits, and they find it very easy to gradually initiate their victims. They initiate easily through sex, and through food in restaurants. Every restaurant has an agent and they work

like a secret service. They are endowed with special powers, so that anything their hand touches, carries negative power. They are very mean and wicked, and many of them are assigned as hotel workers and prostitutes. They have mind blowing seductive powers. They are in the offices too and are assigned against glorious destinies. They dress seductively though they may appear to be gentle, but they are on a mission. Taking an opportunity to have a fling at work, thinking it is cheap sex, is one of the greatest tragedies that could befall a man and mess his destiny up for ever. They are gradually moving into schools to initiate the children through food. It is very easy to initiate children because they wouldn't notice, the spirit would have really flourished and grown wicked before they are aware. Familiar Spirits can be inherited and this manifests early in life. It grows fast in an environment devoid of prayer, for example if the parents don't attend church or they attend but are not spiritual. They don't give a damn, as the initiate could eat the womb of a mother, just because they do not want another child to be born to compete with them. Or a father sharing things in the house partially, and they decide to get him out of Job or make him wretched. These are real life confessions by initiates. Familiar Spirits have a close linkage with the spirit of death and hell, and many of them have a covenant of death and have chosen a day to die prematurely. They also have power covenants, to see things, punish people, and for example make vehicles to summersault. Most times however they capitalise on your vulnerabilities and sins. Familiar Spirits are very wicked and subtle. Many of them unlike the marine witches are very passive and gentle. They look like they would never hurt a fly, until the power of the Holy Ghost falls upon them. They start confessing and revealing their negative achievements. They will never talk or reveal their secrets, if you are not led by the Holy Spirit to touch sensitive issues. If you are led and are probing, asking leading questions, they break down and cry, telling you everything. You can play on their emotions. For example, if the mother has suffered so much labouring to raise them, send them to school. If she decides to punish the mother by eating up an organ, and you mention all these sufferings of the mother. If she reflects and thinks truly, and realises, she bursts into a cry. I met a nurse who came for deliverance. She was sent to torment the life of the husband. The husband was so good to her buying her things and all that. At a point, I recounted all that the husband did and how he loved her. She was touched and started crying. They are in bondage and don't lithe situation but cannot help it. Such wives make very good lovers once they are free. However, if the husband was giving her tough time, she wouldn't even blink. She would never have come for deliverance in the first place nor reveal anything.

The signs of witchcraft covenant are as follows:

1. *Bad dreams.* When you enter a witchcraft covenant, there is pollution in your spirit, and one of the ways you can know you are now linked with the devil is that you would be having nightmares. What you see in the dream is a pointer of the type of covenant you have entered into. If you begin to have sex in the dream, and getting tired when you wake up, it means that sexual demons are attacking your virtues and you are in a sexual covenant, typically from the marine agents. If you see dead people regularly, then you are in covenant with familiar spirits or have been attacked by the grave.

2. *Fear.* When you are in an evil covenant, fear grips you, because they will continue to intimidate you through your dreams and try to dominate you. If you study the word grow thick skin, then they cannot succeed with you. They will try to intimidate you but don't give in.

3. *Sickness.* One of the signs of witchcraft covenant is regular sickness that beat diagnosis. This is combined with bad dreams and fear. It is a sign. You dream regularly about serpents, wild animals or other scary creatures.

4. *Poverty.* When somebody is in covenant with witchcraft spirits, they possess you, and cause you to make errors that work against your greatness. Wrong business decisions, and a waning spirit are common. Then you keep having dreams like wearing rags or dirty clothing, going back to your former house in the dreams and the likes.

5. *Strange Voices.* When you are in covenant with witchcraft and they possess your spirit, you are now one with them. They make you to hear voices that do two things. The first one is that they lie to you. What God has not planned or said, they say it to you to confuse you and mislead you. Disregard every voice that deceives you. The second reason is that they want to deceive you. You may hear a voice saying you would get crippled, or mad, at a particular time. Discountenance all of that, because the faithfulness, love and mercy of God are above all that.

6. *Lust and Evil Sexual Urge.* The plan of the devil is to destroy you and make your life miserable for you. One subtle way to do that is to release lust and evil sexual urge into your life. When you have co-workers of the opposite sex, then you begin to feel lustful, and think about sex, more frequently than usual. Then watch it. There is a need for deliverance and self-control. They might also put a mark on you that will attract the opposite sex, so be careful when you notice such a trend. It is not a testimony, but otherwise.

7. *Marital turbulence.* The marine world uses this a lot in order to destabilise people. Once your marriage is troubled, your peace is taken away. Without peace, there can be no progress. Evil sexual desires, and sex outside marriage can cause all the things we have mentioned, from fear, bad dreams, sickness, poverty, etc. If you can control lust in marriage or even as a Bachelor, you will do yourself a lot of good.

8. *Thoughts of death.* The devil has come to steal, to kill and to destroy (John 10:10). When you have now exposed yourself unconsciously to the devil through food or sex and they have broken through into your spirit man, they can show you different types of lies. If they want you to be guilty of death, then they keep sending images of the

grave, images of dead people, and they keep bringing the thoughts of death into your mind very frequently that if you are not walking in faith, you believe erroneously that the end has come and that you are going to die. It's a crazy lie. They are manipulating you with those images to give you negative faith that will destroy you. Don't accept that! The Bible then says that we should cast down imaginations (2 Corinthians 10:5). Every thought that exhalteth itself against the knowledge of God is not of God. It is of the devil, and an evil imagination.

9. *Untimely and Sudden Death.* If you are unable to control these thoughts, then they become your reality. Then it follows that you become what you believe. If you believe in the dreams and visions of death, be sure that it will come to pass. However, if you have faith to disbelieve it, it will never happen. Witches came to me and said to me, you are guilty of death and sickness. I came out of the grave in the spirit on a certain afternoon during my siesta and the vision cleared. They were showing me graveyards, and dead people, and it was on a regular basis. To make it worse, my wife and my family were not in Europe then. There was no confidant, but I was left with God's promises, which I have come to realise as the greatest virtue and belonging in life. The devil lost completely. As I ignored the devil and continued focusing on Christ, his promises have been getting louder and stronger and stronger by the day.

10. *Failure at the edge of breakthroughs.* These demons will always supervise your life that you will not be able to have a breakthrough. They will frustrate your breakthroughs even before you have them. This is because you are being monitored from the witchcraft coven. It takes fervent prayers and a word of wisdom from God to block them completely and have victory. You need to be closer to God.

11. *Unexplainable behaviour.* Evil covenants will completely deplete your inner strength and change the direction of your destiny. The enemies are trying to destroy you by making you to do things you can never imagine you could do.

12. *Evil pattern.* An evil pattern which is consistent with that of other people in a group you identify with, maybe in your family, community, workplace or school, is a mark of an evil covenant. When students in the same class in school are manifesting the same sickness or behaviour, then there may be a witchcraft agent among them, who is trying to oppress or possess them.

CHAPTER TWENTY-FOUR

HOUSE HELPS AND THIRD PARTIES

By House helps, we mean those people who help you in the house in your daily activities. These includes people who take care of the children, help with cooking and washing. Most times they sleep inside your house and have access to your food, because of the nature of their work in the house. In the past, many of them have been terribly used by the devil to open the door to disaster and tragedy, many times which are irreversible, in the houses where they live. Some house helps are strategically assigned and supported by dark powers to bring down a hardworking and prosperous person. Third parties are similar to these people and may be drivers, gardeners and your relatives. Anyone who is not a member of your immediate family and may not be part of your success story, are strictly known as third parties, although we have had wives or children in the past who have confessed to witchcraft. Mother in-laws and father in laws too in the past have confessed to witchcraft.

A woman had compassion on a stepsister who had challenges financially and socially. She took her to live with the family. They continued living together, until woman lost her husband and second son in a motor accident. The guest sister that came to live with the family confessed that she was a witch. In order to wreak havoc on the family, she was always bewitching the pot of soup and meat. She confessed she was sent to bring affliction upon the family.

Another house help who was hired from another geographical part of the country confessed that she tied the womb of the wife of the employer, and that she made the man in the house to lose his job. Some others are there to seduce the man of the house, form a satanic alliance with him, and scatter the marriage. Once the marriage can scatter, that's the end of his fortunes.

A rich woman had a prosperous husband, and their family lived in a sprawling mansion of very high taste. They were doing fine, and lived happily, until the wife thought it would be easier to bring in a hairdresser. The hairdresser was coming to make the hair, but secretly seducing the man. She succeeded in seducing the man, and the desire for the hairdresser became uncontrollable. The hairdresser had taken that opportunity to bewitch the man to have access to his riches. She succeeded, and the marriage was broken. Out of shame, the man sold his sprawling mansion and packed out of the locality to begin afresh. The scandal was so ridiculous.

Many gatemen have charms and magical witchcraft powers with which they could seduce a woman, especially if the husband is a busy executive, but rich. The target of the gate man is a better life and money. Affairs between the woman of the house are commonplace. The gateman or gardener enjoys the best food in the house and does whatever he likes with impunity. He wears the best dresses that reasonably his salary cannot buy if he eventually succeeds.

These people blend so easily with the rest of the house, that you might never really suspect their activities until they have taken it too far, or they attend a church service and the power of God falls upon them and they manifest under the anointing and confessing. The urgency with which a family needs people to fill these positions may tempt you to overlook the risks involved in taking in a complete stranger that you do not know their foundation or background. There have been many confessions about evil powers making their initiates extremely tired, so that they cannot go to church, or do other things important. You may have a good appointment that will prosper your life, but they get you extremely tired on that day. If a house help always gets tired, you should be having thoughts especially on Sundays. Then if they sleep only during church services or spiritual activities, but active when it's time to gossip, watch it. The house helps are able to strike because the house holders were spiritually asleep. Unfortunately, these agents of darkness go their way as soon as they are suspected or detected.

Matthew 13:25

But while men slept, his enemy came and sowed tares among the wheat, and went his way.

How to Identify Witchcraft Assault in the Home:

1. Changes in attitude or behaviour of your spouse or your children towards you. If there's an affair or hidden activity, there will be a change.
2. When the house helps or stranger suddenly becomes disrespectful.
3. When there is a lack of disrespect for boundaries. There of course should be boundaries. The farm of a father and his soon will always be differentiated by boundaries, even as close as they are.
4. Spending style of the strange one in the household has changed.
5. Sudden financial problems since the stranger came.
6. Frequent illness of the husband, wife and children since the stranger came.
7. Loss of job of members of the family like husband and wife
8. Frequent quarrels between husband and wife.
9. Bad dreams possibly due to food pollution or sex pollution. If the man in the house is sleeping with the house help and at the same time his wife, the three of them are linked spiritually. They not only dream about one another, but the agent is in a position to attack the wife.
10. Sudden attachment between the toddler and the house help. A boy was employed as a house help and the toddler was attached to this boy too intimately. One day, the CCTV caught where he put his organ in the baby's mouth and that one has been enjoying the evil, hence the attachment.
11. Strange movement of appearing and disappearing. Taking too long g when sent on errand in the neighbourhood. This signifies a linkage with someone in the neighbourhood for evil.
12. Sudden disappearance of materials in the household.
13. Reluctance to spiritual activities by the house help. For example, does not like going to church or participating in vigils. Resists the word of God.

14. Strange looks. Not been able to look you straight in the face, and this sign can be exhibited even by your very spouse (Jeremiah 17:5). Bitter truth. There is an adage that says that when a roof is not suspicious, it collapses, or when a house is unsuspecting, it is suddenly set ablaze.
15. Strange utterances, for out of the abundance of the heart, the mouth speaketh (Matthew 12:34)
16. Acts of wickedness.
17. A moody disposition. Possessed people are usually moody when operating in an unconducive environment of aggressive prayers.
18. Particular sitting or lying positions, which are known as covenant positions. They sleep easily and go on astral projections from there.
19. Muttering alone behind the walls.
20. When they exhibit other strange behaviour too numerous to mention here.

How to Win Witchcraft Battle of House Helps and Third Parties:

1. *Prayerfully recruit, if you must recruit a house help or other third parties.* Prayer continuously is important if you are trying to choose a house help. Tell the Lord to show you who the person in question is, mentioning their name.
2. *If you must recruit urgently, try not to recruit a mature lady from a youth to middle age.* This age bracket may be dangerous. This includes people who are still young and sometimes may dress seductively because they are still young.
3. *Comprehensive counselling should be carried out.* Ask them their names. Some names reveal the type of religious background you belong. Where they were employed in the past. Why did they leave? Ask them about their dream lives. Do they dream about waters, and are they afraid of waters? Do they get beaten up in the dream? Do they exhibit fear? Do they have sex in the dream? Do they see themselves frightened by people in their dreams?
4. *Try and observe closely.* It is necessary to observe closely when you have urgently recruited or are not sure if they are possessed. Do they have marks on their faces or other parts of the body? In most cultures, they may have some peculiar marks. Watch out for the traits of fear. The utterances will convey fear no matter how old they are. They don't do good things with faith and confidence. Watch the way they sleep. Many possessed people have covenant positions from which they take off to witchcraft meeting. They may sit with legs stretched and backing the wall. Some may raise their feet on the wall. They may mutter certain things or shout. They could also walk in their sleep. They may wake up in the midnight looking sad, pensive or sad. When you ask, that why are they sad, they won't say able to tell you. They may go solo without talking to anybody and just like to be on their own.
5. *Prayer has a great role to play.* They would not manifest easily if you are not prayerful. I had a personal experience whereby we went for a deliverance program. That afternoon, I took her through the deliverance prayers for she couldn't read or write. That was when the demons started manifesting. I tried my best by being patient with her and trying to deliver her, until I saw that the Lord wanted me to let her go. She stood at the gate of our residence then, as she waved and said bye-bye. Behold it was a dream, and I woke up. She had many animal spirits in her, and they were dangerous animals, though the demon inside her was lying that they were not after me or my

family, that they just wanted to be pushing her about and troubling her. That was true, but the demons were still hiding some facts because they do tell lies. The wild animals I saw including a lion and crocodile was proof that her witchcraft could kill. I was just fresh from the School of Deliverance so I had knowledge.

In such a case, you need to pray with the whole family every night, even if for one hour. Make sure it is sometime between the 12 midnight to 3 am window. Even if he or she wants to project, it won't b possible. Take them for deliverance together with your family too. I once recruited a house help who couldn't speak English Language. As the program began, yet she did not understand what was being said, the power of God fell upon her and she manifested.

Also pray for them in your closet and God will reward you. Pray that God should send his angels of deliverance to help them. Pray also to break their covenants. Pray for God's protection over you and your household. Lay your hands upon your children and pray every night that the power of God should fortify them. Speak to every mountain and valley, because words carry power. Pray and claim good things for yourself. Note any dreams you have about them, including other people in the house with you. Stand in gap for everyone in the house. Love helps in deliverance.

6. *Anointing with oil.* Anointing every person in the house with oil. Organise prayer meetings in the household and your place of work periodically. Also anoint your beds, doors, windows. Sometimes you could give everyone the anointing oil to drink. There should be no preferential treatments. This might make the people you are trying to deliver to get rebellious as the demon will be strengthened.

7. *Watch their relationships with people in the neighbourhood.* Wicked people may seduce your house help with food or money in order to possess them and get at you. Since you are an employer, in every right by law, you can define their boundaries in the context of their work with you.

8. *Try to define your boundaries and do it with great consciousness.* There are certain things you should not allow, depending on your own circumstances. Over familiarity breeds contempt, sometimes. Even between you and your own children, there should be some boundaries. This is not discriminatory, but for your own good as a man or woman of the house. There are certain issues you do not discuss with a house help. For example, gossiping about your husband/wife with the house help is most unwelcome. This brings him/her to the same pedestal as you both. Don't be surprised how he or she begins to address you and has now developed undue confidence in the affairs of the house.

9. *Learn to keep secrets.* Most times a witch may not receive clarity about certain things except they hear you saying those things. It is very important that you keep your secrets secret, regarding your career, marriage and even your family.

10. *Know that the devil occupies an idle hand or mind.* Make sure that you have a plan drawn for every staff and keep them occupied. If they are not going to be busy, then you could allow them do some training to learn something e.g. going to school, hairdressing, or carpentry and agree with the trainer on hours involved, so that you would have a win-win situation.

11. *Show love, don't discriminate.* We never can know what posterity has in the waiting. Let us be fair to every house help or staff. There is a role that love plays in deliverance, when you show love to the deliverance candidate. As much as possible, do the same things you do to yourself and kids to house helps and third parties' event. Though the reality is that it may not be 100%, but at least 70%-95%. The Lord told me some time ago that love and faith are important keys in the ministry of Healing Miracles.

12. *Don't allow loose and indecent dressing.* As an employer, you have every right to determine the type of dress a house help or worker wears at work. When you have a house help who is 25 years old, and likes dressing to expose her cleavage, or likes wearing tight clothing it is not quite right. This is even worse when your wife is a nurse who regularly runs night shifts. The lady performs all the cooking and serving, is now very familiar with the man of the house. People who run night shifts are better off employing part-time staff, as much as possible, or who have closing time and do not live in the same house with you.

13. *Where possible, the CCTV could be installed in the sitting, dinning, or children's bedroom.* A number of witchcraft activities have been captured on the CCTV. A male worker who stripped and told the children to suck his manhood, thereby transferring sexual demons. A Nanny was also caught on camera, who stripped and told the children to suck her breast to initiate them. The breast sucking has been used to initiate several men! I know a man who sucked a lady's breast, and since that time, the spirit of the lady entered into him, instructing him on what to do, and they could kill him. He may be told not to have sex with his wife, or not to try to go to church.

14. *Periodical deliverance of everyone in the household.* This will expose if any child is having an evil seed, as well as exposing any strange influence. Enforce the fasting and don't joke with it.

Prayers to Win Possessed House Helps and Third Parties:

1. Satanic spy, sponsored from the Kingdom of darkness against my home, be exposed and be disgraced in the name of Jesus Christ.
2. Every evil accord between internal and external enemies of my household, be frustrated in the name of Jesus Christ.
3. Familiar spirit attack against my household, scatter by fire in the name of Jesus Christ.
4. Anything that God has not planted in my home, be uprooted in the name of Jesus Christ.
5. By the power in the blood of Jesus Christ, I recover my marriage from the dominion of witchcraft powers.
6. By the power in the blood of Jesus Christ, I redeem mu finances from the coven of witches and wizards in the name of Jesus Christ.

7. Wisdom that exceeds the wisdom of the enemy, fall upon my life in the name of Jesus Christ.
8. Wherever I have sinned and fallen short of your glory, O Lord, have mercy on me in the name of Jesus Christ.
9. Iron-like curses fashioned against my home, be shattered into pieces by the power in the blood of Jesus Christ.
10. Witchcraft altar in my home, be destroyed by the fire of God in the name of Jesus Christ.
11. Mirrors of darkness, monitoring my household, break and scatter into pieces in the name of Jesus Christ.
12. Agenda of the powers of darkness for my family, be frustrated completely in the name of Jesus Christ.
13. Sexual attack against my household in order to scatter my marriage and mu glorious future, be frustrated in the name of Jesus Christ.
14. O Lord arise and let every plan of the evil ones for my destiny be frustrated in the name of Jesus Christ.
15. Every door, open to external attacks in my household, be closed in the name of Jesus Christ.
16. Every Jonah in the boat pf my family, be sent packing by the Holy Ghost power in the name of Jesus Christ.
17. Poverty activators in the journey of my life, be arrested in the name of Jesus Christ.
18. O Lord, deliver my home from the net of marine witchcraft in the name of Jesus Christ.
19. Every bewitched object, serving as a helipad for witchcraft in my home, be destroyed by fire in the name of Jesus Christ.
20. You my children, reject bewitchment in the name of Jesus Christ.
21. Every material that is stolen from me to be used on evil altars against my life, you shall not prosper in the name of Jesus Christ.
22. I cover my house with the blood of Jesus Christ. It shall not be a meeting place for witchcraft in the name of Jesus Christ.
23. O Lord, let your glory overshadow my household in the name of Jesus Christ.
24. Every ritual and sacrifice carried against my home, lose your power in the name of Jesus Christ.
25. Evil tree around my house serving as an altar for the devil be destroyed by the thunder fire of God in the name of Jesus Christ.
26. Witchcraft bird on evil assignment over my house, crash-land and die in the name of Jesus Christ.
27. Every witchcraft agent, spending my money and attacking me, receive the judgement of God in the name of Jesus Christ.
28. Witchcraft agent, polluting my food in order to destroy my destiny, your time is up, be exposed and be disgraced.
29. Every witchcraft food that I have eaten unconsciously, be melted in my abdomen and turn to water in the name of Jesus Christ.
30. Every witchcraft sponsored infirmity in my life, be healed in the name of Jesus Christ.
31. Satanic agent, opening the door to disaster in my home, lose your power in the name of Jesus Christ.
32. Every dangerous pet in our household, harbouring bewitchment, die suddenly in the name of Jesus Christ.
33. Every witchcraft weapon fashioned against my household shall not prosper in the name of Jesus Christ.
34. Witchcraft agent in my household that is reporting me to community coven, be arrested and be disgraced in the name of Jesus Christ.

35. Witchcraft hand over my finances, catch fire in the name of Jesus Christ.
36. Witchcraft arrows of infirmity in my body, I shake you off by fire in the name of Jesus Christ.
37. Every witchcraft robber that is hunting fir the glory of my children be frustrated in the name of Jesus Christ.
38. Every charm and incantation of the gateman shall not prosper over my wife in the name of Jesus Christ.
39. Every indecent exposure and charmed powder and eyeliner of the house maid shall not prosper over the life of my husband in the name of Jesus Christ.
40. Every sexual trap set by witchcraft in order to frustrate my marriage and future be destroyed in the name of Jesus Christ.
41. Evil activity of satanic in-laws visiting in order to attack my family with witchcraft, be disgraced in the name of Jesus Christ.
42. Divide-and-rule tactics of selfish satanic in-laws in order to enjoy my money be disgraced in the name of Jesus Christ.
43. Witchcraft agent, related to me by blood, be exposed in the name of Jesus Christ.
44. Every witchcraft prophecy by any doctor against my health, I cancel you by the power in the blood of Jesus Christ.
45. Anything hidden or buried by witchcraft in my home or in my office, be destroyed by the fire of God in the name of Jesus Christ
46. Every attack against the breadwinner in my house, backfire in the name of Jesus Christ.
47. O Lord arise and restore everything that witchcraft has destroyed in my household in the name of Jesus Chris.
48. Every witchcraft agent visiting my house through astral projection at night, be stuck in space in the name of Jesus Christ.
49. Any man or woman going to sleep to harm me, die in your sleep in the name of Jesus Christ.
50. Let the mission and agenda of poverty activators in my family be terminated in the name of Jesus Christ.
51. Any witchcraft agent in my household, that has swallowed any member of my family vomit us by fire in the name of Jesus Christ.
52. Any charm or amulet fashioned against me or any member of my family, lose your power by the power in the blood of Jesus Christ.
53. Power of enchantments and incantations fashioned against my household, fail woefully in the name of Jesus Christ.
54. Every divination and power of the diviners fashioned against my life, be rendered impotent in the name of Jesus Christ.
55. Every weapon of polluted food against my household, be rendered impotent in the name of Jesus Christ.
56. Every deception, lies, and falsehood, aimed at working against the will of God for my household, be exposed and be disgraced in the name of Jesus Christ.
57. Every power, hiding inside a tree around my house, catch fire and be arrested in the name of Jesus Christ.
58. My glory on any dark altar, receive deliverance in the name of Jesus Christ.

59. Every agent of darkness assigned to reduce my spiritual strength through food, be arrested in the name of Jesus Christ.
60. Arrow of seduction fired against my life from close enemies, I return you back to the sender in the name of Jesus Christ.
61. Every blackmail of the enemy against me and my household, be erased in the name of Jesus Christ.
62. O Lord, open the eyes of my understanding in the name of Jesus Christ.
63. Spirit of counsel, fall upon my life in the name of Jesus Christ.
64. Every witchcraft agent in my household, undergoing astral projection be arrested in the name of Jesus Christ.
65. Animal spirit, manifesting against the plan of God for my life, be paralysed in the name of Jesus Christ.
66. Evil cooperation between internal and external enemies against my success, scatter by fire in the name of Jesus Christ.
67. Holy Spirit, restrain me from exposing myself through vain words in the name of Jesus Christ.
68. I refuse to be caught by satanic traps in the name of Jesus Christ.
69. Any material belonging to me on witchcraft altar, be destroyed by the power in the blood of Jesus Christ.
70. Demonic traffic in my household, closing the heaven of good things against my life, clear away by fire in the name of Jesus Christ.
71. Every battle of the night against my family be household wickedness, scatter in the name of Jesus Christ.
72. I release myself or any member of my family from the chain of the house help in the name of Jesus Christ.
73. Wealth transfer mechanism of witchcraft fashioned against my life, fail woefully in the name of Jesus Christ.
74. Seat of witchcraft in my household, catch fire and burn to ashes in the name of Jesus Christ.
75. Meeting place of the enemy in my household, I seal you up by the power in the blood of Jesus Christ.
76. I withdraw the clock of my destiny from the hand of witchcraft in the name of Jesus Christ.
77. Padlock of darkness fashioned against my womb, or fashioned against my treasure, break and scatter in the name of Jesus Christ.
78. O Lord, show me your plan for my family in the name of Jesus Christ.
79. Wind of the Holy Ghost, blow away my stubborn problems in the name of Jesus Christ.
80. Soul tie to strangers affecting my life, break in the name of Jesus Christ.

CHAPTER TWENTY-FIVE

CURSES.

A curse, simply by definition is a force that works contrary to the love of God, kindness of God, grace of God, and glory of God. Every human being is made for God's glory, and pleasure:

Isaiah 43:7

Even every one that is called by my name: for I have created him for my glory, I have formed him; yea, I have made him.

But,

Romans 3:23

For all have sinned, and come short of the glory of God;

God does have a plan for us, (Jeremiah 29:11) that is written or revealed to make everything work well for us at the end. When man decides not to walk according to this plan, then he is said to commit sin. This sin is disobedience and is also witchcraft (1 Samuel 15;23)

Jeremiah 29:11

For I know the thoughts that I think toward you, saith the LORD, thoughts of peace, and not of evil, to give you an expected end.

The main concept behind curses that we need to understand is that it is sin that brings curses, and that is why the book of the law is there to guide us and give us wisdom. Contrary to what many believe that a curse needs to be pronounced, no it needs not be pronounced in some cases.

Malachi 3:8-9

⁸Will a man rob God? Yet ye have robbed me. But ye say, wherein have we robbed thee? In tithes and offerings.

⁹Ye are cursed with a curse: for ye have robbed me, even this whole nation.

However, if the person offended is really deprived and humiliated and displeased, and they open their mouth and curse, those words give the curse intensity and direction. It therefore implies that every sin you commit is a blank cheque you have given to the witchcraft powers to rough-handle your destiny. A person made a promise to a lady that he was going to marry her. The lady was committed sponsoring him in the higher institution of learning, working hard, buying clothes, coming to cook and believing that she has found a husband, not just that, but that her husband is an Engineer for example. A few weeks to graduation and the young man calls the lady, and after scratching his head, said slowly, how he regrets that he cannot continue with his promises. The lady then bows her head, and says nothing than "well, thank you, but God will judge". Some others will open their mouth and start cursing immediately. Many couples without a child are guilty of this. Many cases of poverty and sickness in marriage are caused by a scenario like this. Some would say, because you have made me sad, you would never enjoy marriage with any human being in life. However, if you are justified and have not really committed a sin, then a curse cannot prosper against you.

Proverbs 26:2

As the bird by wandering, as the swallow by flying, so the curse causeless shall not come.

This scripture makes us to know that every curse has a cause. Curses cannot work against anyone who serves God (a servant) whole heartedly and lives righteously. Every tongue that rise against them shall be condemned. Anyone that curses a blameless fellow does that at his own risk, because he shall be condemned.

Isaiah 54:17

No weapon that is formed against thee shall prosper; and every tongue that shall rise against thee in judgment thou shalt condemn. This is the heritage of the servants of the LORD, and their righteousness is of me, saith the LORD.

The way curses operate, you may even think you are righteous, and a church goer, going to church to pray, but your prayer is sin, and you are cursed. I had a church member, who came for a "Prosperity" program that I organised. She prayed and at night, she had a contrary dream that robbers came to Rob her shop and carted away things. She told me these things and I asked her if she was always giving tithe. She said no, that it wasn't easy to give tithe, because she was selling piecemeal. She was not eligible to pray prosperity prayers because she wasn't giving her tithe contradicting God's word:

Psalms 109:7

When he shall be judged, let him be condemned: and let his prayer become sin.

Ananias and Sapphira gave but with deceit. They were cursed and died. (Acts 5:1-10). God requires loyalty and honesty, and not deceit.

Jeremiah 48:10

Cursed be he that doeth the work of the LORD deceitfully, and cursed be he that keepeth back his sword from blood.

Witches could issue curses against themselves, against one another, against people and against a community. We have examined an overview, about curses, but let's now look at types of curses.

1. *Curses as a result of sin and disobedience to God.* When God has told us in the bible that certain things are sinful and we should not do them, it is better to hearken. When we are not ready to obey them then curses are experienced. This applies to both the written word and revealed word. Almost everyone for example in prison, has committed a sin at a time. They are locked up and the devil stops their destiny for a while, with shame and reproach. It is only the mercy of God that can deliver from such a curse and you need to cry for mercy. We need to keep studying the Bible and do what the word says.

2.

    Joshua 1:8

    This book of the law shall not depart out of thy mouth; but thou shalt meditate therein day and night, that thou mayest observe to do according to all that is written therein: for then thou shalt make thy way prosperous, and then thou shalt have good success, says the Lord.

3. *Inherited Curses.* There are curses which by nature, implication or assignment affect the children in a family line.

    2 Kings 5:27

    The leprosy therefore of Naaman shall cleave unto thee, and unto thy seed for ever. And he went out from his presence a leper as white as snow.

The curse specifically addressed the seed forever. So, it is classified as an inherited or generational curse. Like the ancestral covenant, it carries an evil alternative in the family line. All the people in the family line may be dying prematurely, experience poverty or battle with marital failure. Thank God for the redemptive power in the blood of Jesus:

Galatians 3:13-14

[13]*Christ hath redeemed us from the curse of the law, being made a curse for us: for it is written, cursed is every one that hangeth on a tree:*

[14]*That the blessing of Abraham might come on the Gentiles through Jesus Christ; that we might receive the promise of the Spirit through faith.*

4. *Self-imposed curses.* There are pronouncements a person may make out of frustration or anger. Words, irrespective of the circumstances, once you utter them, they carry power. If you are in a marriage, and you have challenges, but instead of you to keep telling your spouse that the marriage will not succeed, or you even think so, then it won't succeed. Many people operate negative faith when the word of God says:

   Mark 11:23
   For verily I say unto you, that whosoever shall say unto this mountain, be thou removed, and be thou cast into the sea; and shall not doubt in his heart, but shall believe that those things which he saith shall come to pass; he shall have whatsoever he saith.

   This scripture is supposed to bless you, but in every way, when you say something negative because it is your faith and you continue to repeat it, then you become what you believe. That is a self-imposed curse. It may be in academics too. If you believe you cannot pass a course and you keep saying it, then it will happen that way.

5. *Regional Curses.* These are curses placed by witches on a particular area or region, which may be because of a particular abominable object or abominable deed. It doesn't really matter how many people committed the bad deed. We can remember Achan who took the accursed thing (Joshua 7:1) and everybody was cursed, and they lost battles. Terrible herbalists' altars that are been appeased with blood can bring a regional curse. The case of Jonah is another example. He brought misfortune upon the people in the boat, through no fault of theirs but because he was a transgressor. (Jonah 1:1-12). Curses in a region can come as a result of their sins as a group e.g. ritual killing and shedding of blood prevalent in an area. A wicked marine spirit might bring curses upon a group of people.

6. *Marital curses.* There are curses that are rooted in marriage. If a man is cursed for breaking an initial marriage covenant that he won't have kids in life, then the lady that marries him will not be able to have kids. If a person is cursed with poverty, the poverty will manifest, in the life of whosoever marries him, no matter the salary she might be earning. If your spouse is demon possessed and is operating under a curse, you cannot be free from curses. It is important to assist them spiritually to break it and not to show resentment. Any form of adultery in marriage or any sin against your marital vows like lack of financial transparency will only put your marriage in trouble, exposing you to witchcraft. Who shall ascend the hill of the Lord? He that hath clean hands and a pure heart. Avoiding curses is all about being alive to our responsibilities in marriage. The operation of the spirit of poverty does not actually have respect for your income, in as much as the devourer are at work. A knowledge of the life history and cooperation to solve the problem is important. Both should be sincere and go for deliverance. Breaking of covenants and curses go together and they should ask for hanging blessing to be released. Even those things that are happening presently in their marriage should be shaken and released through prayers.

7. *Parental curses.* This is when a parent curses the child out of anger, or does things abominable things implicating a child, or the child himself does things contrary to God's commandments. For example, the sin of incest implicates a child. A child who is disobedient to the parents will be cursed, because the bible says honour your parents, and gives reasons. The reason is that so that it will be well with thee, and that thou mayest live long in the land that God has given thee. A child who does not take care of the parents or who does not care for the parents might be cursed even without the parent saying anything, especially if he or she was raised by a single parent. Quite a lot of people are suffering from the scourge of parental curses. A curse from a spiritual parent might come under this heading too. We notice that all these curses are as a result of sins. A parent is a person in authority ordained by God (Romans 13:1). We need to ask for forgiveness from our parents, and the mercy of God through Jesus Christ our LORD to cancel parental sins.

8. *Occupational curses.* There are curses attached to some occupations, because they violate divine values, or they are absolutely not God's will. Many medical and allied professions violate God's values of family cohesion. A doctor who stays at work almost round the clock without time for his wife and children, and a nurse sleeps in the hospital running night shifts, and spending time with strange men, exposed to temptation. Also, people in the entertainment industry and pilots or sailors, who spend long hours at work, or travel for days Many people in this category have marital challenges. There are some professions like drug peddling, strip clubbing, betting etc. Parents in these professions usually do not raise good children. We need to be careful in the way we operate in our professions, trying to respect scriptural guidelines, so that we do not give way to witchcraft spirits to torment our destinies and that of our children. When you are a healthcare professional, you need to provide a reasonable balance between work and family to deal with such curses. Then pray for God's strength and wisdom. Changing your role e.g. as a Nurse and housewife, you might consider a remote or hybrid role as a "Nurse Assessor", because divine standards should dictate what you do.

9. *Graveyard Curses.* There is a power known as the power of the grave (Psalm 49:15; Hosea 13:14). Witchcraft is closely associated with this power. There are witchcraft powers that meet in the graveyard, and curse people who have offended them and dome something bad to them. They themselves are under curses, because their practice is contrary to what the scripture says. People that practice these things die before their time, or live miserable lives. They chant people's names in the grave at night and put people's pictures in the grave. They exhume corpses for magical preparations and many of them are necromancers or consult necromancers. They are heavily loaded with demons, and whenever you see the graveyard or cemeteries in your dreams, you need to pray against curses and covenants originating from the grave. There are people whose problems as far as they can remember, started at the graveside, as they were attending a burial. Furthermore, in some cultures, if a person dies, but they are not sure of what killed him, they go to his graveside to issue curses. When a will is contestable, the children too in some cultures go to the graveside to "demand justice" by issuing curses. These are all manifestations of the concept of graveside curses. It takes thorough repentance and prolonged prayer and fasting to break the yoke of graveyard curses.

10. _Coven Curses._ There are curses that originate as a result of coven judgement, after hearing a case in the coven. They might curse that the person should die, or suffer sickness, poverty, or the likes. These are very strong curses, but Christ has redeemed us from these curses. If you want to break a curse like this, you need to tarry in prayer and fasting for days, until you have spiritual evidence for example in your dream, or physical manifestation that the prayer has been answered.

11. _Curses as a result of an abominable or curses object or person._ There are curses that befall a person or group of persons because of something or somebody that they are not scripturally supposed to have in their custody, but which they do. This is exemplified by the case of Achan (Joshua 7:1) who took an accursed object, and the children of Israel lost the battle to the enemy. That account says "the children of Israel committed a trespass" even though it makes us to know that it was Achan specifically that took of the accursed thing. A child who steals a ruler in school and brings it to the house qualifies as an Achan. A visitor who visits for a week or two, and sleeps in your house, qualifies as an Achan, and opens the door to curses and demonic traffic. Similarly, it also applies to persons who have offended God, or who are by scriptural standards not to be allowed to be around you. Take the example of Jonah (Jonah 1:1-15). Jonah disobeyed God by embarking on a journey to Tarshish, instead of Nineveh, and was clearly a transgressor. He brought the anger of God upon the rest of the people in the boat. A man who is sleeping with a married woman, qualifies as a Jonah in the boat of his family or employers, under the circumstances. Many accidents have occurred that affected people who did not know about the sin of the offender. But because they offended witches, the judgement is that he must die in a vehicle accident as he travels. This is why you need to pray carefully before you join hands with people in business. Many people are failing in business because of a close business associate who by virtue of their sins or circumstances have opened the door to demonic spirits. Regular prayer as a child of God will always fish them out and deliver you and your family. However, you need to be very attentive and obedient to the Holy Spirit, because they are people you might not suspect or unable to search or tell not to come to your house. Take a family member who is into the occult for example.

12. _Curses as a result of covenant breaking._ Romans 1:31 mentions "covenant breakers" that they are sinners. Covenant breaking is failing to honour an agreement, for example in marriage or business. A man courts a lady, but a few months to the proposed wedding date, he said he was no longer interested. Furthermore, you promised you were going to pay a particular amount for a product or service, but after receiving the goods, you have refused to pay the agreed amount. As an employee, at the time of being employed, you agreed to come to work punctually, and do all your best. Now you are employed, but you are a latecomer, and slothful person. Every agreement with anyone should be documented and witnessed. Don't promise what you cannot deliver!

Ecclesiastes 5:4-5

⁴When thou vowest a vow unto God, defer not to pay it; for he hath no pleasure in fools: pay that which thou hast vowed.

⁵Better is it that thou shouldest not vow, than that thou shouldest vow and not pay.

Covenant breaking is a serious spiritual offence. In the dark kingdom, covenant breaking, no matter how minutes it could attract a death sentence. For example, a witch vows to donate the husband's manhood, and for one reason or the other fails to do so, it may cost her life. That is why they are very mean. You pay dearly for your mistakes.

13. <u>Telekinetic or Psychokinetic Curses.</u> The supernatural concept of Tele kinesis is well known, whereby people could change the motion or state of an object, using the powers of the mind. A little girl confessed one day, how she used the powers of her mind to overturn a trailer to make it to have an accident. It is usually done in close proximity. This means the victim most often than not is seen or heard. Speaking in tongues, living a prayer and fasted life will help to turn their wisdom to foolishness.

Consequences of Curses:

1. <u>Marital problems.</u> Many marital problems that people experience are as a result of curses.
2. <u>Poverty.</u> One major reason why witches and wizards can curse someone is to make them poor. Life can be so frustrating when a person cannot afford the basic things in life.
3. <u>Sickness.</u> Sickness brings pain to the person and the family members. They keep spending money and many people sell their property to heal their Sickness. They lose money or instead of making money.
4. <u>Untimely death!</u> When a person is operating under a curse, they begin to see that they are exposed to death. A sick person without money and without improvement can die easily.
5. <u>Bad dreams!</u> Bad dreams arise as a result of curses. It is a sign that something is wrong spiritually. Each time there are repeated Bad dreams, a person must rise up and act.
6. <u>Misfortunes.</u> One of the main signs of a curse is misfortunes. Getting to the right place at the wrong time, victimisation, loss in business and the likes.
7. <u>Sorrow.</u> When labouring under a curse, a person cannot know peace and joy, but will always be sorrowful. There is a slowdown and generally low quality of life.

How to Receive Deliverance from Curses.

1. <u>Repent from sin.</u> The first step to receive deliverance from curses is to repent from every known sin. Curses cannot prosper in our lives, if we always do good.

2. *Praying through the blood of Jesus.* Jesus died on the cross and shed his blood for remission of sins. The Bible clearly says he hath borne our griefs and carried our sorrows (Isaiah 53:4). We are free by the power in his blood.

3. *Fasting.* It is good to add Fasting to prayer, denying ourselves of food for some time daily. In Matthew 17:21, Jesus Christ said, "howbeit, this one goeth not out but by prayer and fasting". There are demons that supervise curses, once you offend. Some of these include monitoring demons. However, when you fast, with prayer, they leave, and the curses are broken.

4. *Faith.* Faith is the substance of things hoped for and evidence of things not seen (Hebrews 11:1). The Bible makes us to know that Christ has redeemed us from the curse of the law, but we have to receive the promise of the spirit through faith (Galatians 3:13-14).

5. *Restitution.* When you have taken an object that does not belong to you, and you have it in your custody, you might heap curses upon your head, until you return them to their owners. In Genesis 20:2-3, Abraham lied to Abimelech that Sarah was his sister, and Abimelech took Sarah. God quickly appeared to Abraham in a dream to warn him that he would be a dead man. In Genesis 20:7, God offered a solution for deliverance to Abimelech, and that was to restore Abraham's wife back to him, and that Abraham should pray for him, otherwise not only him but his family will bear the consequences.

6. *Changing roles in an occupation.* If a particular role would expose you to sin and curses and give witches an upper hand over your life, then you need to change it. Sin will only strengthen witches against your life. For example, if you are a lady and you work as a "Room Attendant" and some people for example are already holding your hands and offering you money, for illicit relationships, you might consider writing to the management to post you to the kitchen or front desk. As a Nurse, you might want to work as a "Nurse Assessor" or seek a transfer to the Paediatric Ward.

7. *Resign and change your job.* If you were in a sinful job before being born again, you might consider changing it, so that witches will not use that as a legal ground against you. For example, if you were involved in selling Cannabis, or you were working in a Strip Club, or a Brothel, all these are jobs that do not glorify God. Resign as quickly as possible to find a new job, no matter how profitable it is. Many cannot quit easily because of the financial rewards. That is the work of the devil and you need to act fast in order to resist curses and bondage.

8. *Be alive to responsibilities.* We all have responsibilities to ourselves, our marriage, the church of God, our extended family, our professions, and our communities. Try to sit down and ask yourself, what are the expectations of these people regarding me? Then ask another big question, Am I fulfilling these responsibilities. If the answer is No, then you are not far from curses.

9. *Watch what you say during trying and difficult periods.* During these periods of hardship, many say things that they are not supposed to say, out of frustration or despair. In times of difficulty, encourage yourself in the Lord, don't think about negativity, but be positive.

10. *Shun Adultery.* One of the greatest causes of curses in life is adultery. When you start committing adultery, you mind is drawn away from your family, your children, and your future. Many are distracted from their careers and is the beginning of failure for many businesses. The children are cursed, your wife is cursed, your business is cursed. The sin of adultery also brings you to disrepute socially and saps you mentally when you cometh the

realisation of your follies. As you go further into it, you discover it is an emotional burden, but yet it may be difficult to get out of it. Agents are despatched from the marine world in order to curse men and women seamlessly and with their full cooperation.

11. *Honour Parents.* The Bible tells us to honour our parents, and this is because of several reasons. One of it is to avoid curses. God does know that the curse of a parent to a child can be powerful, and he is warning us ahead to honour our parents. Respect their views and always explain to them why you may not be willing to carry out their bidding. Give to them in order to make them happy and forgive you. Do things that will make them happy and bless you. Let every moment with parents be fulfilling.

12. *Ask God for wisdom*. When you walk in wisdom, you will be able to avoid curses. Wisdom will make you to do the right things and make you blameless before man and God. Ask for the spirits leading in all that you do.

13. *Don't enter into an agreement or promises you can't fulfil.* When you make promises to man and to God, think very well, before you commit yourself, otherwise you would commit the sin of covenant breaking. Most of the problems we encounter in life are as a result of broken agreements in business or marriage. When you make a vow in church, make sure you fulfil your vows at the time you have promised to do.

CHAPTER TWENTY-SIX

PROSPERITY AND DELIVERANCE FROM THE SPIRIT OF POVERTY.

The spirit of poverty is one of the most potent, most deadly, and most effective weapons of witchcraft, and is mainly targeted against bread winners, who cannot control their sexual and other satanic appetites. The spirit of poverty has no respect for the enormity or vastness of your possessions, once you enter into witchcraft trap, and it is deployed against you. Poverty can be so demeaning and frustratingly wicked. Once a person loses this wall of defence, the entire life is in shambles, and complex problems develop! It deals with you, not only physically, but mentally and socially. Going by the World Health Organisation's definition of health, as being a state of complete physical, mental, and social wellbeing, and not merely the absence of infirmity or disease, you will see that poverty itself is ill-health. Witchcraft cannot afflict you with poverty, and you think that you are healthy in the real sense of it. It takes a lot of prayers, fasting, and righteous living, to recover back what you have lost. However, restoration is still possible.

What is Poverty?

Poverty is simply defined as physical, mental and emotional depletion. There is serious poverty, when there is no money in the house, you cannot afford what you like to eat or drink, can't meet up with obligations, mental stress, sleeplessness, emotional disorders, disorientation, and sometimes a feeling that life is not worth it. This is why many have committed suicide.

There was a man, many years back, who was rich in money and materials. He had a fleet of trucks for haulage services, and schools and several people were employed by him. Life was good, until he met with a witchcraft agent. He had an affair with this lady, and they were having sex, and the secret relationship was "flourishing". All of a sudden, like Job, in the bible, the trucks started developing problems, one after the other, and one by one, he sold all the trucks. The schools that he had, that were flourishing, they were all in shambles, that he only had less than 5 pupils in the classes. It was then that he confessed to his wife. He had to undergo series of deliverance, and at the end of it all, several prophecies attested to the fact that his sudden misfortune and tale of woes were caused by that strange lady that he slept with.

There is another case of a high-ranking officer in a well-known organisation, internationally. This man was aspiring to be the President in that organisation, until this strange witchcraft agent, entered into his life. He took the lady to a hotel, and the lady, an undergraduate during the encounter, brought out a laptop to and pretended she was on her assignment as she relaxed with the man in the hotel, and was chatting away with him "excitedly". In the process, he revealed some organisational secrets, and promised he was going to fraudulently help the lady to get certain things from the organisation. The man had in his ecstasy undressed completely and was naked, not knowing the laptop camera was on, capturing all he was doing and saying. When the lady was done with this life destroying video, she put off the camera, and got up, telling the man she would soon be back to have sex with him till the morning of the next day. He was happy, not knowing that he was already destroyed.

This lady circulated the video, showing this to-be organisation chairman, naked. The video went viral on the Internet immediately, because the organisation was a great organisation. The man had ascended so high in his career, likewise, great was his fall! He couldn't be installed as the president, he was sacked completely from that organisation. He was also suspended from other international concerns that he was director, or member of the board of trustees, and the likes. He was also relieved of his positions of honour in other social organisations. Back home, he had put a stigma on his wife and children, and life was no longer bearable. He has never been the same because he has continuously lived in poverty.

Pray like this, "every lion of adultery, inside of me, that wants to devour me without leaving a remnant, be arrested by the power in the name of Jesus Christ".

Every man with a brilliant destiny should be very careful, and bond very intimately with their wife. Life can never be the same again, once a man falls into a trap like that. Many have quietly received a death sentence unannounced, from these witchcraft powers. This is why some people die mysteriously and people keep wondering what may have happened to them.

How can witchcraft powers strengthen poverty in a life?

1. *Ignorance about Jesus.* When you don't know the way, you will be lost in the wilderness of poverty, and when you don't know the truth, you will be in the bondage of the spirit of poverty. There is certain information that you need to know about God's plans that will set you free from the grip of poverty. If you are not armed with these, witchcraft will afflict you forever. Jesus is the way, the truth and the life.
2. *Sin.* In James 4:17, the bible says, "to him that knoweth to do good and doeth it not, it is sin". Every transgression against the commandment of the Lord, and anything that is not of faith are all sinful. Doing what is not right and walking against the commandment of the Lord will keep a person in poverty.
3. *Sexual Sins.* I am emphasising on this because of the significance attached to it. It makes it extremely easy for witchcraft to devastate a man's life. 1 Corinthians 6:18 has it that every other sin is outside the body, but that anyone that commits immorality commits it against his own body. This means figuratively that he released the poison of poverty into his own body. Once witches have slept with a man, they have access to his destiny. The same is true, when a wizard wipes a lady's vaginal fluid with a handkerchief or has access to it in any other way.

4. *Unforgiveness.* We need relationships to build people around us, to buy our wares, and to propagate the information about what we sell. If this is the case, then we need to forgive people. Unforgiveness itself is rebellion against God's commandment, and witchcraft.

5. *Refusing to seek God's will in your career.* When you discover God's predestination and will for your life, all you need is to follow it, so that you can seamlessly prosper. Without this, you have not worked with the plan of God, but are working with a false plan, which will only disappoint you.

6. *Not praying on the go.* After seeking the will of God as to the career you need to pursue, you also need God's direction and guidance on the go. Don't forget that when you pray, you break curses and covenants of poverty, as well as bind the spirit of poverty. Revelation of the written word and revealed word is important. Psalm 107:20 says he sent his word, and healed them, and delivered them from their destructions. This you do by prayer and fasting, so that you will receive revelation and guidance to carry on.

7. *Not Giving to God and man.* When you don't give to God, and Rob God in tithes and offerings, you close heavens doors of blessing over your life (Malachi 3:10). When you also don't give to men. Luke 6:38 says give and it shall be given unto thee, not just what you give, but it shall be pressed down and shall run over (overflow). The Bible describes giving as sowing, and when you sow, your harvest brings back in multiple fold. Giving is not just about money. Things like your time, materials, words of advice, words of encouragement can be sown bountifully without minding what it costs you. The Bible says you shall reap bountifully (2 Corinthians 9:6). When you start a new business, you can leverage on the people you have been good to patronise you or support you in one way or another. The Lord promises that when you deal thy bread to the poor and satisfy the afflicted soul, then your light shall rise in obscurity, and thy darkness be as the noon day. He shall guide thee continually and satisfy your soul in drought, and make fat thy bones, and you shall be like a tree planted by the rivers of water.

8. *No adequate time for word study and meditation.* The word of God gives direction and the right leading to all our activities in this world. When you study the word of God, you know his promises for you and pray accordingly. Spiritual guidance is also available to you through the word study.

9. *Laziness.* When you are attacked by witches, they manipulate you and give you a slothful spirit, which makes you weary about being serious in whatever you are doing. In Proverbs 24:33-34, the word of God says, "a little sleep, a little slumber, a little folding of the hands to rest, and poverty will come on you like a thief, and scarcity like an armed man". They also cause sickness, which makes you unable to work. Sickness has been identified as a weapon in the hands of witches that they use to stop people, especially when you have a laudable project on your hands. Suddenly, people begin to fall sick every now and then without any concrete diagnosis being arrived at. Don't just sit down and wallow in self-pity.

10. *Procrastination.* Unaware to many people, procrastination is the thief of time! What you can do today, don't delay till tomorrow. Make every day count. Procrastination is the act of delaying or postponing tasks. If I have a task, e.g. writing a book which I am supposed to do every day, but I choose to do it once in a week, say writing on Mondays only. What I would have achieved in 1 year, will be achieved in 7 whooping years! So, if I am working every day, alongside a fellow who works one daily, then he would be 7 years behind me. Logically, if we work at

the same rate, what I would achieve in 1 year, he won't achieve until after 7 years. He would have given witchcraft an upper hand.

11. *Curses.* Curses can be a cause of poverty in a person's life, be it the curse of inherited poverty, environmental poverty, attitudinal poverty, group or collective poverty, acidic poverty etc. Curses are so terrible and mysterious in the way they manifest.

What are the Manifestations of the witchcraft arrows of poverty?

1. *Tiredness and weakness.* When you feel tired and weak, during the day and can't do anything. People that have this type of experience have been made to work on farms or carry out other coven assignments at night, that they just continue to sleep during the day. Some serve as horses or caramels to higher witches. When you are always tired, you will be lazy.
2. *Sickness.* Witches will make you sick almost every day, from one ailment to the other, once you give way to witchcraft attacks through sin or a careless lifestyle.
3. *Confusion.* Once you begin to witness witchcraft attacks, they will make you afraid through your dreams, and instil fear in you, making you to lose focus and be confused. Another trick is to make you see false visions that don't bear any relevance to the thoughts of God for your life, or strange voices. Once confusion sets in, there will be delayed progress and poverty.
4. *Mysterious losses.* Witchcraft victims experience mysterious losses in business. The refrigeration system of a cold room may develop a fault, and all the sea food perish. A swarm of locusts could be deployed against a farm by witches and wizards. A person who has a fleet of buses may lose everything one-by-one or may be involved in a case of manslaughter through a road traffic accident. They may also be involved in a libel case running to millions of naira in damages.
5. *Mistakes and errors.* Workers in the offices may commit errors that will make them to lose valuable resources or key staff. They may also make spiritual blunders, like the company director that I mentioned earlier on.
6. *Weather disasters.* A terrible wind may just arise and destroy the masts of a Telecommunications concern, just immediately after installation and they are still battling with the repayment of the loan acquired to do the business. These terrible spirits could conjure an evil wind targeted at a particular person. A hot weather may just bring about a poultry disease that will destroy all the chicken in a poultry. The neighbourhood poultries may be unaffected and making hot sales.
7. *Planting of a devourer.* A deviant child, wife, husband or co-worker may manifest physically as a devourer. A husband or wife with a high-end lifestyle, living above the family income qualifies as a devourer. They are just there to increase expenses, but are not able to suggest will bless the marriage in many years. Devouring house helps will waste food, steal food, and steal your materials. A devouring co-worker will borrow money and not return it, will always eat your food during break, will overtake your materials, and even devour your time. Time is also a convertible resource that if you do not manage well, could lead to poverty. Unfortunately, this is the cause of poverty in many lives.

8. *Discouragement.* When you are surrounded by people that discourage you and deflate your faith and confidence, it will be difficult to progress and prosper. When there is lack of emotional support, it would be difficult to prosper. A wife or husband who will never say good things to the spouse, or an employer who will always fault and run down the employee without any encouragement will dry the bones and cause spiritual death financially in each of the cases. Many employees don't know that witchcraft can capitalise on lack of motivation and encouragement to cause poverty in an organisation.

9. *Husband does it all.* Due to cultural deficiencies in some parts of the world, some women have the mindset that the husband is the sole financier in the house and that they need to do nothing than to just take care of the children. This makes the women poor, the family impoverished, and may not allow the man to live long, especially in a depressed economy.

10. *Antagonism.* When witches want to afflict you with poverty, they put an evil mark upon you. This mark may be on the forehead, hands, or face. I mentioned the case of a certain woman, whom the parents offered sacrifices to a tree, in order to have her, because the parents couldn't conceive. She was dedicated to an idol and on conducting deliverance, a mask was removed from her face by angels of God. She had passed out momentarily during prayers. Her complaint initially was that nobody patronised her business.

11. *Sexual perversion.* When witchcraft want to make someone poor, they put upon him the spirit of lust and sexual perversion. They also put upon him the mark of the dog, to attract the opposite sex. A man with the spirit of sexual perversion will find it difficult saving money and will be distracted. He will be limited. A lady with the spirit of sexual perversion may think she's prospering initially. After some time, she discovers she's actually running at a loss, and will live a miserable life. Only repentance and holy living can save her.

12. *Dreams of poverty repeatedly.* When a person keeps dreaming about wearing rags, all the time, and losing money in the dream. He sees himself in the dream being given torn notes or the lowest denominations of coins. He sees himself in the dream in a refuse dump or dirty places. He dreams about damage of materials in his office or dreams that a spoon got broken. He may see a dead person who is long dead sitting on his seat in the office. He dreams about fetching water in a basket. A woman may see her hair unkempt and dirty whilst putting on dirty clothes. A person may dream about armed robbers robbing the house. The dream of seven lean cows swallowing the seven fat cows was also a dream of poverty and famine.

13. *Lack of helpers.* Witches can make you to lack helpers. People will just automatically not want to see you. They could cause scenario that just make people to accuse you falsely. A child may get missing in your neighbourhood, and suddenly, people will believe you are the kidnapper. The rumours will begin to fly around even when you haven't and cannot do anything like that. Rumour mongers are deadlier than the flying witches. Some cultures in West Africa believe that you can have solution to the onslaught of a witch or a wizard, but not a rumour monger. Rumours destroy reputations, and your reputation can be bought or can be sold. Don't have a bad reputation.

14. *When you are in a wrong location.* There are certain locations which has not been destined by God to support your prosperity, maybe because there are people there or circumstances that are not conducive to your growth. God told Abraham to get out of his kindred and his people and not until that time will God bless him (Genesis 12:1).

There was so much famine in 1 Kings 17, that people were so hungry. The only solution from God was for Elijah the Tishbite to change his location, and hide by Brook Cherith, where God appointed some special beings to feed him. These special beings were ravens (birds). Don't ask me where they got the food from, but it was a constant supply, and met his needs as a man of God (twice daily). God knows the specific location where your helpers are if you walk with God.

15. *If you don't know your helpers.* In the same chapter of 1 Kings 17:9, when the brook was dried up, God told Elijah that he should arise and go to Zarephath. The solution here again was location specific. There were neighbouring towns, but God specifically told Elijah to go to Zarephath. Not just that, but he "commanded a widow". How come that out of all the people, it was only a poor widow who was waiting to eat all she had left with her son, and die, that God appointed as a blessing to Elijah! Who are your business partners or helpers? Have you asked God? Know what? The woman was a giver and worthy vessel in God's hands, and God found it worthy to commit the blessing of Elijah into her hands for even greater blessings for her and her son. God tested her, for God loves a cheerful giver. Are you a giver.

16. *You are not a giver.* The woman was a giver, who would not withhold all that she had in this world from a stranger! Moreover, a servant of God. We could also say the woman respected and feared God. Do you have these qualities? Are you willing to give "whatever" is laid in your heart for the sake of the fact that it is the word of God? This woman a widow, gave all.

17. *Are you obedient?* What is God asking you to sacrifice? Are you willing and obedient? The Lord asks me to tell you that if you are "willing and obedient" (Isaiah 1:19), anyhow, you shall eat the good of the land, and not just any cheap things. Obedience is key! God told me something on a particular morning many years back, as I was about to eat a sumptuous breakfast with my wife and children beside me in our bedroom on our very large bed. He said, proceed on a 7 day fast, with no food, no water, and no sex. I was not prepared, but I obeyed instantly, and decided to fast. At the end of 7 days, God gave me a download of my calling and ministry, step by step. What a wonderful appointment so early in the year. God had told me then as a poor civil servant who was only working hard unnoticed by anyone, that "the nations of the world will bless you". I wondered without a clue. When he told me to leave my job that I got after several years of being unemployed, I quit immediately. Many people thought I was insane. They saw me as a foolish person. I dedicated my life wholeheartedly to the work of the ministry, using my gift of deliverance wading through every shame and reproach. My wife was by me, supporting me and my kids that were very tender then. She could have divorced me, because it was not our plan from the scratch. No one is perfect, but without her support, things wouldn't have been easy. Know that I left my Clinical Practice and the income level changed. Most times I hid my face when my mates were coming, and many despised me in no small terms. They believed I would never recover again. I got stronger and more determined. I cried many times secretly and wiped my tears, trusting only in God. I painstakingly gathered a wealth of knowledge in deliverance and healing in the almost 20 years before I wrote this book. Here am I today with this humble presentation, and I hope it goes around the nations of the world and blesses the world.

What to do to overcome poverty:

1. <u>Accept Jesus Christ as your Lord and saviour.</u> He is the way to success, and the truth that leads to prosperity. Jesus came to show the way, and when you follow the way, it shall be well with you.

2. <u>Repent from every sin.</u> Sin will only make you to work against the plans of God for your life. Sin in thoughts, in words, and actions should be avoided.

3. <u>Hardworking.</u> When Mr. Green works one day in a week, and Mr. Blue works seven days in a week, Mr. Blue is most likely to achieve in 1-year, what Mr. Green would achieve in 7 years, if the conditions are same. A person who works harder builds wisdom and experience faster. He is able to overcome witchcraft poverty attacks more easily. Laziness is bewitching yourself!

4. <u>Pray to God to show you the right location and take you there.</u> We have seen from the above that blessings are location specific. Sometimes, working under the same conditions, a change in location could just be all that is needed to change your game for the better. When God chooses your location, you can be sure he has appointed people and gotten ready the resources to bless you there. Pray regularly, so that you wouldn't be used work at night. When you are on fire for God, no witch can overwork you. Pray against disasters and losses as well as against every dream of poverty. The dreams of poverty e.g. by Pharaoh. He appointed Joseph to oversee the food in the land.

5. <u>Prayer and fasting.</u> A praying Christian is always a winner when it comes to living in abundance. Revelation is a function of prayer and Intimacy with God. Revelation leads to abundance and celebrations.

6. <u>Violent faith.</u> When you believe in what God has said, no matter how unrealistic it seems, and you pursue it with all your heart, and utmost confidence, then you shall be blessed. Elijah did not lightly esteem the widow, but believed. Put all your time and resources into the vision of God in your life.

7. <u>Be an unrepentant giver.</u> When you give, you are provoking divine intervention and the blessings of heaven upon your life. Give your money, materials, time, encouragement, and any other thing needed by people around you. Try to meet needs, and when God is leading you to give, don't hold back, but give all. Remember Ananias and Saphira (Acts 5:1-10).

8. <u>Forgive.</u> God has prepared people to bless and support you. However, if you create an obstacle between you and the people God has ordained to bless you, it may be difficult for you to access the blessings. When you learn to forgive and heal spiritually (James 5:16), then you have strength to move on and progress in life. Unforgiveness will give you incurable pains, headaches, sleepless nights and constant emotional problems. True prosperity is difficult under such circumstances.

9. <u>Be very kind and nice.</u> The word of God says let your light so shine that men may see your good works and glorify your father which is in heaven (Matthew 5:16) This will draw many helpers into your life and business.

10. <u>Abstain from sexual looseness.</u> This will only increase the number of demons you have to torment you. It will also attract curses in your life. We have seen how sexual looseness ruined people and how. Run from sexual immorality.

11. <u>Have an independent spirit.</u> A wife who has a wealthy husband should not over-depend on the wife. A man who has a wealthy wife should not depend on the wife financially. Mature children should learn to survive

independently. When this happens, the butter will not be spread too thin anrist.d poverty can be conquered. Witches will seize an opportunity to torment you when there is something you should do but you failed to do.

12. _Encourage yourself in the Lord._ Even when naysayers and discouragers surround you, ignore them and believe in God's word. Make positive affirmations and confess prosperity scriptures. Say good things to yourself.
13. _Discourage every devouring spirit._ There are people who are around you that are wasteful. If this trend is not stopped, you will continue in perpetual poverty. If the trend in the house is wasting food and throwing into the bin, you will be amazed how much you waste every month.
14. _Planning is important._ Don't take both cars out on a day that just husband and wife are going out, because the kids are on holidays. Transactions you can carry out online should be done accordingly, as you don't need to waste fuel and time.
15. _Be at your best._ When you forgive people, relax and plan your life, and there is no stress at all, you are always at peace, and there is progress. Errors are limited. Be your best.
16. _Prevention of diseases._ Adopt a healthy lifestyle, exercise, eat healthy. Try to know what type of food suits your life and circumstances. In a cumulative manner, your health will invariably affect your work physically and mentally.
17. _Don't keep accursed things in your house._ When you keep accursed things in your possession, they can bring poverty into your life, and household.
18. _Laying of hands._ Laying of hands impact upon your life an excellent spirit which makes you to prosper depending on the decree issued when the hands were laid. However, you still need to work very hard, and discover the secrets of your trade.
19. _Absolute obedience._ When God has planned to prosper you and he gives you a set of instructions, then you need to follow strictly the time and specific instructions. When you don't follow precisely, you breach the contract and will not have the expected results. Follow the instructions to the letter.
20. _Save money for incidentals._ There is a need to save some money and make hay while the sun shines, so that when a need arises to spend money, you will not experience poverty. If you fail to plan, you have planned to fail.

Prayers to Disgrace Poverty:
1. Spirit of poverty, lose me and let me go in the name of Jesus Christ.
2. I break every covenant with the spirit of poverty by the power in the blood of Jesus Christ.
3. Every food that I ate in the dream, that is causing poverty in my life, receive purging by fire in the name of Jesus Christ.
4. Every garment of poverty, every spiritual rag upon my life catch fire and burn to ashes in the name of Jesus Christ.
5. Curse of poverty in my life, break by the power in the blood of Jesus Christ.
6. Poverty mindset in my life, receive healing in the name of Jesus Christ.
7. O Lord my father, show me who I am in the name of Jesus Christ
8. O Lord, reveal your assignment in this world to me in the name of Jesus Christ.
9. Helpers of my destiny, locate me by fire in the name of Jesus Christ.
10. Every evil dedication crying against my greatness, be silenced in the name of Jesus Christ.

11. Blood guiltiness in my foundation, bringing poverty upon my life, be forgiven by the power in the blood of Jesus Christ.
12. O Lord my father lift away, every embargo of infirmity against my finances in the name of Jesus Christ.
13. Evil voice misleading me, be silenced in the name of Jesus Christ.
14. I rebuke every spirit of the devourer in the name of Jesus Christ.
15. Foundation of poverty in my life, be destroyed forever in the name of Jesus Christ.
16. O Lord, take me to the divine location where you have deposited my divine allocation in the name of Jesus Christ.
17. Evil mask, chasing away my clients and customers, catch fire and be roasted in the name of Jesus Christ.
18. Evil birds and serpent using my glory to prosper, receive destruction in the name of Jesus Christ.
19. Mark of disfavour upon my life, be broken in the name of Jesus Christ.
20. Evil sacrifice fashioned against my finances, lose your power and backfire in the name of Jesus Christ.
21. Witchcraft bank caging my money, be demolished in the name of Jesus Christ.
22. O Lord my father, show me the secret of my abundance in the name of Jesus Christ.
23. Rituals done by business competitors against my business, backfire in the name if Jesus Christ.
24. Evil covenant assigned to derail my glory, break in the name of Jesus Christ.
25. Arrow of infirmity assigned to hold my destiny to a financial stand still, jump out by fire in the name of Jesus Christ.
26. Every bag with holes programmed into my life, burn to ashes in the name of Jesus Christ.
27. I receive the power to get wealth in the name of Jesus Christ.
28. Family pattern of poverty break and release my life in the name of Jesus Christ.
29. I shall rebuild the waste places of my financial destiny in the name of Jesus Christ.
30. Power of the tail, break and release me in the name of Jesus Christ.
31. Anything representing my finances that is buried by witchcraft, be exhumed in the name of Jesus Christ.
32. Powers drinking the blood of my business and career, receive the judgement of God in the name of Jesus Christ.
33. My staff of bread shall not be broken in the name of Jesus Christ.
34. Every tree of darkness, harbouring bewitchment against my financial prosperity, thunder and fire of God, locate them for destruction in the name of Jesus Christ.
35. O Lord, give me listening ears and obedient heart to your word in the name of Jesus Christ.
36. Every accursed thing or person bringing the judgement of poverty against my life, receive destruction by fire in the name of Jesus Christ.
37. O Lord, command my helpers to help me in the name of Jesus Christ.
38. Spirit of excellence, lifestyle of excellence, baptise my life in the name of Jesus Christ.
39. O Lord, give me a new revelation that will move my finances forward in the name of Jesus Christ.
40. Holy Spirit, buy and sell in my marriage in the name of Jesus.
41. Divine inspiration of the Holy spirit for business and career enlargement, baptise my life in the name of Jesus Christ.
42. Every close associate and hidden enemy making my labour of no financial effect, be exposed and be disgraced.

43. My wealth, come out of the grave of witchcraft in the name of Jesus Christ.
44. I come out of the laps of Delilah in the name of Jesus Christ.
45. Agape love of God, possess me and draw clients to my business in the name of Jesus Christ.
46. Grace and anointing to pray and fast always, fall upon my life in the name of Jesus Christ.
47. O Lord my father, increase my strength in the name of Jesus Christ.
48. O Lord give me the grace to walk according to your will in the name of Jesus Christ.
49. Every dream of picking snail in the dream, I cancel you in the name of Jesus Christ.
50. Every dream of poverty and suffering, I cancel you by the power in the blood of Jesus Christ.
51. Every satanic passion in my life, be cancelled in the name of Jesus Christ.
52. O Lord, make me a positive contributor to the finances of my family in the name of Jesus Christ.
53. I come against every change in weather or climate assigned to ruin my business in the name of Jesus Christ.
54. Epidemic or pestilence that wants to affect my finances for evil, be reversed in the name of Jesus Christ
55. Every spirit of procrastination, operating against my finances, loose your power in the name of Jesus Christ.
56. Iron-like curse, saying my life shall not amount to anything, break and be shattered to pieces in the name of Jesus Christ.
57. O Lord, send your word and enlarge my coast in the name of Jesus.
58. O Lord, let your hand be upon me for career and business promotion in the name of Jesus Christ.
59. Every dwarf spirit and blessing amputator leave my life now in the name of Jesus Christ.
60. O Lord, let your good will in my career and business, be established in the name of Jesus Christ.
61. Father, by your mercy, forgive every sexual sin that is holding my finances captive in the name of Jesus Christ.
62. O Lord, mould my life, by the power in your word and fill me with your blessings.
63. O Lord, send your word and damage every ignorance attacking my prosperity in the name of Jesus Christ.
64. I blast every marine wardrobe and possess my garment of glory in the name of Jesus Christ.
65. Every evil chain, tying me down to the spirit of poverty in my father's house or my mother's house, break in the name of Jesus Christ.
66. Witchcraft padlock fashioned against my finances, I break you with the sword of fire in the name of Jesus Christ.
67. Violent angels of the living God, encamp around my life, career and business in the name of Jesus Christ.
68. Every torn notes or coins that I received in the dream, be destroyed by fire in the name of Jesus Christ.
69. Angels of my blessings, locate my life in the name of Jesus Christ.
70. O Lord my father, position my life for blessings on a huge and global scale in the name of Jesus Christ.
71. Every jinx, every spell, fashioned against my prosperity, break in the name of Jesus Christ.
72. Any person using diabolic means or charms against my prosperity, receive disgrace and be disappointed in the name of Jesus Christ.
73. Holy Ghost bulldozers move into my life and destroy every satanic obstacle in the name of Jesus Christ.
74. Spirit of counsel, baptise my life, guide me, lead me, and direct me towards financial breakthrough in the name of Jesus.
75. My breakthrough shall be irreversible. I am blessed forever in the name of Jesus Christ.

76. O Lord, give me the grace to forgive and forget my customers and clients in the name of Jesus Christ.
77. Miracle of supernatural increase, locate my destiny in the name of Jesus Christ.
78. Mind controlling demons issuing strange commands in my mind, be silenced in the name of Jesus Christ.
79. O Lord my God, anoint my life with your favour in the name of Jesus Christ.
80. Power and anointing that attracts blessings fall upon my life in the name of Jesus Christ.
81. My father, my father, help me to discover your purpose for my life in the name of Jesus Christ.
82. O Lord my father establish me to prosper and flourish like a palm tree in the name of Jesus Christ.
83. O Lord, let your fire of creativity and resourcefulness be kindled in my life in the name of Jesus Christ.
84. Every weapon of the dust, fashioned against my greatness, you shall not prosper in the name of Jesus Christ.
85. Evil mirror of witchcraft monitoring my business or career, break and scatter in the name of Jesus Christ.
86. Evil voice assigned to lead me into the wrong investment or wrong decision, be exposed and be disgraced in the name of Jesus Christ.
87. Spiritual robbers, stealing from my life, be arrested in the name of Jesus Christ.
88. O Lord, let your mercy speak in my life in the name of Jesus Christ.
89. Bewitchment in my hands, catch fire and jump out in the name of Jesus Christ.
90. Arrow of poverty in my hand, catch fire and jump out in the name of Jesus Christ.
91. My father my father, my father, expose every wasteful habit in my life in the name of Jesus Christ.
92. Ancestral chain of poverty break and release me in the name of Jesus Christ.
93. Power in the blood of Jesus Christ set me free from spiritual cobwebs hanging my blessings in the name of Jesus Christ.
94. My head, receive deliverance from every poverty mindset in the name of Jesus Christ.
95. My legs, receive the power of God and take me to the place of my glory in the name of Jesus Christ.
96. Mark of rejection upon my head, be wiped off by the power in the blood of Jesus Christ.
97. Every stagnant river, flow out of my destiny, and let the rivers of living water flow into my soul in the name of Jesus Christ.
98. O Lord, by your spirit, let the people you have commanded to bless my life remember me for good in the name of Jesus Christ.
99. O Lord, arise and advertise my work, career, or business internationally in the name of Jesus Christ.
100. O Lord, repair the vehicle of my destiny, in the name of Jesus Christ.

CHAPTER TWENTY-SEVEN

HEALING AND MIRACLES.

Sickness is another way through which witchcraft punishes its victims. A lot of those people that take ill or are admitted in the hospital Wards have been attacked. They are victims of blood suckers or flesh eaters. Since the bible says the life of the flesh is in the blood, an attack against the blood is against the life, and manifests as sickness. Most witches that have confessed to witchcraft do say that they have eaten someone's heart, or kidneys. A little girl confessed to witchcraft and said that they have eaten the womb of the mother, that she may not conceive after her. Healing involves praying for the sick to be healed, but miracles go further to raise the dead, make shortened limbs grow, Instant bursting of cancer lumps, blind eyes to see, stops the rain, changes the weather, turns water to wine, and all sorts of amazing phenomena, this chapter discusses the basic principles that can achieve these.

As an attack against the spirit of man. Witches may launch an onslaught against a person's spirit. They could shoot the spirit or use evil words to manipulate the spirit. They could put a life goat on their coven and conjure a person's spirit into the goat, and then in turn speak evil words into the goat.

A person's spirit could be summoned and bruised on an evil altar. When the spirit is wounded, then the person is in trouble.

A person could also be injected in the dream, and he will wake up in real life and fall sick, just because of that injection.

Many years back, a woman dreamt that someone sucked her breast in the dream. The following morning, she started having pain in the breast in real life. The case was not followed up appropriately spiritually, and the disease aggravated before the woman died.

Some people are actually tied down with a rope and thrown on an evil altar. I met a man and his wife in an International program where I served as a Counsellor. The woman dreamt that the in-laws tied their son on an evil altar. The man was suffering so much. To make things worse, they were having some issues and were quarrelling.

A teenager was engaging in sex with another teenager. He was around 19 years old back then. He was so captured spiritually by the lady. When they inquired spiritually, it was discovered that the girl was withdrawing his semen. The result was that this boy teenager was having tuberculosis of the lungs and was getting leaner and leaner. However, he was not ready to let this girl go against advice.

At some other times, a sexually perverse man could suck the breast of a witch in real life, and the spirit of the witch would be transferred inside him and speak inside of him, and torment him with infirmity continuously. I saw this in the case of a particular man around year 2011.

A principality could be nursing a baby, through access to the baby at birth. This is another case scenario that I saw in year 2002. The baby was very sick, and stooling and vomiting, until the Lord instructed me to use the anointing oil on the baby's head and to give her some to drink. That was it. She was healed.

An elderly woman was shot from the back in the dream. The next morning, she woke up with a wry neck and facial paralysis. A combination of prayers and physiotherapy healed her.

How do witches make people sick?

1. *By means of sexual covenants.* A witchcraft agent can have sex with a man who is being targeted, and after the ordeal, he falls sick, and is nursed fir a long period before he eventually dies. Relatives of his wife could use this means without the knowledge of the wife, but simply because the wife is connected by blood.

2. *Through direct contact with blood physically or in the dream.* When witchcraft agents have access to your blood in the hospital, they could use it against you, to make you sick or aggravate your illness. The diagnosis brought to the hospital will serve as a mask. A burns patient with multiple burns was brought to one of the hospitals where I worked. He started shouting that they were using nylon satchels to collect his blood. Anytime I moved closer, they stopped. Anytime I moved closer to the Nurses Bay, further from him, they continued. He wasn't a Christian, so they had all the opportunity to attack him.

3. *Through contact with body fluids e.g. semen, breast milk, saliva etc.* This has been explained above with the case of the teenager diagnosed as having tuberculosis. The case of the man who sucked a lady's breast at work and was being tormented through the breast milk that he sucked.

4. *Through impersonation.* They represent you with an animal or graven image on their altar. Whatever they want to do to you, they do it to the animal or image e.g. shooting, or heating with fire. Some are hung at the fireplace. This means that anytime they are cooking, the person experiences a high temperature, or a high blood pressure. It takes revelation knowledge and wisdom under the circumstances to win a battle like this.

5. *Through spiritual tying with a rope.* Once they have possessed a person, they can have unhindered access to your spirit man and tie you. Once you are tied, you experience a great difficulty, and the peace of that person is withdrawn. People like that feel like dying, because the discomfort is much.

6. *Harvesting an organ and sharing it amongst members in the coven.* This is very common in witchcraft confessions. They tell the public that they shared the heart, the womb, or any other organ that they have shared. If it is the blood that they drank to bring about the infirmity, they say it. Many people who are lean and emaciated or weak are having their blood siphoned and drunk.

7. *Through feeding physically in parties, or spiritually in the dream.* In this scenario, the sick person buys a goat or cow, and lays his hand on the live animal, commanding his sickness to be transferred into the animal. After doing this, the animal is killed and the blood is drained into the ground and buried. The cow is cut and fried in irresistibly large chunks and distributed to people.

8. *Through satanic gifting.* A sick person is told to take a clothing that many people identify him with. He then uses it to wipe his head and his entire body, and gifts it to someone. He may use money, instead and use it to wipe his body as he says, "every impending death, I transfer it into this money".

9. *Through sacrifices and rituals on the road junction.* This is another method. They could buy the head of a particular bird, with some white bean pudding and palm oil. He transfers the sickness into the ritual, and places it on the "T" or 'X" junction. Sometimes, they have a quick bath with black soap on the road junction, and anyone that passes there first thing in the morning carries the sickness or death, if he is not spiritual. All he would feel is goose pimples or a feeling of swelling of the head. This type of satanic technology is becoming popular in the United States at this present time, though it is indigenous to Africa. Video and photographic evidence have it that immigrants now practice this in the United States.

10. *Through laying of hands.* Laying of hands is a significant spiritual exercise which can transfer both good and evil virtues. A hand can be laid directly on a person in order to transfer problems or laid on an animal.

11. *Transfer from the seat.* Some place a charm on a seat, and as people come to greet the sick person, and sit on the seat, they carry the evil load.

12. *Through a flying arrow in the air.* Sometimes, certain arrows are programmed into the air against a person. When such an arrow is fired, it might be as if a heavy stone fell on your head, and from that time, you begin to feel a headache. Such arrows can kill.

Signs of witchcraft sent sickness:

1. *Weakness and tiredness which persists.* When you go to the hospital, you may discover that your PCV (packed cell volume) is low, due to the activities of blood suckers and flesh eaters.

2. *Dreams of seeing yourself sick or seeing sick animals in the dream.* Wearing hospital dress or seeing yourself in the hospital environment. When you are being fed by the dead or see dead people repeatedly. When you lose large amounts of blood in the dream. That blood symbolises life (Leviticus 17:11) and that life is flowing out of you.

3. *When you feel that something is getting out of your body.* In this case, you feel light and your head feels light.

4. *When you are emaciating.* This makes you lean by the day, and it is very obvious as people ask you if you are okay.

5. *Disease defies treatment.* When you keep swallowing drugs without improvement, or you keep going for surgery and they keep telling you that you still need further surgery. They have confused the doctors! A curse of infirmity will act in this way, that even your carers are confused!

6. *When you have symptoms going on and off and following an unusual pattern.* Insanity is an example that follow the cycle of the moon. Some people who are diagnosed of mental illness have aggravated symptoms during the full moon. Some have their own following seeing a particular dream object. Others observe their own after a particular traditional festival.

7. *Very strange swellings or other symptoms.* When there is a swelling or discolouration without a fall, or without an explainable cause. These are signs of witchcraft attacks. An attack in the dream sometimes may manifest physically on waking up in the morning.

8. *Diseases that do not have a specific diagnosis.* When you are been attacked by witchcraft and fall sick, when the doctors cannot arrive at a diagnosis, and all they do is keep on testing and testing, and giving you recurrent appointments, then it is not a biological phenomenon, but a spiritual phenomenon.

How do you approach healing?

1. Accept and confess Jesus Christ as your Lord and saviour. Without Jesus, you will never know the way, without Jesus, you will not know the truth and be set free, and without Jesus, you cannot live. "Jesus is the way, the truth, and the life" (John 14:6).

   Say this:

   > Lord Jesus. I thank you for coming to this world to save me. I thank you for the blood you shed for me on the Cross of Calvary. As from today, I make you Lord and Master over my life. I forsake the devil and all his evil works. Thank you, Lord Jesus, for saving me.

   Don't forget that counselling is necessary before ministration of healing.

2. *Jesus the Greatest Physician.* Know that when Physicians cannot arrive at a definitive diagnosis, or a workable treatment, and you are almost dying, you need to cry to the Physician before Physicians. He is Jesus the Greatest Physician.

3. *Repent from every known sin.* Adopt a lifestyle of holiness and righteousness.

4. *Leave behind harmful habits.* When you adopt a lifestyle of holiness and righteousness, there are certain harmful habits that you leave behind, like smoking, drinking, unforgiveness, sexual immorality, hatred, strife etc. This will give you an incorruptible body.

5. *Forgive and let go.* Unforgiveness alone may give you sleepless nights, psychogenic pain, depression, anxiety, hearing strange voices, aggravate high blood pressure, make your heart problems aggravated, reduced productivity, disorders of the autonomic nervous system etc. If you continue this for too long, and not repent, it will have devastating effects. True healing starts with practicing holiness.

6. *Stop smoking and drinking alcohol.* Stop smoking which can aggravate high blood pressure, heart problems, cause lung cancer, risks of abortion, blindness, diabetes, asthma, and all these can shorten your life span. Alcoholism can cause fatty liver, then liver cirrhosis, aggravate blood pressure, kidney disease, worsen diabetes, mental stress, depression, etc.

7. *Read your bible* and note the promises of God for healing and deliverance. Meditate on these scriptures daily and confess them. Confessions (positive affirmations) register in your spirit and ginger your spirit.

8. _Ignore the devil._ The devil will always bring negative thoughts, feelings, fears, doubts, and imaginations into your mind, in order to confuse you, deceive you, and make your healing unrealisable. Imaginations and everything outside the promises of God should be ignored (cast down). 2 Corinthians 10:5 says casting down imaginations and every high thing that exhalteth itself against the knowledge of God, bringing them down to the obedience of Christ. This means you keep believing in the written word of God. This is even more so, if the Lord has given you a promise in your dream or through a man of God specifically addressing your situation.

9. _Think on good virtues_ and be positive always:

    Philippians 4:8

    Finally, brethren, whatsoever things are true, whatsoever things are honest, whatsoever things are just, whatsoever things are pure, whatsoever things are lovely, whatsoever things are of good report; if there be any virtue, and if there be any praise, think on these things.

10. _Pray every day and night_, until something happens. Pray for forgiveness where you need forgiveness and pray for wisdom where you need wisdom. The Bible says in James 4:3 that it is possible to pray for the wrong things such that your prayers are not answered. If you know that you have sinned, for example, adultery and things are now bad, set a day aside first to ask God for forgiveness and mercy, before coming to pray for healing.

11. _Decree and speak to your mountain._ Mark 11:23 says, whosoever shall say unto this mountain, be thou removed and be cast into the sea, and shall not doubt in his heart, but shall believe that those things which he saith shall come to pass, he shall have whatsoever he saith. Cultivate the habit of commanding your infirmity based on what the word of God says. The scripture for example says in Isaiah 53:4 that surely, he hath borne our griefs and carried our sorrows; yet we did esteem him stricken, smitten of God, and afflicted! Then you decree that "father you bore my griefs and carried my sorrows, Lord, take away my infirmity". Luke 10:19 says, "Behold I give you power to tread on serpents and scorpions, and over all the power of the enemy, and nothing shall by any means hurt me". Then you confess that "Father, I receive power to tread upon …………(mention the disorder that you want God to heal). I rebuke and take authority over this disease. It shall not harm me in any way nor kill me in Jesus name. Refer to the book "Miracle Healing" by Alexander Zabadino, on the Amazon Kindle Direct Publishing Bookstore.

12. _Always pray with the name of Jesus Christ._ The Bible says that at the name of Jesus, every knee shall bow, concerning things in heaven, things on earth, things under the earth, and every tongue shall confess that Jesus Christ is Lord to the glory of God the Father (Philippians 2:10). Jesus also says in Mark 16:17 that "in my name shall they cast out devils". John 14:13 also says that "And whatsoever thou will ask in my name, that will I do that the father may be glorified in the Son",

13. _Praying with the blood of Jesus._ Isaiah 53:5 says he was wounded for our transgressions and bruised for our iniquities. The chastisement of our peace was upon him, and by his stripes we are healed. He shed his blood for the remission of sins and set us free from the consequences of sin. A crown of thorns on his head, nails in his hands and feet, 39 stripes on his back, and in all these, shed his blood. He hath borne our griefs and carried our sorrows and this is the justification for our healing (Isaiah 53:4).

14. _Add works to faith._ Without works, faith is dead (James 2:17). In the book of Acts Chapter 3, Peter commanded the man at the beautiful gate to rise and walk in the name of Jesus. The ability to walk was already in him, but he

did not substantiate it or put it into action. But faith therefore is the substance of things hoped for and the evidence of things not seen (Hebrews 11:1). There is every necessity for you to demonstrate evidence that you really want to receive the miracle! It was not until Peter held him by the hand and raised him up, that his ankle bones received strength, and he leaped, and walked. When Abraham was told by God that he would become a father of many nations, he believed in hope against hope and being not weak in faith, considered not his own body now dead at about a hundred years old nor the deadness of Sarah's womb, but was strong in faith giving glory to God (Romans 4:18-20). God answered his prayers, and the promises came to pass.

15. *Laying of hands.* When the anointed hands of a spirit filled person are laid upon a sick person, the anointing of the Holy Ghost flows into the body of the sick person, breaks the yoke and heals the sickness. Most times, devils will jump out, or other unseen spiritual transactions take place which lead to healing.

16. *Anointing with oil.* The Bible says In James 5:14, that is any sick among you, let him call for the elders of the church; and let them pray over him, anointing him with oil in the name of the Lord: In verse 15, it continues, and the prayer of faith shall save the sick, and the Lord shall raise him up; and if he has committed sins, they shall be forgiven him. The oil is a medium that carries the power of the Holy Ghost.

17. *Be under the anointing.* God has people that he has given the gift of the "Working of Miracles" and he justifies and glorifies them (Romans 8:30). The Bible makes us to know in James 5:15, that people brought forth the sick into the streets, and laid them on beds and couches, that at least the shadow of Peter passing by might overshadow some of them. This does not however mean that someone not in that office cannot work Miracles. It all depends on faith, for all things are possible to him that believeth.

Prayers That Heal Valiantly:

1. O Lord, have mercy upon me and heal me completely in the name of Jesus Christ.
2. Judgement of witchcraft over my health and wellbeing be cancelled by the mercy of God in the name of Jesus Christ.
3. Covenant of terminal disease in my life, be broken in the name of Jesus Christ.
4. Covenant of the grave break and release me in the name of Jesus Christ.
5. By the power in the blood of Jesus Christ, I redeem myself from every curse of infirmity in the name of Jesus Christ.
6. Every hidden infirmity in my body, be exposed and be disgraced in the name of Jesus Christ.
7. Arrows of infirmity planted into my life in the dream, come out by fire in the name of Jesus Christ.
8. I break every yoke of infirmity unto death in my life in the name of Jesus Christ.
9. Every torment of the spirit of infirmity in my life, come to an end in the name of Jesus Christ.
10. I bind and cast our every spirit of infirmity hiding in my body in the name of Jesus Christ.
11. Inherited infirmity in my body, be healed in the name of Jesus Christ.
12. Sickness in my life as a result of evil dedication, be uprooted by fire in the name of Jesus Christ.

13. I build a shield around my life against every infectious disease in the name of Jesus Christ.
14. I rebuke every spirit of blindness in my life in the name of Jesus Christ.
15. Witchcraft pot of infirmity hanging on any tree in my environment, be broken by fire in the name of Jesus Christ.
16. Evil altar sponsoring sickness in my environment, be destroyed by fire in the name of Jesus Christ.
17. Covenant of blood suckers and flesh eaters fashioned against my life, break in the name of Jesus Christ.
18. Vulture of death assigned against my life, die in the name of Jesus Christ.
19. Anything buried in the ground taking away my peace, come out by fire in the name of Jesus Christ.
20. Curse of infirmity issued against my life, backfire in the name of Jesus Christ.
21. Every infirmity in my life as a result of witchcraft initiation break in the name of Jesus Christ.
22. Lame spirit hiding in my body, come out by fire in the name of Jesus Christ.
23. O Lord my father increase my faith in the name of Jesus Christ.
24. I arrest every spirit of fear on assignment against my life in the name of Jesus Christ.
25. O Lord my father, send your word, heal me, and deliver me from destruction un the name of Jesus Christ.
26. You the spirit of doubt, lose your hold over my life in the name of Jesus Christ.
27. I cancel every evil clinical prophecy against my life on the name of Jesus Christ.
28. Crowd of evil sympathisers working against my faith and belief system, scatter by fire in the name of Jesus Christ.
29. Witchcraft animal representing me in the kingdom of darkness manifest and receive destruction in the name of Jesus Christ.
30. Grave cloth wrapped over my life, catch fire and be roasted in the name of Jesus.
31. Witchcraft powers diverting my healing virtues, expire in the name of Jesus Christ.
32. Witchcraft attack against my drugs and infusion, expire in the name of Jesus Christ.
33. Any wrong food that I am eating that magnifies infirmity in my life, be purged from my system in the name of Jesus Christ.
34. I come against every false negative or false positive results in my diagnostic tests in the name of Jesus Christ.
35. Evert witchcraft plantation of infirmity in my blood of Jesus Christ.
36. Serpent of infirmity in my body be roasted in the name of Jesus Christ.
37. I reverse any genetic anomaly in my blood in the name of Jesus Christ.
38. Yoke of problem expanders, break and release me in the name of Jesus Christ.
39. I transfuse my blood with the blood of Jesus Christ and I command every agent of infirmity to dry up by fire in the name of Jesus Christ.
40. Anointing of infirmity that entered my body through sex, dry up by fire in the name of Jesus Christ.
41. Embargo of infirmity over my life, be lifted by fire in the name of Jesus Christ.
42. Serpent of infirmity swallowing my finances, wither and die in the name of Jesus Christ.
43. Any witchcraft tree in my environment that is sponsoring infirmity in my life, be located by the thunder and fire of the Holy Ghost in the name of Jesus Christ
44. Anointing of sickness upon my life, dry up by fire in the name of Jesus Christ.
45. Miracle angels of God visit my life for signs and wonders in the name of Jesus Christ.

46. Surgeon angels of God, my life is available, repair every diseased organ in my body in the name of Jesus Christ.
47. Father, in any way that I have sinned against thee, forgive me and have mercy upon me in the name of Jesus Christ.
48. Every seed of cancer or any terminal disease in my life, dry up by fire in the name of Jesus Christ.
49. Wicked coven judgement of infirmity over my life, be overturned by the mercy of God in the name of Jesus Christ.
50. Witchcraft network in charge of my infirmity, scatter by fire in the name of Jesus Christ.
51. I break and lose every witchcraft chain tying me down to any evil altar in the name of Jesus Christ.
52. Witchcraft personality that has vowed not to release me, receive the judgement of God by fire in the name of Jesus Christ.
53. Strange material or object in my household that is causing infirmity in my life, be destroyed by fire in the name of Jesus Christ.
54. Resurrection power of our Lord Jesus Christ, fall upon every sick organ in my life in the name of Jesus Christ.
55. O Lord, arise in your mercy and break every chain and fetter of infirmity binding my life in the name of Jesus Christ.

CHAPTER TWENTY-EIGHT

THE SPIRIT OF DEATH AND HELL.

The spirit of death and hell is one of the most destructive spirits in the kingdom of darkness. The death of a victim is usually the ultimate goal that witches and wizards drive at, after attacking with the spirit of infirmity, and usually they try to fire both arrows at the same time. Majority of the victims of witchcraft attacks and possession battle with the dreams of death which may lead to untimely death or sudden death, or both.

Believers should not joke with the signs of the spirit of death and hell, which primarily is to kill. The power of the grave robs you of your virtues and possessions and swallows them. The power of the grave is synonymous with rottenness and retrogression, poverty and sickness. However, it could also mean physical death to a great extent, depending on the origin of the arrow and mode of release of the arrow. An arrow that entered when a person was present at a graveside of a person related by blood, for a ritual, is different from an arrow that was fired by mentioning your name at the graveside, especially when you are not related by blood.

What are the methods of firing the arrows of death and hell?

1. *Through careless and indiscriminate eating and drinking.* Witchcraft may get you poisoned physically, so that you die immediately or die gradually. They could also poison you spiritually so that you are tormented by evil spirits and possibly fall sick and die someday. The eating pattern that you demonstrate in real life can be used against you in the dream. Bewitched food that you eat physically will be repeated spiritually in the dream. When you ate food physically and you dream about it at night in a strange manner, like seeing yourself in the same restaurant eating dirty stuff, then you were bewitched.

2. *Through the covenant of death.* It is possible to enter into a covenant of death after eating foods sacrificed to idols, or after having sex in an illicit manner. If a married couple make a covenant, and the woman says, any other woman you have sex with shall die untimely as I marry you today. Marriage is a covenant, and part of the covenant is what you say on that day. So, any woman that would have sex with that man shall surely die. I had a candidate many years back, who courted her boss in the office. The relationship flourished and the Pastor wife of the man was not happy about it. The transgressors eventually fell seriously ill and was brought to our church. I knew her history and told her to be praying for mercy. Nemesis caught up with her, because I told her to discontinue the relationship to no avail. Witchcraft agents may offer you cheap sex in order to drag you into the covenant of death.

3. *Curse of death.* Utterances and pronouncements could lead to death. In Joshua 6:26, after the fall of Jericho, Joshua issued a curse that anyone that attempts to rebuild the wall, would do so at the cost of sacrificing their first born and laying the foundation with the loss of their youngest son. In 2 Kings 2:23-25, Elisha cursed the boys that mocked him,

calling him a bald head. Elisha cursed them in the name of the Lord, and 2 she bears came out of the woods and killed 42 of the boys. If you commit a sin and someone curses you the curse of death, except you cry for mercy it will manifest.

4. *Evil dedication.* Some people dedicate themselves to an evil deity for riches or fame. As soon as they seek dedication and are dedicated, they are told how many more years they would live on earth to enjoy the wealth and fame. Many children were dedicated to idols before they were born. The parents may have been having miscarriages and without a child. They now dedicate them to the idols. They usually die when they are grown e.g. by the time they are to get wedded, or graduate from a school.

5. *Flesh eaters.* A department in the witchcraft kingdom are responsible for eating human organs spiritually. They eat kidneys, hearts, brains, wombs, etc. A little girl confessed that she ate the womb of the mother so that she wouldn't conceive a younger one to compete with her. She wanted to enjoy all the care and affection. If the purpose is to kill, they would kill the person. They would just start falling sick and die one day.

6. *Blood drinkers.* There is another department for blood suckers. These are present strategically on motorways and road junctions, as well as hospitals. Since the life of the flesh is in the blood (Leviticus 17:11), they withdraw the blood until the person becomes emaciated, and sick, until they die. Every sign of continuous emaciation should be addressed promptly medically and spiritually. They also cause motor accidents leading to loss of lives. They masquerade in some women to cause excessive menstrual flows or attack during childbirth.

7. *A Lifestyle of Sin and unrighteousness.* Many people are jinxed to commit sin and to make negative decisions that destroy them. In spite of the fact that smoking kills, when I preach against it, some people don't care. In James 4:17, the Bible says Therefore to him that knoweth to do good and doeth it not, to him it is sin. We cannot underrate the part that alcoholism has played in the destruction of souls worldwide. Sexual immorality is another way. In many African nations, the life of many have been sacrificed on the laps of strange women through charms. Imagine a charm that makes a man-eating salt, after having sex in an illicit manner. Or he summersaults and crows like a cock and dies.

8. *Evil summons.* There is evil summons spiritually whereby a person is summoned spiritually to appear inside water in a calabash, or on a wall in a witchcraft covenant. They are then shot or stabbed, with resultant death immediately or after some time. Sometimes the victim answers to his or her name and slumps and dies.

9. *A person may be manipulated into committing suicide by programming the spirit of death.* There have been people that jumped into a river or jumped down from great heights, defying every persuasion. They just wasted their lives.

10. *Through enchantments.* There are witchcraft enchantments whereby a person gets up from the bed at night and walks into the thick forest in order to die. These enchantments are aimed essentially to make people to commit error. It may be in a place of work, whereby a person commits error that leads to death, and people keep wondering how that person committed the error.

11. *During surgical procedures or abortion.* The blood suckers and flesh eaters can attack during surgical procedures. That is why you need to pray very well before embarking upon any surgical operation. Also, you don't tell everybody that you are scheduled for surgery on a particular day, for example.

What are the signs of the spirit of death and hell?

1. *Fear of death.* If you are under the attack of the spirit of death and hell, you will continue to have the fear of death. I had a candidate who was always thinking about sudden death. She tried to cross the road one day. She was hit by a motor bike and seriously injured. She could have died if not for the mercy of God. That is why you should do away with the fear of death but trust God. When you keep thinking about sudden death, you'll become what you are thinking. Think positively and courageously, disregarding every negativity.
2. *Dreams signifying death.* When you dream about dead relatives and dead people, repeatedly and regularly, then the spirit of death is somewhere lurking around. Dreams of seeing coffins, seeing graveyards, seeing dead animals, morgue or mortuary, or when you dream and you see a vulture or owl around your house, or wearing a black dress in the dream or people crying in the dream. The bone of the human skull or a complete skeleton.
3. *When you keep perceiving the smell of a rotten thing.* This is the presence of the spirit of death and hell.
4. *When you hear the voices of people who are dead.* They keep speaking to you.
5. *When the arrow of incurable disease is fired* and you have been diagnosed with a terminal disease or purportedly incurable *disease.*
6. *Suicidal thoughts tendencies.* When a person is thinking that life is so difficult and not worth living, and that the best option is to do something that will end the existence.
7. *Many near death experience.* You miss being hit by a vehicle by a second, or you fell into a deep ditch, or a few days later, armed robbers raided your locality and the bullet almost hit you.
8. *When your intuition keeps telling you.* There is ease and there is serious tension giving you the feeling that something bad is about to happen. People who have died were said to have had a premonition one way or another through their words or actions.
9. *At other times strange signs in the environment.* The dogs may continue to cry violently, or there might be the cry of a cat very loudly in the middle of the night which is heard by everyone and makes everyone in the environment to fear.
10. *Verbal threats.* Demonic spirits may come to you to threaten you that you are guilty of death and infirmity. However, who is it that saith and it cometh to pass when the Lord commands it not (Job 3:37).
11. *There is a transition between this world and another world.* This is reflected in the spiritual experience as people tormented by the spirit of death and hell may see themselves in a strange world different from this world.
12. *Visitation by demons.* People who are about to die experience the presence of demonic spirits, and others like dead relatives that they can see beside them clearly, and who may discuss with them.

Yet in all these things we are more than conquerors through him that loved us (Romans 8:37). He has been threatened in the dream with the judgement of death and sickness. They tried, but God was faithful. In the case of Hezekiah in Isaiah 38, he was very close to death, but God saved him. God gave him another 15 years. If Jesus raised the dead that was totally gone, there is nothing he cannot do. What are the steps to receive deliverance from the spirit of death and hell?

Steps to receive deliverance from the spirit of death and Hell:

1. *Total surrender to Jesus.* Give your life to Jesus by confessing him as Lord and personal saviour.
2. *Repent from your sins.* Every sin potentially can kill and send you to hell fire. The spirit of death and hell thrives on our sins, and if we must be delivered from the spirit of death and hell, we have to let all our thoughts, words and actions be according to God's will.
3. *Consistent prayer and faith works.* As someone who has battled with the spirit of death and hell personally, consistent prayer and faith works wonders. I start with faith. Think about prophecies that were released before the incident that you are being confronted with. The faith you have makes you unbendable to witches and wizards. They will bring all forms of visions of graveyard and dead people to intimidate you and threaten you. They make it very frequent that if you are not demonstrating faith, you may succumb. Many people succumb when the attacks were too much. They will make it so real! If you are a student or a worker, concentrating would be difficult. Very stubborn faith and believe in God's word will change your game.
4. *Confess the word all the time.* Say the word anyhow. Psalm 118:17 says I shall not die but live and declare the works of the Lord. In Isaiah 41:10 it says Fear thou not; for I am with thee: be not dismayed for I am thy God: I will strengthen thee; yea I will help thee; yea I will uphold thee with the right hand of my righteousness.
5. *Pray and fast ceaselessly.* When your prayers are fervent and consistent, then you can make exploits. Just keep praying until God answers. In my own case, I heard that I was guilty of death and sickness with several dreams and visions of death. I was not bothered but kept praying. After a few months, I was having my siesta one afternoon, and all of a sudden, I was lifted upwards from a grave, as if it was an elevator that lifted me out of the ground. When I got to England and alone without my family, the battle continued until they were *defeated.*
6. *Eschew violence.* Violent behaviour kills, and most times when you least expect it. Beware of your associations.
7. *Lifestyle choices e.g. eating and drinking should be done responsibly.* When you don't do things in moderation, it could end your life abruptly. Also try and di routine medical examinations.
8. *Put God first.* Every day as you go out, make sure you pray. There are mornings that God may wake you up even early. I was made to wake up early to go to work on a particular day to go to work early. The Holy Spirit did that in order to save me from irate youth. I had passed the portion of the road before the riot broke out.
9. *Seek knowledge.* The Bible says in Hosea 4:6 that my people perish for lack of knowledge. If that is the case, then knowledge can prolong life. Seek knowledge about medicine and technology amongst others.

10. _News._ Make sure you listen to the news on radio, television, and even on the Internet that will sensitise you to events happening around you.
11. _Learn to pray in tongues daily._ When you are faced with a situation when evil is lurking and that you don't know what to pray about, you pray in tongues, for the spirit helpeth our infirmities (Romans 8:26) for we know not what to pray for.
12. _Speak the words of life into your destiny._ The words that we speak carry power. Mark 11:23 says, that whosoever shall say unto this mountain, be thou removed and be cast into the sea, and shall not doubt in his heart, but shall believe that those things which he saith shall come to pass, he shall have whatsoever he saith. Words carry power and we should learn to decree good things upon our lives always.

CHAPTER TWENTY-NINE

DELIVERANCE OF THE HEAD.

The head, hands and feet are symbolic in deliverance, and these parts of the body have always been targeted and attacked by witchcraft powers. However, we shall first look at the deliverance of the head. There are reasons why the head is important, there are things that you can do to bewitch your head, and there are signs to indicate that the head is under attack, the possible effects of these attacks on the spiritual health and destiny of an individual.

Why is the head targeted by witchcraft?

The head is regarded as the symbol of a person's destiny. The Lord told Moses, certain things concerning anointing Aaron.

Exodus 29:5-7

⁵and thou shalt take the garments, and put-upon Aaron the coat, and the robe of the ephod, and the ephod, and the breastplate, and gird him with the curious girdle of the ephod:

⁶and thou shalt put the mitre upon his head, and put the holy crown upon the mitre.

⁷Then shalt thou take the anointing oil, and pour it upon his head, and anoint him.

Someone might wonder, why was the head anointed. Why was the crown placed on the head? In many traditions across the world, when someone is enthroned as King, the head is treated with dignity and all the rites are done on the head. When hands are laid, they are laid on the head to bless. When the head of an animal or person is severed, that is the end of life. No human being can exist without a head. This part of the human body is so extremely important that the devil not only medically but spiritually attack. The head should be well protected. Unfortunately, the enemy sees it as an object of attack, in order to derail destinies.

How has man made himself vulnerable to witchcraft attacks against the head?

1. <u>Through evil laying of hands.</u> Many people have had a stint with members of the Occult whereby hands were laid consciously or unconsciously. Sometimes evil rings or bangles are worn. They use it to transfer evil spirits, Rob people of stars, or fire the arrows of discomfort or strange behaviour.
2. <u>Barber or Hairdresser's Salon.</u> Some barbers have demonic ways of attacking the destinies of men. Washing the head and allowing the water to run down the hose to a large drum, then using the water for rituals. Some cut your hair in order to bewitch you. Demonic concoctions may be used as hair cream. Still some lay hands and you may think

nothing has gone wrong, except when you get home and you dream about that same Salon, as God shows what was done against you. This is very common courtesy of God's love and mercy. Some hairdressers have bewitched hands that if the Lord opens your eyes, the fingers are serpents.

3. *Inherited bewitchment of the head.* The head may be bewitched as a result of a curse placed upon the head. The manifestation will be seen in the head. We shall see the signs of these manifestations soon.

4. *Covenants might bewitch a head.* A conscious or unconscious covenant may bring symptoms of head bewitchment.

5. *Idol worship.* When you are given to the worship of idols and deities, bewitchment of the head may result. When you receive favours from idols, when it is payback time, they may request for your memory, cognition, or other brain functions as you begin to hear strange voices.

6. *Hard drug abuse.* The use of hard drugs can easily bewitch the head. Unfortunately, there are many of these addictive substances in the world today that are being invented by the youth. A lot of self-destruction is going on that insanity is on the increase. This is usually acquired from peer groups. Parents have a great role to play.

7. *Incisions.* There are black substances believed to give certain magical benefits that are rubbed into incisions made in the head.

8. *Through satanic summons or commands.* A person may be represented by an animal on an evil altar, and they just lay hands on the head of the animal, call the name of the person they want to bewitch, and bewitch the head. He wakes up from his sleep with a heavy headache or confused or both. That will be the beginning of problems.

9. *Wearing hats, caps and headgears of strangers.* I used to have a counselee. The beginning of her problem was the headgear she was persuaded by a friend to use to a function. The very night of the function, she had some funny revelations about the headgear. She had terrible spiritual problems following that period, until she came for deliverance when we met.

10. *Blood Rituals.* When you partake in blood rituals, and someone washes your head with animal blood, that may be the beginning of your problems, unless you aggressively pursue deliverance.

11. *Through food.* A certain man committed adultery and was captured by the woman that she bewitched his head. When they bewitch your head, the main thing is that your thinking and intelligence is attacked. The woman gave him vegetable soup. All that mattered from that moment was that woman he committed adultery with. He, at a stage abandoned his wife and children, and packed all his belongings to live with the woman. At that point, the woman shouted for help. The man eventually went for deliverance and was set free.

12. *Through charms.* There are employers that could bewitch a person's head. Once you are bewitched, you would gladly do any assignment they give to you. It is the wage or salary they give to you that you will gladly accept, no matter how small. These people use charms and enchantments in many forms.

Signs of a Bewitched Head:

1. *Strange Voices.* When the head is bewitched, a person begins to hear strange voices, which sometimes issues strange commands, you may hear strange conversation of things that you don't know about. Demons will continue to speak in your day until you do something about it.

2. *Confusion.* A person suffering from bewitchment of the head will always experience confusion which is mild initially but escalates if nothing is done about it.

3. *Headache and pains in the head.* When the head is bewitched, one of the symptoms is headache or pains in some parts of the head. This pain can be so significant that it adds to your confusion.

4. *Strange movements in the head.* At the time of bewitchment, if a serpentine spirit is programmed into the head, you would feel it moving around in the head. If the arrow of insanity is fired, you have the feeling of a lizard moving in your head. Depending on the type of bewitchment, many things could move inside your head.

5. *Strange behaviour.* A husband with a bewitched head will first start misbehaving. Likewise, a wife! What they didn't do prior to the time, they will start doing it and without apology. Some of these Strange behaviours tend to suicide or self-harm. A kid may hit the head against the wall, or suddenly become dull in class, and the academic performance is grossly affected.

6. *Bad dreams may be experienced.* There is an evil spiritual arrow in the head, with an unstable spirit. The spirit which is the candle of the Lord (Proverbs 20:27) has been hijacked by the enemy. The enemy ceases it and manipulates it due to carelessness on the part of the victim. The result is bad dreams and scary visions.

7. *Error and mistakes.* A brilliant child who is doing well in class, will be prone to errors as soon as the head is bewitched. A person with a bewitched head will notice that they start having errors and mistakes.

8. *Failure.* Once there are errors and mistakes in a person's life, there can't be success, but failure academically, professionally, domestic decisions and others.

9. *Sleeplessness (Insomnia).* Most people with bewitched heads do not sleep and remain awake at night. In some other instances, out of depression, they might sleep all day, though this is not as common as the former. One noticeable pattern however is a disturbed sleep pattern.

10. *Sickness.* There is some spiritual disagreement between the spirit and the flesh, such that the spirit is willing, but the flesh is weak (Matthew 26:41). This is how spiritual healing works, and a merry heart will do good like medicine and heal (Proverbs 17:22).

11. *Noise in the head.* When there is a bewitchment of the head, there will be irritating and sustained noise in the ears, and in the head. All these signs of headache, confusion, and noise in the head constitute a big problem which may result in insanity.

12. *Insanity.* People who are battling with mental issues have the head attacked in various methods outlined above in order to arrest their destinies. The attack of the head is usually used to slow down destinies or stop destinies altogether. The head may be subtly bewitched and you won't suspect. All you will notice is that outcomes are changing. Routine deliverance of the head is necessary. It's like a brain box servicing or engine overhaul!

13. *Memory Loss.* Some people are not totally insane, but they have memory loss. This may start with putting something somewhere in the house, but you have forgotten. In an employment interview, they are asking you questions when you get there. It looks as if they used a duster to wipe your memory.

14. *Uncontrollable anger.* Uncontrollable anger is another manifestation of the bewitched head. It is normal to be angry, but when it becomes uncontrollable and it regresses into fits of rage, yelling and shouting, which they may later regret and sob hysterically, then it is a totally abnormal situation.

15. *Lack of progress.* They may not fail totally, but progress will be slow. One of the indices is that business may be affected, another is that the satisfaction of staff under them or their superiors may be affected.

Conducting the Deliverance of The Head.

The deliverance of the head involves prayers, and specialised deliverance ministrations. Prayers for the deliverance of the head will be outlined at the end of this chapter. However, the head is anointed lavishly with oil, and the following procedure are followed.

1. Rub the oil into the scalp, and command every evil attachment, mentioning one by one - cowrie shells, combs, phylacteries, serpents, evil arrows to come out as they shake their heads vigorously. Command those things with an authoritative tone to come out by fire. Tell them to begin to shake the head as you mention those entities and command them to come out by fire. Command them in another set of prayers and instructions to come out by the power in the blood of Jesus. Then the third round tell them to come out in the name of Jesus.

2. The second time, tell them to anoint the eyes, and you command every stranger in the eyes to come out. Command evil arrows to come out in the name of Jesus Christ. Command them to come out by the power in the blood of Jesus. Command them to come out by the power of the Holy Ghost.

3. The third time, tell them to anoint the ears, and you command every stranger to come out, including serpents, evil arrows, evil spirits, to come out. Command every noise to cease. During deliverance you had an overview of the problems of your candidates, so you address those concerns.

4. The fourth time, tell then to drink the oil, and command the strangers in the tummy to come out. Once again you have an overview of their problems through counselling on the very first day. The people that ate in their dreams, you already know what they ate, and you command those things to come out. If they are marine, you command serpents and fishes to come out amongst others. If they are black witches or victims of black witches, then you command the bird inside anyone to catch fire and be roasted.

5. At this stage do not forget to address infirmity, even though you have addressed it during the healing session. Diseased of the eyes, ears, tongues, speech if you have a patient with a speech related tongue e.g. autism. Wry neck, diseases of the muscles and joints of the neck etc.

CHAPTER THIRTY

DELIVERANCE OF THE HANDS.

The hand is the symbol of a person's prosperity. The enemy does attack the hands in many ways during sleep, physically or set some spiritual traps. People possessed by witchcraft do notice that they may destroy everything they lay their hands upon. Their hands too can bewitch people's food, organs or other things. They are able to wipe away tears.

Psalms 144:1

Blessed be the LORD my strength, which teacheth my hands to war, and my fingers to fight:

The power of God is a restorer and even a restorer of a person's business or career. The hand is the symbol of our work, and the devil takes great interest in attacking the hands.

Signs of a bewitched hand.

1. Strange movement in the hands. Serpents, cockroaches or other insects or worms may be moving in the hands to the extent that you may really have the feeling that such are moving around in the hand.
2. Hotness in the hands.
3. Heaviness and strange feelings in the hands.
4. Damaging objects and materials in your place of work or at home.
5. Diminishing profits.
6. Evil impact on customers. If a hairdresser, the customers may have terrible brains and itching in their heads.
7. Trembling of the hands without any observable reasons.
8. Deformity of the hands and fingers.

Causes of bewitchment of the hands.

1. Using your hands to touch demonic or cursed objects.
2. Cursed hands.
3. Stealing
4. Covenant of poverty
5. Evil dedication
6. Idol worship.
7. Incisions on the hand
8. Evil handshakes

9. Strange attacks in the dream against the hands e.g. knife or razor cuts and touching of poo in the dream.
10. Evil inheritance. Bewitchment, or problems of the hand can be inherited.

Conducting the deliverance of the hands.

Essentially, anyone that is being oppressed by the spirit of poverty, has a disease affecting the hands, or has tendencies to bewitch by touching or laying of hands. There are people whose fingers in the realm of the spirits are serpents. When they work as Chefs, they bewitch the food, and anyone that eats that type of food is in trouble.

The first step in the deliverance of the hands is to have a consciousness of these issues above and a desire to be free from the bondage.

Anointing oil is normally blessed by praying on it, and you pour some on the palms of both hands rubbing them together and praying out loud.

The prayer points to be prayed include:

1. Power of the Holy Ghost, fall upon my hands now in the name of Jesus Christ.
2. Clap your ends as you pray that the blood of Jesus should cancel evil covenants fashioned against your hand.
3. Clap your hands and command every curse of poverty and non-achievement fashioned against your hands to break in the name of Jesus Christ.
4. Rub your hands together, until hot. The deliverance minister will issue a command and all you need to say is Amen. For example, he may command every arrow of poverty to come out in the name of Jesus Christ. He may command every witchcraft serpent to catch fire in the name of Jesus Christ.
5. Pray loudly that every chain of darkness fashioned against your hands to break in the name of Jesus Christ.
6. Pray that evil incisions should lose their power over your hands.
7. Add some more oil and say I pour the blood of Jesus Christ on my hands and rub away every evil mark of witchcraft on my hands
8. Every animal or object programmed into my hands catch fire and release me now in the name of Jesus Christ.
9. You the ring and bangles of spirit husband or spirit wife, on my fingers, catch fire, break in the name of Jesus Christ.
10. Hand of the monkey or any other animal programmed into my hands, catch fire and be roasted in the name of Jesus Christ.
11. My original hand on witchcraft altar, be restored in the name of Jesus.
12. Every evil object that I have ever touched with my hands, I break your power over my hands in the name of Jesus Christ.
13. Let the glory of my hands work be delivered in the name of Jesus Christ.

14. Demonic spirits operating in my hand, be arrested by fire in the name of Jesus Christ.
15. You my hands, receive healing from every disease and infirmity in the name of Jesus Christ.
16. Every arrow of debt fired into my hands, come out by fire in the name of Jesus Christ.
17. Prophesy into your hands, that "you my hands, begin to prosper as from today" in the name of Jesus Christ.
18. Pray again that you my hands, reject bewitchment as from today in the name of Jesus Christ.
19. I destroy every evil cobweb fashioned against my hands in the name of Jesus Christ.
20. Every evil altar cursing my hands, be destroyed by the thunder fire of God in the name of Jesus Christ.
21. Satanic animals programmed into my hands, cockroaches, insects, worms, I command you to catch fire and burn to ashes in the name of Jesus Christ.
22. Every power cursing my hands be rendered deaf and dumb in the name of Jesus Christ.
23. Every evil manipulation by palm readers against my hands, be undone in the name of Jesus Christ.
24. Every satanic timer working against the work of my hands, be destroyed by fire in the name of Jesus Christ.
25. You my hands begin to cooperate with my head as from today in the name of Jesus Christ.
26. Bewitchment by marine spirits upon my hands, be undone by the power in the blood of Jesus Christ.
27. I cancel the effect of any black soap or native concoction that I ever used to wash my hands by the power in the blood of Jesus Christ.
28. Any evil sign of the enemy on my hands, be washed away by the power in the blood of Jesus Christ.
29. Every enchanter, speaking evil words against the work of my hands, I break your power by the power in the blood of Jesus Christ.
30. I release my hands from every witchcraft cauldron in the name of Jesus Christ.
31. Fling your hands and fingers and say I command you evil arrows to come out in the name of Jesus Christ.
32. Pour some more anointing oil lavishly as you say I wash my hands with the blood of Jesus Christ.
33. Witchcraft padlock, fashioned against my hands, break by fire, break by fire, break by fire in the name of Jesus Christ.
34. Every bewitchment of the hands that I inherited from my parents, and grandparents, break and release me in the name of Jesus Christ.
35. Satanic ring of spirit spouse on my finger, I remove you, be roasted by fire in the name of Jesus Christ (Actually try to remove the rings from your fingers)

After praying, you tell them to pause, and immediately you call down the fire of the Holy Ghost, as you issue decrees for evil arrows, evil plantations and witchcraft animals to go out by fire in the name of Jesus Christ. The deliverance minister should move close to the candidate because the manifestation mat be violent sometimes.

CHAPTER THIRTY-ONE

DELIVERANCE OF THE FEET.

The feet represent a person's journey in life and your outcomes. The feet could be bewitched in many ways by witchcraft powers, and with adverse effects on a person's life. The feet could be bewitched in the following ways:

1. Stepping on a bewitched object
2. When you use your feet to trespass or walk on the wrong place
3. Through incisions
4. Attacks in the dream.
5. Ritual baths near the river
6. Ritual baths using blood of humans or animals, or other rituals involving the feet.
7. Tying charms and amulets around the feet
8. Bewitched feet from the womb.
9. Curses issued against a person's feet.
10. Evil laying of hands on the feet.
11. When the dust you have stepped on is used to enchant against you and bewitch you.

What are the effects of bewitched feet?

1. _Wrong positioning._ The person will always make mistakes in the choice of place to work.
2. _Swollen feet syndrome._ The feet will be swollen and painful.
3. When your presence in people's life brings disaster. If a person with a bewitched foot gets married, people might start to die mysteriously in the house, or fall sick.
4. _Work._ If a person with bewitched feet starts work in an office, they may cease to make sales, or a terrible fire incident may happen in the office.
5. _Friendship_ with a person with bewitched foot may cause problems for the sad friend and disasters in their lives.
6. _Co-tenancy._ When you live in a house and things all of a sudden begins to go bad, a person with a bewitched foot is likely to have packed in. They didn't bargain for it, but they bring misfortune even as they are part of the misfortune.
7. _Sickness._ It is not possible for you to carry a demonic spirit as tenant in your life, without having strange experiences. Sickness is one of such.
8. _Failure in marriage._ A person with a bewitched foot carries a negative influence which disorganises. They are at the receiving end.
9. _Sorrow._ This is the ultimate result when everything goes wrong. There is sorrow.

10. <u>Disfavour.</u> People are quick to recognise a negative aura. This brings untold disfavour, and employers will not like to see you around because everything is not going fine with them.
11. *Remotely controlling the feet.* They might call someone in his sleep and tell him to go to the bush, or go to the river to drown, or go to a bridge and jump. Those people will stand up without hesitation and go.

How to conduct deliverance of the feet:

It is assumed that the person has given his life to Jesus Christ and confessed him as Lord and personal saviour. It is also assumed that you believe in the death and resurrection of our Lord and saviour Jesus Christ and the power of Christ to deliver to the uttermost.

> *John 1:12*
> *But as many as received him, to them gave the power to become the sons of God, even to them that believe on his name.*

Prayers for deliverance of the feet:

1. Witchcraft padlock, fashioned against my feet, break in the name of Jesus Christ.
2. Witchcraft attack against my life's journey, backfire in the name of Jesus Christ.
3. Witchcraft clock working against my life's journey, catch fire and be destroyed in the name of Jesus.
4. Power of evil incisions fashioned against my feet, break, by the power in the blood of Jesus Christ.
5. Every evil voice controlling my journey in life, be silenced forever in the name of Jesus Christ.
6. Evil chains fashioned against my feet, break and release me by the power in the blood of Jesus Christ.
7. By the power in the blood of Jesus Christ, I redeem myself from every curse fashioned against my feet.
8. Mark of disfavour on my feet, be wiped away by the power in the blood of Jesus Christ.
9. Every bewitchment of the dust under my feet, be reversed in the name of Jesus Christ.
10. Power of rejection, working against my life anywhere I go, break in the name of Jesus Christ.
11. Anything programmed into my feet, that is affecting my marriage, be deprogrammed in the name of Jesus Christ.
12. Cobwebs fashioned against my feet, clear away by fire in the name of Jesus Christ.
13. Every evil covenant I entered into unconsciously by way of trespass, be broken by the power in the blood of Jesus Christ.
14. Anything representing my feet on witchcraft altar, be withdrawn by fire in the name of Jesus Christ.
15. Evil worm, serpent, cockroach, lizard, or other animals programmed into my feet, come out by fire and die in the name of Jesus Christ.
16. Evil storm, following my life everywhere I go, be still in the name of Jesus.
17. Every power of the air attacking the journey of my life, be arrested and be bound in the name of Jesus Christ.
18. Blood covenant working against my feet, break in the name of Jesus Christ.
19. Lay your two hands on your feet and command them "You my feet, take me to the place of my glory" in the name of Jesus Christ.

20. Begin to stamp your feet on the ground, and I shake off every satanic entanglement fashioned against my feet in the name of Jesus Christ.
21. Sing like this: break my yoke, break my yoke, Holy Ghost fire break my yoke.
22. Every witchcraft yoke fashioned against my feet, break in the name of Jesus Christ.
23. Pour the anointing oil lavishly on your feet and as you rub your feet, say I rub off every infirmity, by the power in the blood of Jesus Christ, and I command every spirit of infirmity to depart in the name of Jesus Christ.
24. Evil decrees, and evil pronouncement fashioned against my feet, be cancelled by the power in the blood of Jesus Christ.
25. Inherited bondage in my feet, break in the name of Jesus Christ.
26. Witchcraft control against my feet, break and release me in the name of Jesus Christ.
27. Every evil connection between my ears and my feet, be broken by fire in the name of Jesus Christ.
28. Remote control of witchcraft fashioned against my feet, be destroyed by fire in the name of Jesus Christ.
29. Arrow of infirmity that entered through my feet, come out and go back to your sender in the name of Jesus Christ.
30. Every foot of Achan, in the camp of my life, troubling my destiny, receive the judgement of God in the name of Jesus Christ.
31. Every bewitchment fashioned against the feet of my children, receive deliverance in the name of Jesus Christ.
32. Deliverance power of God, locate the feet of my husband in the name of Jesus Christ.
33. Every foot anointed by the devil to work against me in my place of work, receive deliverance in the name of Jesus Christ.
34. Arthritis in my ankles, in any joint of my feet, receive healing in the name of Jesus Christ.
35. My feet (touch your feet with your hands), you shall not take me to the place of destruction in the name of Jesus Christ.
36. You my feet, refuse to cooperate with the evil agenda of the dust against my life and destiny in the name of Jesus Christ.

CHAPTER THIRTY-TWO

THE HOLY GHOST BAPTISM.

The Holy Ghost baptism is a significant and an important encounter, whereby the Holy Spirit comes upon you and gives you power.

Acts 1:8

But ye shall receive power, after that the Holy Ghost is come upon you.......

This power does not come immediately you receive Christ, but you need to continue in the study of the word of God, meditation, prayer, and fasting. The more intimate you are with the study and meditation in the word of God, then the more you act and believe.

John 1:12

But as many as received him, to them gave he power to become the sons of God, even to them that believe on his name:

Receiving Jesus and believing in his name, brings the power of the Holy Ghost, as you earnestly wait in faith to receive it with the evidence of speaking in tongues. During the Baptism of the Holy Ghost, the power of the Holy Ghost is kindled and many unusual things begin to happen. After the baptism of the Holy Ghost, a believer cannot be the same again! The Bible says in Acts 1:8, above, that it gave them the power for witnessing. Witnessing requires boldness in everything, and the Holy Ghost gives that as well.

Acts 4:31

And when they had prayed, the place was shaken where they were assembled together; and they were all filled with the Holy Ghost, and they spake the word of God with boldness.

During deliverance ministrations, which normally is carried out with the candidates fasting, many evil works are destroyed. Chains are broken, evil plantations uprooted, satanic padlocks broken, spirit spouses jump out, witchcraft spirits depart, evil covenants are broken, evil masks removed, evil marks of disfavour rubbed off, and there is increased hunger and thirst for the word of God and the things of God.

Isaiah 58:7-8

⁷Is it not to deal thy bread to the hungry, and that thou bring the poor that are cast out to thy house? When thou seest the naked, that thou cover him; and that thou hide not thyself from thine own flesh?

⁸Then shall thy light break forth as the morning, and thine health shall spring forth speedily: and thy righteousness shall go before thee; the glory of the LORD shall be his rereward.

The Holy Ghost baptism is usually conducted when the fasting and prayer is at its peak during the deliverance program.

How to conduct the Holy Ghost Baptism:

The baptism of the Holy Ghost follows a procedure. The following are the procedure:

1. *The candidate must desire it and wait for it.* Acts 2:1 makes us to note that they were waiting in one accord in a place. When a person desires him knowing the benefits as you shall learn shortly, then the main hurdle is overcome. Once you hear his voice (word) and desire him with all your heart, then you have opened the door. He requires that you open. In as much as you are willing to open, then he enters. He is knocking. Will you open to him? (Revelation 3:20)
2. *Seek assistance.* It is good for you to join a local church and discuss it with your Pastor or ministers, if they did not previously raise it. According to what God told me, he said that during Evangelism, if somebody has given his life to Christ, then I should try to see that he receives the baptism of the Holy Ghost. Many who have given their lives to Jesus remain powerless or may even backsliding without the Holy Ghost baptism. A Pastor would discuss with you how you can go about it.
3. *Appointment day.* Usually, some Pastors decide to conduct a Holy Ghost Class, whereby we gather on allotted days of the week to receive teachings and pray for the baptism of the Holy Ghost. In some other cases, it is done during the deliverance week.

A typical schedule for the Holy Ghost baptism:

1. *Opening prayers.* Binding territorial powers, pray for open heavens, loose people that are tied, etc.
2. *Praise worship session.* Sing solemnly the songs of deliverance, songs of encouragement, songs of healing, and songs of Holy spirit. This paves way for the Holy Ghost gradually. This goes on for about 30 minutes.
3. *Word exhortation.* Different scriptures are cited and thoroughly explained to teach the process and significance of the Holy Ghost baptism.
4. *Prayer Points.* Prayer points are raised militantly after the word study, up to 50-100 prayer points, calling upon the Holy Ghost to be released, and every hindrance to be removed. This runs for another 30 minutes or 45 minutes and stimulates and paves way further for the Holy Ghost. This is followed by songs about the Holy Spirit, in worship or warfare style for about 30 minutes as well. After these, the candidates are well charged and prepared to receive.
5. *Receiving.* Essentially to receive it, the candidates are told to be silent for about five minutes immediately after the warfare or worship songs. Some would even have started speaking in tongues before you tell them to. Teach them to listen to an inner nudge. There is an inner prompting, and an inner voice that you should follow and repeat after. It might not really make sense to you but say it. The power of the Holy Ghost comes down as soon as you are relaxed and open to him, he enters into you. Anything can happen at this stage. Many demons begin to jump out, chains are broken, evil arrows fly out, spirit husbands surrender, and marriage certificates are distributed. Tell them to be attentive as some may see visions about what is happening at that time. Make provisions for protection of the candidates, so that the demons do not for example angrily make then to sit on a nail or confuse them to run into the main road. Lock all exit doors. If you are receiving the baptism for the very first time, ministers should be around to guide you until you gain spiritual momentum and enter into the spiritual super-highway.

6. *Laying of Hands.* Some candidates need to be impacted by laying of hands (Acts 8:17; Acts 19:6). The Deliverance Minister needs to be led anyways for the bible says we should not lay hands suddenly on anyone (1 Timothy 5:22).

7. *Anointing with oil* (James 5:14-15). When you anoint a candidate with oil, the power of the Holy Ghost is imparted and they begin to speak I'm tongues. As demonstrated in James 5:14-15, any act that can bring about the impartation of the Holy Ghost can be employed to do deliverance, healing and miracles.

8. *Through your breath.* This is one method that works effectively that many ministers ignore. Jesus Christ demonstrated it in the Bible (John 20:22).

9. *Other means as led.* The Holy Spirit is a spirit that you cannot predict sometimes. He may lead you in any way to impart the anointing. I went to minister in a service when invited by a Pastor colleague on a certain morning. The spirit of God told me to point to people on the last two rows and command the Holy Ghost to fall upon them. That was what I did, and the whole place was in pandemonium to the glory of God. Satan was terribly discomfited. On another time, the Holy Spirit told me to use my suit to wipe the candidates, and that was it. I was just passing amidst the candidates, and as I got to a certain lady, the Holy Ghost told me to step on her big toe with my own big toe. The power of the Holy Ghost so fell upon her that she manifested greatly.

10. *Follow-up.* During a weekly deliverance session, this process is carried out usually between 9am - 1pm. The difference in a Holy Ghost Baptismal Class is that it runs once or twice a week, until the candidate receives the baptism. The Holy Ghost Baptismal Class is highly encouraged for every new convert. We shall see the importance of the Holy Ghost Baptism and the reason why every believer must receive the Holy Ghost Baptism.

The Importance and Works of the Holy Ghost in a Child of God.

1. The Holy spirit convicts you of sin and informs your decision to want to give your life to Jesus (John 16:7-8).

2. The Holy Spirit helps you to maintain a Holy living (Galatians 5:16) and makes you to hate sin and hunger and thirst for righteousness. Once you hunger and thirst for righteousness, through practicing what you read in God's word, you will be filled continuously (Matthew 5:6).

3. He makes you to have zeal for the word of God, and gives understanding of the word of God, especially if you meditate (1 John 2:27).

4. The Holy Spirit makes you bold to resist sin anywhere. He gives you the desire to practice Holy living (Acts 4:31).

5. The Holy Spirit makes you to want to pray. He makes you have a desire to want to pray (Ephesians 6:18).

6. The Holy Spirit teaches you to pray, for we know not what to pray about. helps you to pray (Romans 8:26).

7. He gives us revelation. The Holy spirit knows all things and teaches all things. He reveals what is to come. When you pray, he speaks to you in dreams, visions, and many other ways, even at different times to establish his purpose for your life and take good care of you (Hebrews 1:1; John 16:13)

8. The Holy Spirit calls you according to predestination. We all have been predestined to follow a pathway and to arrive at a destination in life. One morning, very early in the day, he gave me an instruction to proceed on a 7-day dry fast that I shouldn't take food, drink or have sex for seven days. I was excited because I love hearing from the Holy Spirit. At the end of seven days, I heard the phrase "Evangelism and Miracles" as my core ministry, and

other things like para-ministerial assignment, my mentor, etc. were revealed to me. Subsequently I was given a download of the scope and purpose of my ministry.

9. When the Holy Spirit calls you, he will give you gifts to operate in that calling and ministry (1 Corinthians 12). The Holy Spirit will normally tell me to go into a fast and tell me why I am fasting. At other times he could tell me to go to a prayer mountain to ask for specific things. He would give me some assignments from time to time. All these work towards the fulfilment of your ministry and higher calling. Don't ignore any of them. He would passively bestow you with the gifts, but when it will manifest, you will be amazed. The first time that I laid hands on a deliverance candidate, I was so surprised at the violent manifestation. It is necessary for you to develop the gifts through prayer and use of the gifts on a daily basis. Yes, DAILY. Make sure you find an opportunity to use it daily even if you are on a secular job. I would normally Evangelise in the morning before going to work. Others would arrange a program in their church in the morning. I use my counselling gifts on the go, through calls or WhatsApp messages. The more you use it, the more it gets better, the more you expand. It's a worthy obsession!

10. The Holy Spirit will not leave you nor forsake you. He will always back you up. When you are making mistakes, he will always correct you. He will always return you to the tracks when you are making a mistake. He also makes covenant with you concerning your family. He sees to their welfare. The calling of God cannot exclude your family. Wives or husband who say that God only called their spouses are mistaken.

CHAPTER THIRTY-THREE

HOW TO MAINTAIN YOUR DELIVERANCE.

Matthew 12:43-45

⁴³When the unclean spirit is gone out of a man, he walketh through dry places, seeking rest, and findeth none.

⁴⁴Then he saith, I will return into my house from whence I came out; and when he is come, he findeth it empty, swept, and garnished.

⁴⁵Then goeth he, and taketh with himself seven other spirits more wicked than himself, and they enter in and dwell there: and the last state of that man is worse than the first. Even so shall it be also unto this wicked generation.

When a person is delivered and restored divinely, he still needs to maintain the deliverance, as the bible makes us to realise in the scripture above. The demon is not happy to realise that he has now been driven from a place that he once lived in. He roams about in dry places. He has gone out, but he is still at the door waiting for the slightest opportunity to re-enter and bring problems much than at the first time, as soon as the door is opened. He is not happy that he is homeless.

What is the slightest opportunity that he is waiting for?

1. <u>When there is no genuine repentance</u>, and he notices that your mind is still not right, you still utter vain words, and commit sin. Now that the door is now open, he brings 7 more wicked spirits with the belief that it would be difficult to cast out 8 other spirits. Repentance from sin is the greatest deliverance that God told me one day as I drove to work.

2. <u>When your sins are not confessed.</u> When you have committed a sin and you find it difficult to confess it, it remains with you and sooner than later, you have a desire to commit another sin. However, if you confess your previous sin, not only that you receive God's mercy for that, since you have exposed the devil, he is unlikely to come again. If you stole and you confess that you stole, you wouldn't like to commit another sin like that.

3. <u>Unforgiveness.</u> When you harbour unforgiveness and cannot forgive, then it will be impossible for you to receive deliverance. One of the conditions for you to receive God's forgiveness and deliverance is to forgive those who have sinned against you. There are many disorders health wise that are pertinent to the issue unforgiveness e.g. mental stress, cardiovascular disorders, sleeplessness etc.

4. _Moments of despair._ For example, when you are down on cash, or have a symptom like a stomach ache the devil make you think about negative possibilities like anticipating suffering. If your mind is fixed on the possibility of suffering, you will suffer, because you become what you believe.
5. _A cursed object._ An object that you acquired sinfully, after your deliverance may return you to square one. Think about your work implement, the clothing you wear, the symbols on the clothing, where you bought them from etc.

How do you maintain your deliverance?

1. _Resist the devil._ After your deliverance the devil will bring a lot of temptations for you to return to your formal state e.g. adultery. There might be a desire in your flesh to reconnect with that person and commit sin. That is when you feel like taking alcohol that you have decided not to take. There is a need to resist the devil with all your power.
2. _Study the word of God and meditate._ There's a need to study the word of God and meditate. The word of God will give you guidance about the steps to take in life and what to do when you are confronted with difficult situations.
3. _Share testimony_ about what God has done for you. Revelation 12:11 says they overcame by the blood of the lamb and the word of their testimony, and they loved not their lives unto death. When you tell people what God has done for you, it keeps it established in your spirit, and makes you to keep abreast of all fears.
4. _Pray ceaselessly._ There is an anointing that is released with prayer, and it gives you further revelation and victory. There should be times that you have separated for fasting and prayer.
5. _Be Obedient._ Note whatever God shows you during prayers and be obedient. God is interested in guiding us to achieve success.
6. _In times of despair_ when you are down emotionally, trust in the power of God to work absolutely and to give you what you want. If you fear and the devil knows this, he will add to your fears and enter your life through that avenue. If the devil knows that you are afraid of headache, the next thing is to tell you to sit at home. The first day he succeeds and makes you think you are not fit to go to work for the whole week.
7. _Confess the word of God._ Bless your lives with the promises in the word of God for you. In Isaiah 41:10 God says "Fear thou not; for I am with thee, be not dismayed; for I am thy God: I will strengthen thee; yea, I will help thee; yea, I will uphold thee with the right hand of my righteousness. Then you tell God, father I thank you. I trust in thee, because you will help me.
8. _Be a praise addict._ Thank God for what he has done and what he could do. Spend quality time praising God because he inhabits the praises of his people (Psalm 22:3).
9. _Monitor your dream life meticulously._ Anything that is happening in your life or that is about to happen will be shown to you in the dream, so you need to get a notebook and write the dreams, seeking to interpret and act.
10. _Always cover yourself with the blood of Jesus Christ._

11. *Have faith.* Do not be shaken or perturbed. When you have faith, regardless of the things that you see and are afraid of, anything can happen for good.
12. *Join a life church.* There is a great spiritual covering that it offers when you are in the midst of God's children. It helps you to learn from other people. There is the opportunity of making great contact.
13. *Remove cursed objects or return them back to their owners or burn them e.g. fetish materials.*
14. *Alter your food choices.* There are times that God has warned me against taking certain food substances in order to help my complete healing. A brother was told by God to desist from taking certain food substances. The Lord told him, that is my covenant of good health and long life for you. This means that your food choices may hinder your deliverance.
15. *Reduce your association with poisonous people.* There are people whose attitudes are not in line with the scriptures, who continue in their bad habits like smoking, drinking and fornication. If you don't reduce your association with them, they can return you to square one.
16. *There may be a need to decisively and urgently relocate.* If you live in a red-light district where there are pubs, beer parlours, brothels, and virtually an "Empire" of prostitution or other vices, then you may want to relocate. It is also not good for you to bring up children in that environment. Bad communication corrupts good manners. If you tend to lust, then you cannot live in a place where you have prostitutes.

Prayers to Maintain Your Deliverance:

1. I subdue every spirit of the flesh in the name of Jesus Christ.
2. O Lord, forgive me every sinful thought that keeps invading my mind in the name of Jesus Christ.
3. I shall miscarry my testimony in the mighty name of Jesus Christ.
4. I break and scatter revert reinforcement of demonic spirits against my life in the name of Jesus Christ.
5. Power of negative thoughts, loose me and let me go in the name of Jesus Christ.
6. Altar of doubt in my life, receive destruction by fire in the name of Jesus Christ.
7. Every yoke of evil dedication that has vowed not to let me go, break, in the name of Jesus Christ.

8. Environmental spiritual battles fighting my deliverance, Scatter in the name of Jesus Christ.
9. Evil hand joined in hand that wants to work against my deliverance, Scatter by fire in the name of Jesus Christ.
10. O Lord, confound the wisdom of the enemy in my life in the name of Jesus Christ.
11. Every power assigned to enforce evil covenants in my life, receive the judgement of God by fire in the name of Jesus Christ.
12. Every evil voice assigned to relocate me for destruction, shut up on the name of Jesus Christ.
13. Every member of my family giving me evil advise, be silenced by the power of the Holy Spirit in the name of Jesus Christ.
14. Evil powers trying to gain access into my life through the ear gate, receive disgrace in the name of Jesus Christ.
15. O Lord, build your wall of fire around me, against the onslaught of the adversary in the name of Jesus Christ.
16. Masquerading enemies assigned to take me back to square one, be exposed and be disgraced in the name of Jesus Christ.
17. I soak myself in the blood of Jesus. The devil shall not overpower me in the name of Jesus Christ.
18. I forgive all the people that have offended me to the bottom of my heart, O Lord, forgive me and deliver me completely in the name of Jesus Christ. Mention their names one by one.
19. Every spirit of poverty that is fighting my deliverance, be arrested in the name of Jesus Christ.
20. Any cursed object within my house or in my vicinity that is working against my complete deliverance, lose your power in the name of Jesus Christ.
21. Every demonic traffic in my environment working against my complete deliverance, Scatter by fire in the name of Jesus Christ.

22. O Lord, reveal to me, every food that I am eating that is working against my complete deliverance in the name of Jesus Christ.

23. Every evil covenant crying against my testimony, be broken by the power on the blood of Jesus Christ.

24. Every evil habit that wants to return into my life, I break your power in the name of Jesus Christ.

25. Satanic revival targeted against my testimony scatter by the power in the blood of Jesus Christ.

26. O Lord, give me the grace to overcome evert temptation in the name of Jesus Christ.

27. O Lord my father, separate me from every friend or associate that wants to return me to my vomit in the name of Jesus Christ.

28. Every power of mammon assigned to return affliction into my life again, be arrested by fire in the name of Jesus.

29. O Lord, I ask for mercy, have mercy upon me in the name of Jesus Christ.

30. O Lord, send you word and deliver me from every destruction lurking around my life in the name of Jesus Christ.

31. I decree, I stand as a mountain in God's house, I shall not be removed in the name of Jesus Christ.

32. Every evil thought and imagination that is working against my deliverance, clear away by the power in the blood of Jesus Christ.

33. Every discouraging sight assigned to work against my deliverance, and destabilise me emotionally, be wiped off my memory in the name of Jesus Christ.

34. I die to fleshly enticement, I refuse to be deceived in the name of Jesus Christ.

35. I reject every evil imagination assigned to trouble my mind, in the name of Jesus Christ.

CHAPTER THIRTY-FOUR

WHEN THE MARRIAGE VOW BACKFIRES.

When couples are joined together, there is a marriage vow that is made, across all Christian denominations. This vow says that,

"I ....take you............................ to be my wife (husband) to have and to hold from this day forward, for better for worse, for richer, for poorer, in sickness and in health, to love and to cherish, till death do us part, **according to God's Holy law,** and this my solemn vow."

Proverbs 18:22 states that:

Who findeth a wife, findeth a good thing, and obtaineth favour of the Lord.

The vow however can be broken, and can backfire, when the **"Holy law"** according to your vow is compromised. This results to disfavour, instead of favour, and affliction, instead of the Lords goodness.

What does it mean for something to backfire?

It means that an expectation, an objective, or goal has an opposite or negative result for one or both parties. This depends on individual expectation at the time the couple agreed to get married, and at the onset of marriage. It may also mean that the expenditure of time, emotions, money, or other resources have gone down the drain, and yielding regrets.

It is sad to note that many marriage vows are backfiring, and marriages hitting the rocks, in many parts of the world. Evangelists have a greater challenge on their hands at this time as it has never been. The devil is finding the marriage institution a soft-landing space to ravage and destroy destinies in a very subtle manner. One of the most potent weapons in the hands of the devil to destroy the destinies of men and women as well as their future is the weapon of "illicit sex" or "extramarital sex". This is widely known as infidelity, cheating, or adultery in many climes. It is one of the most destructive acts in history.

1 Peter 3:7 states

Likewise, ye husbands, dwell with them according to knowledge, giving honour unto the wife, as to the weaker vessel, and as being heirs together of the grace of life; **that your prayers be not hindered.**

What is the picture of marriage, that God has in mind?

We shall try to see what God has in mind, when he instituted the marriage institution.

Genesis 2:18

And the Lord God said, It is not good that man should be alone; I will make him an help meet for him.

Colossians 3:18-19

¹⁸wives, submit yourselves unto your own husbands, as it is fit in the Lord.

¹⁹husbands, love your wives, and be not bitter against them.

1 Corinthians 7:3-5

³Let the husband render unto the wife due benevolence: and likewise, also the wife unto the husband.

⁴the wife hath not power of her own body, but the husband: and likewise, the husband hath not power of his own body, but the wife

⁵defraud ye not one the other, except it be with content for a time, that ye may give yourselves to fasting and prayer; and come together again, that Satan tempt you not for your incontinency.

Hebrews 13:4

Marriage is honourable in all, and the bed undefiled: but whoremongers and adulterers God will judge.

When we consider the above scriptures, we can make certain conclusions about God's will for marriage. We should first note that the marriage institution is for mutual cooperation, and the wife is a help meet. She should render support. A marriage cannot stand, if the support of the woman is lacking. The man should ensure that he wins the support and cooperation of his wife. That is why as has been stated earlier in 1 Peter 3wins your prayers may be hindered.

The first thing that the bible says in Colossians 3:18 is that wives should submit to their husbands. The power of a woman is in submission. This does not infer a master-servant relationship as many husbands or wives misconstrue. What it means is that a woman should reason with the husband and as much as possible give honour to the husband in decision making. In 1 Peter 3:7, the bible also says men should honour their wives. Honour is reciprocal!

The bible also talks about the conjugal conduct of husbands and wives. It says that a w husband or wife does not own their body, but the partner. It goes further to say that it is only the partner that should have access to their body and the marriage bed should be undefiled.

Prayer and fasting are given an important place in marriage. God wants couples to pray, and only prayer is the condition that can make couples to abstain from sex, just for a moment. It encourages that they should quickly come together again to avoid the devil tempting them. This means that conjugal union was put in place by God to prevent inordinate affection and adultery.

All these ideas have been disregarded by husbands and wives. There is no submission in marriage, and couples don't love and honour one another. The Bible sees the husband as the head of the family (Ephesians 5:23). However, many women ignore this fact, just as many men abuse the privilege and make it to mean a master-servant relationship. Conjugal commitments have been shirked. We are in an era where couples are more committed to the strange man and strange woman. One thing however is that illicit relationships are not founded on a covenant. If there is any commitment, it should be towards your marriage. This is what men and women have despised and lost their marriages and by implication their future. Eventually they lose out with the strange man or woman, after losing their marriage. If they remarry, it will never be the same. Adultery, cheating or infidelity as it has been called, can only be described as a suicide mission. Each time you break a vow or covenant, there are repercussions!

How Has Witchcraft Been Able to Invade Marriages?

With reference to witchcraft invasion of marriages, call it open doors to witchcraft invasion in marriage if you like, there are many ways. In dealing with this complex topic, I will like us to have behind our minds the scripture in:

> 1 Samuel 15:23
>
> For rebellion is as the sin of witchcraft, and stubbornness is as iniquity and idolatry. Because thou hast rejected the word of the LORD, he hath also rejected thee from being King.

The main issue here about witchcraft is the **rejection of the word of the LORD.** Unfortunately, the consequences of this stubbornness and rebellion, could flow from generation to generation within the same family. Someone might ask that in what ways? Terrible witchcraft starts from denying the other party sex, whether he or she knows or not. The bible says you are not the owner of your body. It is one of the greatest robberies that can ever happen. The second one like it is denying your spouse money or for example, food, for a just cause. Blackmailing is another act of witchcraft within the context of marriage.

What are the main manifestations of witchcraft in marriage? Good question!

1. _Possession by marine spirits._ When our parents have worshipped marine spirits, we are possessed by marine spirits. These spirits are violent and stubborn and find manifestation in the marriages of their victims. Unfortunately, a good marriage cannot thrive on stubbornness, violence, or other traits exhibited by marine spirits.

2. *Evil covenants.* A person with a satanic agreement or accord will always find it difficult to obey the commandments of the LORD. If a person is under any evil covenant (refer to "Covenants" in this book), it will be difficult to have a good marriage until that covenant is broken. An evil covenant could bring about strange behaviour, a wicked disposition, disobedience, violence and many more. Signs of an evil covenant have been mentioned earlier on in this book.

3. *Curses.* When you allow a curse to prosper in your marriage usually because of a broken agreement with a suitor. For example, you promised marriage and you eventually broke the heart of that person. Even if the person does not curse, you attract a curse upon your life. The Bible says there is no peace for the wicked (Isaiah 48:22). The only solution is genuine repentance and pray to break the curse. There have been instances where environmental curses have affected marriages.

4. *Evil spiritual marriages.* An evil spiritual marriage means you are joined in a marriage relationship to a demonic spirit. The major sign is having sex in the dream, and you see a personality come to you on the dream, demonstrating marital gestures, making promises to you and generally trying to play the role of a husband. It enjoys making love and giving you an arousal that occurs indiscriminately and randomly. This will make you to be vulnerable to extra marital affairs. The spirit spouse also makes you react unseemly to your spouse and quarrels may be common.

5. *Excessive love of money.* There are periods in marriage when things may be a bit difficult financially. Remember you made a vow of "for better for worse". If you love money in excess, then you wouldn't be able to fulfil your vow. Marriage requires understanding, moderation, and contentment.

6. *Unforgiveness.* This will give way to the devil in your marriage. We cannot but offend one another, and if marriage must continue and peacefully too, each party needs to be able to forgive, whenever there is a rift, and move on.

7. *Worldliness.* The Bible observes that though we are in the world, we as children of God should not be of the world (John 17:14). The love of the world consists of the lust of the flesh, in our feelings, emotions and imaginations; the lust of the eyes in our environment and the things that we see; and the pride of life in form of our ego and desire to occupy positions and Lord it over people. All these will not allow us to enjoy marriage.

8. *In-laws.* In-laws can introduce witchcraft into marriage and we should not play sentiments here. What is wrong should be seen as wrong, and a spade should be called a shade irrespective of whosoever. The knowledge of God must be exalted. Bear in mind that a member's greatest enemy are members of his own household (Matthew 10:36). In the present and the future, only you will bear the consequences of your actions. Be wise.

9. *Association.* The types of friends you keep can bewitch your marriage by misleading you. A lot of spouses that were good initially, was suddenly influenced by the wrong friends and started misbehaving. Watch the types of friends that you have and never share your matrimonial secrets with friends.

10. *Enchantment.* Witchcraft can creep into your marriage through enchantment. Household wickedness, strange men and women, envious friends, relatives of your spouse sometimes may be quietly attacking and cannot be trusted.

11. *Adultery.* This is also known as cheating or infidelity. It is the greatest type of problem in marriage accounting for the major reason for divorce worldwide. Try and run away from it. It pays nobody no good. It shall be discussed in the next chapter.

12. *Poverty.* Finance is another issue that leads to a break-up in marriages worldwide. When a couple together find it difficult to meet up with their financial obligations, it is most frustrating and can make a marriage to fall apart. This may be because of a reckless spending habit, or that one or both couples are not in employment. Couples should discuss their circumstances and plan their spending very well. Try to find something to do, that brings money in. Whatever your hands find to do, do it diligently.

13. *Environment.* A bad environment can influence good partners and a promising marriage negatively. There are many things happening in your environment that the devil may suggest to you that it is a model and you should emulate. Don't look at what is happening around you, or how couples are relating. Don't even copy couples in your church, but read your bible, pray to God and keep focusing on God's plan for your lives.

14. *Fake Pastors.* There are different types of Pastors with different exposure, and different anointing. The Pastor is there to advise, but act on your conviction, because there are so many fake Pastors out there. I pray your marriage shall not be bewitched in Jesus name.

15. *Evil inheritance.* If your parents struggled with marriage, your father was a polygamist, or your mother married up to 4 times, when you are married, you should be careful too. A child from an abusive marriage can inherit the demons of their parents, evil covenants or curses. This is a sure means through which marriages are bewitched.

16. *Culture and tradition.* There are cultures around the world that contradicts the word of God. There are cultures that encourage male domination and chauvinism, even when God says that husbands should love their wives. However, your wife comes back from a 12-hour shift and is still expected to do the cooking, while the man was at home all day. Some traditions and religions still encourage polygamy. Polygamy is a major cause of envy and household wickedness, and as Christians we should separate from the influence of a bad culture or tradition which makes you to go contrary to God's word. In some traditions too, the female children spend more time with their parents than with their husbands and children. Follow God's word, and not faulty precedents.

17. *Civilisation.* In as much as men should treat their wives fairly, the slogan of "women emancipation" has been over flogged. Many women societies and Non-Governmental Organisations are teaching rebellion, in the name of women emancipation. We are in an era where women have abandoned the need for intimacy with their husbands and focus more on the use of vibrators. There are laws that are unfair to a gender and there is no agreement with God's word.

18. *Consultation with mediums.* When there is consultation with mediums and false gods, all they can achieve is to mislead you. Certainly, those evil Priests may be able to "see" what may happen, but they can't give you a solution and many times their ideas are false. Don't believe their visions and solutions they offer.

19. *Rumours.* There is no way you can avoid rumours, because people will always peddle rumours. Even when they see your husband with his immediate younger sister, some friends would tell you that they saw him in a hotel. They may tell you they saw your wife in the marketplace smiling at the butcher! So, what does that connote. Rumours can destroy your marriage if you care to listen to them and attach weight to it. Rumours can poison your spirit and scatter your joy. May your joy not be scattered in Jesus name.

20. *Soliciting advise from the wrong quarters.* When you have issues, don't allow anger to overwhelm your spirit, but pray earnestly to the Holy Spirit for leading and guidance. The Holy Spirit will lead you. Find time for meditation and

deep thoughts. Try and wait for the right time to discuss it with your spouse. Maintain a low voice devoid of arrogance, because the way and manner may sometimes say what you don't mean, and mean what you did not intend to say. This way, you could mend the breach and move ahead. You can go to discuss it with your Pastor. Don't ridicule your spouse in the presence of the Pastor. In the next exercise we will now see how couples can assess their marriages and solve problems amicably.

THE MARRIAGE DELIVERANCE SCORE SHEET.

This score sheet contains some expectations in marriage. Couples should come together to assess one another and score their level of satisfaction with the marriage based on the attitude and behaviour of the other spouse.

No.	Marital Virtue	Score max 10
1.	Support for one another. How do you rate his or her support?	
2.	Submission to one another (Ephesians 5:21). How much understanding does he/she show?	
3.	Communication. Assess how good you are able to connect when you are not in the home at work or when you have travelled. It also includes non-verbal communication and body language.	
4.	Looks and attraction. How much does he/she align with your definition of good looks?	
5.	Care. How much does he/she care?	
6.	Companionship. How much does he/she spend time with you considering available time?	
7.	Problem sharing and solving. How much does he/she share your challenges?	
8.	Emotional fulfilment. Overall, how much are you fulfilled emotionally?	
9.	Word of God. In your own opinion, to what extent do you study God's word?	
10.	Prayer life. What score do you attach to your prayer life as a couple?	
11.	Bonding. How much does he/she bond compared with how he or she bonds with the children/job?	
12.	Taking responsibility. What is the score you would give to this aspect?	
13.	Sexuality. How much are you satisfied with your sex life?	

14.	Financial transparency. Do you know how much his/her income is each month?	
15.	Financial contributions. When you rate his/her financial contributions in relation to monthly income.	
16.	Maximisation of potentials. Is he/she exploring all income opportunities?	
17.	Confidentiality. How good is he/she in keeping marital issues confidential?	
18.	How much does he/she rate you over outsiders or third parties?	
19.	Unforgiveness. How much is he/she willing to forgive?	
20.	Networking. How good is he/she at Networking to the benefits of the family?	

All these attributes show factors that could build a good marriage. There could be more, depending on your goals in marriage. It is expected that you add to the questions, if desired, type it and reproduce it.

The spouse is the examiner in this case, and he or she is expected to score the other partner with a lead pencil, on a 10-point scale. It must be in all fairness. For example, a spouse who is spending a lot on drugs, cannot be expected to do their best financially under the circumstances. However, the person may score a low mark if he/she can get a better job. Once the score is given and the score sheet completed, then the score sheet is submitted to the partner you have assessed. Let that person defend his/herself, for the benefit of doubt and to Foster understanding. Most times a partner will realise why the other one is behaving the way they are behaving. The scores can be changed, after the explanations on both sides.

Couples should try and calculate the scores on each side. Since there are 20 points in this case, and you had a maximum of 10 points in each, there is a maximum of 200 marks which you convert to a percentage score. We recommend a 70% pass mark.

If a partner scores very low on a particular item, then you look for ways of solving the problem together which is a product of faith and works (James 2:20).

Steps to Deliverance:

1. *The first step is for both partners to give their lives to Jesus Christ* by saying these few words,

   Lord, I believe you are the saviour of the world who came to die for me, show me the way and deliver me. I make you Lord and saviour over my life today and reject the devil and all his evil works. Thank you, Lord Jesus, for coming to save me. Amen.

2. <u>The next step is to make a resolve to say bye-bye to sin.</u> In James 4:17, the bible says, "to him that knoweth to do good and doeth it not, it is sin". Sin separates from God, hinders prayers and perverts destinies. We need to allow our conscience to lead us. Don't ignore your conscience. Think about what you can do to right the wrongs on your score sheet. He that covered his sins shall not prosper, but whosoever confesses and forsake them shall receive mercy (Proverbs 28:13).

3. *<u>Make a thorough word search in the bible</u>*, dwelling on the key words of the areas of your weakness. If it is lack of submission, then you go to YouTube and search "submission in marriage". There will be many messages on the subject that you may listen to severally. The concordance is another resource for you to learn more about your area of weakness and work on it, based on the scriptural knowledge. Discuss with your spouse, any challenges you may have.

4. *<u>Set realistic goals that you want to achieve.</u>* Map out strategies that could help you to achieve these goals. There are certain things that need to leave your life, and certain things you must allow.

5. *<u>Fasting and prayer</u>* is very important, in that it kills sin in your life. When you are fasting and flesh is weak, the spirit is exalted and you can make exploits in the spirit. Prayers are easily answered. There is a special anointing that brings revelation when you pray and fast. Depending on the situation, demons can jump out when you have given yourself to fasting and prayer for a long time. Prayers are effective when you pray a prayer point repeatedly for at least 1 hour every day. In the case of a partner who does not have much to contribute financially in marriage, he could pray against the spirit of poverty and non-achievement, for days. Don't forget to write down the dreams that you have when you pray. There should every attempt to cast out demonic spirits troubling your marriage.

6. *<u>Go for Counselling.</u>* Every couple should have a Counsellor and should try and seek help whenever there is a problem. There could also be some form of support from a psychotherapist, but let everything you do be in line with the word of God.

7. *<u>Sexual Intimacy</u>*. This will often help your marriage and cement your bond as husband and wife. It boosts confidence and grows a relationship. Sexual Intimacy can bring progress in a marriage and should not be seen as a means to punish your partner. Some partners ignorantly see it as a way of punishing the other partner.

8. *<u>Communication</u>*. When you are not in the same place, for example your husband/wife has travelled to another town or country, you should still keep in touch, in the very least. For example, you may want to say good morning to your partner, or chat or gist with them. Also, you may want to ask a question or give a report of what happened in the children's school earlier in the day. Communication also includes been able to express yourself to your partner non-verbally. For example, if I am in a place like the bank or hospital, my wife does not need to talk. We have agreed gestures we use to communicate and I know when she doesn't want me to go ahead with something. Sometimes a plumber may come to the house to do a piece of work and I am trying to pay all the bill. She just needs to make a gesture and I would know that I should give him a partial payment, and not all.

9. *<u>Care for one another.</u>* It is your responsibility to care and show concern for your partner, when he or she is sick, or when he or she is going through a challenging time, or bereaved. Console them, speak kind words and spend time with them. Don't just greet him/her casually and run inside the room and say, "good for him". Remembering

you too might be challenged at some point. Your care goes a long way in making your spouse heal after a major catastrophe.

10. *Don't drain your partner emotionally.* Some partners are toxic and Nagy. If you do this you end up draining your partner emotionally, and they cannot concentrate and think constructively. This might lead to mental issues and might lead to other medical issues like blood pressure. Someone can give a spouse high blood pressure. If you keep nagging, you may kill him/her prematurely and the load becomes you own. Very few spouses would like to assist you in financing children from another relationship. If at all, they do it sceptically.

11. *Be financially transparent.* When you are financially transparent, your husband/wife knows how much you earn on a monthly basis and both of you can calculate how much is available per time, and how much you need to spend and how much you need to save. No matter how tight the budget may be, try and save for the dry season. That is called financial discipline.

12. **Cooperation.** Cooperation is supporting your partner to overcome a difficult task. Sometimes the car may break down and needs repair. If you are in a position to, then help. If the wife too is facing challenges, maybe from her family, and she needs to do certain things, then cooperate. This may not be only financially, but show some concern and bring reasonable advice. Stand by them all through.

13. **Forgiveness.** There is no perfect marriage anywhere, and we are bound to offend one another. The great solution if you want to move ahead and progress is to forbear and forgive (Colossians 3:13). When you forgive, you don't continue talking about the offence of your partner, and neither are you seeking to revenge. Act as if that offence was never committed. Laugh it off and say, "we are moving forward in Jesus name". And so, shall it be!

14. **Enhanced spirituality.** Find time to pray and fast together as a family. Also find time to study the word of God together. Create an avenue to ask questions and foster deeper understanding. Make sure you attend a church that meets your needs and never miss church programs for any reason. The mere fact that you find yourself in the midst of people you identify with is golden, and you learn more in your interactions with people, instead of being alone at home.

Deliverance Prayers That Will Bring Joy into Your Marriage:

1. Witchcraft powers, manipulating my marriage, lose your power in the name of Jesus Christ.
2. Evil wall, created by the powers of darkness between me and my husband/wife, collapse by fire in the name of Jesus Christ.
3. Anyone, holding on to the blessings of my marriage, be tormented by fire and release it now in the name of Jesus Christ.
4. I break every covenant of destruction, fashioned against my marriage in the name of Jesus Christ.
5. Covenant of sorrow, fashioned against my marriage, break in the name of Jesus Christ.
6. Covenant of untimely or sudden death, fashioned against me or my husband/wife, break in the name of Jesus Christ.
7. Any witchcraft covenant demanding for the blood of any of my children, be broken by the power in the blood of Jesus Christ.
8. Every demonic in-law attacking my marriage, be exposed and be disgraced in the name of Jesus Christ.
9. Lord, break me and removed me, and let the glory of my marriage appear in the name of Jesus Christ.
10. Agape love of God, envelope my marriage in the name of Jesus Christ.
11. Covenant of spirit husband/wife, break and release my marriage in the name of Jesus Christ.
12. Every curse issued by spirit husband/wife against my marriage, break and receive disgrace in the name of Jesus Christ.
13. Evil dedication to spirit husband/wife on my life, break in the name of Jesus Christ.
14. Evil dedication to the waters affecting my marital joy and fulfilment, break in the name of Jesus Christ.
15. Covenant of the river goddess fashioned against my Children, break in the name of Jesus Christ.
16. Everything that spirit spouse has stolen from my marriage, I recover you now, in the name of Jesus Christ.
17. Marine serpent attacking my marriage, be roasted by fire in the name of Jesus Christ.
18. I dissolve every spiritual marriage and possess my divine blessings in the name of Jesus Christ.
19. I destroy every evil marriage certificate given to me by spirit husband/wife in the name of Jesus Christ.
20. Every family that I have under the waters, that I belong to spiritually, be destroyed by the consuming fire of God in the name of Jesus Christ.
21. Evil altars in the marine kingdom caging the glory of my marriage, be burnt to ashes by the thunder fire of God in the name of Jesus Christ.
22. I command spirit spouse, to be tormented by fire, walk out of my life and be arrested in the name of Jesus Christ.
23. I cancel every sexual covenant between me and spirit husband/wife in the name of Jesus Christ.
24. Every weapon, fashioned against my life by spirit husband/wife, you shall not prosper the name of Jesus Christ.
25. Every attack from the waters against my marriage, backfire in the name of Jesus Christ.
26. Familiar spirits on assignment against my marriage, receive disgrace in the name of Jesus Christ.

27. Familiar spirit mark upon my children, be wiped away by the power in the blood of Jesus Christ.
28. Familiar spirits mark upon me or my wife/husband, be wiped away by the power in the blood of Jesus Christ.
29. Familiar spirit network on assignment to destroy my marriage, Scatter by fire in the name of Jesus Christ.
30. Lord, give me the grace to forgive and to forget completely, every sin that my husband/wife has committed against me in the name of Jesus Christ.
31. God of New beginnings, appear in my marriage by fire in the name of Jesus Christ.
32. Every door shut against my marital blessings by the spirit of disunity, be opened in the name of Jesus Christ.
33. Wisdom of the wicked, against my marriage, turn to foolishness in the name of Jesus Christ.
34. I receive the power of the Holy spirit to expose the game of the evil adviser on assignment to destroy my marriage in the name of Jesus Christ.
35. Every buried blessing in my marriage, be resurrected in the name of Jesus Christ.
36. Every dead virtue in my marriage, receive the breath of life in the name of Jesus Christ.
37. I break the power of enchantments, fashioned against my marriage in the name of Jesus Christ.
38. Any power, sponsoring evil agenda against my marriage, I render you impotent forever by the power in the blood of Jesus Christ.
39. Let the raw anger of God, fall upon the gathering of satanic in-laws planning to scatter my marriage in the name of Jesus Christ.
40. Satanic in-laws that tasted or ate the provisions during our traditional wedding, planning evil against our marriage, the anger of God is upon you in the name of Jesus Christ.
41. Evil power, waiting for me in the future, in order to make the boat of my marriage to capsize, be arrested now in the name of Jesus Christ.
42. Evil sacrifice done at the Riverside against the glory of my marriage, lose your power in the name of Jesus Christ.
43. I withdraw my wedding gown from every marine witchcraft altar in the name of Jesus Christ.
44. I decree, you my marriage, you shall be fruitful in the name of Jesus Christ.
45. My marriage shall become paradise on earth and bring forth the glory of God in the name of Jesus Christ.
46. Evil bag on witchcraft tree, swallowing the finances and blessings of my marriage, be located for destruction by the thunder fire of God in the name of Jesus Christ.
47. Every garment of poverty, prepared for me and my husband/wife, catch fire in the name of Jesus Christ.
48. Mark of disfavour upon my marriage, be cleansed brother power in the blood of Jesus Christ.
49. Every evil decree, every evil ordinance written by witchcraft powers against my marriage, I wipe you away by the power in the blood of Jesus Christ.
50. Every idol upon any evil altar, representing me, my husband/wife, or the glory of our marriage, catch fire in the name of Jesus Christ.
51. Satanic gift that I received on the day of my wedding that is crying against the glory of my marriage lose your power over my marriage in the name of Jesus Christ.

52. Evil ritual or sacrifice that I part-took in on the day of my wedding, consciously or unconsciously, lose your power in the name of Jesus Christ.
53. Any activity I part took in on the day of my wedding that brought a curse upon my marriage, lose your power over my marriage by the power in the blood of Jesus Christ.
54. Every evil flow from my environment into my marriage, dry up from your source in the mighty name of Jesus Christ.
55. Every inherited demon in my life, attacking the glory of God in my marriage, be evacuated by fire in the name of Jesus Christ.
56. Lord, deliver me from inherited evil attitudes and behaviour in the name of Jesus Christ.
57. Satanic visions, assigned to misguide my marriage, be exposed and be disgraced in the name of Jesus Christ.
58. Every spirit of doubt, working against my marriage, lose your power in the name of Jesus Christ.
59. Arrow of fear in my mind, jump out by fire in the name of Jesus Christ.
60. I cancel every evil prophecy issued against my marriage by the power in the blood of Jesus Christ.
61. Lord, erase from my mind, every satanic culture and tradition affecting my marriage in the name of Jesus Christ.
62. Evil celestial altars raised against my marriage in the heavenlies, crumble by fire in the name of Jesus Christ.
63. Evil terrestrial altars, raised against my marriage, be located for destruction by the consuming fire of God.
64. Earthquake of God's deliverance, locate and destroy every marine altar erected against my marital destiny in the name of Jesus Christ.
65. Concluded work of darkness in the Indian Ocean against my life, scatter by fire in the name of Jesus Christ.
66. Evil principalities and powers in the oceans, targeting much marital joy for evil, be made blind and paralysed in the name of Jesus Christ.
67. Global satanic revival against my marriage, ministry, and calling, be buried in the name of Jesus Christ.
68. Every garment of shame and reproach, prepared for my marriage, catch fire in the name of Jesus Christ.
69. Every evil altar erected against the glory of my marriage, scatter by fire in the name of Jesus Christ.
70. Evil voice, confusing me in marriage, be silenced in the name of Jesus Christ.
71. Satanic power, issuing evil instructions against me, I bind you and render you dumb in the name of Jesus Christ.
72. Lord, impact upon my life the spirit of unity and cooperation in marriage in the name of Jesus Christ.
73. Lord, give me a good team spirit in the name of Jesus Christ.
74. Holy Spirit, give me solutions to the problems in my marriage on the name of Jesus Christ.
75. Lord, give me the spirit of discernment and wisdom in the name of Jesus Christ.
76. Spirit of brokenness and humility, fall upon my life in the name of Jesus Christ.
77. My efforts and sacrifices in marriage shall not be in vain, and another shall not take my seat in the name of Jesus Christ.
78. Spirit of error, on assignment to waste my years of commitment to my marriage, come out and be arrested in the name of Jesus Christ.

79. Curse of barrenness, fashioned against my marriage, break in the name of Jesus Christ.
80. I deliver my marriage from the hands of the wasters in the name of Jesus Christ.
81. Strangers in my marriage, be exposed and be disgraced in the name of Jesus Christ.
82. Hook and catch of the strangers in my marriage, be broken in the name of Jesus Christ.
83. Every resource that I have lost through disobedience in my marriage, I recover you in the name of Jesus Christ.
84. Evil forces that want to tear my marriage apart, lose power one-by-one in the name of Jesus.
85. Every attempt of the enemy to use my children to frustrate my marriage, be frustrated in the name of Jesus Christ.
86. My children, refuse to cooperate with the agenda of witchcraft for your life in the name of Jesus Christ.
87. Lord, send your word, heal my marriage, and deliver my marriage from every destruction in the name of Jesus Christ.
88. Untimely death shall not separate me from my husband/wife, we shall enjoy one another till old age in the name of Jesus Christ.
89. Arrow of sudden or Untimely death targeted against my marriage, backfire in the name of Jesus Christ.
90. Every unhealthy suspicion in my marriage, be put to shame in the same of Jesus Christ.
91. Every communication gap in my marriage, be mended in the name of Jesus Christ.
92. Spirit of misunderstanding in my marriage, lose your power in the name of Jesus Christ.
93. Every deceptive spirit, using me against the glory of my marriage, lose my marriage and let me go in the name of Jesus Christ.
94. I conquer every lust of the flesh that is working against my marriage in the name of Jesus Christ.
95. I conquer every lust of the eyes, working against my marriage in the name of Jesus Christ.
96. Financial miracle that will put an end to marital affliction in my life, locate my marriage in the name of Jesus Christ.
97. Every stupid mentality promoting poverty in my life, cometh an end in the name of Jesus Christ.
98. Inherited infirmity assigned to end my life and my marriage, come to an end by the power of the Holy spirit in the name of Jesus Christ.
99. Curse of sickness attacking my marriage, be broken in the name of Jesus Christ.

Deliverance Prayers That Will Bring Joy into Your Marriage continued:

1. Cycle of physical and spiritual amnesia in my life be broken in the name of Jesus Christ.
2. Every marital problem transferred, into my life by laying hands, expire in the name of Jesus Christ.
3. Miracle that parted the Red Sea, let it happen in my life and marriage in the name of Jesus Christ.
4. Evil spiritual river of my in-law's house, flowing into my life, dry up from your source by fire in the name of Jesus Christ.
5. Every effect of evil laying of hands on my life and the life of anyone in my family, expire in the name of Jesus Christ.

6. Evil agreement that I entered into unconsciously on the day of my wedding, be cancelled by the power in the blood of Jesus Christ.
7. Evil mark, that was placed upon my life on my wedding day, I wipe you off by the power in the blood of Jesus Christ.
8. Witchcraft attacks at night, fashioned against my conception and safe delivery, backfire in the name of Jesus Christ.
9. Any power aborting testimonies in my marriage, you are a liar, lose your power in the name of Jesus Christ.
10. Every curse of separation and divorce working against my marriage break in the name of Jesus Christ.
11. Marine serpent of strange behaviour in my life, attacking God's plan for my marriage, come out with all your root in the name of Jesus Christ.
12. Every door, open to spiritual robbers in my marriage, I close you forever in the name of Jesus Christ.
13. Calamity, disaster, tragedy, and destruction shall not be my lot in marriage in the name of Jesus Christ.
14. Every defilement of my marriage bed, be washed by the power in the blood of Jesus Christ.

CHAPTER THIRTY-FIVE

DELIVERANCE FOR ELIGIBLE SINGLES

There are many singles who are eligible and searching, but cannot find, and are being delayed. Some eventually find someone, but they may not be compatible with one another. When a gentleman or lady gets married to the wrong person, it can really be a lifetime trouble. Once a person marries the wrong person, your progress in life may be on hold. There are even people that wedded on the appointed day, but never knew they married the man or the woman that will someday end their life. The issue of the person to marry should be done painstakingly, so that you wouldn't live to regret it all your days.

Things to Note in Choosing a Partner.

Note that a beautiful woman will not necessarily make a good wife, because the bible says beauty is vain (Proverbs 31:30), but a woman who fears the Lord is to be praised. When you need a wife, think be careful and don't be deceived by beauty, but rather consider character. Have it at the back of your mind that marriage is a lifelong contract. Don't think about the possibility of a divorce.

There are many wrong teachings that say that a parent cannot lead a child to marry a particular person. This is a lie from the pit of hell. Most parents who are spiritual receive revelations from God concerning the husband or wife of their children. A parent is an authority ordained by God over a child.

> Romans 13:1
>
> Let every soul be subject unto the higher powers. For there is no power but of God: the powers that be are ordained of God.

God says you should honour them that it might be well with thee and that you may live long (Ephesians 6:3)

It would be a different case though if your parent says it is because they are rich or because they are friends, or from the same town, then you need to prayerfully consider it, if it goes well with you. However, if not, it cannot be, and you need to let such a parent realise that.

Another thing is that do not use the financial status of a man in the present to choose, but rather think about his prospects and what he wants to become. His ambitions. The fact that a man is wealthy does not mean that he will be kind to you. The beginning does not usually determine how things will end. We should note that we should not despise the days of little beginnings (Zechariah 4:10). Better is the end of a thing than the beginnings (Ecclesiastes 7:8). What a woman should look for is character.

A man or woman that is from your race or tribe is not necessarily be God's will for your life. Don't judge by race or ethnicity. A man from your country may not be God's will for you. Sometimes, deceivers and fake prophets are all out there that prophecies may fail (1 Corinthians 13:8). A lady was deceived by her pastor, telling her that a particular young man was God's will. She came to me for guidance. I told her not to follow what the pastor said. Some days later, she dreamt that the young man was drunk and lying on the floor. Yet some days later, she broke the heart of that sister, telling her he was not interested in marriage any longer. She was deceived by the pastor.

The bible encourages us to test all spirits (1 John 4:1) for false prophets are gone out into the world. What you should do is to confirm from 2 or 3 sources and by their character and behaviour to you during courtship. Never compare your situation with your friend's. Everyone has a different character and things that define them in life.

Also note that makeups do not attract real Christian men. As a lady, if you want genuine men, you may not really apply make-up.

> 1 Timothy 2:9
>
> [9] in like manner also, that women adorn themselves in modest apparel, with shamefacedness and sobriety; not with broided hair, or gold, or pearls, or costly array;

God does not respect make ups, and it shouldn't be applied.

Note that a spend thrift is not a good husband material. The way he is spending lavishly is how he would spend when you are married and people like that don't have savings.

A lady came to me one morning and shouting and rejoicing. I asked her was happening and she said she just saw her suitor in the dream. I asked her the dream she has, and she said she had sex in the dream. Sex in the dream is the attack by spirit spouse that steals from you and shifts your date of marriage further. It is something you pray against, and does not call for celebration in any way.

What Are the Causes of Delay in Marriage?

I was part of a special ministration to people who were 50 and above and were single. I have attempted to do some form of focused group study for that population based on my activities I that program.

Evil covenant. Some men and women have covenants that bring evil spirits into their lives. This causes strange behaviour in the victim, which tends to be repulsive. In as much as the evil spirit and the strange behaviour remain with you, marriage might be difficult.

Curses. This is an evil force or influence that always works against your expected blessings. It cancels your blessings. Anything contrary to obeying the word of God attracts a curse. A curse is forever on any promiscuous man or woman, because they will never enjoy marriage. Once you are given to having multiple sex partners, as a single no lady or gentleman will marry you. If your own is lying, no one is interested in a dishonest future partner. In James 4:17, the bible says to him that knoweth to do good and doeth it not, it is sin. What is that thing that you are doing that is not good? Repent now and get a suitor.

Evil dedication. When you are dedicated to an idol, or evil spirits, they are attached to you, and they will do you no good, and to mess up your life, making you repulsive to suitors. Their presence inside you may make you prone to committing errors and misbehaving to your spouse to be. This is another reason why some are having a delay. Only deliverance can help.

Spirit spouse. A spirit spouse comes to have sex with a person in the dream. It is a demon of the opposite sex, that spiritually stands between you and your intended and physical suitor. They transfer toxins into you through sex that makes you repulsive to suitors or make you to commit mistakes. They get you sexually aroused and uncontrollable sexually. This sexual habit may put you into trouble with suitors. The marriage certificate of many brethren has been seized by spiritual spouse, because when you have a spirit spouse and go for deliverance to break the covenant, any physical marriage you are trying to enter will meet with problems.

Pre-marital sex. This is why many men and women that are eligible are unmarried. If you are loose as a lady, a man will take advantage of you until you completely loose value. Then he could date you for many years and use you, and at the end, dump you. If you offer free sex, most men will dump you eventually. There is also the tendency for you to feel guilty and leave at the slightest provocation, because of your own feeling of unworthiness. You should be able to control yourself sexually. However, if a lady controls herself sexually, then the young man sees you as valuable and always looking forward to that day that he will marry you.

Character lapses. If for example you are too lousy and talk anyhow, then this is a character flaw that will make you repulsive. If you are too parasitic depending on people for financial or material gains which become overwhelming, even as you are not yet married, then they tend to break the relationship. The spirit of greed in you will release you and tell you they are not good enough, making you not realise your own error. Smoking and drinking are not only sinful but are repulsive to many Christians.

Parental influence. There are parents that influence the marriages of their children negatively for selfish reasons. For example, for the mere fact that someone helped you financially, or you are friends, or you come from the same place, is not enough reason for such to automatically qualify as a spouse to your child. Parents like that seem to be uncooperative to another relationship that comes through for that child. It takes prayers and wisdom after a long time to change their minds and be pacified. Some parents could be very troublesome, hindering their children.

Wrong counsel. Words can lead you, as well as mislead you. In a materialistic world, if you are not careful, you will make a mistake that you will forever regret. Most friends tend to favour people who are wealthy or in positions of influence. Be very careful where you receive counsel from.

Unemployment. The trend is for women to be in a place of financial security, whilst the man too does not want to marry a liability. A good job increases your chances of getting a suitor. If you are not yet stable financially, your marriage can crumble due to incessant quarrels occasioned by poverty. Many people are still not married due to the fact that they are unemployed.

Unforgiveness. If you are the unforbearing and unforgiving type (Colossians 3:13) that finds it difficult to overlook the other person's flaws, then your marriage may be delayed. Even when you are married and you still continue with unforgiveness, then it will be difficult to enjoy the marriage.

Materialism. If a single person is materialistic, and has the love of material things, he or she will never get satisfied with a partner. As soon as he/she gets a richer person then the interest shifts to a new lover and continues like that. People like that never get married and settled.

Peer influence. A group of friends could influence one another so as to influence their choice who to marry or their beliefs about marriage. When this happens there might be a delay in marriage because they are trying to conform to a certain value.

Evil spiritual marks. An evil mark could be placed on someone's head, hand, back of neck, or other parts of the body. This makes the brother or sister to be repulsive to suitors. In some people, all they need to do is to pray against evil marks, and their marriage will manifest immediately.

Evil odour. Many brothers and carry odours which are very strong and repulsive. This scares suitors away. The odours are easily noticeable and strongly negative.

Occupation. You could hear a suitor saying only if her job does not entail night duties, it would have been better. Some would say "only if his job does not entail travelling around for weeks it would have been better". Some would say, "only if the job does not involve performing on stages or acting" it would have been better. The day you reconsider your stance about some vocations, that probably could lead to answer prayers. There are some vocations that give you away. Some people too so not enjoy their marriage because of their occupations. There are occupations where over 50% of them are divorced after a few years of their marriage.

Please note that almost all the above listed factors wouldn't just delay your marriage, but can lead to the wrong partner.

Choosing the Mr. Right or Miss Right.

This is a task that only Holy Spirit can effectively perform. Since it is something of a lifetime benefit, it should be handled with patience, and carefully. First and foremost, you should surrender to Jesus Christ. He says "I am the way, the truth, and the life, no one cometh unto the Father but by me.

Surrender to Jesus Christ by confessing him as your Lord and saviour. Say Jesus I thank you for coming to save me and giving your life for me on the cross of Calvary. I confess you as Lord and saviour over my life as from now, and I forsake the devil and all his evil works. Thank you, Jesus.

The next thing is to repent from any known sin. What is sin? James 4:17 says "to him that knoweth to do good and doeth it not, it is sin. There are certain things that conscience tells you are not right before or after doing them. These are the things we are referring to. You go to the house of the boy, and he was fondling you. Sin. You lie to your parents that you are going to work, but you have spent the day at the other end of town with a married man in a hotel. All these lies will work against your destiny. Even emulation, wanting to be like that person is sin (Galatians 5:20). Going by these opinions of peer groups about marriage is a sin and an illegality. If you have lust, the devil will use it against you by bringing that person to have sex with you in your dream, and it will affect your prospects of revelation of a suitor.

The next want to do is to study the word of God, meditate upon it, and observe to do according to all that is written therein. Then you shall prosper and have good success.

Enrol in a singles program where you learn more about things that border on dating and courtship. These meetings are held once or twice weekly. Also, you may want to avail yourself of various resources online regarding various topics. These programs are opportunities for you to meet with people. God will most of the time lead you to people you already know as your partner, once you qualify spiritually.

Prayer and fasting. Some fasting till around 12 noon or 2pm daily is not a bad idea. If possibly take it till 6pm on Fridays, and once in a month, you may do a 24-hour fast. Pray earnestly that reveal the bone of bone and flesh of your flesh. That God should connect with that person, and that all obstacles on your way should give way. These 3 points are key, though others will be added at the end of this chapter. As you pray, totally surrender to the will of God, and don't have any other expectations concerning anyone in your heart, because God may answer you according to the idols of your heart (Ezekiel 14:4).

Forgive. If you do not forgive, then devil will use it against you. For example, the person that is supposed to be your divine partner may be seen in your dream pursuing you. Cleanse your spirit and operate in dominion. The devil will use your sins to pervert your dream life.

Make positive affirmations. For example, in Isaiah 41:10, God has given you promises there. Learn the scripture by heart and always use it creatively on a daily basis, saying "Father I thank you, for you are with me, and you will help me. I thank you for strength, and wisdom you will give unto me. I thank you because you shall reveal my husband/wife to me.

Romans 12:10 Be kindly affectioned one to another with brotherly love; in honour preferring one another. Don't apply lipstick, mascara and eyeshadow. There is no point wearing artificial hair. Let all your make-up be that of a good and kind spirit. Be humble, and gentle. Be of a broken and contrite spirit (Psalm 51:17), though as wise as a serpent (Matthew 10:16).

Know your spouse. Once you have fulfilled all the conditions above, then you need to pray daily. Each time you pray, you are knocking the windows of heaven. After praying the prayers for the day for about an hour or two, you keep quiet and be still. Psalm 4:4 recommends that after prayers, you should be still. This quiet period enables you to search your spirit. The word of God is dropped into your spirit quietly as a thought. Sometimes you hear a single word, which might be the name, or even the street where your suitor lives. All these are clues which as time goes on get clearer to you. In the course of the day, as you pray daily, the likelihood for a response to your requests increase. All of a sudden, you could receive a word in your spirit. Learn to disconnect from your surroundings and close your eyes. Focus on things happening inside you.

In Psalm 19:2, we know that day unto day uttered speech, and night unto night sheweth knowledge. When you sleep, in your dreams, you might see someone giving you a rose, you may see the image of your suitor smiling and well dressed, you may hear a voice, call his name or her name, you might see both of you on a large, well-kept lawn. You may see him lifting your hand. It is also possible for God to tell you to do something regarding marriage e.g. the Holy spirit may tell you to visit her parents to give the bride price. Then you visit their home and make your intentions known. The Holy Spirit will never mislead you. Mind you, any dream of actual wedding is not a good dream, or that you got pregnant for someone or that a lady got pregnant by you. All other dreams signifying a relationship in construct or content that relates to marriage is a confirmation.

Third parties can also catch a revelation of your suitor. Parents of the bride or groom may have a revelation in some way. For example, if a son in future will have two suitors and one would be fair and the other dark. The Lord can show the father a revelation showing two of them, but that the dark lady is the right one. Even though he doesn't know anyone from Adam, he can advise and make an informed decision.

The sibling's pf the bride or groom could also catch a revelation about the right husband or wife for their sibling. Be open to family and friends soliciting their prayers.

Once you know the person with a reasonable degree of certainty, then you have received a lifelong ticket, and you should congratulate yourself. When you are praying for a partner, you need to pray until something is revealed to you. You can be confident in moving closer and sharing you time and thoughts. A further confirmation is that the person will flow along with you, or in some cases may be indifferent.

After this time, you should privately talk to your Pastor, as a man, and he will tell you the next steps, especially if the sister is in your church. If not, you need to book an appointment with her pastor. Ladies generally don't like making the first move, if God reveals to them. In that case, the lady should tell her Pastor, and the Pastor would know how to invite the gentleman for a talk.

The Pastors of both the bride and groom should be aware and relate to one another. At a point, the brother and sister tell their parents. Both the bride and the groom should create time to visit either parents and their families. It is customary in Africa to take a small gift for the parents and this is not out of place in Europe and America too.

The courtship continues with the knowledge and consent of the parents as a mark of honour to the parents. This is not to say that there wouldn't be objections one way or the other. Let either parents know, especially if they are Christians that that is God's choice, and nobody on earth is perfect. Parents should try and respect their children's choices. Many parents eventually succumb to the wish of the duo.

The time of courtship is for both to re-discover one another and know one another more intimately. They are also to start planning their future. For example, how many children they want to have, career preferences, and everything that the brilliant future holds.

FINDING YOUR DIVINELY ORDAINED PARTNER:

1. Lord my father, unveil my divinely ordained partner in Jesus mighty name.
2. Every evil marriage pattern in my ancestral line, break and release me in Jesus name.
3. I break every covenant with spirit husband/wife, working against my marriage, break by the power in the blood of Jesus.
4. I withdraw my marriage certificate from every marine witchcraft altar in the name of Jesus Christ.
5. Serpent of sexual immorality in my life, be destroyed by fire in the name of Jesus Christ.
6. Every stranger sitting on my seat in marriage, be unseated in the name of Jesus Christ.
7. Lord, give me the profitable employment that will mend every broken wall in my marital journey in the name of Jesus Christ.
8. Every peer group and unprofitable friends that the devil is using against my marital joy, scatter in the name of Jesus Christ.
9. Lord, give me the grace to recognise and mend every character flaw in my life in the name of Jesus.
10. Lord, give my parents the grace to understand your vision for my life in the name of Jesus Christ.
11. My father and my God, give me the grace to always forgive other people in the name of Jesus Christ.
12. Lord, give me grace to disgrace every evil sexual desire in the of Jesus.
13. Every satanic environmental pattern working against my marital plans, be scattered in the name of Jesus Christ.
14. Mark of rejection upon my life, be wiped away by the power in the blood of Jesus.
15. I destroy the power of inferiority complex in my life in the name of Jesus Christ.
16. Arrow of error that wants to manifest against my marriage, jump out and backfire.
17. I come against every doubt in my mind in the name of Jesus Christ.
18. Holy spirit, be strong and mighty in my spirit in the name of Jesus Christ.
19. Every blasphemy of the enemy, against my marital plans, be rendered null and void in the name of Jesus Christ.
20. I diffuse every demonic pressure mounting on my head and working against my blessings in the name of Jesus Christ.
21. Lord, release your perfume of marital favour upon my life in the name of Jesus Christ.
22. Lord, your word says beauty is vain. Deliver me from the vanity of beauty in my marriage choice in the name of Jesus Christ.
23. I refuse to choose my destroyer as husband/wife in the name of Jesus Christ.
24. I refuse to be misled in marriage by the deceitfulness of riches in the mighty name of Jesus Christ.
25. Lord, take away every mantle of depression away from my life in the name of Jesus Christ.
26. I remove the ring of spirit spouse from my finger in the name of Jesus Christ.
27. Evil covenant in my mother's side, saying no to my marital plans, be broken by the power in the blood of Jesus Christ.
28. Unconscious covenant working against my marital joy, be broken in the name of Jesus Christ.
29. Environmental evil covenant, break and release my marriage in the name of Jesus Christ.

30. Every evil barrier standing between me and my divinely ordained partner, collapse in the name of Jesus Christ.
31. Every power using my face to attack my suitor, be arrested in the name of Jesus Christ.
32. Every battle of uncooperative in-laws mounting against my marriage, be dismantled in the name of Jesus Christ.
33. Lord, let there be a holy soul-tie between me and my divinely ordained partner in the name of Jesus Christ.
34. Any power, cursing my marriage, be rendered dumb in the name of Jesus Christ.
35. Envious witchcraft monitoring my marriage plans, lose your power in the name of Jesus Christ.
36. Cultural embargo mounted against my marriage, be destroyed in the name of Jesus Christ.
37. Religious barrier mounted against my marriage plans, crumble in the name of Jesus Christ.
38. Satanic voice assigned to confuse my decision, be silenced in the name of Jesus Christ.
39. I bury every opposition against my marriage plans in the name of Jesus Christ.
40. Every demon that wants to pollute my heavenly vision, I break your power in the name of Jesus Christ.
41. Yoke fashioned against my revelations, break in the name of Jesus Christ.
42. I receive the grace for discernment in the name of Jesus Christ.
43. My father and my God, where I am unable to receive your message clearly, reveal it to my true friends and relatives in the name of Jesus Christ.
44. Light that the enemy cannot comprehend, locate my life in the name of Jesus Christ.
45. Lord, let the fire of agape love for my divinely ordained partner be ignited in the name of Jesus Christ.
46. Father Lord, give me multiple signs to recognise my divinely ordained partner in the name of Jesus Christ.
47. Lord, let there be a magnetic pull between me and my divinely ordained partner on the name of Jesus Christ.
48. Lord, use my picture to overwhelm my divinely ordained partner in the name of Jesus Christ.
49. Lord, show me what more that I need to do to enter into the centre of your will for my marriage in the name of Jesus Christ.
50. Power of charms fashioned against my marriage, be destroyed by fire in the name of Jesus Christ.
51. Every sacrifice at the road junction against the divine revelation of my divinely ordained partner be nullified in the name of Jesus Christ.
52. Evil voice confusing my divinely ordained partner, be silenced in the name of Jesus Christ.
53. Group of evil advisers fashioned against my revelation of my divine partner, scatter in the name of Jesus Christ.
54. Lord send your word and make a way for me where there seems to be no way in the name of Jesus Christ.
55. Satanic padlock fashioned against my marriage plans be broken in the name of Jesus Christ.
56. Anointing for divine revelations be released upon my life and my divine partner's life in the name of Jesus Christ.
57. Angelic helpers of my marital destiny, appear by fire in the name of Jesus Christ.
58. I refuse to be replaced by another in the name of Jesus Christ.
59. Lord, I surrender to you, take control of my marital plans in the name of Jesus Christ.
60. Holy Spirit, you are the great matchmaker, arise and do something marvellous in my life in the name of Jesus Christ.
61. Satanic wax blocking my ears from hearing God's voice, be melted away by the fire of the Holy Ghost in the name of Jesus Christ.

62. Satanic cataracts preventing me from seeing cleat visions and revelations, be removed in the name of Jesus Christ.
63. Thou voice that broke the cedars of Lebanon, make a way for me in the valley of my marriage decision in the name of Jesus Christ.
64. I prophesy against every mountain standing against my marriage plans, be made plain in the name of Jesus Christ.
65. Every love potion that I have taken unconsciously that the enemy is using to misdirect me, I break your power in the name of Jesus Christ.
66. You my divinely ordained partner, be released from witchcraft bondage in the name of Jesus Christ.
67. Evil angels in the third heavens withstanding the revelation of my divinely ordained partner, I break your power in the of Jesus Christ.
68. Every negative utterance that I ever made that is working against the journey of my marriage be nullified by the power in the blood of Jesus Christ.
69. You my divinely ordained partner, come out your hiding place and appear to me by fire in the name of Jesus Christ.
70. You my divinely ordained partner, come out of the prison of darkness in the name of Jesus Christ.
71. Thou glory of the living God, be revealed in the name of Jesus Christ.
72. I walk in power into the realms of destinies fulfilling revelations in the name of Jesus Christ.
73. The voice of the Lord that shaketh the wilderness, shake every wilderness holding down my divine partner in the name of Jesus Christ.
74. The voice of the Lord that discovered the forests show me my husband/wife to be in the name of Jesus Christ.
75. Power in the voice of God, lead me to the husband/wife that you have chosen for me in the name of Jesus Christ.
76. The voice of the Lord that divideth the flames, destroy evil veils disallowing me from knowing my divinely ordained partner.
77. Every curse of error and mistake preventing me from making the wrong choice in marriage, be broken in the name of Jesus Christ.
78. The Lord that sitteth upon the floods, take control of every problem arising against my marriage plans in the name of Jesus Christ.
79. Thunder in the voice of God, scatter every power gathered in the spirit realm against my marital journey in the name of Jesus Christ.
80. Miracle that parted the Red Sea, happen in my marital fears and hopelessness in the name of Jesus Christ.

CHAPTER THIRTY- SIX

DELIVERANCE FROM THE SPIRIT OF INFIDELITY.

When you imagine your wife/husband, sneaking out at night to have sex with the next-door neighbour, packing the stuff at home to please and satisfy the strange man/woman. Many times, people will tell you we saw your husband at a hotel somewhere or in a public place messing around. How would you feel if your husband/has slept with almost all the men/women in the office? How would you react if you trust your husband, and keeps swearing he doesn't have money, only for you to discover he opened a big shop for an undergraduate, and even bought a van for deliveries, yet he keeps telling you he has no money. A woman was into adultery and was denying it. They called a native doctor to the scene, who invoked magical powers, and she confessed that none of the children the husband laboured so hard to raise, was his. In another account, a Pastor's wife fondly referred to as "Mummy" was having affairs with most of the males in the church and was the cause of powerlessness due to her harlotry. How would you feel if you discover that the house maid is 5 months pregnant for the so called "man of the house"? Wouldn't it sound funny if you discover that your mother is sleeping with your husband? How can it be heard that the woman of the house sleeps with the gardener, driver and other staff? To even burst the bubble the gardener is trying to brag that he is the father of your last two kids? How would you feel to discover that madam gives them the best of the pieces of meat that you have at home? How does it sound when a neighbour is jokingly but truly telling you that he has had your wife or husband, several times? There was this public figure whose wife was sleeping with almost every man she came across. The show of shame is endless in the world of the cheating partner!

One may wonder, what then can be done. It would shock you to know that many mother in-laws are actually supporting this show of shame, for what they will benefit financially, especially if the poverty mentality is there. A millionaire who was poor till the age of 45 or 50, would still have a poverty mentality based on their past life experience. Most times it is only obvious to the couples. For example, if you are a man and go in to your wife you would know if she has been cheating. A cheating partner is a liar and would always tell lies for sympathy from people around. At the end of the day, you would be blamed. These behaviours are not normal and are deeply spiritual! If there is an allegation of divorce against a husband or wife, whom would you expect the children to go with? The wife, isn't it? A knowledge of these will help you to think about dealing with the problem. Some couples that cheat come to a realisation that the act is bad, but they cannot give it up. It is a bondage, and spiritual. Remember that your vow is "for better for worse", and that God hates divorce (Malachi 2:16). Cheating is a sin like every other habit like alcoholism and smoking, and should not be treated in such a way that it becomes a storm in a teacup. Whether the man or woman is the cheat, great wisdom is required by the other party to handle the situation. It is even easier for a woman to handle a cheating husband than a cheating wife.

The Agenda of Sexual Demons in The Christian Home.

A lady was possessed and was a serial cheat. She confessed that she was sent to the life of the husband to make him sorrowful all his life. She went further to confess that she was sent to make the man poor and spiritually bankrupt and so that the anointing of God upon his life would be dry. The only thing that they could do in order to succeed in this bid was to attach a spirit husband, a sexual demon into the life of this man to torment his destiny. Obviously, if he is always emotionally unstable, he won't progress in life, even though he had a colourful destiny. Sometime a period of separation could help couples and they can come back together again to the glory of God. The spirit husband is a sexual demon that can be programmed into a family to stop their progress except they move close to God and God intervenes.

In the case above, the woman was "sent" by her mother who was a witch. It would have been a different thing if she confessed that she decided to deal with the husband. Mothers have a physical and spiritual influence through the placental route. A mother through the blood connection could link a child or any other person linked by blood. A woman like that, if she is from a polygamous marriage would not only have access to her daughter. She has access to other wives in the polygamous setting to kill them, make them insane or do other things, and nobody would know. She was connected to her husband through sex, and the other women too were connected through sex. All of them were connected. This particular woman was said to have been boasting to have control over the polygamous family after the death of her husband. She was a confirmed witch. Many of them Use church activities as a cover, especially in non-Pentecostal churches.

There have been cases of men that were into adultery, and infected their partners with venereal diseases, apart from beating the women always. One thing that spirit wife does to men is to make sure they do not have a good job, or when they have one, they will make them to commit errors and will be sacked. Most times the spirit wife would have sex with a man a night before his employment interview, and he can be sure he will never have the job. The result is that since ladies love financial security, it takes the spirit of God to make then stay. Eventually the marriage results in a divorce! Imagine a poor man at the same time is possessed by a sexual demon, looking for sexual partners all over the place. A poor man, a nuisance, and a notorious man.

Psychologists and sociologists have tried to study the causes of infidelity. They say it is due to anger or resentment due to wrongdoing on the part of their partner, the love has gone cold and they are not interested, terrible in-laws, poverty, small organ, low self-esteem, opportunistic cheating, covetousness, inferiority complex, association, environment, distance relationships (marriages), and when needs are not met. All these are factors that could predispose to cheating when the main factor is present. Medical or social science can never get to the root of the issue, and that is why no matter how rich a woman is, she can still have sex with her gardener. A man can leave the wife in his house and choose a mistress in a slum nearby, which is very ridiculous. At that point he gets desperate that he doesn't mind packing his belongings to that slum. Is that love? It is a high-level witchcraft attack and could be due to a spell.

What then is the root cause? They are sexual demons, that excite men and women sexually. Most common of these is the Spirit husband, though other sexual demons abound. The spirit husband or wife appears to the victim in their dream and sleep with them injecting toxins into their lives spiritually. There is a blood linkage so to say between husband, his wife, and the spirit husband. The result is that there is a fierce competition between the physical husband and the spiritual husband. The wife may cooperate with the spirit husband to afflict the physical husband. Spirit husbands operate from the spirit realm and if the spouses are not spiritual people, anything can happen along the line.

How can a spirit spouse enter a person?

A spirit spouse can possess a person through the following ways: evil inheritance from a parent, through a covenant with an idol, by way of a curse, indecent dressing, extramarital sex, evil laying of hands, lust, evil dedication, enchantment, witchcraft attacks and mark of evil attraction.

Characteristics of a Cheating Spouse:

The likely tendencies of cheating partners vary from person to person and due to the lineage, circumstances, and background. However, the following are common, but not exhaustive.

1. <u>*Shying away from sex.*</u> One of the first signs that a cheating partner will show is to shy away from conjugal union for several days in a row.

2. *Abusive and insulting words* that portrays the partner has lost respect. Most times a cheating woman for security sake will like to date someone more influential than their spouses.
3. *Toxic behaviour and hatred* to the spouse.
4. *Breakdown of communication.* A cheating spouse is not interested in communicating with you. They give short responses to whatever you are saying.
5. *Unexplainable hatred* towards the spouse which could be transferred to the children sometimes. He or she sees nothing good about the blessed union from God which is their original marriage.
6. *A cheating partner is an unblinking liar.* They tell lies to cover their wrong doings, but for an intelligent spouse, this lies will be defective, but you don't need to flog it for too long.
7. *A cheating partner lives a confused life.* Whatever money they get from the trade is usually squandered.
8. *Excessive carnal desire and lust*, outside marriage.
9. *Blackmailing.* A cheating partner usually loves blackmailing and spreading propaganda in order to discredit the spouse. One of the blackmails is he/she is lazy and boring on bed. They blackmail to their family, in laws and friends.
10. *Comparison.* One of the characteristics of a cheating spouse is that they start comparing you with other men/women, out of covetousness.
11. *A cheating partner sometimes may put on a facade of false kindness* and humility to cover or douse any suspicion from friends and family.
12. *A cheating partner is usually aggressive* in their conversation with their spouse or anyone they suspect has knowledge of their escapades, to cover their guilt.
13. *An adulterous spouse is shameless.* They are possessed by sexual demons and just like a mad man who is possessed. He goes to the gutter to drink dirty water and sees nothing wrong with it.
14. *Sudden consciousness about their looks*.
15. *A cheating partner can curse*, expressing their innermost ill intentions.

Consequences of Infidelity on the person who has a spirit spouse:

The victim of infidelity is the wife or husband of the cheating partner. This evil happens suddenly. You may continue to wonder if it is true, until the attitude and behaviour of the cheating partner establishes it. The following are the effects on the victim.

1. *Low selfesteem.* The first thing a victim will experience is a low self-esteem, no matter how highly placed you may be.
2. *Depression.* If you allow it to overwhelm you, it will throw you into depression. Pray and also go for psychotherapy.
3. *Loneliness.* Since your supposed partner is now withdrawn, then you are a lone ranger in the house. Loneliness is the word. Even at work, or outside the house, it is there in your spirit.
4. *Shame and reproach.* This will be experienced and if you allow this to overwhelm you, then you make enemies for yourself, because it is not hidden. People will lightly esteem you.

5. *Mental torture*, which could make you to hear strange voices. There have been cases of people who virtually went mad because of a heart break.
6. *Aggravation of medical conditions* like a heart disease or high blood pressure. I know 2 cases of a toxic relationship that led to an elevated blood pressure, then stroke, until they passed on. The psychological burden of infidelity on the victim can be enormous. If you are a cheat, think about the harm you are doing, or you may likely cause an innocent person, and repent.
7. *There is no peace.*
8. *Quarrel with in-laws*, especially the unbelieving in-laws. They would always like to be on the side of their son/daughter, no matter how terrible the case may be, and no matter how you try to allow the truth to prevail and peace to reign.
9. *Concentration problems* which impact upon productivity.
10. *Children and Parental separation.* If the victim is the husband, the children would like to take sides with their mum, especially if they are still young. When the victim is the wife, it even makes it worse for the man invariably.
11. *Children seeing you as a threat.* Another common social epidemic is that you may have children who are not your biological children, under your roof. As the child grows up, he/she sees you as a threat and enemy, no matter how kind and tolerant you may be. Wisdom is required.
12. *Poverty.* There is a satanic triangle established between the husband/wife/spirit spouse. They are joined by blood, and this gives access to the spirit spouse as a spiritual entity to work against the success of the marriage through hatred between both of them, negative inspiration, sickness and more.
13. *A temptation to retaliate.* This will add to your problems, as you will strip yourself of God's assistance, once you commit sin. It will erode your conscience, especially if you didn't plan that are not disposed to doing such. Continue in your righteousness, and the righteous shall be as bold as a lion, but the wicked flee when no one pursueth (Psalm 28:1).
14. *Tendency towards suspicion*, and sometimes these suspicions are not correct.
15. *Misunderstanding.* A victim may be misunderstood and hated by the public who do not understand what is happening.
16. *It is not uncommon to see a strange man/woman in your dreams,* because you are connected in your dreams. For example, anyone wearing your dress in the dream tells tales, or you see them competing with you in the dream, or their face appears to you in the dream

Steps to Deliverance from The Spirit of infidelity:

1. *Accept Jesus Christ as your Lord and saviour.* Confess that *"Lord Jesus, I thank you for coming to this world to save me. I make you Lord and saviour over my life as from today and forsake the devil and all his evil works. Thank you, Jesus.*

2. *Run from sin.* What is sin? The bible says in James 4:17 that to him that knoweth to do good and doeth it not it is sin. There will be temptations in an adulterous situation, and adultery has been the cause of murder in many cases. Learn to control yourself. He that hath no rule over his own spirit is like a city with broken down walls (Proverbs 25:28). Be temperate and kind. Be angry but sin not (Ephesians 4:26).

3. *Study the word of God meditatively.* Study the word of God and think about how it applies to your situation. Psalm 4:4 encourages us to be still when meditating. The word of God will filter into your spirit, not only to comfort you, but can come as instruction, doctrine, correction or reproof (2 Timothy 3:16).

4. *Pray harder.* We are dealing with a deeply spiritual problem that may have physical dimensions. Ephesians 6:12 says we wrestle not against flesh and blood, but against principalities, against powers, against the rulers of the darkness of this world, against spiritual wickedness in high places. Prayer is needed with fasting on a regular basis, mainly to break the covenant of the spirit spouse, cast out the spirit spouse, pray against curses, pray against marine witchcraft influence, and destroy the ring and certificate of spirit spouse with your husband/wife. Remember to pray against charms or diabolic materials, because they may actually use charms to seduce an innocent man or woman and make them commit immorality. They continue to renew the charm in as much as they continue to have sex.

5. *Casting down imaginations.* The Bible in 2 Corinthians 10:5 encourages us to cast down imaginations, thoughts, and feelings of failure and disappointment, and bring them down to the obedience of Christ. This means we should only focus on the word of God. Study a lot of God's promises and focus on them.

6. *If you see him/her with the opposite sex*, keep your calm. God says he will fight for you and you shall hold your peace (Exodus 14:14). The temptation can make the devil to strike and do crazy things, but be a fool for Christ and you shall glorify God in the end. I know about couples who said they were travelling, but had to come back home to pick something and caught their spouses in the very act. They did nothing but just picked something and went out immediately. Nothing can be more humbling and conscience racking to a cheating partner. Silence!

7. *Strengthen connection with the children.* The children are the link between husband and wife, and you can use this fact to your advantage. Buy things that will interest the Children, put in films that will interest them, and the children move towards you and everywhere us sparked with joy. Your partner definitely wouldn't like to be the odd one out and will gravitate towards you.

8. *Make use of moments of least resistance.* No matter how vile a cheating spouse may be, they have moments of least resistance, especially if you can put on a gentle "saintly look", and not an aggressive look. This is the moment to strike with your tender loving kindness. Please note that a merry heart doeth good like medicine (Proverbs 17:22). Good words lead to a merry heart. Learn to speak kind words in all sincerity and not deceptively.

9. *Go for deliverance programs and retreats.* It will amaze you how God can use these programs to do great things in your lives. Initially a cheating spouse may not be interested when the poison of infidelity is still strong, but like a

drug, the effect of the poison gradually wears away after some time. Some continue without any remorse, whilst some quit infidelity after some time. However, be sure that once you have a grasp on the way to manage it, then you are okay. If you don't treat with wisdom and patience, a divorce can terribly devastate your destiny.

10. *Make long promises.* For example, I will buy an iPhone14 for you in about 6 weeks when I have my bonus! Don't think that how can I buy something for someone cheating on me. The way we think is not the way God thinks. This keeps them in suspense as they try to please you in order to get this. It is also possible to use short term promises, but worth it. For example, a woman may say, in two weeks' time, I prepare your best food for you. It has to be a very special dish. One of the doors to a man's heart is food. This might be your winning g point even if he engages in sex outside.

11. *Avoid the intervention of in-laws.* Some in-laws don't have anything good to offer apart from deception and lies. A mother-in-law who has something to benefit from her cheating daughter will always add to the problems at hand. Some of them too were very terrible adulteresses in their earlier years in life.

12. *Learn to smile.* Put on smiles even when a cheating spouse insults you, and turn it into a joke, walking away.

13. *Learn to walk away from anticipated arguments.* Anytime you perceive there may be argument or unhealthy confrontation, then you walk away. Instead of creating a scene that neighbours will stare at you, or try to be nosy, it's better you walk away. It is also good for your mental health.

14. *See this trial of your faith as a time to be a better version of yourself and develop in value.* If you get distracted, depressed and devastated, there is every likelihood that you may depreciate and start living a useless life. That is the agenda of witchcraft for your life. However, you can reverse the agenda. How? Enrol in a time-consuming intensive training program, that will not only occupy your mind and prevent you from destructive thoughts, but make you a higher earner. Learn to earn. You can commit yourself to a mentoring program online. Make your life more exciting and more profitable. Never resort to alcoholism or contemplate suicide. Be creative. Life is not about what happens to you, but the way you react to it. When life throws a lemon at you, at all costs, make a lemonade.

15. *Take care of your health.* It is most likely that the new development may bring you mental challenges, affect your blood pressure, and other indices. Take good care of yourself. Don't allow the devil to have the last laugh in your life. It might be sometimes necessary to book an appointment with a psychotherapist.

16. *Keep back information.* A cheating spouse can be very dangerous that you cannot share every secret with them, unfortunately. Don't share information about your progress with then because they want you down, and not promoted. This is a serious witchcraft problem, though some fake Pastors may still encourage you to share every information. Get it to sink in that even under a normal marriage, you may not need to share every information like Abraham. He did not discuss with her wife what he was to do to Isaac, as an example. A dangerous spouse can use information about your progress against you. He/she can also divulge to strangers to mock you.

17. *Learn to look away sometimes even when you saw them.* No man that warreth entangleth himself with the affairs of this world.

18. *Think about lovely things for your marriage.* Plan a good holiday with your family in a distant town. A marriage embattled with infidelity may manifest greatness subsequently if you handle the case prayerfully very well.

19. *Watch your utterances.* Don't commit yourself to what you cannot fulfil. Don't be abusive in such a way that it can be used against you in the future.
20. *Separation.* It might be beneficial to separate for a while. Many are oblivious of this fact and go for divorce. When you are separated, you have not committed yourself to a divorce, and it is just for a while. However, if absence does not improve your commitment to one another, which is rare, then the courts may advise a divorce. For example, you may apply for a course in another country or sign a job contract in another country. A period of separation usually makes you to value what you have and make an informed decision. It might not be possible to value what you have until you lose it, and separation is a good experiment to test that.

For public speaking engagements, mentorship, or communication with the author, please contact through: abayomi.olugbemiga@gmail.com

Prayers to Bury the Spirit of Infidelity:

1. I return the ring of spirit spouse, and I cancel every evil agreement in the name of Jesus Christ.
2. My inner beauty, begin to glow in my life in the name of Jesus Christ.
3. Lord, erect a hard wall, against me and the strange man/woman the devil has anointed to scatter my marriage in the name of Jesus Christ.
4. Father Lord, let there be an irreconcilable difference between my husband/wife and the strange woman and man, in the name of Jesus Christ.
5. Strange man/woman, sucking the milk and honey of my marriage, lose your appetite in the name of Jesus Christ.
6. Every man or woman that has vowed that my life and my marriage will never enjoy peace, be divinely relocated in the name of Jesus Christ.
7. Let every strange man/woman putting on my clothing in the dream be stripped naked in the name if Jesus Christ.

8. Every situation or circumstance imposed upon my marriage by the strange man or woman, be reversed in the name of Jesus Christ.
9. Demonic spirit, using my marriage to torment me, be arrested in the name of Jesus Christ.
10. By fire by force, I withdraw the key of my marriage from the hands of the strange man in the name of Jesus Christ.
11. Oil of gladness from the almighty God, be released upon my marriage in the name of Jesus Christ.
12. Fetish power and confidence of the strange man/woman over my marriage, break in the name of Jesus Christ.
13. Every virtue in my life, confiscated by the powers of darkness, because of my jealousy and envy, I recover you in the name of Jesus Christ.
14. Covenant of distraction and poverty against my marriage, break in the name of Jesus Christ.
15. Dominion of familiar spirits over my life, through sex, break by the power in the blood of Jesus Christ.
16. Every satanic virtue transfer through sex, that is responsible for non-achievement in my life, be reversed in the name of Jesus Christ.
17. Every stranger, secretly intruding into my marriage, receive disgrace in the name of Jesus Christ.
18. Padlock of the strange man/woman, fashioned against my wife, husband, break by fire in the name of Jesus Christ.
19. Every grip of stubborn strange man/woman on my marital glory and dignity, lose by fire in the name of Jesus Christ.
20. God of justice, arise and judge the attack of the enemy against my marriage in the name of Jesus Christ.
21. Evil decision from the coven against my marriage, be disgraced in the name of Jesus Christ.
22. Evil marriage pattern of my in-law's house, you shall not manifest in my marriage in the name of Jesus Christ.
23. Pollution in my life, and in the life of my wife/husband, be washed by the power in the blood of Jesus Christ.
24. Huge blessings bombard my marriage in the name of Jesus Christ.
25. Altars of darkness, manipulating my wife, catch fire and burn to ashes in the name of the name Jesus Christ.
26. Seduction of the strange man/woman against my marriage, fail woefully in the name of Jesus Christ.
27. My marriage, you shall not cooperate with the agenda of the strangers in the name of Jesus Christ
28. Evert strange man/woman that has swallowed my life, vomit me by fire in the name of Jesus Christ.
29. Any padlock of sex, that the strange man or woman has used to lock my consciousness, break in the name of Jesus Christ.
30. Every vulture of infidelity waiting to prey on my destiny, be roasted by fire in the name of Jesus Christ.
31. Satanic wisdom, operating against my marriage, be turned to foolishness in the name of Jesus Christ.
32. Serpent of God in my life, swallow the serpent of demonic magicians on assignment against my marriage in the name of Jesus Christ.
33. Lord my father, take away every reproach in my marriage in the name of Jesus Christ.
34. Lord, send your word, and give me a solution to the problem of infidelity in my life in the name of Jesus Christ.
35. Lord, visit every demon of mental infirmity in my life with your fire in the name of Jesus Christ.
36. Grace for salted words in my marriage, fall upon my life in the name of Jesus Christ.
37. Serpent of infidelity in my marriage, die in the name of Jesus Christ.

38. Lord, cage every strange man/woman assigned to trouble my marriage in the name of Jesus Christ.
39. Every demonic gift of the strange man/woman, mesmerising my husband/ wife, lose your appeal in the name of Jesus Christ.
40. Bewitched food that was used to lure my husband/wife into adultery, loose your power in the name of Jesus Christ.
41. Evil covenant, evil bond, evil contract between my husband/wife and strange woman/man, be broken in the name of Jesus Christ
42. Witchcraft personality, using my wife against me, lose your power
43. Satanic conspiracy against my marriage, scatter by fire in the name of Jesus Christ.
44. Anything strengthening the strange man/woman against my marriage, be destroyed in the name of Jesus.

CHAPTER THIRTY-SEVEN

DELIVERANCE FROM WITCHCRAFT ATTACKS AGAINST YOUR CONCEPTION.

My wife and I went for a retreat in Ibadan, Nigeria, in the year 2013. We engaged on a twenty-eight-day white fast, as led. After the fast, in the beginning of March, the Lord spoke, 'Power to make women to conceive and deliver safely, has been released to you today". The Lord thereafter gave me further directions in a church that God used me to establish in the year 2010. Till date, many have given glory to God, based upon this covenant. The Lord spoke through prophecy then, how he was going to use me in this ministry in foreign lands. My wife who has been a Nurse/Midwife has joined me in this ministry, supporting with her expertise and years of experience.

The problem of infertility is a common one, and can be so devastating, especially if it happens to a newlywed couple. Infertility is a condition whereby the male or female reproductive system is dysfunctional, and pregnancy cannot be achieved after at least about 12 months of regular unprotected sexual intercourse. Infertility can be primary or secondary. Primary Infertility is when a pregnancy has never been achieved by a person, and secondary Infertility is when at least one pregnancy has been achieved. To solve the problem, the approach should envisage, and encompass the prevention, diagnosis, and treatment of infertility. Generally, couples should try everything they can to achieve conception as early as possible, though conception and safe delivery has been recorded at 74 years!

Social and Psychological Aspects.

Infertility can be demoralising, for example in your place of work, when the staff have an occasion to bring their children for a party, and you cannot bring your own child. When they are discussing about parenting, you have to keep quiet or pretend as if you are not listening. If you bring your younger brother or sisters' child and somebody asks the child, is she your mummy? The child looks right and left for a moment and shakes his or her head, saying "no". How frustrating and how embarrassing can that be? Sometimes? The boredom of being alone, without nobody to keep you company can be so frustrating. When you are now advancing in age and people are sending their children on errands, but you have none to send.

Sometimes, even your own partner could pass some derogatory comments as if it is your fault. The blame is usually put upon the woman, and she is always sad. There was a case like that, and the woman was always accused of not being able to conceive and produce kids. She always lived a guilty and sorrowful life. Somewhere along the line, they met a doctor who advised that the husband does a sperms count. That was it! The man's spermatozoa were deformed, either having two heads, or no tail, or other strange forms. To the glory of God, she's a happy mother today. God has turned against her reproach. In-laws can also be lacking reason and understanding, always blaming one side than the other. When surely there is hope, a bad in-law can scatter a marriage. In other cases, polygamy is the other option, which may be hidden to the wife initially. Sometimes a woman may double date and eventually make it official. It is so sad leaving someone you loved so much. It may take long to heal, but it is not impossible. Brothers or sisters in law may insult or abuse you directly whenever a quarrel arises. The frustration can be overwhelming especially after many years. However, of eventually your prayers are answered, the joy is even much more overwhelming. It is worth the efforts.

In the society, people lightly esteem you. They sometimes call in their children from your apartment into their room, so that you would feel lonely. Some sing and call you names to your hearing. Anytime you have a disagreement with your partner, which is common, this is the peak of frustration and rejection, especially as a woman. The problem of infertility is usually felt by the woman in most cases than does the man.

The mental stress is much, that most women who are infertile become paranoid. They feel that everything that anyone is referring to them even when they are not. A person could be so depressed that nothing matters in life at the moment depression sets in. Many take solace in their places of work if they have a job. If not, the problem is worse. A tendency to commit adultery may be observed in some, and it makes the relationship very dry between husband and wife. Faith is one thing that couples need to develop to keep them going in the storm. It will also usher in miracles sooner than later. Bad emotions will affect secretion of hormones and affect ovulation, making it haphazard. When a person believing God for the fruit of the womb is emotionally devastated, it doesn't help.

Witchcraft Attacks Against Conception in Females.

There is a medical consequence for most witchcraft attacks. That is what we shall examine now.

1. <u>Flesh eaters and blood suckers.</u> When blood suckers and flesh eaters are on rampage, the uterus, fallopian tubes, and ovaries are the objects of attack. There have been instances where witches confessed that they ate someone's womb. That type of womb will be physically present, but the myometrium (womb muscle) could be

weak, that it cannot hold a foetus to term. There will be miscarriage. That is when you have an ovarian failure whereby the ovarian function is deficient at an early age, affecting the production of oestrogen and affecting the menstrual cycle and ultimately conception. Hormonal balance is a major cause of infertility, and fundamentally, this should be addressed. Flesh eaters also could cause a disease like polycyclic ovary affecting hormonal production as well. Witches can also suck the blood in the ovaries or uterus thereby affecting the functions of this organ. The foetus needs blood to develop, and anaemia can cause pre-term birth, developmental problems and low birth weight.

2. *Inherited witchcraft.* When witchcraft is inherited, things like fibroid follow depending on the covenant inherited and the purpose of the covenant. Fibroid occupies space in the womb, depending on the size, and is another factor that prevents conception and can cause miscarriages. Massive fibroid will not allow the foetus to be well implanted and grow freely. Many anomalies of the reproductive organs and system are transferred by witchcraft. Inherited diseases like hypertension and diabetes could also affect the conception and development of a baby.

3. *Eating in the dream* is another form of attack by witchcraft. When you eat in the dream, usually because there is a blood connection or initiation, they use the food to poison your spirit, affect your emotions, or introduce infections. Infections of the reproductive system are detrimental to conception. An infection of the womb, affecting the fallopian tube can block the tube, thereby preventing movement of the released ovum into the uterus for fertilisation, and conception.

4. *Spirit husband.* Spirit spouse normally comes to have sex with a woman, thereby causing a miscarriage. There have been instances where a woman will dream of having sex, and spontaneously, abortion will follow. I had a counselee, who was a victim of serial attacks by a spirit husband. She kept having miscarriages and unable to have a baby. Spirit husband can also feed a woman and cause misconception. Spirit husband can make a woman to be promiscuous through an evil covenant, and people like this will lack the degree of Intimacy required for conception in certain couples. It is not just coming together, but what is the emotion. This affects hormonal levels, and the reproductive system as a whole.

5. *Dream attacks.* I had a counselee that saw the mother in-law come to press her womb in the dream. She woke up and was bleeding. However, she quickly raised an alarm, and we prayed for her. She also went to the hospital that the baby was saved. Others won't be lucky, and many people have been victims of violence in their dreams leading to an abortion they did not want. They could also attack with a cancer of any of the reproductive organs, leading to dysfunction and unfruitfulness.

6. *Curses.* There are people that are cursed by household witchcraft or other groups. The curse will never allow them to have a child. Many times, the curse is from the spouse, due to a broken marriage covenant with other partners prior to the present marriage. People under this description could have testicular cancer, or other problems. They may behave strangely and loose helpers.

7. *Evil dedication.* When a person is dedicated, there are serious linkages to Evil altars. They have the presence of demonic spirits in them. This is why it is important to ask your parents about the history of your life so that you can break every yoke of evil dedication.

8. *Evil covenants.* Evil covenants open the door to demonic spirits, including blood suckers and flesh eaters. These spirits attack the pregnancy. One common way through which witchcraft initiates and torments the sick is through food. This is why it is important to be careful about what you eat and where you eat it.

9. *Evil summons.* A person can be summoned in the dream. If they succeed in their summon, it means that they have access to the mother and the foetus. This is we tell pregnant people to pray very well before they sleep.

10. *Evil possession.* When a person is possessed, they don't have the control over certain aspects of their lives. This leads to strange behaviours. There are ladies that enjoy serial abortions which affects their wombs, and ability to conceive. Some of them were victims of surgical scarring or cross infections. A surgical scar is formed, when during abortion, a wound is formed which heals with a scar. The scars are fibrous, and like nylon, and cannot easily allow a foetus to remain and grow. The result is that they cannot a baby. Evil possession is also the cause of bad habits like smoking and drinking alcohol, and all these have terrible consequences on the ability to conceive and give birth to a baby.

11. *Environmental attacks*. Watch where you spread your underwear or how you dispose your underwear. There is a department in the kingdom where they go about, collecting menstrual pads or vital things like placenta if you don't dispose of them carefully. They use these things to transfer your virtues and afflict you. Many are childless or are having stubborn problems in life, simply they were careless with some items they could have been more careful with.

12. *Indiscriminate and careless of drugs.* This can affect hormonal balance and lead menstruation problems. Drugs can also cause miscarriages, and birth defects for defects for your baby. Some drugs e.g. nicotine in smokers have been found to damage the fallopian tubes and uterus. Nicotine can disrupt ovarian function affecting the ovum necessary for conception. Do you want to continue smoking? Study the literature of every drug you take. You may be surprised that many drugs have negative effects on lactating and pregnant women.

13. *Age.* Women should be aware that for men and women sexual function decline with age. They should try to be serious about the issue. The female sexually is maintained until about the age of 38 years when it begins to decline until menopause.

The Effect of Stress Ovulation.

A major factor to consider in order to conceive quickly is the issue of stress- physical and to a large extent, emotional stress. Emotional stress affects the secretion of hormones because it is neutrally mediated. This can cause hormonal imbalance necessary for ovulation. If this happens, then the date that you ovulate – release your "egg" is affected, leading into corresponding changes in your menstrual cycle and the date that you menstruate and intervals between menstruation dates. An irregular menstrual cycle makes it difficult for you to determine the likely date of ovulation that you can come together with your husband and conceive.

Stress Factors Affecting Fertility.

Many factors can cause emotional stress, irregular menstrual cycles and failed conception.

Pressure from toxic in-laws is the most disturbing factor. Many of these people are not patient enough and if you give them a chance and don't take the bull by the horns, they frustrate you and spiritually sit on your miracles for as long as they are allowed to trouble your life. Let them know that God is in charge and will never fail you. The next one is your spouse himself or herself. Most immature spouses are unable to contain. It can be easily felt that they are becoming withdrawn and uncooperative. This may subtly open the door for strange behaviour like domestic violence, being jittery and even adultery. When a partner does that, it is the beginning of destruction. This is not a battle you can fight by quarrelling. It requires great commitment and unity. The ovulation window (those 2 days of likely ovulation) of the wife should be celebrated specially and no time for resentments. The third cause is financial concerns. When there are bills to pay, of you are not careful, you are overwhelmed by the pressures placed upon you by your needs. Husband and wife come back home with a headache, and tiredness. No one even remembers the ovulation date, yet they keep praying and fasting. Know ye not that faith without works is dead? (James 2:20). The pressure of health issues can also affect you. The fibroid, low sperm count, ovarian failure etc. Don't you know that our God is a miracle working God and he answers when you trust him with all your heart? (Jeremiah 29:13). Why don't you decree and speak to that mountain? (Mark 11:23). Whosoever shall say unto this mountain, Be thou removed and be cast in to the sea, but shall not doubt in his heart but shall believe that those things which he saith shall come to pass; he shall have whatsoever he saith. The experience with miscarriages and what people are saying about you can also bring emotional stress. The Bible admonishes us to cast down imaginations and let all our thoughts be brought to the obedience of Christ (2 Corinthians 10:5). Whatsoever things are true, pure, just, honest, lovely and of good report should grow and multiply in your spirit (Philippians 4:8). When you have marine witchcraft oppression and you don't pray and break their power, it brings about career issues which also give you a lot of emotional stress. No one is happy if their job is not doing well. Prayer will give you revelation, and revelation will lead to your celebration in Jesus name. Couples should pray more when everything seems not to be working as expected. Stress and anxiety are not beneficial but will limit you. What are you doing with it then? Let us see what we can do to get the right ovulation date.

Determination of Ovulation Date.

Certain methods could help you to most accurately determine the day of ovulation and increase your chances of conception. The first one is an increase in the basal body temperature. The basal body temperature is your body temperature when you are not sick, and you have had a period of rest. When as a Christian, you are sensitive in the spirit, you should be able to detect that slight increase in temperature you need to know the time of your miracle. This can be easily detected when you wake up in the morning, or after a long rest and you wake up for a vigil. Secondly, some people have "ovulation pain" at the time of ovulation. This pain is a mild pain or discomfort that could be felt on one side of the lower abdomen (position of the ovary), or sometimes on both sides of the lower abdomen during ovulation. When you feel this, then it is miracle time, and you need to come together. The third method is the "ovulation test kit". Search this online to give you the various names based on the Country you are doing your search, and it will give you the corresponding prices, anything from about $10 upwards. It detects a surge in the luteinizing hormone (LH) and predicts the two most likely days you can ovulate. There are different types of it that we cannot exhaustively discuss it here. Search online! The man must be prepared to make the best advantage of the wife's ovulation date, in terms of nutrition, mental and emotional alertness. If it comes at a time there is a misunderstanding, it is better you settle the misunderstanding and forget from the depth of your heart. The blessings of God are far from quarrelling couples unfortunately. Where there is unity, are the blessings of Jehovah (Psalm 133:3). This is not just true for making babies, but for wealth acquisition and any other blessing.

The fourth method is the detection of increase in the volume of cervical mucus that you see or feel in your cervix. It becomes clearer and more slippery more like raw egg white. When you touch with two fingers it doesn't break easily. One major sign is that you feel wet, at that period. It means you are set for a miracle baby. You shall receive yours after reading this chapter in the mighty name of Jesus. The fifth method is the use of "ovulation apps". These are apps with built in algorithms (system) that predict ovulation dates based on certain information you feed into the system, like your basal body temperature. Once it senses an unusual increase, it will let you know. It may also be the LH levels from the predictor test kit. This is another good method.

The sixth and most popular method is calculating your ovulation date taking track of the date of your menstruation. This is most reliable for people who have a regular menstrual cycle. However, people who have fertility problems do not have regular periods and need to use this method in conjunction with other methods earlier stated. It is believed that ovulation occurs 14 days to the end of your menstrual cycle. If you have been recording for a few months and you have an average cycle of 30 days, then you draw a 30-day calendar, and go to the end of it (day 30) and count 14 days backward. That will automatically give you day 16 on your calendar. This means you are good to go, a day or two before day 16, which is day 14 or 15. When you have sex on day 14 or 15, then as the ovum comes out, the sperm on time welcomes it on point. The sperm can live for 5 days, inside the woman, but this also depends on the conditions inside the woman e.g. acidity, alkalinity, temperature, the mucus which helps it etc. It also partly depends on the quality of the sperm. Some spermatozoa may just die after 2 or 3 days. Ideally, sex 2 days before the ovulation is appropriate

Having known how to track the most likely ovulation day, please don't forget it. This is your game changer. If you miss it, it is like someone missing a bus! If you are believing God for a baby, it is not only the responsibility of the woman to calculate the ovulation date. Both the husband and wife should collaborate.

Causes of Infertility in Males.

The whole blame of fertility is put mostly on the females, who then feel guilty. Research and experience have shown that this is not always the case. Sometimes, the infertility comes from the males, and infertility from the male may be more suspect and treatment medically than the females. The causes of infertility in the males are quite to that of the females, but different in manifestation because the organs and Physiology are different. What are the causes of infertility in the males and how can they manifest.

1. _Direct witchcraft attacks._ Confessions have been made by witches, that they "took" the manhood of someone. Such a person will find it difficult to maintain an erection, abnormal spermatozoa (with two heads, or no tail) or have low sperm count. People like that have a low sperm count. The case of low sperm count is very common, and every couple with fertility challenges should first consider a sperm count amongst other things. There have been cases where these attacks came from a former girlfriend, who was offended. In another episode, the mother of the man confessed in tears, "I ate his manhood". In another episode, the mother said, "I donated his manhood". In order for witches to acquire power, they usually have to donate something like the manhood of the son or husband, the womb of their daughter, other virtues or the life of a close person.
2. _Conscious evil covenants._ A man's manhood can be placed under an evil covenant by a former girlfriend or the mother, in exchange for power or as a punishment. Who was the girlfriend that asked you strange questions, who always held a strange handkerchief anytime you had sex, or who touched your manhood with it. A covenant with an agent who has a spirit husband could take a manhood. The same person will be bringing herbs to you and collecting your money. This is why it is not good to engage in adultery or fornication.
3. _Curses._ A curse may manifest in many ways in order to misconduct and errors. A man under a curse or even a woman at that, will always have a cause automatically to quarrel or fight with the wife or the husband when the ovulation time is approaching. This will make them to miss conjugal Union and likelihood of conception. I know a couple, that they will always quarrel anytime something good is coming for them to celebrate. Effects of a curse! It could also be due to a curse sometimes.
4. _Evil dedication._ This may cause a man to be weak and loose desire to have sex. When a man's sex drive and appeal is down most time, it is a big problem. Many of these men are sick always and emaciated. They look very frail and sickly. First of all, he needs spiritual care to break that evil dedication. Is your husband like that?
5. _Satanic spiritual odour._ The powers of darkness can act in many ways. I have seen couples who are indeed repulsive to one another. One partner often perceives a smell that makes the other partner strongly repulsive! Some do say, "what is smelling like this"? God has given some male animals a perfume to attract the female for sex and conception. Animals like the he-goat and male lion exhibit these behaviours. It is God's strategy for

attraction. Pheromones are secreted by some female animals e.g. rabbits, ants, deer and mice to attract males during oestrus or heat. Male animals can detect it from a distance. What is your strategy to induce and attract your partner and break the yoke of darkness? Everything is not prayer.

6. _A rough past._ Many men used their life roughly in the very early reproductive years, having sex indiscriminately. Even as married men believing God for a child, they still commit adultery. This is foolishness.

7. _Self-imposed rituals for money or fame._ Some men have entered into evil agreements for power and fame. This has taken their manhood consciously or unconsciously. As a wife, you have to be prayerful to discover the cause of infertility. Some of them are simply shocking. Most of the time, the solution of a problem lies in knowing the cause. There are many secrets that many are carrying in their heads, you may never know who is who.

8. _Unconscious evil covenant._ Many men entered are evil victims of evil Unconscious covenants. This may be through food in that canteen, and your destiny has been attacked. The barber can also do this. If you are in the habit of visiting herbalists, sorcerers, spiritualists because you want to know what the future holds or for other so-called benefits, you may have been short-changed. Where did you go in the past that an evil transaction occurred? Try and remember. You need to pray.

9. _Environmental evil altars._ There are evil witchcraft altars in every street, council area, village, town, city etc. These altars decide on the affairs of the residents. If you are a drunkard, you may be a victim. If you normally eat from a restaurant run by an agent by an agent, you and others may be victims. This type of problem will affect many people in the environment. If you have noticed that in the same vicinity, some couples are experiencing miscarriages, delayed conception, childlessness, then look no further. It is a collective captivity of an environmental cause.

10. _Attack on your garments._ As a couple entertaining visitors regularly in your household, you don't spread panties, singlets, boxers and other underwear carelessly. Spread them on a rack in your bedroom and lock your bedroom when you are away. This is also to cover your secrets. Witches use your secrets against you. Witches use these materials to put conception on hold or deny you of it for ever because of your ignorance. There is a price to pray ignorance, and ignorance is expensive. You can't afford to be ignorant. In the environment too, don't spread underwear outside, but inside.

11. _Occupational causes._ Heat and stress do not support the production of healthy sperm. Spermatozoa is the cell that fertilises the ovum. When the seminal fluid from the prostate and mixes with it, it becomes "sperm". These fluids offer nourishment and protection to spermatozoa. It also helps them move very effectively. When you work in a bakery, where you are exposed to heat, it can affect the quality of your sperm. When your mainly sedentary and you can sit on a seat for several hours without standing, there is so much heat generated in between your thighs as well as well stress. You might need your job if this is affecting you. Don't always sit heating up your testicle. You can stand and attend to customers sometimes. This is also good for muscles and joints.

12. _Medicines like anabolic steroids._ Anabolic steroids are variations of the male hormone testosterone and mostly used to enhance muscle development and athletic performance. Other people like musicians and security

officials also use them. Examples include nandrolone, methandostenolone, and stanozolol. They are capable of shrinking the testicle and interfering with reproductive functions. They cause erectile dysfunction.

13. *Erectile dysfunction (ED).* This is a condition characterised by inability to achieve or maintain an erection firm enough for a satisfactory sexual intercourse. This can be caused by cardiovascular diseases, diabetes mellitus, neurological disorders, hormonal imbalance, medications (anabolic steroids, nicotine), stress, anxiety, depression, or relationship issues. Among other things, couple should try to resolve ant relationship issues when believing God for a child. Relationship can cause irregular menstruation as well as erectile dysfunction both of which work against effective conception. ED can be cured treating underlying cause if a disease. There are also lifestyle changes e.g. quitting smoking and alcohol. Good nutrition will help. Run from medication that are harmful. Seeing a doctor and a psychologist would help, and where drugs and lifestyle changes have failed, you may consider a penile implant.

14. *Age.* Reproductive ability reduces with increasing age in both men and women. With advancing age, the sperm reduces. A man is most virile at the age of 30 years up till 45 years when sexual function starts to decline, though it varies from person to person. The use of recommended supplements by your doctors, and good nutrition will help a great deal.

Role of Nutrition in Reproduction.

Nutrition has a wonderful role in reproduction and has profound effects on fertility in males and females. However, this important topic is often neglected by couples believing God for a child. What are things to note about nutrition when believing God for a child?

Obesity. Obesity is excessive accumulation of body fat which poses a risk to health. It is measured by the body mass index (BMI) which is the value when you divide the body weight in kilograms by the height in metres squared. The normal value is fixed at 30 Kilograms/metre^2. In males, high a BMI reduces testosterone levels, and sperm quality. A low BMI leads to reduced sperm production. In females, overweight or underweight causes unstable hormone levels and menstrual irregularity which leads to conception problems.

Vitamins, minerals, antioxidants and enzymes lead to improved reproductive health in both men and women. Foliate, iron, zinc, vitamin D and Vitamin C optimise fertility and are good for improved fertility. Uncontrolled blood sugar e.g. diabetes in males can lead erectile dysfunction and reduced sperm quality. In females, excessive blood glucose disrupts hormone balance and leads to menstrual irregularities and problems with conception. Antioxidants like fruits, vegetables, and nuts protect reproductive cells from damage, and in males brings about improved sperm health. In females it enhances improved egg health.

Omega-3 fatty acids. This is found in oily fishes like the mackerel and salmon, and walnuts. They have anti-inflammatory properties and improve reproductive function, by supporting hormone production and reduce inflammation in both males and females alike. Alcohol, caffeine and nicotine are not good for reproductive health because they reduce fertility. A good hydration can be achieved by drinking water, fruit juices and beverages rich in electrolytes. When the body is well hydrated, it improved the consistency of the cervical mucus, and allows sperm to move freely and easily into the uterus. In males, hydration improves sperm volume, sperm quality, and libido. When the body is dehydrated, there is a high density of spermatozoa which tend to shrink in shape with reduced movement. This is detrimental to a good conception and might cause infertility. Husband and wife need to drink considerable quantities of water.

Aphrodisiacs are another group of food, herbs and drugs which increases sexual desire, arousal or performance. Examples of aphrodisiacs include chocolate, eggs, cod fish eggs, avocados, almonds, maca root, saffron, and different types of bitters. The list is endless depending on culture, beliefs and personality. In Nigeria, West Africa, Ogbono a kind of soup that is very good as an aphrodisiac. Viagra is also good. Men with cardiovascular diseases should use aphrodisiacs with caution, because the excitement of sex can make you to overshoot physiological limits, though this is uncommon. It can however be used freely by people without cardiovascular diseases.

Assisted Reproductive Technology.

When natural conception has failed, there are medical procedures that could be employed to assist reproduction. The procedure can be done to produce multiple births if there are no age-related risks or other medical related risks in carrying the baby to term and delivering the baby safely. In other words, if it is safe enough, you could tell your reproductive technician in some cases that you need twins or triplets.

In some cases, it is possible to pre-select the sex of all the babies to be born. If you can carry 3 babies and you want 2 males and one female combination, it is possible by his grace. The only downside is that it is a bit expensive for some couples. A determined couple could prayerfully seek the face of God concerning finance and other things that God should lead them to a place where it will be successfully done. It is not all the time that it is successful, depending on age, diagnosis and treatment protocol. The success rate is usually between 30%-40% in Nigeria. It is almost the same success rate in other countries plus or minus, but is considerably more affordable in Nigeria.

There are seven aspects of Assisted Reproductive Technology that I would like to mention here. These are:

1. **In-vitro Fertilisation (IVF).** The egg is extracted and fertilised by the sperm in a laboratory. This means that the egg and sperm are collected and fertilised under laboratory conditions and nurtured till implantation.
2. **Intra-cytoplasmic Sperm Injection (ICSI).** A single sperm is injected into an egg to facilitate fertilisation. It is often used when the male factor infertility is present, or when conventional IVF has failed.
3. **Intra-Uterine Insemination (IUI).** This is when specially prepared sperm directly is placed into the uterus around the time of ovulation to improve the chances of fertilisation. IUI may be used as a treatment for certain types of infertility such as male factor infertility or unexplained infertility.
4. **Gamete Intra-Fallopian Transfer (GIFT).** This is when eggs and sperms are transferred into the fallopian tubes, then the fertilisation occurs naturally.

5. **Zygote Intra-fallopian Transfer (ZIFT).** In this method, a zygote is transferred into the fallopian tube instead of the uterus.
6. **External donation of egg or sperm.** A situation may arise when the husband or wife cannot produce a viable sperm or egg for reason of age, disease or injury. Under such a condition, sperm or an egg can be donated by younger people for example, but the woman may still carry it in her womb.
7. **Surrogacy.** The sperm and egg may be okay, but when the womb is weak, absent or dysfunctional, another woman entirely could be paid to help them to carry the baby after implantation. It is an option under the IVF treatment.

Faith and Conception.

Conception after waiting for a long time, amidst the ridicules, pain, shame, and hopelessness requires faith. In Romans 4, Abraham had faith

> Romans 4:18-20
>
> [18]Who against hope believed in hope, that he might become the father of many nations; according to that which was spoken, so shall thy seed be.
>
> [19]and being not weak in faith, he considered not his own body now dead, when he was about a hundred years old, neither yet the deadness of Sarah's womb:
>
> [20]He staggered not at the promise of God through unbelief; but was strong in faith, giving glory to God;

Faith is all about believing in hope against hope. It is also about believing who has promised, to be able to perform that which he has promised. Faith is reckless trust and confidence in the word of God, proclaiming that you are strong, even when you are weak (2 Corinthians 12:10). Where do you get the word of God from? From the scriptures, once it is written. Then you address the spirit realm, both angels and demons, that it is written. What you believe is what you become, and as a man thinketh on his heart, so is he. Don't entertain any doubts or fears, but cast down every imaginations, feelings and thoughts that may male you fearful (2 Corinthians 10:5).

When you walk according to faith in the word of God, you shall have favour all around and shall be strengthened. Study the word of God and affirm them positively and confidently. Speak to your mountain without doubt but believe that you shall receive that which you have said and it shall be real and come to pass (Mark 11:23). Learn how to count your blessings and increase your strength.

Each time you doubt, fear and are down cast, you are losing to the devil. However, when you have absolute trust and confidence in God, he will come through for you. When you are contemplating Assisted Reproductive Technology, it is faith that will fund it, if you don't have the money. Faith will direct you to the right person that will make it successful. Faith will perform that miracle of conception. The overall miracle is faith from one point to another. One practice of faith is to choose the name of your baby that you and your husband/wife will be calling one another at home e.g. Daddy/Mummy Joy. Faith is calling those things which be not as though they are (Romans 4:17). Another one is to buy your baby things and keep them in the house. Use Cusson's baby oil and perfume in your house.

A practice of the children of the prophets is to work in the midst of children in church or if possible, you could be a teacher of the children somehow. Make sure you bless children a lot and interact with them heartily. There is an angelic ministry to children and one of the works of the angels is to bless people that bless the children. (Matthew 18:10). Read more about faith in chapter 20 of this book.

Sex to Maximise Chances of Conception.

The Lord told me one day, that the reason why some people do not conceive is because of the way that they have sex. The voice said that men do not insert their organs completely into the vaginal cavity. I pondered over this statement for some days and was able to come up with some facts. The first one is that if you do not insert deeply and ejaculate, the sperm is splashed usually around the vulva and the entrance of the vagina. This is far from the fundal area or adjacent parts where the zygote is usually implanted. The second fact is that the distance that the spermatozoa need to travel before they can fertilise the ovum as it comes out is reduced. The third fact is that the time needed for both ovum and spermatozoa to come into contact is considerably reduced. The spermatozoa is still of high quality and fertile when it meets the ovum because there is very little delay in meeting the ovum.

It is easy to achieve. Be well prepared mentally and emotionally. Then be in a conducive place without distractions. You could chat and talk and have a prolonged foreplay until the man is "rock solid". The woman must have been well stimulated as well. Then at this point, insert all the way as much as you can, going down fully and finally When you are just about to ejaculate, move deep down as far as you can go, and hold it until you ejaculate. Don't come out in a hurry. Wait for a while so that you can get the best in terms of volume of semen ejaculated. Then when you are satisfied you can come out but with the woman still lying down. You may give her two pillows under the pelvis to aid movement by gravity of the spermatozoa.

When you are a human being and not a dog, don't do dog position during sex. If you are not a bricklayer, don't do wheelbarrow. These different perverted positions waste a lot of semen, and majority of the spermatozoa die without an opportunity at fertilisation. Sexual perversion is a sin that could limit your chances.

Facilitating Effective Conception:

1. <u>**Surrender to Jesus.**</u> If you must know the way, and if you must know the truth, you need to surrender totally to Jesus. A life of true surrender to Jesus is the first step. Say I surrender my life to Jesus and make him Lord and master over my life. I forsake the devil and every dark work. Thank you, Lord Jesus, for saving me.
2. <u>**Repent from every sin.**</u> Sin is a destroyer. Don't commit adultery. Let the sperm be for your procreation. Don't drink and smoke. Remember your sperm count. Don't worship idols, because you may join to spirit wife. Anything that is sinful will hinder you, so don't be given to sin.
3. <u>**Forgive your spouse and other people.**</u> They devil tries to bring a gap between husband and wife spiritually if they quarrel all the time. Many couples miss their ovulation period because of quarrels.
4. <u>**Confess your designs and reconcile with God. 1 John 1:9**</u> says if we confess our sin, he is faithful and just to forgive us and cleanse us from all unrighteousness. Don't allow your conscience to tie you die to one spot.
5. <u>**Prayer and Fasting.**</u> Prayers for forgiveness of sins, prayers for mercy, God's favour, divine grace, divine strength, directions and wisdom. Pray to break covenants, curses and evil dedication too. Go to curses and covenant in this book.
6. <u>**Husband and wife should find time to rest adequately**</u> and do everything to control your emotions. Be happy always and praise and listen to music (Isaiah 61:3). The garment of praise takes away the spirit of heaviness. Good words facilitate a merry heart, which does good like medicine.
7. <u>**Visit your doctor (Jeremiah 8:22).**</u> A doctor is learned in that field and can give you advise about what to do and what not to do. He can advise you on lifestyle changes or give you drugs or medicine. Both husband and wife should go for tests e.g. sperm count. Don't hesitate to share problems. Use your medication religiously. Try and find out and understand reasons why you are not fertile.
8. <u>**Eat good food.**</u> Eat a balanced diet. Don't eat food too rich in carbohydrates. Take aphrodisiacs if your sex drive is low. Don't drink and don't smoke! Take a lot of water.
9. <u>**Have faith in God and be patient.**</u> With God, nothing shall be impossible. Confess God's word regularly. Listen to faith messages and practice faith.
10. <u>**Deal with stress.**</u> Emotional stress is dangerous and will only disrupt your hormonal balance. It will affect your menstrual cycle leading to lack of conception. Find time to cool down and enjoy yourself, possibly by the beach or some other places.
11. <u>**Have faith.**</u> Faith can do anything. This is why you need to have faith. Faith is absolute trust and confidence in God. You have got to know the will of God for your life according to his word.
12. <u>**Exercise.**</u> Exercise is good for the body. It tones your muscles and enhances your mental capabilities. It makes blood to flow, as well as hormones and enzymes.
13. **Prayers for Miracle Conception:**

1. You my womb, receive deliverance from the jaws of flesh eaters and blood suckers in the name of Jesus Christ.
2. Witchcraft covenant saying no to my conception, break by the power in the blood of Jesus Christ.
3. Covenant of death fashioned against my conception and safe delivery, break in the name of Jesus Christ.
4. Any power that I have been dedicated to that is holding on to my womb, lose my womb and let me go in the name of Jesus Christ.

5. Let my menstrual cycle receive correction by the power in the blood of Jesus Christ.
6. You the spirit of fear, release my ovulation in the name of Jesus Christ.
7. Every doubt arresting my ovulation, clear away in the name of Jesus Christ.
8. Holy Spirit, teach me the secret of my conception in the name of Jesus Christ.
9. Let the spirit of fear working against my hormonal levels release my hormonal levels in the name of Jesus Christ.
10. Let my husband's penis receive strength in the name of Jesus Christ.
11. Erectile dysfunction working against my conception, receive healing in the name of Jesus Christ.
12. Father Lord, show us the secret of our conception in the name of Jesus Christ.
13. Let the sperm count of my husband be restored in the name of Jesus Christ.
14. Hidden medical problem causing barrenness in my life, be healed in the name of Jesus Christ.
15. Angels of the living God, remove every blockage in the fallopian tubes of my wife in the name of Jesus Christ.
16. I command every testicular infection to receive healing in the name of Jesus Christ.
17. Every barrier between my sperm and my wife's ova, be crumbled in the name of Jesus Christ.
18. Lord, make me to hate every food that is giving me low sperm count in the name of Jesus Christ.
19. Let my sperm cooperate with my wife's ova in the name of Jesus Christ.
20. Lord, show me the food that I need to take to boost greatly my power for conception in the name of Jesus Christ.
21. Every fibroid in my womb hindering my conception, catch fire and be melted in the name of Jesus Christ. I withdraw my conception virtue from every witchcraft altar in the name of Jesus Christ.
22. Lord, ginger me by the Holy spirit and move me impulsively to have sex with my wife that will lead to conception in the name of Jesus Christ.
23. Let my undescended testicles descend in the name of Jesus Christ.
24. Holy spirit, enter into my life and make me produce sperm with good shape and high quality in the name of Jesus Christ.
25. Lord, increase the quality and strength of my ova in the name of Jesus Christ.
26. Yoke of barrenness in my life, break by fire in the name of Jesus Christ.
27. Every activity of spirit child in my marriage, be frustrated completely in the name of Jesus Christ.
28. Lord, show me if you want me to carry out Assisted Reproductive Technology in the name of Jesus Christ.
29. Spirit of the living God, show me the clinic that will handle my assisted reproduction procedure in the name of Jesus Christ.
30. Lord, show me the doctor that you want to help with my assisted reproduction in the name of Jesus Christ.
31. Lord, touch my organs to function the way they should in the name of Jesus Christ.
32. Lord, let there be normalisation of my hormonal levels in the name of Jesus Christ.
33. Evil pattern of conception in my father's house and mother's house, be broken over my life in the name of Jesus Christ.
34. Let every ovarian failure in my life be reversed in the name of Jesus Christ.
35. You my womb lining, receive healing in the name of Jesus Christ.
36. Lord, melt away every excess fat tissue saying no to my conception in the name of Jesus Christ.

37. Every inherited reproductive problem, loose me and release my miracle on the name of Jesus Christ.
38. Every chemical substance hindering my conception, be neutralised by the power in the blood of Jesus Christ.
39. Lord, kill every cancer cell hindering reproductive in my life in the name of Jesus Christ.
40. Any witchcraft power, attacking my womb with spontaneous abortion, lose your power in the name of Jesus Christ.
41. Parental curse, attacking my conception, break in the name of Jesus Christ.
42. I release my baby from evil environmental altars in the name of Jesus Christ.
43. Every power using dreams of pepper, tomatoes and palm oil to attack my conception, be arrested in the name of Jesus Christ.
44. Every nutritional problem against my conception, be healed in the name of Jesus Christ.
45. Lord, restore my wasted years in the name of Jesus Christ.
46. Every physical and spiritual resource that I need to conceive, O Lord give to me in the name of Jesus Christ.
47. Every evil counsellor assigned to mislead me, be silenced in the name of Jesus Christ.
48. Resurrection power of God, fall upon my life and my spouse's life in the name of Jesus Christ.
49. Every negative confession that I made against myself, be erased by the power in the blood of Jesus Christ.
50. Every ritual that the enemy has done against my conception, lose your power in the name of Jesus Christ.
51. Evil hand, joined in hand against my conception, be frustrated in the name of Jesus Christ.
52. Every curse in the life of my spouse responsible for barrenness in my life, be broken by the power in the blood of Jesus Christ.
53. Evil dedication in the life of my husband responsible for barrenness be broken in the name of Jesus Christ.
54. Evil hands upon my life, saying no to my conception, wither in the name of Jesus Christ.
55. I come out of the cage of barrenness in the name of Jesus Christ.
56. Spirit of patience, fall upon my life in the name of Jesus Christ.
57. Lord, inhabit my praise and give me a miracle in the name of Jesus Christ.
58. Every wall of separation between me and my husband/wife, crumble in the name of Jesus Christ.
59. You heaven over mu conception, open in the name of Jesus Christ.
60. I bind every evil influence against my conception in the name of Jesus Christ.
61. Miracle that parted the Red Sea, happen in my life in the name of Jesus Christ.
62. I enter into the vehicle of conception and safe delivery in the name of Jesus Christ.
63. I come out of the bus stop of barrenness in the name of Jesus Christ.
64. Foundational grave of unborn babies, loose your power over my unborn baby in the name of Jesus Christ.
65. Every witchcraft weapon fashioned against my conception shall not prosper in the name of Jesus Christ.
66. Every witchcraft bird flying because of my conception, cash-and-carry and die in the name of Jesus Christ.
67. Charms of envious witchcraft fashioned against my conception, disobey your users in the name of Jesus Christ.
68. Power of enchantments over my life and my conception, disobey your users in the name of Jesus Christ.
69. Lord, send your word and destroy the power of doubt, assigned to kill my miracle in the name of Jesus Christ.

70. Expectation of the wicked against my conception, power of the Holy Spirit, frustrate it in the name of Jesus Christ.
71. Angels of the living God, trouble every trouble of my pregnancy in the name of Jesus Christ.
72. Every judgement of witchcraft against my conception, I cancel you in the name of Jesus Christ.
73. I release myself, from the grip of the tormentors in the name of Jesus Christ.
74. Everything that the enemy presented in exchange for my miracle, lose your value in the name of Jesus Christ.
75. Anointing of miscarriages over my life, dry up by fire in the name of Jesus Christ.
76. I confess every sin of previous abortion and ask for forgiveness on the name of Jesus Christ.
77. Seed of spirit husband in my life, be destroyed by fire in the name of Jesus Christ.
78. I bear on my body the marks of the Lord Jesus, then spirit spouse should not trouble me and my baby in the name of Jesus Christ.
79. As I shout 21 Halleluiah, let every evil wall against my conception fall to the ground in the name of Jesus Christ.

CHAPTER THIRTY-EIGHT

POWER OVER THE ENEMIES OF YOUR SAFE DELIVERY.

There is a song that is women attending ante-natal classes in Nigeria usually sing. The song sings, O Lord, let me deliver safely, and let me be heard, and let the voice of my baby be heard, on the day of my delivery. This song gives us the meaning of safe delivery. Safe delivery is when on the day of your delivery, people congratulate you and you reply to them heartily. As you are replying them, your baby is crying as babies normally do.

When a woman conceives, it takes a lot of procedure and work for the baby to develop normally without hitches, and the mother gives birth without any casualties or tales of sorrow on the day if delivery. The physical and emotional health of the mother is of utmost priority. A pregnant mother should be registered on an ante-natal program ideally close to their place of abode. There are tests to be carried out before you put to bed. These include blood pressure tests to know the blood pressure to be able to monitor pre-eclampsia. Blood tests to determine if there is anaemia, or infection in the blood, urinalysis to see if there is protein or infection in the urine, screening for chromosomal anomalies, glucose screening and Ultrasound scan to determine the expected date of delivery, position of the baby in the womb and birth risks etc. Tests are very important in pregnancy.

However, there are different types of witchcraft influence that could interfere with the normal delivery and the health and safety of the mother and child. We are in a wickedly wicked world. These are the likely influences:

1. _Evil covenants._ When there is an evil covenant in place, the mother notices negative influence and different kinds of signs during pregnancy. There could be sudden unexplained bleeding. This is a sign that something is wrong with the baby or the mother and is an emergency. Spotting is different though and could not be an emergency but should not be underplayed. An evil covenant is usually a dark agreement that is either conscious or unconscious. It may result into an evil pattern or evil cycle. Some do have a covenant of death.

2. _A curse._ A curse is an evil force that follows someone for wrongdoing, or as a consequence of evil deed previously by the pregnant woman. This is why it is always good to ask for mercy and forgiveness during pregnancy. Pregnant woman should also do good to avoid curses. Curses push away good things and can make you to have disfavour as a pregnant woman. For example, a pregnant woman could fall and get injured seriously. Falls should be watched against during pregnancy. A curse could manifest as a high blood pressure during pregnancy and eclampsia after the baby is born.

3. _Evil dedication._ Some women were dedicated to evil spirits as children. Such women grow with the demons they were dedicated to and have different types of experience. Those spirits give them evil dreams and they fall victim to different types of diseases and mishaps. They keep seeing the object they were dedicated to in their dreams or hear strange voices intimidating and threatening them. Evil dedication could bring about anomalies that could manifest in their lives e.g. obstructed Labour.

4. *Direct witchcraft attack*: Different types of witchcraft attack could manifest in the dream at the time of pregnancy. Eating in the dream, injections in the dream, seeing tomatoes and pepper in the dream, seeing dead relatives during pregnancy, dreaming to see yourself in the midst of familiar or unfamiliar people. Pursuing a person in the dream, having sex in the dream which may result to spontaneous abortion and bleeding. Tell any dreams that are creating fear to a man of God.

5. *Environmental witchcraft attacks*: This is common in women who over-relate with people. Women that eat anyhow, you can buy food anywhere, you interact and reveal your secrets, you take anything given to you to eat or use. All these overfamiliarity opens your life to attacks and you don't know who is who. Someone may say all these restrictions are too much in the name of deliverance. I pray they will never attack you, for you to learn your lesson the hard way.

6. *Blood suckers and flesh eaters*. These spirits like to suck blood, and they will normally act immediately and cause the pregnant woman to bleed immediately. Some keep appearing to you in the dream, showing you palm oil, pepper, tomatoes, red clothing, red candle, and other red materials. On the day of delivery, of you don't pray, study the word and have faith, then they attack. Some hospitals themselves are altars of blood suckers. A doctor who is randy and sleeping with their agents has the spirit though he may not know. All he will see is that people are dying or loosing blood in his hospital. Try and investigate before registering in the wrong hospital. Some houses also are altars. When you live in a house where your neighbour was shot on his way from work, and a few weeks later, another person had an accident, still a month later another was stabbed in a riot, leaving only you that hasn't experienced anything like that. Then you need to fight spiritually. An African proverb says the death that is killing your colleagues is also referring to you as a parable. The activities of blood suckers or drinkers of blood (Isaiah 49:26)

7. *Inherited witchcraft.* Some are unfortunate to have inherited demons. In as much as you do not cast them out, they will always be manifesting in your life. Worst is familiar spirit. They keep saying all sorts of things that you will die on a particular day. Once you fear that statement, you technically have agreed with their plans. The Bible thereby says we should cast down imaginations (2 Corinthians 10:5). One of the hardest tasks to encounter in deliverance is to be kidding with ab enemy that is already inside. No other thing to do than to fight them through prayers. When your mother when she was having you and your siblings had terrible experiences, you need to pray.

8. *Evil summons.* A pregnant woman could be summoned from a coven. If you commit immorality with a woman's husband and you are pregnant, she can summon you. She is connected through sex to her husband, and because she is connected to you through her husband, she has the key to your life. She can summon you and pass any judgement that she likes, including death. A wicked mother in-law can summon you too, if you are not in good terms. Blood connections make way for evil summons and other witchcraft attacks.

9. *Polygamous witchcraft.* When two or more wives are under the same or different roofs in the name of religion or culture, expect jealousy, envy and hatred. This leads to physical and spiritual attacks. They all want to have the lion share of the man's property. Some women kill the step wife in order to achieve her goals or do some other evil. There is no peace that we have that equals the peace we have in Christ.

10. *Consultation of mediums.* When you consult mediums, you are indirectly consulting demons. Basically, you have consulted with demons, and you have established a connection with them. They can do anything to you or the baby. We are all aware that the devil has no good gift, but he has come to steal, kill and destroy (John 10:10).

11. *Poor Nutrition.* When the nutrition is poor, the baby will not be well nourished, as well as the mother who is carrying the baby. Anaemia is a common problem in pregnancy that mothers should try to take balanced diets to ensure good nourishment. If the baby is not well nourished, there is every possibility of having very low birth weight, and poor brain development. The mother may be feeling dizzy, weak and tired during pregnancy. Because the blood is inadequate, complications are common, and often there would be a need for blood transfusion. When blood is inadequate, and the mother bleeds excessively, it could cost life. Loss of appetite, tiredness and dizziness during pregnancy should not be overlooked.

12. *Stress.* Too much of stress during pregnancy can cause spontaneous abortion or raise the blood pressure of the mother continuously. Pregnant mothers should rest adequately during pregnancy.

13. *Age of the mother.* Any age 36 years and above, mothers should be careful. At advanced ages, town planning will save you from unwanted pregnancy e.g. injectable and loops. These last for years. Go to your hospital for advice. If you get pregnant at an age above 36, then take a lot of rest, good nutrition, and go for regular check-ups.

14. *Inappropriate healthcare.* In most cases, Inappropriate healthcare can be very dangerous before the birth of the baby and during birth. Mothers should pray to seek the face of God, before they decide to register in a facility. Both husband and wife should join hands to pray to seek God's face.

Foetal and Neonatal Death.

An unsafe delivery is mainly due to spiritual factors on the part of the mother, or due to ignorance. As we have seen, the mother and father of the unborn child(ren) have a great role to play as soon as the baby is conceived and they know it, or the pregnancy test is positive. However, some children are possessed, either as inherited or acquired at the time the mother is pregnant. Once again, I would like to reiterate that the mother has a big role to play in ensuring that she has a safe delivery. In some cases, a baby reincarnates in a satanic way. Babies like this in Nigerian culture have their ears or other parts of the body serrated. When they are born, they are born with the same marks and sickly nature. These reincarnated babies are known as "Ogbanje" by the Igbo in Nigeria, and Emere or Abiku by the Yoruba. They come with all sorts of styles if they find themselves in a prayerless family. Prayer warriors are their masters. In some instances, they are very powerful, to the extent that they threaten and intimidate their parents. They come with different kinds of death covenants. Some mothers also enter into covenants on their behalf, that their baby would die, or they are going to die with their baby.

Foetal death is death before birth, whilst neonatal death is when a baby dies shortly after birth. Both of them spiritually could be due to:

1. *Covenants on baby or mother's side.* When the mother is careless in what they eat, who touches them, or their interactions in the environment, dark spirits could be programmed into the baby in order to attack the parents. Some babies simply inherited the spirits.
2. *Curses.* Parents that had strong agreements with other partners but broke up cruelly will always struggle with curses. The curses most times cause barrenness or death of their babies.
3. *Evil dedication.* Evil dedication of the mother can attract demonic traffic during childbirth and affect both mother and child. An evil dedication means there is an evil covenant, which spiritually will have terrible effects.
4. *Direct witchcraft attacks.* The baby could be attacked directly by witchcraft from the mother's womb, through curses, incantations, enchantments and others, with long lasting bad effects on the long run
5. *Environmental witchcraft.* There are people with evil power that monitor babies in the womb.
6. *Blood suckers and flesh eaters.* Blood suckers and flesh eaters is another department of the dark kingdom from which attacks can come. They usually make the mother to bleed in excess and attack the baby in the womb. They also eat the flesh and cause diseases of organs.
7. *Inherited witchcraft.* Familiar spirit babies that have stubborn yokes belong to this category.
8. *Evil summons.* A person could be summoned to a witchcraft coven and satanic judgement passed over the baby. This is why it is good to pray for mercy, whilst in pregnancy.
9. *Hospital witchcraft.* There are witchcraft agents in the hospitals, starting from occultic doctors who have ab assignments to collect blood, or nurses and other staff who may be blood suckers or spiritual vampires.
10. *Polygamous witchcraft.* When there are several wives and there is polygamous witchcraft, all the wives may not be happy about the fact that the one is pregnant among them. This may bring about witchcraft attack and envy.

What is the work of witchcraft as seen in the hospitals?

Foetal death

1. *Foetal distress.* When the baby is has an abnormal weight, because a gluttonous spirit was inside the mother, making her to be predisposed to eating carbohydrates. It may be a big struggle and the baby dies in the process of that struggle, because he or she is tired due to lack of nutrients or water.
2. *Umbilical accidents* whereby the umbilical cord is compromised that there is a cut in the supply of nutrients and oxygen, which could affect the baby's brain functions. For example, the umbilical cord winds round the neck of the baby, suffocating the baby to death, or the umbilical cord ties and forms a knot, or there is a rupture of the umbilical cord.
3. *Placental abruptness* is when the placenta separates from the womb before the baby is born leading to a cut in blood and nutrient supply leading to foetal death.
4. *Mother's health status.* Conditions like high blood pressure and gestational diabetes could pose problems. Pre-eclampsia could lead to high blood pressure and give rise to eclampsia after birth. Pre-eclampsia in pregnancy is

characterised by high blood pressure, headaches, blurred vision, and could often damage the liver and kidneys. Eclampsia is one of the greatest causes of death in mothers after birth. The effects of seizures in the mother could cause brain damage, foetal distress, pre-term birth, and retarded growth of the baby.

5. *Foetal anomalies* known as congenital malformations could affect vital organs like the heart, leading to foetal death at the time of birth.

Causes of Neonatal Death.

The neonatal period if a baby is the first 28 days after birth. This is a period of great development and transition from the intra-uterine life to the external world. 75% of deaths of babies and attacks usually occur during the first week of life. The following are the causes of death of babies in the neonatal period.

1. *Premature birth.* Premature babies are vulnerable and often die from infections, respiratory problems, lack of warmth, and other factors. Smoking is one of the causes of Premature birth. Attack of spirit husband sleeping with the mother during pregnancy is the most common cause. The mother wakes up with bleeding from the private part, and that's it.
2. *Birth asphyxia.* Owing to the oxygen debt and lack of oxygen supply, the babies usually die in the first few hours of life. Some end up with a damaged brain, known as cerebral palsy.
3. *Congenital anomalies* could kill in-utero and after birth. Hole in the heart, malformations of the lungs, and the intestines could kill a baby in the first few hours of life. This is mainly due to foundational witchcraft attack.
4. *Respiratory distress syndrome.* This is when the lungs are not well developed and cannot support respiration. The baby dies shortly after birth as a result. Evil covenants or curses could lead to this.
5. *Infections.* When the amniotic sac and the chorionic sac (chorioamnionitis) are infected, it could lead to the death of the baby or speech and hearing delay. It could make a baby to be born pre-term, arrest development and cause cerebral palsy. When the mother of the baby has been eating in the dream, it could lead to this.
6. *Sudden Infant death.* The baby dies in the neonatal period often without a known cause. Usually, it is suspected to be due to suffocation of the baby. However other factors could be responsible. This could be due to spiritual attacks by foundational witchcraft or environmental witchcraft.
7. *Intra-cranial haemorrhage.* During birth, if the mother is not calm enough, the baby's head could be injured. Also, when the obstetrics methods are faulty, the baby's head could be injured leading to intra-cranial bleeding and death.
8. *Multiple births.* Most multiple births are usually pre-term and are born with vulnerable. In most cases, it takes an extra for them to survive. Mothers should avoid stress and ensure good nutrition once it proven that you have multiple babies in you.

How to Trust in Jesus for A Safe Delivery.

Only Jesus has power over situation on earth. He paid the price on the cross of Calvary. The Bible says he hath borne our griefs and carried our sorrows. Trusting in Jesus for a safe delivery has to do with faith and works. Faith is activated by your actions, as you substantiate what you hope for (Hebrews 11:1). Faith is the substance of things hoped for, and the evidence things not seen. Heaven requires evidence that you merit what you have seen. What you want or God has promised it to you.

What are the things you need to know?

1. Surrender your life to Jesus.
2. Repent from sin, because sin will separate you from God's love, grace and except you repent (Isaiah 59:1).
3. Forgive, so that you can be forgiven (Matthew 6:12).
4. Confess your faults to one another that you may be healed (James 5:16). Forgiveness with a pure heart and clean hands ensures perfect healing.
5. Study and meditate in the word for prosperity and good success (Joshua 1:8). The instruction, correction, reproof and doctrine you need, are all in the word of God (2 Timothy 3:16). Study the word and be innovative with the word. The word itself has creative powers, because all things were made by the word (John 1:3), and God called those things which be not, as though they were (Romans 4:17). The word of God applied in faith can bring something from nothing. It can create.
6. Pray always and make your wishes known to God. There are certain things you will never receive until you make a request for it. David enquired of the Lord in 1 Samuel 30:8, saying, "Shall I pursue after this troop"? Shall I overtake them? And he answered him, pursue; for thou shalt surely overtake them, and without fail recover all. Your own prayer could be, Shall I go for a Caesarean Section because of my age, or for the safety of my baby? Then the Lord may tell you categorically or show you a sign that you should go ahead or not, for everyone that asked receiveth; and he that seekers findeth; and to him that knocked it shall be opened (Matthew 7:8). What then do you pray for? Essentially, you pray to break covenants, curses, evil dedication, divine assistance of angels, arrest demonic spirits, fir God to reveal the secrets of the enemies and so on.
7. Speak to your problems. Jesus told them in Mark 11:23 whosoever shall say to this mountain, be thou removed and be cast into the sea, and shall not in his heart, but shall believe that those things which he saith shall come to pass; he shall have whatsoever he saith. Every good thing that you earnestly rejoice at, and you believe, not doubting, you shall receive. When you exhibit fear, technically you are saying you believe in the evil imaginations the devil is putting in your mind, and that is why you are afraid. The Bible tells you to cast then down to the obedience of Christ, choosing rather the testimony of Jesus Christ, which is the word of God.
8. Make positive affirmations. Amongst many others, I recommend Isaiah 41:10 for a pregnant woman believing God for safe delivery. Say "I will not fear, for the miracle working God is with me; I shall not be dismayed, for he is my God, he will strengthen me, he will help me, because he loves me, yes, he will uphold me with the right hand of righteousness". As you say it, remember that Satan was an angel created by God, and the creature cannot overpower his creator. Impossible! The affirmations will be stronger the more you see God on the throne as the Almighty.

9. Have faith. Do not fear, do not doubt. Believe only in the testimony of Christ, which is the word of God. Think possibilities, speak possibilities, act the word of God.
10. Anoint yourself with oil or let your Pastor do it. Let him pray with you too. The prayer of faith shall heal the sick (James 5:14-15).
11. Have a day at least, that all you pray for is revelation, because revelation is power. Revelation shows you what is in the dark and leads you as to what to do and what not to do. If there's a food you love to eat, that is dangerous, the Holy Spirit will tell you. If you have a bad habit, he will expose it so that you can change. If he wants you to attend a particular hospital, he will let you know. Anything that keeps intruding into your mind, does not contradict the word of God, and gives you peace is from the Lord, irrespective of what people may think, say or do. Follow it.
12. Make sure you choose your doctor prayerfully, so that you don't fall into the hands of an occultist or drinker of blood. Many hospitals are altars of the devil, because of the desire of many to get rich overnight. Keep praying to God until he reveals something to you until you are satisfied.
13. Don't shy away from your doctor(s). You need his advice at this time like never before. You could take his mobile number and that of some nurses. Don't be shy to ask, so that you can receive. Call them or send messages to them to ask them questions. Confirm their advice online and follow suit. If you entertain any doubt or fear, do not hesitate to ask them.
14. Eat a balanced diet. Don't take too much of carbohydrates which will make your baby too big. An overweight baby will only give you problems at the end of the day. A balanced diet is also good for the health and development of the baby. Don't forget that anaemia is one of the greatest problems of a pregnant mother and the child to come. Take a lot of water. Smoking and drinking are no go areas.
15. Do not be unduly righteous. In Jeremiah 8:22, God wants you to consult a Physician. If that is the case, then do not reject a Caesarean Section if it is what will help you and save you from untimely death. Respect medical advice. If blood transfusion will help you, take it, and do not allow ignorance to kill you. Don't delay, because the difference between life and death could just be 2 minutes.
16. Have regular blood pressure checks. Have a sphygmomanometer at home to check your blood pressure. However, not everyone with a high blood pressure has pre-eclampsia, but the risk is higher. Don't joke with it. If it is high, you are having headache, dizziness or swelling of the feet, eyes and hands, then quickly see your doctor and tell him. You will need to test your urine for protein to confirm if there is pre-eclampsia. Eclampsia is one of the greatest killers during or after childbirth. Note also that an unusually high blood pressure can make you bleed excessively during childbirth. Blood pressure checks shouldn't be toyed with during pregnancy.
17. Don't throw yourself off balance with fear, during labour that you are not relaxed. Keep confessing God's word and believe good things. This way you won't fear, and you will be calm. Many women injure their babies because of fear, and may fracture the skull, leading to haemorrhage or bleeding inside the head of the baby. If you don't relax enough, there is every indication and temptation to give you episiotomy. This means cutting you with a scalpel to allow a smooth passage of the baby.

18. Seek knowledge. You need to read extensively as well as watch and listen to YouTube videos. I expect you to view different you tube videos on all the things discussed in this chapter and in this book. If possible, I expect you to also confirm the things in this book with your doctors.
19. Avoid physical and emotional stress. Stress can aggravate your blood pressure, and as well lead to a miscarriage. During pregnancy, don't carry too heavy things. Don't think about too many things but cast all your cares on God (1 Peter 5:7). If you do your exercises, make them very mild and make sure someone is with you.
20. Exercise. Exercises especially walking exercises within limits of pain or stress are desirable daily. This helps circulation and, in a way, helps maintain your weight. Gentle stretching exercises prepare your body for labour. Pull up your ankles and relax; whilst sitting on a mat with your legs stretched on the mat, incline your body forwards and backwards gently, stretch gently rotating to the right side and left side, turn your neck to the right and left. Low impact swimming is good if you have access to a swimming facility. Hydrotherapy with water of a suiting temperature is good for relaxation and calming the body down. Play with the water but be very careful of the risk of a slippery surface and a fall which is not good. Playing with water is best done when you are lying on a couch, then your husband uses a shower head to release the water and bath you. At the point of labour, you could be on the bed and water is poured on you too. Stroking massage, or gentle palmar massage is another thing that can relax you during labour. When the baby arrives and you are at home, continue with pelvic floor exercises, stretching, walking and breathing exercises. This time you can use weights to strengthen your muscles. Go to YouTube for more enlightenment on these exercises.
21. Monitor your dreams. There is a need to have a dream register where you record all your dreams. You can always refer to whatever God has told you at any time. God reveals secrets through dreams that will make things easy for you (Job 33:15).

Prayers for Safe Delivery:

1. O Lord, deliver me in your mercy from the power of blood suckers and flesh eaters.
2. Familiar spirit covenant, demanding fir my life, or the life of my baby, break by the power in the blood of Jesus Christ.
3. Every hand bill of obituary prepared for my life, catch fire and burn to ashes in the name of Jesus Christ.
4. Every demon that is assigned to arrest my breath or that of my baby, be arrested in the name of Jesus Christ.
5. Every witchcraft device, programmed to hinder my safe delivery, be burnt to ashes in the name of Jesus Christ.
6. Any wicked boasting power, monitoring my life for tragedy on the day of my putting to bed, go blind in the name of Jesus Christ.
7. Covenant with the grave fashioned against my life, break in the name of Jesus Christ.
8. Every blood sucking demon, waiting to waste my blood on the day of my delivery, receive disgrace in the name of Jesus Christ.
9. I reverse any congenital malformations fashioned against the life of my baby in the name of Jesus Christ.

10. Holy Ghost, go before me to the hospital where I will deliver, and prepare the hearts of the people for me in Jesus name.
11. Every curse attacking my success on the day of my delivery break in the name of Jesus Christ.
12. Every sacrifice carried by the enemy against my safe delivery I break your power in the name of Jesus Christ.
13. O Lord, give my doctors and nurses excellent wisdom to deal with every obstacle standing against my safe delivery in the name of Jesus Christ.
14. Every attack in the hours of the night against my safe delivery backfire in the name of Jesus Christ.
15. Witchcraft altar fashioned against my safe delivery, be destroyed by the thunder and fire of God's judgement in the name of Jesus Christ.
16. Holy Spirit, open my understanding and disgrace every plan of the enemy against my safe delivery in the name of Jesus Christ.
17. Black cloth put upon me in the dream, I remove you and set you ablaze in the name of Jesus Christ.
18. Evil spirit that wants to enter my doctors and nurses, be arrested in the name of Jesus Christ.
19. O Lord my father, reveal to me the hospital where you have given me the grace to deliver safely in the name of Jesus Christ.
20. Every power threatening my pregnancy with abortion, be arrested in the name of Jesus Christ.
21. Father Lord, let me have favour with all my doctors and nurses on the day of my delivery.
22. Healing angels of God, lay your hands upon my life and destroy every yoke of high blood pressure in my life in the name of Jesus Christ.
23. I rebuke every spirit of gestational diabetes on my life in the name of Jesus Christ.
24. My efforts shall not be in vain in the name of Jesus Christ.
25. I break every dark covenant that wants to manifest in my life against my safe delivery in the name of Jesus Christ.
26. Evil pattern of child delivery on my father's side or mother's side that wants to manifest in my life break in the name of Jesus Christ.
27. Witchcraft animal in my environment crying evil cry against my pregnancy in the hours of the night, be wasted in the name of Jesus Christ.
28. Evil mirror, monitoring the development of my baby, shattered into pieces in the name of Jesus Christ.
29. Evil restaurant polluting my life and my pregnancy, be exposed and be disgraced in the name of Jesus Christ.
30. Astral projection against me and my baby, be frustrated in the name of Jesus Christ.
31. O Lord, hide me and my baby in your secret place against every attack of witchcraft in the name of Jesus Christ.
32. I bear on my body the marks of the Lord Jesus Christ, therefore me and my baby cannot be troubled in the name of Jesus Christ.
33. Power to tread upon serpents and scorpions, fall upon my life in the name of Jesus Christ.
34. I cancel every evil clinical prophecy against me and my baby in the name of Jesus Christ.
35. I over-rule every negative witchcraft decision against my safe delivery in the name of Jesus Christ.
36. Funnel of darkness prepared for my blood and that of my baby, be destroyed now in the name of Jesus Christ.

37. Labour Room bewitchment that wants to manifest on my day of delivery be destroyed by fire in the name of Jesus Christ.
38. Every hidden altar, in the hospital where I have registered to deliver my baby, destroyed by the power on the blood of Jesus Christ
39. I arrest every spirit of fear attacking my safe delivery in the name of Jesus Christ.
40. I close the door against every evil imagination, thoughts and feelings intruding into my life in the name of Jesus Christ.
41. O Lord, teach me your word, and make me to deliver safely in the name of Jesus Christ.
42. I Anointing for prayer, fall upon my life in the name of Jesus Christ.
43. I ask for forgiveness and mercy concerning every sin that I may have committed against God in the name of Jesus Christ.
44. Every attack of spirit spouse at the time of my delivery, be paralysed in the name of Jesus Christ.
45. O Lord, renew the right spirit within me.
46. I cast out every devil hiding in my body in the name of Jesus Christ.
47. Anointing for supernatural revelations overshadow my life in the name of Jesus.
48. Lay your hands on your womb and say, you my baby, receive the fire of God in the name of Jesus Christ.
49. Every glory killer on assignment against my baby, fail woefully in the name of Jesus Christ.
50. Angels of the living God, reposition everything that need repositioning in my womb in the name of Jesus Christ.
51. I come against every umbilical cord compression in the name of Jesus Christ.
52. You my baby's placenta, you shall not be detached in the name of Jesus Christ.
53. You my womb, receive deliverance from every flesh eater in the name of Jesus Christ.
54. Every medical condition hiding in my body that wants to manifest against my safe delivery, in the name of Jesus Christ.
55. I arrest every spirit of seizure that wants to manifest in my life on the day of my child's delivery, be impotent in the name of Jesus Christ.
56. Attack from the waters against the life of my baby, backfire in the name of Jesus Christ.
57. You my head, refuse to harbour bewitchment on the day of my delivery in the name of Jesus Christ.
58. Any drug that wants to work against me and my baby, be exposed and be disgraced in the name of Jesus Christ.
59. O Lord, strengthen me and renew my youth in the name of Jesus Christ.
60. Environmental battles against my safe delivery, scatter by fire in the name of Jesus Christ.
61. Every desire for harmful substances like smoke and alcohol in my life, die in the name of Jesus Christ.
62. Father Lord, because you forgave me, I forgive everyone that has offended me irrespective of what they did to me. Thank you, Jesus.
63. Every fiery dart of the enemy fashioned against me and my baby, backfire in the name of Jesus Christ.
64. Nutritional disease fashioned against my pregnancy be healed in the name of Jesus Christ.
65. I rebuke every spirit of premature birth in my life in the name of Jesus Christ.

66. Every witchcraft tree growing against my safe delivery, be uprooted in the name of Jesus Christ.
67. Conspiracy in the third heavens against my safe delivery, scatter in the name of Jesus Christ.
68. O Lord, send your word, heal me and deliver me from my destructions in the name of Jesus Christ.
69. Evil voice confusing my destiny, be silenced in the name of Jesus Christ.
70. Evil clinical prophecy released against my life, be cancelled by the power in the blood of Jesus Christ.
71. Every environmental curse working against my life be cancelled by the power in the blood of Jesus Christ.
72. Wickedness of the wicked on my day of delivery, backfire in the name of Jesus Christ.
73. Every demon that is following me about in order to wreak havoc on the day of my delivery be arrested in the name of Jesus Christ.
74. Lay your hands on your tummy, and pray, you my baby, receive the power to push out on the day of my delivery.
75. Every infection in my womb that wants to affect my baby, be healed now in the name of Jesus Christ.
76. Witchcraft mark on my tummy, be wiped away by the power in the blood of Jesus Christ.
77. I come against any birth injury to me or my baby on the day of delivery in Jesus Christ name.
78. I cover myself and my baby with the blood of Jesus Christ.
79. Evert witchcraft embargo mounted against my safe delivery, be dismantled in the name of Jesus Christ.
80. I arrest every spirit of death assigned against me and my baby in the name of Jesus Christ.

Printed in Great Britain
by Amazon